The Tyranny of Change

The Tyranny of Change

America in the Progressive Era
1890–1920

SECOND EDITION

John Whiteclay Chambers II

RUTGERS UNIVERSITY PRESS
New Brunswick, New Jersey, and London

First published in 1992 by St. Martin's Press,
New York, New York
Reprinted in 2000 by Rutgers University Press,
New Brunswick, New Jersey

Library of Congress Cataloging-in-Publication Data

Chambers, John Whiteclay.
    The tyranny of change : America in the progressive era,
  1890–1920 / John Whiteclay Chambers II.
      p. cm.
    Includes bibliographical references (p.) and index.
    ISBN 0-8135-2799-6 (alk. paper)
      1. United States—Politics and government—1901–1953.
  2. Progressivism (United States politics).   3. United
  States—Politics and government—1865–1900.   I. Title.

  E743.C39 2000
  973.91—dc21   99-054338

Manufactured in the United States of America

To my children
Bret, Jeff, Michael Adam, and Tacy

Contents

Preface to the 2000 Edition

As the twenty-first century begins, the Progressive Era, that exciting period of awakening and change at the dawn of the twentieth century, continues to provide vital insights about the birth of modern America. Indeed, the sense of new possibilities inherent in the commencement of a new century offers readers in 2000 some commonality with Americans in 1900. Then as now, people welcomed a new century with a mixed sense of anticipation and apprehension, expressing concern about accelerated and seemingly uncontrolled change and articulating some doubts but many more hopes about the future.

Because the years around the beginning of the twentieth century proved so important, historians continue to explore their diverse aspects. The political reforms that gave the Progressive Era its name and original time frame have been long established, but much of the new scholarship has examined the social and cultural dimensions of change. Some investigates the gendered meanings of reform, the roles of race, class, and sexuality in turn-of-the-century politics, and the environmental impacts of Progressive-era policies. Just as frequently, the new social and cultural scholarship ignores the political history of the period, sometimes disregarding the very concept of progressivism. Whether highlighting or ignoring progressive reforms, scholars have pushed the origins of modern America back to the Civil War and the implications of this era forward into the 1930s. Consequently, the periodization has become so fluid that Elisabeth Israels Perry, president of the Society for Historians of the Gilded Age and Progressive Era, concluded in 1999 that "setting the era's chronological boundaries seems to depend on the personal interests, perspectives, and values of each historian."

Despite such diversity, however, the concepts of a progressive impulse or ethos and a Progressive Era continue to be relevant. There were, after all, unique aspects to the period around the turn of the century. Americans in other times have worried that they were entering what Woodrow Wilson called "a very different age." Those living in the Progressive Era were right to think so. The period included the confluence of several time-specific, transformative developments. Among these were the proliferation of an urban-industrial economy, the influx of unprecedented numbers of new immigrants, the emergence of large and extraordinarily powerful corporations, and a new view towards the role of the national government. Depending on their situation, groups of Americans chose different strategies to respond to these changes as they sought to maintain or improve the realization of their security, status, and ideals, but there were also some common responses.

A core element in the Progressive Era to those who called themselves progressives and to many others was a purposeful intervention that ultimately contributed to a stronger role for government. Although its origins dated back to efforts by agrarians and others in the late nineteenth century, the modern American regulatory state began only with the new positive views toward somewhat more centralized government and the assortment of federal regulation adopted in the Progressive Era. Progressives differed over what they hoped to achieve by such legislation. Indeed, they were so diverse that they represented, as often noted, "no unified movement . . . but rather a hodgepodge of coalitions working for changes that often contradicted each other." Nevertheless, a strong reform ethos certainly dominated the period. Despite definitional difficulties, the democratic ideal played an important part in the ideology and rhetoric of those who called themselves progressives—or radicals. So did the desire to mobilize "the people," either directly or behind active government, to restrict private activity when it threatened the public interest. Historians have long focused on the progressives' expansion of government; a key area of research today is exploring more fully the impact of the era's reforms upon the diverse peoples of the United States.

As the new supplemental bibliography to this volume makes clear, some of the most influential scholarship on the era in the past decade has emphasized the importance of the state in the changes of the period. The focus has been particularly on the relationship between new political structures and methods of influence and their consequences for particular groups: farmers, industrial workers, women, immigrants, minorities. Much of the work has shown how the power of government at various levels could be used to benefit newly organized groups (or how such groups could themselves learn to benefit from changes in the system). Other studies have shown, however, how groups could use the powers of government repressively, as in the disfranchisement and legal segregation of African Americans in the South or in the intensive wartime campaign of psychological mobilization of the masses and vigorous suppression of dissent during and immediately after World War I.

The confidence of many reformers in "the public" as the hope of democracy did not survive long after World War I. Wartime propaganda, subsequent public relations techniques, and consumerist advertising helped to transform the dominant intellectual concept of the public from active agent of social change to passive object of external forces. The optimistic, pragmatic attitude of many of the progressive elites had contained a strong element of self-righteousness and a willingness to use governmental control as a means for social improvement. By the end of the Progressive Era, the original idealization of the public had been succeeded by a more cynical view of malleable public opinion and manipulated masses.

Yet much of the new scholarship on topics stretching across the late nineteenth and early twentieth centuries has, in exploring social and cultural history, countered such a cynical view about the men and women of America. We now see much more clearly how people, individually and collectively, sought effectively to maintain control of their lives amidst the powerful and sometimes repressive change around them, with or without relying upon government.

Perhaps nowhere is the role of human agency clearer than in the recent detailed studies of how black women dealt with such challenges. To expand their autonomy, Atlanta's female black domestic servants and washerwomen, as Tera Hunter has shown, drew strength from secular and religious working-class organizations and personally and collectively joined in on-the-job labor activism. (Many of them also partook of after-hours leisure, particularly dancing, despite the fact that it was looked down upon by white employers, city officials, and conservative members of the black middle class.) Farther north, young southern black women migrants, who at the turn of the century became live-in domestic servants in Washington, D.C., resisted the total control of their lives reminiscent of slavery. Between 1900 and 1920, as Elizabeth Clark-Lewis has revealed, these young black women transformed domestic service in the nation's capital by insisting on certain changes. They wanted to live in their own places instead of those of their employer, to wear their own clothing rather than uniforms, and to have time off on Sundays. Their success in achieving these changes contributed to their own sense of dignity and personal power. It also contributed to the further development of community awareness among African Americans and ultimately helped these young women make a transition to self-employment.

A useful device in analyzing the effects of subjugation on African Americans, women, and other marginalized groups has been the broad concept of a "politics of opposition," encompassing not a single strategy or goal but a continuing spectrum from avoidance to protest and resistance. This concept can be applied to an array of middle-class and working-class responses. Middle-class black women, for example, struggled, often in the face of exclusionist policies by white women, for women's suffrage, urban settlement houses, missionary work, community welfare, and social reform in general. As black women and men sought to improve the situation of African Americans in an increasingly segregationist society, they also pushed for antilynching laws, better education in black schools, and full civil rights.

The knowledge we now have about the activities of these black reformers expands and transforms our understanding of progressivism and the era. It acknowledges the active roles of black men and women in improving their situation rather than portraying them as passive or marginal. If one moves from a political or ideological focus to a broader definition of reform, then African Americans can be seen as reformers, working through black churches and volunteer organizations to strengthen their own communities and institutions even while whites disfranchised them and legalized racial segregation.

White Americans put a white face on some of the crucial aspects of opportunity and status in the emerging urban-industrial economy, as

Jacqueline Jones puts it. One was the ideal of technological progress, which relied upon increasingly complicated kinds of machines. The skilled labor required by the new technology was often restricted to certain groups of white men and occasionally white women. (Although in a few cases, such as mine workers in West Virginia and Alabama and briefly among packing-house workers in Illinois, white men and black men worked together in the same jobs.) The other ideal was one of fashion and glamour, an ideal that relied upon youthful white women to provide appealing images in advertising and entertainment and to serve as clerks to sell merchandise to consumers, the vast majority of whom were women.

Identification and analysis of "whiteness"—of the creation of white racial identity—has recently become an important historical subfield. Some historians have asserted that in response to their anxieties about industrialization white workers of different ethnic groups constructed or accepted a powerful new concept of "whiteness," which ensured them status by defining their identity as superior to that of blacks and other groups defined as non-white. Scholars now debate the concept and investigate its impact on race relations, including increased segregation, anti-black violence, and immigration restriction that marked this period. Meanwhile, historians also continue to explore the more tolerant and humanistic sides of working-class life and culture and to examine middle- and working-class efforts at interracial and interethnic cooperation for mutual benefit and to fulfill America's democratic ideals.

For women as well as many other groups, the Progressive Era left an ambiguous legacy. Activist women enlarged the public sphere to include women in leadership and other policymaking roles in a number of national and international organizations. After more than half a century, they obtained the vote. At the same time, middle-class white women activists often accepted prevailing racial prejudices and failed to cooperate with black and immigrant women. There were difficulties in linking women reformers across class lines. For white middle-class women reformers usually favored protective labor legislation and government "pensions" for mothers who had no male support, working-class women activists often viewed unionization and child-care provisions as more effective in improving their lives. In achieving laws controlling wages, hours, and working conditions for women and providing for mothers' pensions, many middle-class women reformers chose to reject the idea of women's equality with men and of economic independence for women. Instead, they accepted the prevailing concept which emphasized women's main role as that of mother not worker. Yet the Progressive Era also saw the emergence of the modern concept of feminism which embraced complete equality and autonomy for women. While legal rights and protection were the focus of most women reformers, other women imagined emancipation in more mundane ways, such as the advertised ability of consumer goods and styles to improve one's life.

Popular culture, particularly since possibilities for the mass consumption of goods and of leisure entertainment proliferated in the cities of the early twentieth century, has been among the most resourceful areas of recent historical research. In the study of the working classes, while labor historians have studied the workplace, scholars of popular culture have tended to emphasize domestic and leisure activities. Working-class women, for instance, developed a sense of autonomy aided by romance and adventure novels, films, fashions, and a new emphasis on sexual pleasure. Working-class male identities, on the other hand, were often defined by neighborhood networks, street gangs, and the camaraderie of saloons rather than by the nature of their work. Once again the new emphasis has been on people or groups as active agents, choosing among different courses of action. Immigrant groups—Russian Jews, Catholic Irish, Italians, Poles, Mexicans, Orthodox Greeks, Buddhist or Confucian Chinese or Japanese—shaped and controlled their lives even within the harsh economic, geographic, and social limits of the dominant culture.

A new focus on popular culture in the dynamic industrial cities has identified what Timothy Gilfoyle has labeled a culture of "civic sociability and democratized urban leisure." Appealing to consumption of fantasy, novelty, and desire, the entertainment centers—arcades, cabarets, vaudeville halls, nickelodeons, and movie palaces—and the spectacular displays in the new department stores epitomized a new urban culture and "modernity" itself. Victorian definitions of morality, class, and gender were deeply eroded. Americans' favorite new form of entertainment, the movies, challenged and also reinforced some existing stereotypes within film genres as different as anti-authoritarian, slapstick "Keystone Kops" comedies, racist anti-Indian westerns and anti-black melodramas such as *The Birth of a Nation*, and hysterical wartime propaganda films.

Fluid and fragmented, American urban culture was in fact enriched by ethnic, class, gender, and regional differences. The cities and their mosaic of neighborhoods provided unprecedented opportunities to escape traditional controls of family and community. Despite limited incomes, many young men and women chose to buy a measure of independence, whether living in their own place or simply going out for after-work entertainment. Studying the use of urban leisure time, especially nightlife, historians like Gilfoyle, Joanne Meyerowitz, George Chauncey, and Madeline Davis have found a wide variety of subcultures, activities, sexualities, and contested social landscapes. The multifaceted development in the new industrial metropolises produced fragmentation and resistance to human-imposed order, developments that were bewildering and even frightening to some. To the aging expatriate novelist Henry James, writing in 1907 about his brief return to New York from London, the new urban life in America was "invented" and full of "chaos." Living in New York City, James complained, was a "struggle in a void."

United States participation in World War I, America's first major armed intervention in Europe, demonstrated the newly industrialized nation's ability to play a major world role. But the aftermath showed the continuing strength of America's political isolationism as well as peace-oriented internationalists' desire for new and better forms of relations among nations. Much recent research continues to criticize U.S. expansionism in the Caribbean and the Pacific in the late nineteenth and early twentieth centuries, while shedding new light on the manner and impact of such actions. In keeping with the new emphasis on cultural history, we are also learning much more about the role of racial and gendered attitudes in U.S. expansionism and in the debate over imperialism and colonization in turn-of-the-century America.

More broadly, our understanding of both foreign and domestic developments is being enriched by comparative transnationalist studies. From the prize-winning 1998 book by Daniel Rodgers, *Atlantic Crossings: Social Politics in a Progressive Age*, for example, we learn how reformers, conservatives, and radicals in the United States, France, Great Britain, and Germany interacted across national borders. This transnationalism helped to affect what was similar and what was different in these nations as they responded to the changes of rapid urban-industrial growth. Other studies situate changing developments affecting women, immigration, capital flows, and other major phenomena in a global context. All of these confirm that turn-of-the-century Americans were hardly unique in the challenges they confronted or in their ambivalence towards the swirl of change as they faced the new century with a combination of anxiety and courage.

As they reconstruct and interpret the dynamic era around the turn of the twentieth century, historians continue, naturally, to debate the causes, nature, and meaning of the change and continuity in what they judge to be the most important events of the period. They select their evidence, test their interpretations, make their assessments. For many, progressive reform still holds a central place, seeming to provide some coherence despite its variety, contradictions, and exclusivity. Yet, much of the new research has expanded beyond progressivism and its core, the middle class. The study of industrial workers, farmers, women, non-whites, and immigrants offers a more complex and contentious picture of American society. This pluralistic view demonstrates the frequent clash of interests, between and within various groups, in a rapidly industrializing economy and an ethnically and racially divided society.

The divergence of historical interpretation should not be disheartening, for our understanding of the past is an open-ended process. One of the valuable aspects of studying the Progressive Era is its clear demonstration of this. The divergent views by different historians invite those who would understand the era to probe it more deeply themselves. Critical analysis is required of the interpretations and the evidence upon which they rest. A true intellectual voyage into the past requires a healthy (but not nihilistic) skepticism and an open, questioning mind.

As we explore the Progressive Era, we need to continue to ask questions, analyze explanations, and make judgments. This calls of course for careful weighing of the evidence, logical analysis, and reasoned, if often tentative, conclusions. The value of the historical method and the insights it offers derives from true intellectual engagement with the past. This is never richer than in such important historical periods as the Progressive Era, where the reward is increased knowledge both of the emergence of modern America and of a method of analysis which can also prove useful in facing the challenges of the future.

For suggesting a reprinting of the second edition of *The Tyranny of Change: America in the Progressive Era, 1890–1920,* I would like to thank Elisabeth Israels Perry, Kathryn Kish Sklar, Robert W. Cherny, and others at the annual meeting of the Society for Historians of the Gilded Age and Progressive Era in April 1999. My thanks also to the wonderful people at Rutgers University Press, especially Marlie Wasserman, the director, and Leslie Mitchner, associate director and editor in chief, who followed through on that recommendation and took such care in publishing this book; Anne Hegeman, who shepherded the book through production; and Amy Rashap, who worked on marketing it.

Finis Dunaway, a doctoral candidate at Rutgers University, served as photo researcher and helped me obtain the cover photograph from the Bain News Service Collection at the Library of Congress.

Patrick Wilkinson graciously agreed to interrupt his work on his doctoral dissertation on the period at Duke University to help prepare a supplemental bibliography of some of the important relevant works published in the past eight years. My thanks to him for doing such a splendid job. Space limitations precluded our including more of the extensive scholarship covering the period.

Thanks also to my colleague Nancy Hewitt for her suggestions, and special gratitude to William H. Chafe, dean of the Faculty of Arts and Sciences and Alice Mary Baldwin Professor of History at Duke University, for his advice and friendship over these many years.

I continue to dedicate this book to my children, Bret, Jeff, Michael Adam, and Tacy, with my love and my hope that they and my grandchildren, Colby, Tyler, Chelsea, Ben and Samuel, will help to build a better future for Americans and all humankind.

Preface to the Second Edition

In the final decade of the twentieth century it may come as a considerable surprise that the beginning of the now dwindling century still has much to tell us. Modern America was born in those early years, and we are heirs of many of the institutions, attitudes, and problems of the Progressive Era.

Between 1890 and 1920, the forces accompanying industrialization sent the familiar nineteenth-century world plummeting toward extinction. A land of family farms and scattered settlements was eclipsed by a modern nation of giant corporations, huge factories and office buildings, and sprawling tension-filled cities. Class, ethnic, and racial violence rocketed warnings throughout society. The women's movement and new cultural attitudes cracked the norms of the staid Victorian age. Industrialization, urbanization, modernism—all seemed to be driving society into an unknown future.

"There has never been a time in the world's history in which blind social forces have been so strong," declared Harvard philosopher Ralph Barton Perry in 1916. Indeed, many Americans believed themselves in a tyrannical grip of change. Yet they were not deterred and sought purposefully to take control of the direction of change. The result included many painful failures as well as some measures of success. We are still living with many of those results. America today is to an important degree the product of the legacy of the Progressive Era.

My primary purpose in the second edition of this book is to reexamine and explain the developments of the Progressive Era, a period of widespread reform and readjustment that reached its peak in the ten years between 1907 and 1917 but whose roots and immediate ramifications extended over nearly three decades at the turn of the century, from 1890 to 1920. I have expanded the scope of this edition to include both the 1890s and the period 1917 to 1920, during and immediately after U.S. participation in World War I. Throughout the book, I have augmented the political and economic emphasis of the first edition with information and insights produced during the past decade, particularly those from the new social and cultural history and women's history. Recent scholarship and experience have also led to a greater understanding of the power of conservative attitudes and institutions and the impediments to significant reform, let alone radical change. This too has informed the second edition of this work.

The Progressive Era holds particular significance because it represents America's first full-scale attempt to come to terms with the rapidly emerging multicultural, urban, industrial society. Western "modernization," which has been described as a process of change in which social institutions have been altered to adapt to mechanization and rising economic productivity, touched virtually every aspect of American life in those years. The transformation to a more cosmopolitan, urban society caused great social and economic shifts and much personal trauma. Furthermore, significant ambivalence permeated this transitional era, tension between seeking change — the idea of progress was, after all, part of the American creed — and wanting to preserve traditional ways of life, especially traditional values concerning individual liberty and opportunity, personal and national morality, and pride in the Republic.

"The march of events rules and overrules human action," President William McKinley asserted at the turn of the century. But the forces of change can sometimes be vulnerable tyrants. There were, for example, many roads to "modernity." Long-range processes such as industrialization may shape broad conditions, but they do not dictate the adoption of particular policies or determine precise results. People choose among alternatives as they understand them. Determined individuals try to make and remake institutions. My treatment of the Progressive Era combines the large forces of "modernization" and "traditionalism" with the actions of particular men and women.

The people who shaped the attitudes and institutions of modern America in its formative years stride the pages of this book. This volume seeks to explain, for example, the role of J. P. Morgan in the formation of supercorporations such as United States Steel, Jane Addams in the origin of modern social work, Douglas Fairbanks and Mary Pickford in early motion pictures, Theodore Roosevelt in the creation of the Panama Canal and U.S. hegemony in the Caribbean, and Woodrow Wilson in America's entrance into World War I and his vision of a new world order.

The new social and cultural history focuses on the experience of masses of average people, and this edition stresses their experiences as workers, consumers, family members, group members, and citizens. Some who played particularly important roles are featured in this book. They are as diverse as Theda Bara, the first Hollywood symbol of the highly sexual *femme fatale*; Margaret Sanger, creator of the controversial modern birth control movement; Ida Wells-Barnett, who roused the African-American community to a crusade against lynching; Leonora O'Reilly and Rose Schneiderman, working-class founders of the Women's Trade Union League; James "Jim" Thorpe, Native American Indian athlete who was the major winner in the newly revitalized Olympic Games in 1912; and evangelist William A. ("Billy") Sunday, one of the most popular preachers of the early twentieth century.

Americans sought to master the sweeping forces of change by what I call a "new interventionism." This represented an unprecedented willingness to intrude into the economy, society, and world affairs. The new interventionists believed that intelligently directed effort could affect change and manipulate the environment for the improvement of society. This new attitude challenged and modified nineteenth-century beliefs in a self-regulating marketplace, unrestricted individualism, and a foreign policy of political and military isolationism.

The Victorian idea of inevitable progress had to be abandoned. It was based on developments in science and industry that created possibilities that had scarcely been dreamed of, but, as people came to learn, were not all for the better. The most famous group among these interventionists was the moderate reformers who called themselves progressives. They gave their name to the era and to the particular spirit of the times. The progressive ethos — a mixture of pragmatic, piecemeal reform and an idealistic, quasi-religious vision of efficient democracy — inspired millions of middle-class Americans to some social activism. It dominated national politics for a decade.

Among historians, the nature of the Progressive Era remains a major source of controversy. My interpretation emphasizes that the developments of this period did not result solely from the action of progressives. Major contributions were made by radicals, conservatives, and important nonprogressive movements, including the corporate reorganization and consolidation movement, the labor movement, the women's movement, and the movements for both cultural homogeneity and ethnic pluralism. This study also stresses the role of private voluntary associations, as well as governmental agencies, as mechanisms for achieving directed change. It examines the role of reformers and others who worked for change not only in the political and international system but also in the private sector: in education, medicine, law, religion, and social and family relationships.

This edition also incorporates recent scholarship that has, to some extent, shifted away from a focus on progressivism itself — now generally accepting the reform "movement" as pluralistic — to the context in which reformers operated. In that context, this edition emphasizes a dramatic change in politics — the contraction of the electorate, the decline of old party loyalties, and the explosion of aggressive, politically active pressure groups. The book also demonstrates how even more substantial change occurred in the organization of economic and social power, as local, informal groups so characteristic of small-town and agrarian society were superseded as the basic framework of American life by immensely larger, hierarchically structured formal organizations — most prominently, large corporations and expanded government. In addition, this edition shows how there emerged in that era a culture of consumption — a set of ideas and values that emphasized the importance of the ongoing acquisition of goods and services that was promoted as offering both a new frontier of economic expansion and a new mechanism for individual happiness and fulfillment. Like the modern corporation, the political pressure group, and the regulatory state, the consumer culture is part of American legacy of the Progressive Era.

In the decades between 1890 and 1920, Americans contended with a host of problems in an urban, industrial society. Among these were dangers posed by overcrowding and violence in the cities and by an increasingly polluted environment, problems of mass unemployment and numerous bankruptcies caused by an untamed business cycle, challenges posed to opportunity and to democracy by the emergence of giant corporations, and tensions caused by racial, ethnic, and class divisions. Equally pressing were issues of gender and sexuality as society was confronted with challenges to prevailing norms about gender roles, the status of women, the nature of the family, definitions of masculinity, and appropriate social mores. Domestically, Americans wrestled with the challenge of "modernism" to traditional values and ways of life, with concepts of a dominant national culture or cultural pluralism. Internationally, the United States sought to redefine its place and its foreign policy in a world in flux.

Understanding the nature of the Progressive Era provides significant insight into the nature of reform, social change, and continuity in America. The power of particular groups fluctuates somewhat over time as economic and political situations differ. As a result, periods of reform have appeared cyclically on the American scene. Examination of the Progressive Era allows us to view an entire phase of a reform cycle and to probe both its origins and accomplishments. As men and women seek to master change, their solutions are not always inevitable or even desirable. Some of the solutions reached in the Progressive Era, such as the juvenile court system, community zoning, and federal regulatory commissions, are being challenged today. Yet others, such as the community chest, chambers of commerce, consumer protection, investigative journalism, urban playgrounds, worker's compensation, environmental conservation, the city manager system, direct election of U.S. senators and other key federal officials, and women's suffrage, have retained widespread support. In foreign affairs the penchant of the American presidents during the era for using the nation's growing economic and military means in support of expansive national goals has also left a divided legacy. Whatever reassessment Americans may make of the legacies of the period, to understand the Progressive Era is to understand the origins of modern America.

The Tyranny of Change

CHAPTER 1

Crisis of the 1890s

America prides itself on progress, and there was a great sense of national exhilaration in many of the developments of the final quarter of the nineteenth century. Yet the growth of great cities, the inpouring of millions of immigrants, the sudden rise of giant industries, and the rapid acquisition of an island empire led many people to question whether these innovations did not threaten America's prized tradition and ideals. Many Americans felt themselves caught up in a swirl of uncontrolled change.

The dual nature of the emerging urban, industrial society was beginning to become clear by the end of the nineteenth century. "Modernization" (or what Americans liked to identify as continued "progress") brought major problems as well as substantial gains. Vastly increased economic production and national wealth was often accompanied by harsh urban life, brutal factory conditions, a scarred environment, and an unprecedented concentration of economic power.

The strains of transition from agrarian society to industrial nation, together with massive flows of immigration and internal migration, intensified tensions among classes, races, and ethnic groups. In regard to gender relations, "modernization" brought forth additional efforts by the women's movement to improve women's status and usefulness to society and to give women their share in directing public as well as their own private destinies.

Americans were also confronted with dilemmas of making politics and government as a whole more responsive to the wider needs created by the new urban, industrial order. How could allegiance to the nation and adherence to principles of American democracy be reconciled with declining voter participation and the proliferation of new interest groups? In the global arena, what role would an industrializing United States play in a world soon to face major challenges from revolutionary nationalism in China and Mexico, communist revolution in Russia, and from aggressively expansionist industrializing Germany and Japan?

The final decade of the nineteenth century dramatized the hopes and fears of Americans about the course of industrial "progress." The "gay nineties" of popular lore were a time of adventure and excitement. Mustachioed men in derby hats promenaded along tree-lined streets with elegant women in high-buttoned shoes, bustles, and flowing lace dresses. In melodious harmony, people crooned the new popular songs like "Daisy" and "The Sidewalks of New York." At the local saloon patrons could still enjoy a free lunch with frosty mugs of beer that cost only a nickel. When the World's Fair opened in Chicago in 1893, people came from all over the country to marvel at the achievements of technology and the evidence of rapid progress demonstrated at the "great white city" erected by the lakefront.

"Life in the States," an English visitor reported in 1900, "is one perpetual whirl of telephones, telegrams, phonographs, electric bells, motors, lifts, and automatic instruments." Enthusiastic admirers of technology, most Americans applauded these inventions. Mammoth new factories delivered thousands of new products: steel girders for skyscrapers and bridges, metal tubing for bicycles, glass for large windows, copper wire for new electrical sources of light and power. Technological improvements enabled people to break through age-old barriers of time and space. At speeds of more than a mile a minute, trains carried travelers across the country in a few days instead of the months it had taken by wagon or coach. Telegraph lines sped words from one coast to another in moments. Mass production provided more goods to consumers at cheaper prices in a national marketplace linked by a network of rails and wires. Henry Adams, a Harvard historian and the descendant of two presidents, mused that "the new American — the child of incalculable coal power, chemical power, electric power, and radiating energy — must be a sort of God compared with any former creature of nature."

Yet many Americans feared the future, for such rapid modernization seemed to be a mixed blessing. Adams himself worried that the nation's dynamic technology might be out of control, spinning it away from its fundamental beliefs and heritage. The benefits of industrialization came with considerable dislocation, suffering, and jeopardy to American society. The unrestrained growth of industry devoured resources, blackened the skies with smoke, and wore down workers in factories and sweatshops. Intensive ten- and even twelve-hour workdays contributed to one of the highest industrial accident rates in the Western world.

Industrialization also seemed to be dividing the country into hostile classes: the extremely wealthy and the very poor. The new industrial rich — plutocrats, many people called them — obtained unprecedented wealth and lived in opulent splendor. In 1900 the steel magnate Andrew Carnegie, shuttling between his baronial mansion on New York's Fifth Avenue and his castle in Scotland, made a tax-free profit of $23 million. At the same time, factories, mines, and railroads employed millions of unskilled or semiskilled workers. Steelworkers worked twelve-hour shifts six days a week and earned an average of $450 a year, barely enough to make ends meet. Women earned less than men: in garment district sweatshops in New York City, they were paid only $5 for a six-day workweek, averaging $260 a year (see Table 1).

The nation seemed to be acquiring a large, unruly proletariat composed largely of recent immigrants from southern and eastern Europe. The growing cities were centers of discontent and seemed to threaten an America that had been dominated by a homogeneous rural or small-town Anglo-Saxon Protestant culture. Those who feared the influx of Catholic and Jewish immigrants into the cities, nativists like the Congregationalist minister Josiah Strong, warned that "the city is the nerve center of our civilization. It is also the storm center. . . . The city has become a serious menace to our civilization."

The 1890s were a time of disastrous events that evoked deep foreboding among Americans. The year 1893, which marked the opening of the World's Fair, also ushered in the worst depression the country had yet experienced. Some 500 banks and 15,000 businesses failed. Hundreds of thousands of people were thrown out of work without savings or relief. For the first time large numbers of tramps roamed the countryside. In one of the first mass protest marches on the nation's capital, a group of jobless men, led by Jacob Coxey and calling themselves "Coxey's Army," marched on Washington, vainly urging federal relief. They were arrested. In Chicago, railroad management, seeking to break a strike of Pullman workers and trainmen, obtained

Table 1
Comparative Value of the Dollar

Since 1913, the Consumer Price Index (CPI) has been a statistical measure of the average change in prices over time of basic consumer goods and services. The CPI indicates a thirteenfold decline in the value of the dollar between 1913 and 1990.

	1913	1990
Consumer Price Index:	10	131
Comparative value of the dollar:	$1.00	$0.07
Comparable purchasing power:*	$1.00	$13.00

Source: Computed from figures prepared by the Bureau of Labor Statistics, U.S. Department of Labor, printed in the Council of Economic Advisers' *Annual Report to the President, 1991.*

*To determine comparable purchasing power in current (today's) dollars of a particular amount, divide the new CPI by the old, then multiply the ratio (in this case 13) by the old dollar amount. (Thus it would require $13.00 in 1990 to purchase the same goods and services that $1.00 would buy in 1913.) Carnegie's $23 million personal profit in 1900 would therefore be comparable to $299 million in 1990; his steelworkers' average annual wage of $450 would be comparable to $5,850.

assistance from the police and from U.S. cavalry sent by President Grover Cleveland. Before the strike was broken, the city echoed with the sound of gunfire and the crackle of flames from burning railroad cars. In the steel town of Homestead, near Pittsburgh, a bitter strike broke into open warfare. When managers at the Carnegie mill dispatched a flotilla of rafts carrying private guards across the Monongahela River from Pittsburgh to land at the town, strikers fired on them with rifles and cannons. Ten persons, mainly workers, were killed in the strike, and an extremist tried to assassinate Henry Clay Frick, the manager of the mill. Industrial violence, crime, disease, and extensive urban poverty challenged American ideals of freedom, democracy, and a relatively classless and harmonious society.

Even in the rural heartland, the Midwest and the South, protest erupted. Populist farmers rose up against the dominance of eastern industrialists, financiers, and railroad tycoons. In 1896 agrarians gained control of the Democratic party in a futile attempt to capture the presidency. Comparing the Populists to the radicals of the French Revolution, a hysterical eastern editor warned that "the Jacobins are in full control. No large political movement in America has ever before spawned such hideous and repulsive vipers."

The crises of the 1890s led large numbers of Americans to wonder whether their belief in a self-regulating society was not contributing to the destruction of that society. Reluctance to intervene in the marketplace seemed to encourage blind social forces. However, the noninterventionist ideal of a free, unregulated marketplace and a limited role for the state had become a major tenet of the national creed in the nineteenth century and was not easily modified. This concept reinforced long-held beliefs in individualism, liberty, and opportunity and suspicion of concentrated power, whether in the state or in the form of private monopoly.

The marketplace ideal, most fully articulated in 1776 in *The Wealth of Nations* by the Scottish economist Adam Smith, coincided with what many Americans already believed: that free individuals pursuing their own self-interest also contributed to the general good of the community. In a famous passage Smith asserted that "the individual intends only his own gain [but is] led by an invisible hand to promote an end which was no part of his intention." Like the colonists who rejected the crown's grant of a monopoly on tea to the British East India Company, Smith challenged excessive mercantilist regulations as inefficient and oppressive. Neither government nor any individual, he argued, had enough wisdom to direct the complex economic life of a nation. Instead, Smith presumed a natural economic order in which competition among producers would generate the most efficient economic growth and the most adequate goods at the most reasonable prices, to the benefit of society.

Smith's conception of a self-regulating economy was readily adopted by Americans and applied to society as well. It reinforced a belief in individualism that had been encouraged by the opportunities available in America because of a shortage of labor and an abundance of land (exactly the opposite of the situation in Europe). Individualism had also been given divine sanction by evangelical Protestantism's emphasis on individual regeneration and self-worth. Furthermore, when the British government sought to expand its authority, colonial rebels like Patrick Henry, John Adams, and Thomas Jefferson adopted concepts of natural law and certain unalienable natural political rights that belonged to all people and could not be abridged by governments. Individualism and self-regulation had thus helped provide intellectual justification for the American Revolution and the American experiment in democratic government.

The economic growth and industrialization of nineteenth-century America took place in a nation that increasingly emphasized the value of unrestricted individualism, a free and open market economy, and a laissez-faire system of limited government. The admonition of Jeffersonian and Jacksonian democratic agrarians was that the government that governs least governs best. Federalists like Alexander Hamilton and Whigs like Henry Clay who advocated a positive governmental role through active economic promotion found themselves running against a popular trend. Emerson, Thoreau, and the transcendentalists emphasized individualism and restricted government, and so did the classical liberal political economists of Europe and one of the most powerful new concepts of the nineteenth century, Darwinism. As applied to society by sociologists like Herbert Spencer in England and William Graham Sumner in the United States, Darwin's theory of biological evolution through natural selection explained social change through natural evolutionary laws and the "survival of the fittest." These theorists, who became known as social Darwinists, defended the automatic functioning of society as being in the best interests of the country's evolutionary progress. They hammered away against proposals for government intervention for either promotion of economic growth or temporary amelioration of hardships as detrimental to natural progress and ultimately futile. In the second half of the nineteenth century, British visitor James Bryce observed that laissez-faire had become "the orthodox and accepted doctrine in the sphere both of Federal and of State legislation."

Social Darwinism reinforced ideas already fairly strongly held and justified practices already established. It supported the conservative temper of many Americans at the time and then added seemingly scientific justification to the faith in progress that most Americans felt because of the economic abundance, opportunity, and individual advancement in the United States. It justified those who argued for a stable and unmanipulated currency and opposed protective legislation for workers and consumers and government interference in the marketplace. Furthermore, skepticism of government seemed to be reinforced by exposés of widespread political corruption at all levels, from the Tweed Ring in New York to the Grant administration in Washington. Unlike their British counterparts, American economists, clergy, business people, and others tended to assume that principles of individualism, competition, and governmental inefficiency were laws of God and that the social and economic growth and increasingly higher standard of living of the United States were part of a divine plan. Like previous generations, they believed that Americans were a chosen people. In a textbook on political economy published in 1870, the economist Francis Bowen asserted that laissez-faire meant "'things regulate themselves' . . . which means, of course, that God regulates them by his general laws, which always, in the long run, work to good."

Although in practice laissez-faire was accompanied by much governmental promotion—land grants to railroads, protective tariffs, stable currency, and antiunion action to aid industry—the idea of the self-regulating marketplace and society attained the peak of its strength in the nineteenth century, when it was enshrined in both thought and law. But even as it reached its apex, the dramatic changes it encouraged began to undermine popular faith in the marketplace ideal. Without restriction or purposeful social direction, industrialization, urbanization, and immigration seemed to threaten American traditions of individualism, competition, and opportunity and the ideal of a democratic, relatively classless society of independent producers. In the crisis of the 1890s many people began to doubt that industrialization would cure its own ills.

A New Kind of Growth

Closing the Frontier

An era of westward growth seemed to come to an end in 1890, when the Census Bureau reported that an unbroken moving line of settlement no longer existed in the United States. The disappearance of America's western frontier, which for 300 years had served as a symbol of economic expansion and opportunity, was a blow to the nation. Even more than in other frontier societies—western Canada, Argentina, Brazil, and Siberian Russia—the American West and the rugged frontier life had become part of the nation's self-image. In 1893 the historian Frederick Jackson Turner warned that the end of the frontier threatened to curtail American uniqueness, individualism, democracy, and economic growth.

The last frontier had been conquered swiftly. After the Civil War, Americans in great numbers had pushed into the trans-Mississippi West, settling the treeless expanses of the Great Plains, the wooded valleys of the Rockies, and the drier regions of the Southwest. By 1900 the population of the West had quadrupled, reaching 17 million, and the frontier had disappeared.

The federal government had promoted, but not directed, settlement of this region. It granted public land to railroads to help finance construction of transcontinental lines. The first was completed in 1869, and by 1893 four railroads linked the West Coast with the East. Railroads and speculators acquired the best land, but many settlers obtained their farms free from the federal government under the Homestead Act of 1862.

In support of white settlement, the government also intervened to restrict, and often eliminate, the Indians. By 1890, thirty years after the white invasion of the plains began, the buffalo herds and the plains culture had been destroyed, and the decimated tribes were confined to reservations. The triumph of numbers and technology had been assisted by the Indians' inability to overcome centuries of tribal rivalry and unite against the whites.

The tribes had resisted destruction. In 1862 the Santee Sioux in western Minnesota rose against invading whites, killing nearly 800. Cheyennes attacked miners and settlers in Colorado. Whites in turn slaughtered Indians. In the Sand Creek massacre in Colorado, militiamen killed more than 200 men, women, and children in a dawn attack on a Cheyenne village. Pressed by eastern reformers, the government attempted a new "peace policy". of putting the Indians onto large reservations where they would be out of the way of white settlement and missionary agents could Christianize them and teach them farming. Lack of funds and outright starvation on the reservations led to many outbreaks of violence in the 1870s and 1880s. In the 1870s, twelve military campaigns to return tribes to the reservations cost the lives of 948 soldiers, 460 civilians, and an estimated 4,500 Indians. In 1876, Sioux warriors led by Sitting Bull and Crazy Horse annihilated General George A. Custer's force of 264 men at the Little Big Horn. The Sioux, like the Nez Percé and other tribes, were forced back to the reservations by the army and by the virtual extinction of the buffalo herds on which their society depended. The surrender of Chief Joseph of the Nez Percé in 1877 captured the Indians' despair and resignation:

> I am tired of fighting. Our chiefs are killed. . . . The little children are freezing to death. . . . I want to have time to look for my children. . . . My heart is sick and sad. From where the sun now stands I vill fight no more forever.

A final outburst came at Wounded Knee, South Dakota, in 1890, when whites, alarmed by the spread of a millenarian movement known as the

Ghost Dance, attacked a Sioux village, killing several hundred men, women, and children in the last tragic massacre of the Indian Wars.

Having defeated their warriors, the federal government tried to assimilate the Indians into American culture. Beginning in the 1870s it sought to destroy the authority of the chiefs and abolished the tradition of dealing with the Indians through treaties as if they were semisovereign domestic nations. Instead, the Indians were brought under federal jurisdiction.

The publication of Helen Hunt Jackson's book *A Century of Dishonor* (1881) contributed to the growth of a movement to ameliorate the conditions that were decimating the Indians. The resulting Dawes General Allotment Act of 1887 endeavored to convert them into small yeomen farmers by granting a 160-acre homestead to every Indian who agreed to work it. This attempt to coerce "Americanization" of the Indians was a disaster from the start. The tribal community was important to them. Many were swindled out of their land allotments, a loss to individual Indians and to their tribes. By 1920 the Indians had lost two-thirds of their land, and the majority were paupers.

In their place, the whites pushed into the West. Prospectors and mining companies moved into California, Nevada, Idaho, Arizona, and the Dakotas in search of gold and silver, copper, iron, and coal. The cattlemen soon followed, bringing steers from Texas to the railheads in Missouri and Kansas in the 1860s and 1870s and to the grazing lands of the Great Plains in the 1880s. They gave the urbanizing country a string of new frontier heroes and villains: Jesse James, Billy the Kid, Calamity Jane, Annie Oakley, Wild Bill Hickock, and Buffalo Bill Cody, the professional hunter and showman who brought cowboys and Indians to the theaters of the East even as the frontier culture was dying. Last came the farmers: lower-middle-income Americans from nearby farm states or Scandinavian or German immigrants, "sod-busters" who broke open the tough, matted, arid grasslands with new steel plows and brought wheat to the prairies of America.

The rapid settlement of the trans-Mississippi West was a source of great pride but also of anxiety, for it seemed to signal the limits of economic growth as well as the end of the frontier. Some members of the eastern elite, like the young Theodore Roosevelt, feared that the loss of the frontier experience would accelerate the flabbiness and materialism that they saw accompanying the rise of an urban, industrial, heterogeneous society.

The Blight of Racism

Like the Indians, other Americans—blacks, Hispanics, Asians— suffered from an intensified pseudoscientific racism, a doctrine that held that there were inherent differences among human racial and ethnic groups that determined cultural or individual achievement. The dominant national view in America at the turn of the century was that all other peoples were inferior to the white race and indeed to persons of western European descent. Anglo-American whites denied African Americans, Hispanics, and Asians their rights as citizens through a combination of legal restraints, physical segregation, and violent intimidation.

In the late nineteenth century these oppressed and largely impoverished minorities were clustered in particular regions. In the South, where nine out of ten African Americans lived and where they constituted about 40 percent of the region's population, blacks were the lowest-paid workers. They eked out a wretched existence as agricultural workers in the cotton fields for annual incomes of less than $400 a year or as tenant farmers who resided and worked on other people's land for a portion of the sale of the crop. These sharecroppers often lived in a kind of peonage, tied to the white planters by long-term contracts and to local merchants by long-term, high-interest debt.

In the last two decades of the nineteenth century, as some blacks moved into southern towns and began to compete with white laborers, and in some areas to vote, every southern state legally formalized a system of racial segregation (known as Jim Crow after a popular black-face minstrel show song) in virtually all public places to separate and castigate blacks as inferior. This policy was upheld by the Supreme Court under the new "separate but equal" doctrine (segregation was not unconstitutional discrimination if separate accommodations for the races were equal) in the case of *Plessy* v. *Ferguson* in 1896. Jim Crow laws helped restrict blacks to the lowest-paying jobs. They also encouraged disfranchisement of African Americans. To avoid possible political alliance between poor black and poor white voters, conservatives in the 1890s — and later many southern progressives — began to deprive African Americans of the vote through new state laws requiring voters to pay a poll tax and pass a literacy test administered by local white registrars. Consequently, the number of eligible voters in Mississippi, the first state to adopt this program, plunged in two years from 257,000 to 77,000. Reinforcing disfranchisement and segregation was a dramatic increase in repressive violence; during the 1890s an average of nearly 200 lynchings occurred each year. Some blacks, most prominently the aged abolitionist Frederick Douglass, publicly protested the new oppression. Some fled the South: 10,000 migrated to Chicago between 1870 and 1890. Most, however, sought strength and solace within the institutions of the black community — kinship networks, fraternal lodges, women's organizations, and the black schools, colleges, and churches.

In the growing oppression of blacks and lack of support from the federal government to which they had turned for protection from state and local repression, African Americans created separate self-help organizations to deal with the increased discrimination. Excluded from white associations, black editors, teachers, farmers, and doctors organized their own groups to promote their interests. Black leaders held two major conferences in 1890 to discuss the problems facing their race; unfortunately, the groups involved were too divided internally to build an effective coalition against the increased discrimination and disfranchisement.

When the men's initial efforts failed, black women with education and social standing, already leaders in African-American women's clubs and in fund-raising and social welfare within the black churches, met in Washington, D.C., in 1896 to found the National Association of Colored Women (NACW). Their aim was to combat growing racism, to meet the changing needs of the black community, and to build a national network among African-American women who were currently separated along denominational, community, and ideological lines. In 1898 black women and men joined in Rochester, New York, in the formation of the National Afro-American Council in protest against increasing racism in America.

People of Spanish origin suffered discrimination and repression, particularly in the West and Southwest of the United States. Mexican Americans in Texas and California were employed as migrant farm or ranch hands or railroad laborers, or, in the cities where they were increasingly segregated into urban neighborhoods called *barrios*, in jobs as low-paid day workers. With racism and anti-Catholicism on the rise in the 1890s, discrimination against Chicanos increased and riots against them occurred in a number of Texas towns. The situation was somewhat less oppressive in Arizona and New Mexico where Spanish-speaking Americans were relatively few in number and included a prosperous existing Hispanic business elite. Small communities of Cubans existed in New York City and, particularly, in Key West and Tampa, Florida. Founded largely by émigrés during the long struggle for independence from Spain that culminated in 1898, these communities came to include prosperous Cuban businesses especially in the cigar industry.

Chinese immigrants to America, who began arriving in the United States from Canton, China, during the California gold rush that began in 1849, first sought wealth in the gold fields. Among the few thousand erstwhile entrepreneurs, those who did not return to China settled mainly in San Francisco and established Chinese-owned laundries, restaurants, and fishing businesses. In the 1860s, thousands of less skilled and moneyless immigrants, recruited in poorer rural areas around Canton, came to help build the western roadbed for the first transcontinental railroad. This immigration, primarily of young, single male workers, continued to grow in the succeeding decades and reached 123,000 in the 1880s. Anti-Chinese sentiment on the West Coast, fueled by racial, cultural, and economic antagonism resulting in part from wage competition,* led Congress in 1882 to adopt the first major immigration restriction legislation in the nation's history. The Chinese Exclusion Act prohibited the immigration of Chinese laborers and denied them the right of naturalization. Many had already returned to China and others were forced to leave. Those who remained in the United States lived in segregated districts of the towns and cities of the Pacific coast. In the 1890s, Japanese laborers would begin to immigrate to the West Coast and would become the latest victims of anti-Asian prejudice.

Mass Immigration and Migration Chains

The majority of the immigrant work force that stoked America's manufacturing industries, worked its mines, and expanded its railroad lines came from Europe. Pilgrims to prosperity, 12 million people rode steamships across the Atlantic to the United States between 1870 and 1900; nearly another 9 million arrived in the first decade of the twentieth century. They came for various reasons: for political and religious freedom and the promise of economic opportunity. Until the 1890s most of these immigrants came from the countries that had sent immigrants before the Civil War: Britain, Ireland, Germany, and the Scandinavian countries. Beginning in the mid-1880s, however, increasing numbers began to arrive from southern and eastern Europe.

The "new immigrants" came from Italy, Austria-Hungary, Russia, Poland, the Balkans, and Greece. They were pushed from their homelands by economic, religious, and political oppression. As landlords consolidated and mechanized their agricultural holdings, millions of peasants and villagers lost their traditional livelihoods. Many fled to neighboring cities. Others set out to find employment in the growing nations of Canada, Argentina, Australia, and the United States. By 1893 they surpassed the "old immigrants" in number and made up the bulk of the new arrivals in the United States each year. They came with high hopes, like Mary Antin, author of *The Promised Land* (1912), who remembered the glowing letters her father, a Jewish teacher and storekeeper, had sent back to Russia from Boston:

> In America, he wrote, it was no disgrace to work at a trade. Workman and capitalists were equal. . . . The cobbler and the teacher had the same title, "Mister." And all the children, boys and girls, Jews and

---

*Although the Chinese laborers were generally paid lower wages than white laborers, additional antagonism against them came from the mistaken notion that they were "coolies," that is, contract laborers (contracted in China to work in the United States for less than prevailing wage rates). A "coolie trade" did exist in Peru and Cuba, but not in the United States.

Gentiles, went to school! Education would be ours for the asking, and economic independence also. . . . So at last I was going to America! The boundaries burst. The winds rushed in from outer space, roaring in my ears, "America! America!"

Traditional interpretations of the immigrant experience have been significantly modified since the 1970s by detailed studies of particular ethnic groups using the methods and concepts of sociology and the new social history. Previously, the standard emphasis was on "self-made" individual decisions and strategies by the immigrants, starting with the decision to relocate and continuing through choices made in order to adapt to American society. In the new scholarship, the role of individuals is still seen as important, but social historians now focus on broader structural influences and group-sustained strategies, which restricted and guided decisions by individuals and families.

In its broadest aspect, the new immigration history views migration within a larger geographical-economic framework. Immigrants were part of a vast labor flow within an evolving global economic system — one that attracted displaced rural dwellers from peripheral areas to become, at least temporarily, workers in the predominant economic center.

Contrary to the well-established stereotype of the "huddled masses," the majority of the new immigrants, while poor, came not from the poorest classes but from the lower and lower-middle levels of their societies. These were not dispirited impoverished people, but typically strong, ambitious young men and women from overcrowded peasant villages. Similarly, the illiteracy of the new immigrants has been overstated. Almost three-quarters of the immigrants between 1900 and 1910 reported that they could read or write (only a 10 percent drop from 1880). Although the literacy rate was highest among people from northern and western European nations, there were only a few groups among the immigrants from southern and eastern Europe that were illiterate.

Nor were the immigrants as traditionally pictured: uprooted from their environments and stripped of their old identities as they ventured alone into the New World. Rather, as the new studies show, decisions about migration as well as the actual transplantation usually took place within migration chains from villages or regions in the Old World to specific towns or city neighborhoods in the New World. The vast majority of immigrants already had relatives or compatriots in the United States and were on their way to join them. Indeed, the earlier arrivals often paid the newcomers' way across the ocean (60 percent of the new immigrants in 1909 so reported). Such collective migration patterns also applied to Mexicans moving into the Southwest and to Asians immigrating to the West Coast.

Another new insight is that the majority of immigrants to the

Awaiting processing and approval from American immigration officials, hundreds of new immigrants jam the "pens" in the Main Hall at New York's Ellis Island which was the chief immigration station in the United States from 1892–1943. (*Edwin Levick/William Williams Collection/New York Public Library*)

United States at the turn of the century *intended* their stay to be only temporary until, after a few years of work, they could save enough money to return home to an improved position for themselves and their families. With such an aim in mind, some Italian and Slavic laborers saved as much as 65 percent of their monthly earnings. Young Irish women who temporarily emigrated to America to earn money for a dowry and to liquidate family debts were common enough in County Longford to merit a special name: "redeemers."

Although the majority of new immigrants permanently settled in America, significant numbers left (with a departure rate of 35 percent for Croatians, Poles, Serbs, and Slovenes; 40 percent for Greeks; and more than 50 percent for Hungarians, Slovaks, and Italians; the rate among Asian immigrants was much higher — more than two-thirds — due to their expulsion).* Among immigrants who left voluntarily, many

---

*Even Jews, driven from czarist Russia by government-organized massacres (pogroms), as well as economic adversity, returned, at least temporarily, to eastern Europe at a rate of 20 percent between 1880 and 1900.

took advantage of improved and cheaper steamship transportation to return home temporarily during slack periods. Both temporary migrant workers and those who settled permanently in the United States maintained close contact with the people left at home, sending them letters, photographs, and even remittances.

In the United States the immigrants became urban villagers, clustering in the industrial cities. That made them more visible than previous immigrants and more closely identified with the problems of the big cities. Although the foreign-born never exceeded 15 percent of the American population (compared to 22 percent in Canada and 30 percent in Argentina in the same years), the immigrants and their American-born children represented a significant part of the population in some areas. In 1900 between two-thirds and three-fourths of the population of Massachusetts, Rhode Island, Wisconsin, and Minnesota had at least one parent born outside the United States. In cities like Boston, New York, Chicago, and Milwaukee, immigrants and their children were a majority of the population.

Traditional interpretations of the incorporation of immigrants into American society focused on assimilation and attainment and stressed the importance of initiative and skill. The new social history emphasizes both adaptation and maintenance of ethnic culture and stresses the structural and collective context in which both occur. American industry needed millions of manual workers for its expanding manufacturing and mining sectors, and most of the immigrants at the turn of the century entered and remained part of the working class for the next half century. Despite these commonalities, conditions differed. Expansive local economies such as in New York and Chicago, and smaller more volatile growing cities such as Atlanta and San Francisco, offered more opportunity for movement than tighter less expansive markets in Boston, Philadelphia, or many small one-company towns.

For a variety of reasons, jobs in the manufacturing and mining industries were often allocated along ethnic lines. Native-born American and West-European workers obtained jobs that were more stable and better paying (on an average of 10 to 25 percent better a 1909 study disclosed) than those held by members of new immigrant groups. Ethnic divisions in the labor market, however, sometimes had positive aspects, for example, in helping immigrants to obtain a foothold in the economy and later to achieve some socioeconomic advancement. Most immigrants obtained jobs through networks of kin and compatriots. From letters and other sources of information, immigrants often knew when they left their home country where they would work and at what wages. Within a few days after their arrival, they were employed at a job secured for them by their relatives or friends. Manual workers frequently worked in labor gangs, composed of people from the same nationality or even region — in some cases with immigrant labor bosses (*padrones* among Italians) hiring them out. Many American industrial employers relied upon ethnic-based hiring either directly in their departments or through the widespread use of subcontracting preparation of a partly finished product.

Consequently, the pioneers of each ethnic group obtained an area of a local economy, such as a specific trade or service, and, thereafter, this ethnic enclave provided succeeding immigrants from that country with jobs and mutual support. Although precise specializations often varied according to locality and migration chain, historian John Bodnar has given some illustrative examples: Italians dominated construction gangs and barber shops in Philadelphia, Pittsburgh, and Buffalo; in Pennsylvania, nearly 70 percent of Slovak men were employed in mining coal; in New York City, Serbs and Croats were heavily engaged in freighthandling; in Chicago, Polish women dominated restaurant and kitchen jobs which they preferred, rather than being employed as domestic servants. Ethnic compartmentalization occurred even within a particular plant, encouraged by management and often by workers themselves.

Of course, every ethnic monopoly meant the exclusion of others. In the North, black men lost control to immigrants of the few trades (such as barbering) that they had dominated for years. With the exception of railroad sleeping-car portering, they were unable to establish new monopolies. Facing continued discrimination and sporadic employment, they spread across a number of jobs and industries, almost always in subordinate, nonsecure, and poorly paid positions. Consequently, blacks were less able than the immigrants to place their children in ethnic enclave employment.

Some immigrant groups were particularly able to find or carve out ethnic subeconomies consisting of ethnic-owned enterprises that employed many workers of the same immigrant origins. According to Ewa Morawska, a leading immigration scholar, although the reasons for this varied historically and for particular groups, the most successful of the new immigrants at the turn of the century were Jews, Greeks, Chinese, and Japanese, with Cubans, Koreans, and Dominicans among the most successful since the 1960s.

For Jewish immigrants in the Northeast, this ethno-economic clustering initially resulted in part from a timely matching of skills — 65 percent of Jewish foreign-born men had been skilled craft workers in eastern Europe — to the demand for similar or at least transferable skills in the expanding garment and related industries in the major cities in which they settled. The garment enterprises in New York and other major northern cities were owned primarily by German Jews, most of whom had settled in America half a century earlier. They hired thousands of Jewish immigrants who, fleeing from Russian pograms, found their way to America and the garment industry through a migra-

tion chain of kinship and village contacts much like that of other immigrants. On a smaller scale, patterns of Jewish economic enclaves were
being formed in numerous other cities and towns across the country by
earlier settlers who extended help to subsequent immigrants by employing them or setting them up in business.

The pattern with Greek Americans and small business was comparable, but that of Chinese and Japanese Americans was different. Studies of the two Asian immigrant groups have concluded that beyond
their achievement-oriented cultural values, it was prolonged, enforced
segregation in an enclave economy (and the maximization of family
resources within that enclave) that enabled the turn-of-the-century
immigrant generation to build the economic base for the later educational and entrepreneurial advancement of their children, many of
whom, nevertheless, remained confined within their ethnic enclaves
until after the Second World War.

In the early twentieth century, already fearful of many of the
effects of uncontrolled urbanization and industrialization, many native-
born Americans regarded the new immigrants from southern and eastern Europe as another threat to traditional society. Prejudice and a
pseudoscientific racism that assumed a hierarchy of races led many
people to view the cultural and religious minorities—predominantly
Catholic and Jewish—as belonging to "inferior Slavic and Mediterranean races." More than one commentator spoke in menacing terms of
"new swarms" of European immigrants "invading America." Concerned about the declining birthrate among native-born Americans,
patricians like Henry Cabot Lodge warned of "racial suicide" and the
overwhelming of the native "racial stock" by immigrants and their
large numbers of children. A vigorous new anti-Semitism led to discriminatory barriers in housing, hotels, clubs, and offices. Representatives of conservative labor unions like the American Federation of
Labor warned that "pauper labor" undermined wage rates and the
country's standard of living. Many native-born Americans connected
immigrants with urban crime, disease, labor violence, and radicalism,
fearing the impact of a new, "unruly and inferior" urban proletariat.

Nativists who opposed the new immigrants sought to acculturate or
"Americanize" those who were already in the country and to limit the
number of new arrivals. As mentioned earlier, the immigration restriction movement began in California, where agitation led Congress to
prohibit the immigration of Chinese laborers in 1882. In the 1890s the
American Protective Association and the Immigration Restriction
League joined the American Federation of Labor, the Daughters of the
American Revolution, and other newly formed nationalistic groups in
pressing for a literacy test that would keep many of the new immigrants
out of the country.

Massive immigration did not, however, subvert American culture.

The new immigrants did not force significant changes in the structure or direction of American family, religious, or political life. Rather, they and their children usually adopted many of the patterns of the predominant Anglo-Saxon culture. But at the time the nativists feared their impact and linked them with many of the problems of the developing cities.

The Rise of the Metropolis

The cities became the focus of the new America. As the southern plantation and the northern family farm had symbolized the agrarian society of the years before the Civil War, so the industrial city emerged, for better or worse, as the symbol of the transformation of American society. The urban population grew from 20 percent in 1860 to 40 percent in 1900. Rural hamlets became small towns; towns and trading centers grew into medium-sized cities like Minneapolis, Omaha, Cleveland, Pittsburgh, Detroit, and Jersey City. In the urban, industrial heartland of the Northeast–North Central region, an entirely new type of city emerged: the modern, industrial metropolis.

The big industrial cities of the North differed in form and function from the old mercantile cities. Previously consisting of a few hundred thousand people clustered in an area of half a dozen square miles, cities like New York, Chicago, Philadelphia, and Boston grew to encompass several million people in areas of up to 40 square miles. Technology altered old constraints. Instead of walking to work, people could commute by horsecar and, beginning in the 1890s, electric streetcar. As wealthier residents moved to the periphery in "streetcar suburbs," the poor remained trapped in the urban core. The outward movement segregated large cities into rings and enclaves differentiated by income and ethnicity and, concomitantly, by rates of crime and disease.

Within the cities, soaring land values encouraged property owners to seek maximum land use. Downtown, where the streetcar lines converged, a central business district developed. Structural steel frameworks and elevators enabled builders to change the skyline of America's cities. Skyscrapers soared above church steeples and the mass of three- to five-story buildings. The downtown area housed the new department stores, banks, professional and office buildings, theaters, restaurants, and hotels that catered to the growing numbers of people who came to the hub of the city to work, shop, and find entertainment.

The city could be exciting. Rural life had been characterized by monotony and isolation, but urban dwellers saw new sights and faces almost every day. Entertainment could be found in playgrounds, beaches, parks, dance halls, vaudeville theaters, baseball fields, museums, libraries, ice cream parlors, or the ubiquitous saloons, which served not only as drinking establishments but also as political and social clubs for many members of the working classes.

But danger and disease also lurked in the cities. The high price of land contributed to urban congestion, although the housing patterns varied. In Philadelphia and Baltimore, where the tradition of home ownership remained strong, contractors built mile after mile of row houses. In Boston and Newark they put up four-story buildings with wooden decks. But in New York high rents forced as many as 400 people to jam themselves into tenements designed for fifty, in which a four-room flat might house fifteen. Dark and foul, the tenements of New York's Lower East Side produced one of the highest mortality rates in the world. Thousands died from typhoid, diphtheria, and tuberculosis. In the notorious Hell's Kitchen on New York's West Side, one reformer, Rev. Walter Rauschenbusch, declared that "one could hear human virtue cracking and crushing all around." Fires destroyed large areas of the cities, including virtually all of Chicago in 1871. Street crime was commonplace.

Startled by the growth of urban poverty and industrial violence and stunned by the angry mobs that roamed the cities during the draft riots of the Civil War and by the great railroad strikes and riots of 1877, several cities and states increased their means of social control. They expanded their police forces and revitalized the militia (now renamed the National Guard) as a defense against mob violence, providing urban militia units with formidable armories patterned after medieval castles with turrets and slotted windows.

Confronted with such poverty and violence, reformers began banding together to improve urban conditions. Some sought to save both the souls and bodies of troubled urban dwellers. The Young Men's Christian Association (YMCA) and the Salvation Army set up residential hotels that also served as religious, cultural, and recreational centers. A more secular movement established settlement houses. The first, Hull House in Chicago's immigrant tenement district, was founded by Jane Addams, a young woman from a middle-class Illinois family who rejected the traditional homemaker role to become the founder of modern social work. Many of the immigrant groups formed their own mutual aid societies, and the needy poor also received aid from Catholic churches and Jewish synagogues. Within Protestantism, a number of concerned clergymen, such as Rauschenbusch and Washington Gladden, founded the social gospel movement, which stressed social ethics and ministered to the needs of the urban poor.

When municipal governments had difficulty coping with sanitation, water supply, urban transportation, and public relief, upper- and middle-class citizens often joined in civic reform associations to obtain governmental action. Led by business and professional people, these so-called good government groups did much to establish and expand professional public health, fire, and police departments, ensuring proper authority and responsibility in those agencies. In many cases this also meant unseating urban party bosses like William M. Tweed of New York City.

Urban political "machines" were often based on a combination of the votes of poor and working-class inner-city ethnic constituents and the financial support of local contractors and other urban business interests. Reformers accused party "bosses" who ran the machines of manipulating voters and of maintaining power and enriching themselves through padded city contracts, kickbacks, and other forms of graft. However, the reformers were often most concerned with increased taxes on property owners. Most of them ignored the role of municipal political machines like Tweed's in providing assistance to the poor and to ethnic groups and in making the fragmented system of city government work.

Urban reformers of the post–Civil War period often formed permanent organizations that acted as supplemental political vehicles for accomplishing what the constituted governments could not do. They also began to expand the powers of government and modify the policy of laissez-faire in areas like public health, where they recognized the need to intervene in the marketplace to exert some control over the water supply, garbage and sewage disposal, inspection of milk and meat, and treatment of infectious diseases in order to protect the public welfare.

The Age of Industrialism

The Supremacy of Industry

Industrialization transformed America within a single generation. By 1900 the United States had emerged as the manufacturing giant of the world, surpassing Britain and other industrializing nations. The change from small shops to the factory system had begun before the Civil War, especially in textiles and iron manufacturing. But in the decades after the war, entrepreneurs dramatically expanded production by establishing the factory system and mass production in a growing number of industries. America's factories boosted real gross national product (the sum total of goods and services produced) by 120 percent, an average annual gain of 4 percent, between 1870 and 1900. By the turn of the century, the value of manufacturing goods exceeded that of agricultural commodities. The United States had become an industrial nation.

This phenomenal boost in manufacturing production came from a triple revolution: in transportation and communication, in production, and in marketing. Railroads and steamship lines created a national and an international market by linking the areas that supplied raw materials and commodities with the industrial regions and the growing urban centers. Drastically reduced transportation costs enabled large, efficient producers to undersell local manufacturers. Steel mills in Pittsburgh could outbid local ironmongers in Philadelphia, New York, and even London. The telegraph provided business with the means of communication and the information required to operate across such distances.

Swiftly developing technology and new sources of power made possible the production revolution that supplied this expanded market. New mining techniques and refining processes provided basic ores. Coal, the major new energy source, replaced waterfalls, horses, mules, and oxen. New processes like the Bessemer and open-hearth methods of making steel improved both the product and its production. (By 1900 the United States was producing more steel, and selling it more cheaply, than Britain and Germany combined.)

Inventions created completely new products, especially for urban consumers. Alexander Graham Bell, educator of the deaf and experimenter in acoustics, demonstrated the first magnetoelectric telephone in 1876. The same decade saw the development of the first adding machine with printed totals, the cash register, celluloid, and electric dynamos. In the 1880s patents were granted for numerous electrical appliances: fans, flatirons, stoves, and sewing machines. An electrical engineer, Thomas Alva Edison, built a research laboratory in Menlo Park, New Jersey, not far from New York City, saying that he intended to turn out "a minor invention every ten days and a big thing every six months or so." A distinctly American concept and a distinct success, Edison's invention factory developed marketable products on a regular basis. The "Wizard of Menlo Park" and his associates produced the phonograph (1873), the incandescent electric light bulb (1879), an improved motion picture projector (1895), and a host of other inventions that helped change the nature of life in America.

A revolution in the structure of American marketing linked the new mass production industries with the emerging mass markets. Before the Civil War, wholesale merchants had managed the distribution of manufactured goods to retailers and consumers. In the postwar era, mass production manufacturers began to circumvent the old system of distribution. In the 1880s and 1890s, Singer (sewing machines), McCormick (reapers), and Remington (typewriters) pioneered in building national and even international marketing operations that included traveling salespeople, franchised retail dealers and repair shops, and branch offices to coordinate supplies. When butchers in the East resisted switching from locally slaughtered beef to the products of the Chicago meatpackers, Gustavus Swift bought his own refrigerated warehouses, sales offices, and retail stores. He was able to undersell butchers who had cattle shipped live to the East because, since 60 percent of each animal was inedible, he saved transportation costs by slaughtering in Chicago, where it could be done in volume, and then shipping the meat to market in refrigerated cars. Expansion from production into distribution (and sometimes backward into raw materials) was called vertical integration, and this technique was employed by a number of Swift's imitators, who made Chicago the meatpacking center of the country and Milwaukee and Saint Louis the dominant producers of beer for the national market.

Mass production, however, has its pitfalls. Through extensive use of costly high-speed machinery, manufacturers could turn out millions of units, from steel rails to cigarettes, at a fraction of the average cost per unit for smaller manufacturers. Taking advantage of the cost savings from economies of scale (reducing unit costs and thus increasing profits through large scale production), mass producers expanded their markets by underselling competitors. But when the supply of goods outstripped immediate market demand, as often happened, prices plummeted. American steelmakers increased output from 3 million tons to 30 million tons between 1870 and 1900, and the price of steel rails dropped from $100 to $12 a ton. Consumers benefited from the expanded number of goods and the long-term decline in the overall price index, which dropped 25 percent between 1873 and 1896. But many of the men who ran the high-volume industries complained that mass production had undermined the basis of workable price competition, thereby weakening the foundations of the self-regulating marketplace.

Although many people believed that industrial competition benefited society by maintaining low prices, the managers of railroads and other capital-intensive, high-volume businesses bemoaned the increasingly harsh price wars as "cutthroat" or "ruinous" competition. Adam Smith, they said, had presupposed a market in which small firms freely entered and left. Smith had assumed that when manufacturers could not sell at a profit because of a temporary oversupply of goods, they would close down until shrinking volume caused prices to increase to a profitable level, at which point they would resume production. But in times of intensive competition for declining markets, the new industrial giants would sell below the costs of production, rather than shut down, in order to pay some of their enormous overhead expenses, such as interest on indebtedness (the cost of building a steel mill in Pittsburgh, for example, increased from $156,000 during the Civil War to $20 million in 1890).

The intensive price-cutting competition, which often drove prices below cost, led many entrepreneurs in the mass production industries to seek to ensure profits through other means. Some, like the steel magnate Andrew Carnegie, became increasingly competitive, shaving costs by cutting wages and streamlining procurement, production, and distribution. Some tried to expand their markets through extensive advertising and sales campaigns at home and, especially after the depression of the 1890s, abroad. But many sought to avoid price competition by joining with their rivals to intervene in the marketplace in order to control price fluctuations and ensure profits. Beginning in the railroads and spreading into industry, these interventionists tried a variety of means ranging from cooperation to consolidation. "I like a little competition," explained J. P. Morgan, a Wall Street banker who financed many consolidations, "but I like combination better."

The Origins of Big Business

Combination produced big business and the largest supercorporations the world had ever seen. An organizational revolution transformed American business. Before the Civil War most businesses had been small shops or firms owned by a single proprietor or a few partners. The largest, the New England textile mills, were companies that had been created with $1 million. But in the late nineteenth century new entrepreneurs built a number of behemoth corporations backed by hundreds of millions of dollars and controlling many plants and thousands of employees. Railroads provided the prototype for large-scale, widespread, hierarchical business organization. But the new form of organization soon spread to mass production industry as industrialists sought to extend their power and control the market for their goods.

Attempts to limit price competition began with pools (or cartels, as they were called in Europe), loose agreements in which a number of rival firms agreed to fix prices and allocate markets. Pools were formed among railroads and in the meatpacking, tobacco, and electrical equipment industries, but they rarely functioned well because they could not be legally enforced. Anglo-American common law did not support combinations in restraint of trade. Instead, business turned to other forms of consolidation: acquisition, merger, and the trust.

John D. Rockefeller organized the first and most famous of the trusts, the Standard Oil Trust, in 1879. The former Cleveland bookkeeper and wholesale merchant had entered the petroleum refining industry at its start and had quickly become the largest refiner of kerosene illuminating oil in America. Chaotic conditions and wildly fluctuating prices frequently cut profits in the industry, and ruinous price wars were common. Rockefeller's Standard Oil Company of Ohio cut costs through efficiency, but it also used its power to obtain secret rebates from railroads, drive competitors out of business, and influence state legislatures. By the mid-1870s the company had eliminated or absorbed many of its competitors through a process of consolidation known as horizontal integration.

Then in 1879 Standard Oil and its forty leading rivals organized a trust in which the voting stock of the operating companies was turned over to a board of trustees headed by Rockefeller in exchange for trust certificates. The trustees of the new Standard Oil Trust set policy for an organization that controlled 95 percent of America's refined-petroleum output. Profits averaged 19 percent a year for the next decade and a half. When the state of Ohio convicted Standard Oil Company of violating its charter, the trust moved to New Jersey, which in 1889 became the first state to make it legal for a corporation in one state to control a corporation in another. In that year the Standard Oil Company of New Jersey was created as a holding company, a paper corporation with its own board of directors, which held the majority of voting stock in various operating companies and could thus set common pricing and market policies for them.

The Challenge of the Trusts

Although the great majority of American businesses remained highly competitive, the emergence of a significant number of giant industrial monopolies became the focus of substantial public concern in the late nineteenth century. Like industrialization itself, the creation of big business stimulated both pride in American power and achievement and anxiety about the ramifications of this new development. There was also much confusion because many people considered all giant firms monopolies when many were not.

Proponents of consolidation claimed that big business was inevitable, stemming from mass production technology, new sources of power, better organization, and the ability to market goods throughout the United States and the world. They also maintained that big business represented progress, creating more jobs and increasing the standard of living by making more products available at cheaper prices. "To stop co-operation of individuals and aggregation of capital," Samuel Dodd, chief attorney for Standard Oil, declared, "would be to arrest the wheels of progress — to stay the march of civilization."

But many Americans worried about these new concentrations of capital, especially their power. "Relations between rival railroad systems," Louis D. Brandeis, a social reform lawyer, complained, "are like the relations between neighboring kingdoms. The relations of the great trusts to the consumers and to their employees is like that of feudal lords to commoners or dependents." At first, cartoonists portrayed the trusts (which came to represent all of big business) as grasping octopuses or bulging moneybags with high silk hats as they loomed menacingly over society. Gradually, public sentiment built against the trusts. Farmers, workers, owners of small businesses, socially concerned ministers, and journalists began to accuse railroad consolidators and industrialists like Rockefeller of being "robber barons" who obtained their enormous wealth and power by predatory means, especially local price cutting and exclusive selling of contracts to retailers, which forced competitors out of business. Some critics believed that the benefits of mass production could be achieved by medium-sized firms. Many worried about big business's control over competition and the marketplace, claiming that the trust destroyed opportunities for others to become independent businesspeople.

Such powerful changes as those represented by the emergence of big business, the massive influx of immigrants from southern and eastern Europe, and the dramatic expansion of urban, industrial cities, posed fundamental questions about the nature of American society. The Victorian idea of inevitable progress had been based in part on the spurt of scientific knowledge and rapid technological change. These seemed to create possibilities that had scarcely been imagined. Yet, by the turn of the century, it was becoming clear that many of these were not for the better. Industrialization was providing a mixed legacy.

CHAPTER 2

Prelude to the Twentieth Century

New Jobs, New Roles

The sweeping forces of industrialization, immigration, and urbanization transformed the nature of work and the work force. Although millions still labored on farms and in villages, the greatest increase in jobs came in urban areas —in factories, offices, retail shops, and department stores. Increasingly, America became a nation of wage earners. At the time of the Civil War, only slightly more than a million people worked for hourly wages; the majority of white Americans were self-employed on farms or in small shops or other businesses. On the eve of World War I, in 1914, however, more than 7 million persons worked for someone else for wages, and millions more were salaried employees paid by the week or the month. America was becoming a nation of employees.

Factory Labor

The nation's factories drew workers from many sources. Some were skilled artisans displaced by industrialization. Many had been unskilled day laborers. And the sons and daughters of farmers left the land in droves for jobs in the factories. Increasingly, however, the least skilled, heaviest, dirtiest, and most dangerous jobs were done by immigrants or by nonwhites.

As people moved from the work routines of the farmer and artisan to factory discipline, the nature of work changed. Mass production and the factory system divided labor into simple, repetitive tasks. Managers used incentives and coercion to adapt rural people to the pace of the machines they operated. Published work rules, bells and whistles, constant supervision, and the piece-rate system, which paid workers on the basis of their output, encouraged productivity. So did fines, suspensions, and firings. Monotonous factory work diminished the sense of

25

self-worth of many workers, who also resented the dependence fostered by the wage system. Many skilled trades and the apprentice-master system were eliminated or greatly modified. "You can take a boy fresh from the farm," lamented a machinist with thirty years of experience, "and in three days he can manage a machine as well as I can."

Speed of production and lack of safety devices led to one of the highest accident rates in the industrialized world. Steelworkers labored twelve hours a day, six days a week in front of the furnaces. Men and women in the nation's factories put in a workweek that averaged sixty hours. Pittsburgh, with its miles of steel mills, seemed to one visitor to be a city "like hell with the lid taken off."

The transformation of work affected workers in different ways. Because of limited alternatives, many accepted factory conditions, particularly because of the wages, which exceeded those in rural areas of the United States and Europe. Since prices dropped throughout most of the last third of the nineteenth century due primarily to increased production, *real* wages (the purchasing power of wages) climbed until the late 1890s. However, during periods of unemployment, which were frequent, laid-off workers received neither wages from the company nor economic compensation from the state.

An additional incentive for accepting the wage and factory system was the prospect of upward socioeconomic mobility. Though seldom experienced, the "rags to riches" myth celebrated in American folklore and the popular novels of Horatio Alger was widely believed. People pointed to Andrew Carnegie, who rose from immigrant factory worker to steel magnate and multimillionaire. Recent studies disclose that although Carnegie was a rare exception, a significant number of people did improve their socioeconomic status somewhat during the period.

Some of those who moved upward were immigrants. Giuseppe Tuoti opened a real estate office in Manhattan in 1885, and his business prospered as Italian immigrants saved their earnings and bought stores and tenements. Within a few years Tuoti had formed a company to develop the town of Woodbridge, New Jersey, as a suburban retreat for Italians and others fleeing Manhattan's slums. Soon he expanded his operations to Staten Island, Brooklyn, and the Bronx. By the time he retired, in 1924, Tuoti had become one of New York's leading real estate magnates, a self-made millionaire. Many other immigrants won a measure of economic success. In America a Warsaw tailor became a dressmaker; a Pinsk peddler flourished as a storekeeper; a talmudic scholar from Vienna became a leading lawyer.

Small gains in status were much more common. Recent statistical research shows that in some cities one out of five white men, native-born and immigrant, moved from blue- to white-collar occupations in a single decade, the 1880s. Furthermore, many unskilled workers moved into semiskilled positions, and their children often moved on to skilled jobs. A laborer's son might become a factory worker, his grandson a machinist. By sending many members of the family to work and living frugally, while putting money in a savings account each week, some families of unskilled and semiskilled workers bought relatively inexpensive houses and became property owners. The realization that improvement was possible may have helped to alleviate the massive discontent caused by the trauma of industrialization.

In some industries, wage cuts and layoffs led to violent episodes, as workers rebelled against management's attempt to impose what many workers considered egregiously unfair conditions. The great railroad strikes of 1877, the Homestead strike of 1892, and the Pullman railroad car strike of 1894 all led to pitched battles between strikers and police. In 1886 violence flared in Haymarket Square in Chicago during a demonstration in support of the eight-hour day. Someone threw a bomb into the ranks of police, killing half a dozen. Police then fired wildly into the crowd, causing more casualties. Four alleged anarchists were executed for the "massacre."

Some attempts were made to form labor-based political parties, but on the national level the Greenback Labor party of 1878 – 1884 and the National Labor party of 1888 were never able to do more than elect a handful of members to Congress.

Although most workers remained outside workers' parties and unions, labor's most significant response to the new conditions was to develop national organizations. The earliest national confederations of workers — the National Labor Union (1866 – 1872) and the Knights of Labor (1878 – 1893) — organized skilled and unskilled workers and opposed the wage system, seeking alternatives such as consumers' and producers' cooperatives. The most influential unions, however, did not try to eliminate the wage labor market but accepted the corporate industrial wage system and sought to limit competition among skilled craft workers in order to achieve higher wages and better working conditions. The railroad brotherhoods (engineers, conductors, and firemen) and the trade unions, which in 1886 formed the American Federation of Labor (AFL), used their economic power, through strikes and boycotts, to better their conditions.

Following the example of big business, organized labor attempted to protect itself against the more extreme effects of market forces by enrolling all the workers in particular trades — carpenters, teamsters, brewers, railroad workers. American labor, craft-conscious rather than class-conscious, only rarely before the 1930s organized all workers in particular industries regardless of whether they were skilled or unskilled. As leader of the AFL, Samuel Gompers, an English immigrant cigar maker, abandoned socialist goals for what he called "unionism pure and simple." Under his direction the AFL grew from 150,000 members in 1886 to 500,000 in 1897, when it represented nearly 60 percent of the union members in America. Labor, like business, challenged and helped to modify the free-market system through the organization of interventionist forces.

A New Middle Class

Among the most rapidly growing areas of the economy was the service sector; the number of white-collar jobs in offices and stores increased dramatically. Clerks and salespeople, typists and secretaries may not have earned the same incomes as members of the middle class, but their attire and surroundings made them feel that they were part of it. In addition, large numbers of salaried workers were employed in the expanding areas of education and government. Staff, supervisors, and managers in the new corporations provided part of the new salaried middle class, as did the growing numbers of professionals — lawyers, doctors, engineers, teachers. Increasingly, the new middle class eclipsed the old middle class of artisans, skilled workers, shop owners, and small manufacturers. The new middle class (of salaried and non-propertied workers) grew eightfold from 1870 to 1910, from 33 percent to 66 percent of the entire middle class. Still, middle-class white-collar workers remained a minority (only 20 percent) of the total male labor force in 1910.

New Roles for Women

Women, important as ever to the rural farm economy, also became a significant part of the urban industrial work force, but the new system generally separated home and work. Furthermore, traditional family responsibilities continued in the new urban life, and many women were caught in the middle, seeking to fulfill two sets of responsibilities at the same time. Young single women had worked for wages in the earliest New England textile mills. During the Civil War they temporarily replaced men in many factories and stores. In the postwar period they found work as domestic servants in private homes. Increasingly, women were employed as workers in commercial laundries, canneries, garment factories, and cigarette and textile mills. They also worked in clerical positions in offices and sales jobs in department stores and as switchboard operators for the expanding telephone network. The factory system employed women from lower-income families. Most middle-class women did not work for wages in the nineteenth century. Neither did most married women, although in poor and working-class families they often provided meals and did laundry for paying boarders because their own families lived at or below subsistence levels. Furthermore, many married women in such families took in home work, making garments and other items on a piecework basis.

In the 1880s, young women replaced boys and young men as telephone operators. Males were seen as too rude and unreliable, so the company selected
young women for their courteousness and reliability. By the turn of the century, as seen in this photograph at the Courtland Exchange in New York City,
rows of female operators remained plugged into their switchboards for nine or
ten hours a day, handling 200 to 300 calls an hour at a weekly wage of seven
dollars. Women could become supervisors (seen here standing behind groups
of operators) and a few even became chief operators (seated at the desk, far
right). But positions above that, from district traffic chief and division superintendent to the president of the company, were held exclusively by men. (*AT&T
Archives/Bell Labs*)

Because of their race and gender, African-American women had a
unique subculture, one not shared entirely by either black men or
white women. Blacks as a whole demonstrated a communal solidarity
that grew out of both their African heritage and the exploitation of
their labor by whites, first as slaves and then as low-paid menial
workers. In economic terms, African Americans were seen by most
white employers as a pool of relatively inexpensive labor. In the late
nineteenth century, black women, like most black men, were largely
excluded from the new economic opportunities and remained engaged
mainly in labor-intensive cultivation of the cotton crop in the South.
The second major area for black women in the paid labor force was
household domestic service, first in the South and then, beginning in
the early twentieth century, in the North. Whether fieldworkers, laun-
dresses, or domestic servants, black females remained tied to over-

whelming wage-earning and child-rearing responsibilities. They helped to maintain the family structure (most black families in the late nineteenth century — 86 percent in 1880 and 83 percent in 1900 — were two-income families with both husband and wife residing at home) that with religious and educational institutions served as the anchors of black community life. Despite their limited income, African-American women had considerable informal influence over young people and adults of all ages in their own communities through their reputation as spiritual counselors and healers. Yet they also suffered the negative impact of poverty. As a result of poor nutrition, abysmal health conditions, and inadequate medical care, a black mother at the turn of the century could expect to see one of every three of her children die before age 10 and to die herself before the youngest left home.

Within the comparatively small black middle class, women worked for pay outside the home to a much greater extent than middle-class white women, finding opportunities as teachers, professors, journalists, or nurses in black schools, colleges, newspapers, and hospitals (which were founded in several cities beginning in the 1890s). Among the most famous were Ida Wells-Barnett, the daughter of Mississippi slaves and a former teacher, who edited her own newspaper in Memphis, Tennessee, and who in 1892 galvanized the black community in a crusade against lynching; Mary Church Terrell, Oberlin College graduate, Washington, D.C., schoolteacher and woman's club activist and pacifist; and later Mary McLeod Bethune, daughter of former South Carolina slaves, a schoolteacher, who founded and served as president of a small black college and who became nationally prominent in the 1930s as an administrator in one of the federal government's youth programs. Whether in their employment or as members of religious, professional, or business associations, such as the black woman's club movement, middle-class African-American females also saw themselves as crusaders for their race and for a better society much more than most white professional women and reformers, many of whom refused to cooperate with the black women, either because of personal hostility or to avoid alienating the white South.

With more than 90 percent of African Americans living in the South, 80 percent in rural areas, and with their own history of exploitation, restrictions, and repression, blacks reacted to the industrialization and urbanization of the era differently from other Americans. As historian Jacqueline Jones has explained:

> In their poverty and vulnerability, black people experienced these historical economic transformations in fundamentally different ways compared to whites regardless of class, and black women, while not removed from the larger history of the American working class, shouldered unique burdens at home and endured unique forms of discrimination in the workplace.

In factories, offices, or private homes, the average wages of women, white or black, were about half those of men and usually less than were needed for expenses. Poor working conditions and low wages encouraged some women, such as the Irish collar makers and laundry workers in Troy, New York, to join the emerging labor movement and participate in strikes. Yet the presence of women in factories provoked anxiety among male workers, who feared competition for jobs and lowered wages. A prevailing concept, which historians have labeled the "cult of true womanhood," stressed domesticity and submissiveness as the proper womanly characteristics and emphasized women's roles as wives, mothers, and homemakers.

In addition to inferior wages and exclusion from many job categories and professions, women in the late nineteenth century still faced legal codes that, despite recent modification to give wives control over their earnings and inherited property and increased rights over their children, still discriminated against them in numerous ways, from denying them independent access to credit to precluding them from voting.

Beginning in the 1840s, middle-class women like Elizabeth Cady Stanton and Susan B. Anthony founded a women's movement as the start of a major collective search to define and ensure a position for women in society that was not subordinate. They sought not only suffrage but fully equal citizenship and autonomy, or individual self-determination. The expansion of the economy in the post–Civil War era created new jobs for women outside the home and offered at least second-class employment opportunities for increasing numbers. In 1870, 15 percent of American women worked outside the home; in 1890, 20 percent did. Society was forced to recognize the disparity between the reality of working women and the ideal of exclusive homemakers. Female academies and women's colleges like Mount Holyoke, Wellesley, Bryn Mawr, Vassar, and Barnard, most of them founded after the Civil War, helped to prepare women leaders and provided for more assertive intellectuality and greater self-assurance in their occupations. Some women found jobs as nurses and schoolteachers, and a handful broke employment barriers to become physicians and professors, primarily at women's colleges but sometimes at predominantly male universities.

A Victorian Moral Code

The so-called cult of domesticity, a widespread belief that idealized the home as the "woman's sphere," was one aspect of a disciplined and prudish code of personal behavior that took its name, Victorianism, from prevailing views in England and America during the long reign of Britain's Queen Victoria (1837–1901). Victorian morality placed extreme emphasis on industriousness, modesty, sobriety, and self-control.

Although often violated in practice, the Victorian code, with its great stress on morals, manners, and proper behavior, served to create visible distinctions among social groups and classes. For the upper and middle classes, it comfortably encouraged and solidified an increasingly self-righteous and intensely moralistic outlook. In functional terms the Victorian moral code also served as a standard (albeit often a double standard more indulgent of men than of women) by which elites and the middle classes sought to control a turbulent, multiethnic, urban, industrial society.

Victorianism had a particular impact on women. Since they were seen as morally superior to men, they might acquire some powers to enforce this moral code. For example, women provided important leadership in the campaign against the proliferation of saloons and the increasing consumption of alcohol. In 1874, Frances Willard, deploring the economic and physical impact on the family of alcoholic husbands and fathers, founded the Women's Christian Temperance Union (WCTU). By 1900 the WCTU had 500,000 female members (men were banned from membership), making it the largest women's organization in the country.

Yet the Victorian moral code was more often directed at controlling women's behavior, especially their sexual behavior. In a growing urban society alarmed by increasing prostitution and venereal disease as well as, from a different perspective, the declining birthrate among the middle and upper classes, a number of crusaders became greatly concerned with the idea of limiting extramarital sex and at the same time encouraging larger families. In the Comstock Act of 1873 (named for public virtue crusader Anthony Comstock), Congress passed a law against the dissemination of "obscene" materials, which were defined to include information about contraception. Many states went even further, forbidding the sale of condoms or diaphragms and prohibiting abortion (which under previous common law had generally been permitted until the sixth month of pregnancy, the normal time of "quickening," or the first felt movements of the fetus in the womb).

Women and the Public Sphere

In the second half of the nineteenth century, women, particularly those from the middle and upper classes, increasingly entered the public sphere — if not yet the electoral arena and public office — as they addressed issues of concern to them and to the larger society. The old ideal of republicanism helped drive a demand for woman suffrage and full citizenship. By the 1890s some progress had been made, including women's access to education and limited toleration in the professions as well as some rights over their own property. Yet women still lacked the vote and also suffered under the double standard of morality, which prohibited sexual indiscretions by women while tolerating those of men.

Women also played an increasing role in social reform. By emphasizing their nurturing and morally superior roles as wives and mothers, upper- and middle-class women expanded their sphere to include the application of domestic values to the larger society. Fostering a vision of a "maternal commonwealth," women in the Women's Christian Temperance Union, the Young Women's Christian Association, the growing number of women's clubs and social work groups, and other organizations redefined Victorian domesticity to include a public role for women. These included major efforts to aid the poor, particularly women and children, through improving their opportunities and controlling the dangerous environment in which they lived.

The most striking symbol of the change among middle-class women in the late nineteenth century was the emergence of the college-educated, generally unmarried, self-supporting "new woman." Nearly half of all college-educated women in the late nineteenth century never married, and those who did married later than most other women. A new lifestyle of the female career woman, in professions such as teaching, nursing, and social work, emphasized intellectual and economic independence. Visually, this was personified in a new style of dress, look, and activities in the 1890s: the fresh, athletic, and slightly rebellious "Gibson girl" (an image created by artist Charles Dana Gibson for *Life* magazine in the 1890s). This new woman played tennis and golf and rode a bicycle in simpler, more practical clothing — a tailored suit or a long dark skirt and blouse or "shirtwaist" rather than the old trailing petticoats and beribboned gowns.

Challenges to the Victorian conception of woman's proper sphere frightened many people, who often linked these to other social problems. Many traditionalists feared that employment outside the home and the drive for women's rights undermined the family and contributed to social instability. They were especially alarmed by declining birthrates and soaring divorce rates, which they blamed on the changing status of women as well as on increased prostitution and venereal disease. Most historians and demographers have instead emphasized conscious choices for improved health, greater autonomy, and a higher standard of living as explanations for the drop in the overall national birthrate, which declined from 52 per 1,000 population in 1840 to 33 in 1900, 30 in 1910, and 28 in 1920. The trend to smaller families was particularly evident among the largely Protestant upper and middle classes.

"Divorce crisis" was the term applied in the first decade of the twentieth century when discussion of this "social problem" was most intense. The divorce rate nearly doubled, from one in every 21 marriages in 1880 to one in every 12 by 1900. In response, state legislatures enacted more restrictive marriage laws that raised the age at which young people could marry without their parents' consent and required premarital medical tests and public notice of prospective marriages. The legislators also tightened up divorce laws, reducing the legal grounds for divorce, diminishing judicial discretion, and increasing the waiting period before remarriage.

Manhood in Modern Society

Modern economic and cultural trends also posed challenges to some of the traditional notions and rites of maleness. Despite important variations across class and ethnoreligious lines, manhood in Western culture was, before industrialization, still linked with skills, prowess, and authority often stemming from ownership of at least some piece of property and traditions of the hunt, artisanship, and agriculture, as well as responsibility for the family. (Even male slaves, without property and with little ability to protect their families, found ways within the slave community to demonstrate their manhood and their importance to themselves, their wives, and their children, for example, through their skills at hunting and fishing.) However, as industrialization created new working and middle classes, specific patterns of male behavior came to depend particularly heavily on social class. Traditional male roles were fundamentally changed, as industrialization heightened the importance of gender. For men it increased the importance of defining and fulfilling the criteria of manhood.

Gender distinctions increased in many ways. Industrialization created many more factory jobs for men than for women, even as numbers of women and children entered the paid work force. The workers in heavy industry in particular — mines, metalwork, construction — were overwhelmingly male. Pride in physical prowess was an important aspect of working-class masculinity. Much of the industrial work in the nineteenth century did demand great strength and stamina, but the main growth in the twentieth century was in technology that lightened tasks, diminishing the importance of physical strength. Male strength was being replaced by machines. As the "steel-driving man" John Henry declared in the popular folksong: "Well a man ain't nothing but a man. And before I'd let that steam drill beat me down, I'd die with my hammer in my hand."

As artisans, tradesmen, and farmers were replaced by machines, many former skilled workers joined the ranks of propertyless wage earners; as a result, fewer working-class fathers had skills or real property to pass on to their children. Many saw this lack of property and hence control as the greatest loss of their importance and their manhood. Even more, in an industrial system in which workers had lost much of their independence and were closely watched and directed by their supervisors, how could such workers see themselves as manly?

Creating a new concept of masculinity provided some answer, stressing elements that had been important and adding new male attributes. Increased sexual activity and at an earlier age was one answer, evidenced by the rising rates of illegitimate births in the nineteenth century. Another was assertion of patriarchal authority within the family; indeed, the authoritarian father, one strict in discipline who ruled primarily because of his position as the main breadwinner, remained pervasive within working-class culture until well into the twentieth century. Inability to fill that role, particularly if the wife was forced by economic or other circumstances to work outside the home, was frequently seen as the failure of a man. Failure and resentment, at times accompanied by alcoholism and uncontrolled bouts of rage, sometimes led to physical abuse or neglect of wives and children. However, collective action—worker uprisings—against wages or working conditions did help to create a link between protest and a sense of self and collective bonding.

While many propertyless males continued to associate manhood with skill and strength, they also increasingly claimed freedom from control, if not at work, at least outside the job. The roughness and physicality of the working-class style of manhood became more evident, in emphasis on sexual conquests, drinking, rowdiness, and contact sports. Outdoor group sports, particularly football and baseball, spread rapidly among working-class males, who could find in them a pride in physical prowess and skill.

Increasingly, new leisure time activities in the late nineteenth and early twentieth centuries were divided by sex. A vigorous subculture developed among working-class male youth, designed to prove masculinity through drinking, fighting, "womanizing," and engaging in rough contact sports—from amateur boxing to sandlot football—generally watched by predominantly male audiences. Working-class bars, pool halls, boxing arenas, and racetracks, were heavily masculinized. Indeed, apart from courtship, there was little male-female contact in leisure.

Middle-class patterns were more complex, but the rise of men's clubs and fraternal organizations reflected the increase in gender distinctions in leisure activities. While upper-class men frequented all-male social clubs, masses of other white men participated in fraternal organizations. In 1897 the *North American Review* proclaimed the last third of the nineteenth century the "golden age of fraternity" and reported that nearly 6 million of the 19 million adult males in the United States belonged to such bodies, the largest of which were the Odd Fellows (810,000), Freemasons (750,000), Knights of Pythias

(475,000), and Red Men (165,000). Indeed, the flow of urban middle-class members into fraternal organizations had actively reformed them from drinking clubs to more morally acceptable institutions. With their opportunities for male bonding and their elaborate, secret, and primitive-oriented initiation and advancement rituals (linked to Indian lore or medieval knighthood, for example), these lodges may have offered men a way of effacing the religious values and emotional ties associated with women and child rearing. Instead, by affirming their manhood and worthiness, the ceremonies may have helped prepare them for the relentlessly aggressive and competitive demands of the masculine workplace. This may have been the deeper meaning of initiation into the fraternal organizations for men in a rapidly changing urban, industrial society in which male roles and definitions of manhood were rapidly being transformed.

More and more middle-class men worked in the bureaucracies of business, and the imagery of ownership and independence as badges of manhood declined in validity. For managers, professional men, and the masses of new clerks and salesmen, income replaced ownership of productive property as the criterion for measuring economic self-worth. This led many men to associate their manhood with specialized knowledge. The middle-class-oriented educational system reinforced this view by largely excluding girls and women from the classical curricula as well as the scientific and mathematical training increasingly important in the economy; instead, women were channeled into religious and moral training and were educated in domestic skills and cultural refinements such as music, art, and language.

School sports were aggressively male, particularly high school and college football and baseball. The rise of such widely played sports helped to bring middle-class males to the same association of manhood with athletic prowess that the working class had developed. In general, however, the middle class had an aversion to violence. The emphasis in the late nineteenth and early twentieth centuries was on rationality and the importance of intellectual skills and moral self-discipline. Only by taming aggressive urges, young males were taught from boyhood, could they master themselves and grow into the chivalrous husbands and beneficent fathers who represented the ideal of the middle class at the turn of the century. The wife — the "better half" — served as the agent of moderation, morality, and "culture." In imitation of the upper classes, the middle class developed a more genteel, family-oriented recreational pattern that included croquet, tennis, and, as a pallid substitute for horseback riding and the hunt, bicycle riding. The ideal in middle-class marriages was increasingly the acceptance of a mutual rather than a patriarchal relationship between husband and wife. Women won domestic rights to own property independently, to control their own earnings, and to divorce. Educated and responsible, in charge of the tasks of running the home and rearing the children, often performing volunteer work in religious or social groups, middle-class wives were ideally seen as equal partners.

The difficulties of male self-definition in the middle class at the turn of the century were complicated by a world of changing economic and social relationships. The middle-class model of manliness was a man who could steer carefully between being too weak — soft, emotional, willing to succumb to grief or fear — and too strong — overly yielding to his destructive, animal nature. In public as in private relations, this meant competing yet, at the same time, maintaining decent consideration for others, suppressing violent impulses, and not subordinating spiritual values to materialism.

Increased Consumption

New middle-class and working-class urban dwellers were the targets of an expanded material culture that increasingly emphasized consumption of new goods and services. Palaces of consumption, called "department stores" because they offered wares in many different departments, encouraged the purchase of everything from ready-made clothing to metal housewares. Their window displays in particular helped to educate consumers to current fashions. Neighborhood "chain stores," such as the first F. W. Woolworth "five- and ten-cent" store, which opened in 1879, eschewed the elegant and expensive marketing of the department stores for a cheaper, "no-frills" approach.

Entertainment also became a major industry, with many new activities vying for consumer dollars. The development of the "safety bike" with equal-sized wheels, pneumatic tires, and coaster brakes caused millions of Americans to take up bicycling in the 1890s. Spectator sports attracted growing crowds. Professional baseball offered an outdoor spectacle for urban residents and by the 1890s filled new stadiums with crowds of up to 60,000 people. Working-class men and women went on "dates" to vaudeville shows, dance halls, "dime" museums, "penny arcades," and grand new "amusement parks" with exotic shows and mechanical rides such as those built at Brooklyn's Coney Island, Atlantic City's boardwalk, Philadelphia's Willow Grove, and Los Angeles's Venice Beach. Wealthier couples could attend theaters, recently built symphony halls and opera houses, and impressive new museums of art and natural history.

Farmers: The Vanishing Yeomen

Although agricultural productivity continued to grow in the late nineteenth century, agriculture's importance declined rapidly. With increasing mechanization — especially the use of mechanical reapers and threshers — and the expansion of farm acreage from 500 million to 800 million acres between 1870 and 1900, agricultural production grew dramatically. But because of mechanization, this leap in output was accomplished by a smaller number of workers. In 1850 some 60 percent of the population was engaged in agriculture; by 1900 the proportion had dropped to 40 percent. Over the same period, agricultural output fell from 40 percent to 20 percent of gross national product.

Many American farmers found themselves in difficulty in the late nineteenth century. With the vast expansion of agricultural production, the price of commodities generally declined, falling by 50 percent between 1866 and 1900. At the same time, farm mortgages increased as farmers brought new land into production and bought new equipment. Agrarians complained of high interest rates, freight rates, and prices for agricultural machinery, which were kept artificially high by means of the protective tariff (a customs duty on imported goods designed to protect domestic producers rather than to raise revenue). Caught between falling commodity prices and rising costs, many farmers went bankrupt. Farm tenancy (the farming of land owned by others) increased nationally from 26 percent of all farms in 1880 to 35 percent in 1900. The rise was particularly dramatic in the cotton and wheat states. The yeoman farmer, the symbol and hope of America in the Jeffersonian era, became an anachronism in a land of large-scale production. An increasingly urban nation looked on small farmers as a relic of the past, while the farmers became radicalized because of their plight and turned to political action to save themselves and their vision of America.

The Weakened Spring of Government

Government was ill prepared to cope with the major forces that were transforming the country. Suspicion of power, a legacy from colonial times, had led Americans to limit central power, fragmenting it through the federal system and the checks and balances on the branches of government. The Jeffersonian-Jacksonian ideal of a limited state and the policy of laissez-faire combined to restrict the functions of the national and state governments. Traditionally, Americans had relied primarily on voluntary private associations rather than public authorities to deal with most of their collective problems. Compared with other nations, the United States had, according to a visiting European scholar, M. I. Ostrogorski, only "a weakened spring of government."

Popular Politics

The humorist Mark Twain was fond of saying that it was a good thing Congress had not been present when God said, "Let there be light," because otherwise the world would have remained in darkness. Like many others, Twain belittled the politicians in Washington. While the powerful currents of industrialization, urbanization, and immigration were changing the nature of American society, both major parties ignored the problems due to both lack of understanding and timidity. Because Republicans and Democrats were so evenly divided, with control in each house of Congress fluctuating between them, they evaded new issues and avoided bold actions that might have uncertain effects. The result was a politics of dead center in which neither major party sought to disturb the status quo. "The Republican and Democratic parties were like two bottles," the English observer James Bryce commented. "Each bore a label denoting the kind of liquor it contained, but each was empty."

Paradoxically, at a time when government seemed so superficial, the political participation of Americans reached its highest point in the country's history. In the last third of the century, the turnout of eligible voters reached 80 percent nationally and 95 percent in certain sharply divided states in the Midwest. In those days, in addition to being a ritual affirmation of democracy, politics, as Michael E. McGerr has shown, was a form of popular entertainment, almost a spectator sport. In addition to their political role, election campaigns through widespread public participation were also expressions of martial spirit, leisure, personal identity, communal life, and class theater. On a hot summer day in 1876 a local paper in a small Indiana town reported that a political rally held during the week was "a spectacle no foreign fiesta could equal."

Sectional and cultural differences also help to explain why most people remained intensely loyal to the two major parties despite their ineffectiveness. The divisions that had led to the Civil War continued to shape the polity for generations after the war's end. The Republican party was strong in the North and among the restricted black voters in the South. The Democratic party was strong in the South and among certain urban, ethnic-based political machines in the North. In a few midwestern and Middle Atlantic states, the parties were evenly matched. Memories of the Civil War and religious and ethnic values proved more important than class or economic issues in determining how most Americans defined their political loyalties. Seeking to enjoy their own cultural traditions, Irish and German Catholics, Jews, and Lutheran and Episcopalian Protestants, members of "liturgical" churches that emphasized ceremony, ritual, and well-defined dogma preferred to keep government out of their private lives. They tended to support the Democratic party, which in the North took a more tolerant view of cultural pluralism. In part, these groups reacted against the Republican party's attempts to use the power of the state to regulate ethical behavior and to create a "virtuous" society, for example, through state and local laws controlling the use of alcoholic beverages and the observance of the Sabbath on Sunday. The Grand Old Party (GOP), as the Republicans called their organization, appealed especially to evangelical, "pietistic" Protestants, such as Baptists, Methodists, Presbyterians, and Congregationalists who emphasized personal reformation, inner regeneration, and "right behavior" over ritual and dogma.

The Growth of Government

In its limited fashion, the federal government gradually began to expand its functions and to shift from issues related to the Civil War and Reconstruction to policies promoting economic growth and some feeble attempts at regulation. To encourage settlement of the West, Congress provided land for settlers and the railroads. To encourage industrial growth and high wages, it maintained a substantial protective tariff against foreign competition. Both major parties supported tariffs, although most Democrats wanted lower duties, which would benefit agrarian consumers. Reaction against corruption, the spoils system (which rewarded partisans with federal jobs), and the assassination of President James Garfield (the assassin was embittered at being rejected for a patronage political appointment, and the assassination helped to mobilize public sentiment for reform of the entire patronage system) led Congress to establish the federal civil service system at a time when the number of civilian federal employees was soaring—it increased from 53,000 in 1871 to 230,000 in 1900.

A wave of protest against combinations in railroading and industry and their dominant influence in the marketplace forced the government to take some regulatory action. In 1887, Congress prohibited pooling (the secret fixing of prices among ostensible competitors) by the railroads and established the first federal regulatory agency, the Interstate Commerce Commission (ICC), to determine whether freight rates were reasonable. Without rate-fixing authority, however, the ICC was soon reduced to a statistics-gathering bureau by adverse court decisions.

A trust was a combination of companies in which the stock was controlled by a central board of trustees that could control prices and limit competition. Federal actions against trusts proved ineffective. In 1890, in response to public pressure, Congress passed the Sherman Antitrust Act, which outlawed combinations in restraint of trade and provided for triple damages upon conviction. Perhaps intentionally, the law was too vague to be effective. Congress had acted partly to avoid more radical state action, especially in agrarian regions. The lawmakers did assert federal jurisdiction over interstate commerce and the national marketplace, and they moved to limit the trusts, but they left it to the executive and the judiciary to decide what would be done.

The Supreme Court emasculated the Sherman Act as it applied to business. It took a limited view of the interstate commerce power (the constitutional authority of the U.S. government to regulate commerce that crosses state lines) when it ruled in favor of the sugar trust in the *E. C. Knight* case (1895). The Court, however, proved quite willing to use the antitrust act against labor unions (*In re Debs*, 1895) and upheld injunctions against strikes that obstructed interstate commerce. While upholding formal consolidations like the sugar trust, the Supreme Court invalidated pooling or cartel arrangements among independent companies in the *Addystone Pipe and Steel* case (1899). Nineteenth-century conservatives believed that the judiciary rather than the other popularly elected branches of the federal government should weigh the claims of conflicting groups and determine the proper equilibrium among the rights of individuals, the sanctity of private property, and the welfare of the community. But many Americans expressed discontent about the ineffectiveness of all of the branches of the national government in dealing with the issues of industrialization.

Politics in the Depression Decade

Grover Cleveland, a conservative New York lawyer-politician, who was the only Democratic president between 1861 and 1913, first won the presidency in 1884. In 1892, following considerable labor and agrarian discontent, Cleveland returned and defeated his successor, Republican Benjamin Harrison of Indiana, winning the solidly Democratic agrarian South and eight northern states. Cleveland was almost immediately confronted with the onset of the worst economic depression of the nineteenth century. The downturn began in 1893 with a financial panic stemming from excessive speculation, particularly in railroad stocks. Loss of cash, credit, and confidence helped to push the economy downward for nearly four years. Railroads, banks, and thousands of businesses failed. Industrial unemployment ranged from 20 to 25 percent. Farm prices dropped more than 20 percent, and farmers' incomes suffered accordingly.

In the wake of such suffering, and the protests that accompanied it, the conservative Cleveland and his advisers clung to a laissez-faire philosophy, arguing that government could do nothing to alter boom-and-bust economic cycles. The main action the administration did take was to focus on saving the gold standard (U.S. dollars were then redeemable in gold or silver), which was being jeopardized by large numbers of foreign and American investors cashing in their investments for gold and thereby draining the U.S. government's gold reserves. To reassure financial interests, Cleveland first overrode western silverites and others favoring inflation and forced Congress to stop the government's program of regularly purchasing large amounts of western silver. Then, in 1895, when the government's gold reserves were down two-thirds to $41 million, Cleveland appealed directly to two Wall Street bankers, J. P. Morgan and August Belmont, who agreed to lend the government $62 million to purchase 3.5 million ounces of gold, half of it from foreign sources. The gold purchase deal helped end the gold drain and saved the gold standard (it also earned the two banking houses a substantial profit). But Cleveland's focus on the gold standard and his dealings with the bankers at the same time that he was authorizing the use of force against the Pullman strikers in Chicago and against Jacob Coxey's unemployed demonstrators in Washington was seen by many as evidence that the administration was overly callous at a time of widespread suffering.

Nor did other branches of the federal government provide adequate relief. Although the Democrats controlled Congress from 1893 to 1895, the Wilson-Gorman Tariff of 1894 only slightly lowered customs duties (and hence the prices paid by consumers). A divided Supreme Court declared unconstitutional the only radical portion of the tariff bill, which established the first federal peacetime income tax (there had been one during the Civil War) and placed a 2 percent tax on the incomes of the very wealthy. The inability of the federal government to respond to the substantial social and economic problems exacerbated by the depression of the 1890s led many Americans to conclude that laissez-faire philosophy had to be modified and replaced by more vigorous public and private leadership.

Populism: The Agrarian Revolt

Plagued by declining incomes and mounting debt even before the national depression began, many farmers and villagers in the South and the West demanded governmental action to ease their plight. "The fruits of the toil of millions," the platform of the newly formed People's party declared in 1892, "are boldly stolen to build up colossal fortunes of a few." The Populists attacked the eastern moneyed interests and the gold standard they supported and demanded unlimited coinage of silver to boost commodity prices through inflation of the money supply. Despite much confusion and moralistic rhetoric over whether the nation's currency should be backed by gold alone or by silver as well, the basic issue was whether the federal government should actively intervene in the economy and use its power to aid groups, like farmers, that were hurt by industrialism. The Populists also urged federal ownership of the railroads, government loans on crops and land, an eight-hour day for labor, direct election of U.S. senators, and a federal income tax on the new sources of wealth.

Taking up the Populists' standard, William Jennings Bryan, a Nebraska congressman, won the Democratic party nomination for president in 1896 in a repudiation of Grover Cleveland's policies. A powerful orator, Bryan challenged eastern financiers and corporate managers — and the Republican party — in ringing biblical terms: "You shall not press down upon the brow of labor this crown of thorns. You shall not crucify mankind upon a cross of gold." The "great commoner" enlisted millions in his crusade, but he lost to a former Republican congressman and governor of Ohio, William McKinley. It was a crushing defeat for the agrarians. Although it is seldom recognized as such, L. Frank Baum's masterpiece of children's fantasy, *The Wonderful Wizard of Oz* (1900), may have contained a subtle, symbolic allegory of the populist revolt. It told, after all, of the unmasking of a fraudulent wizard by a little girl from Kansas, a farmer, an industrial workman, and a cowardly lion (the pacifist politician William Jennings Bryan?) who followed a yellow (golden?) brick road but were saved by Dorothy's magic *silver* shoes (Hollywood later changed them to ruby red) in the Land of Oz (ounce?).

Although few Americans realized it at the time, Bryan's defeat marked the last bid of the nation's farmers for leadership of a national reform movement. It also ended an era of political stalemate and timidity, ushering in a period of a strong Republican majority and some bold new political leadership that addressed many contemporary issues, particularly ones that concerned business and other increasingly well-organized interest groups.

McKinley as President

McKinley had won the presidency by combining traditional Republican support from business, farmers, and Union veterans of the Civil War with new backing from many industrial workers and urban immigrant groups, primarily those opposed to the groups and positions of the Democratic party. In the depression of the 1890s, the Republican party, emphasizing national leadership and prosperity combined with some ethnic representation, was able to saddle the Democratic party with the aura of instability and hard times and put together a powerful northern- and western-based coalition. The GOP built an organization that could command votes, raise money, and mobilize public opinion. It dominated national politics for the next thirty years.

As chief executive, McKinley foreshadowed the "modern" presidency by reorganizing and invigorating the executive branch. By actively leading the party and the government, he abandoned the more passive role of the previous "caretaker" presidents. Aiding him was the economic recovery, which began in 1896, spurred by a combination of prices bottoming out, increased business confidence resulting from the Republican victory, and new discoveries of gold in Alaska and South Africa that expanded the money supply without panicking conservatives concerned with silver-fed inflation. Moving to enact his campaign promise, McKinley obtained a higher tariff, allegedly to protect wages as well as prices in American industries. But he also instigated a process of reciprocal tariff reductions with other nations in an effort to expand foreign markets for American goods. In the area of labor-management strife, McKinley sought to provide an alternative solution to resolving violent railroad strikes, such as the Pullman strike, by obtaining from Congress an administrative structure for government mediation. He was also considering some kind of government regulation of monopolies, but a crisis in Cuba and consequent war with Spain in 1898 turned his attention to foreign affairs.

The Taste of Empire

New Directions

"Barriers of national seclusion are everywhere tumbling like the Great Wall of China," an American historian observed in 1898. By the turn of the century, Americans had joined the Europeans and the Japanese in the international competition for commerce, colonies, and prestige. Exercising new-found strength, the United States defeated Spain in 1898 and gained not only a major role in the Caribbean and the western Pacific but recognition as a world power as well. Expansionists hailed the end of America's largely self-imposed exclusion from international affairs. "The policy of isolation is dead," the *Washington Post* declared. "A new consciousness seems to have come upon us — the consciousness of strength, and with it a new appetite, a yearning to show our strength. . . . The taste of empire is in the mouth of the people."

This new outward thrust posed a challenge to American traditions. In the past the United States had maintained a realistic, limited foreign policy. Isolated, protected by broad oceans and relatively weak neighbors on either side, and enjoying a large domestic market, Americans paid little attention to events abroad, reacting to those that affected them rather than trying to shape international developments. The United States saw itself serving primarily as a moral example to the world, a beacon of democracy. In the late nineteenth century, however, American policymakers became more willing to embark on foreign adventures.

Expansion was not new to Americans, who had justified their westward conquests as part of a divinely ordained "manifest destiny." But overseas imperialism was different. The acquisition from Spain of an empire of thickly populated islands such as Puerto Rico and the Philippines, which the United States intended to administer as colonies, not as potential states of the Union, led many traditionalists to accuse the nation of departing from its unique mission. As the philosopher William James put it in 1898, in the early days of the war with Spain:

> We had supposed ourselves . . . a better nation than the rest, safe at home, and without the old savage ambition, destined to exert great international influence by throwing in our "moral weight." . . . Dreams! Human Nature is everywhere the same; and at the least temptation all the old military passions rise and sweep everything before them.

Fueling America's new expansionism was a growing sense of what the nation could and should accomplish in the role of world power. The idea of mission remained strong, and the descendants of those who had sought to convert the Indians now carried the Bible to "heathens" in Hawaii, Japan, and China. The evangelist Dwight L. Moody echoed the buoyant optimism of many Christian Americans in 1887 when he organized the Student Volunteers for Foreign Missions and called for "the evangelization of the world in this generation." America's traditional sense of itself as the exemplar of free democratic institutions was augmented by social Darwinism, which, as interpreted by imperialists on both sides of the Atlantic, meant that it was the responsibility of the Anglo-Saxon race ("the white man's burden," Kipling called it) to "civilize" and "uplift" the nonwhite peoples of the world.

Industrial growth gave Americans a new sense of power, but the depressions of the 1870s, the 1880s, and especially the 1890s caused many in industry and government to look for new markets abroad. Exports leaped from $34 million to $1.5 billion during the last three decades of the century. Many prominent Americans saw foreign economic expansion as necessary to great-power status as well as beneficial to national prosperity. "The trade of the world," Senator Albert Beveridge declared, "must and shall be ours." The desire to extend and protect foreign commerce and to be a great power led to the modernization of the U.S. Navy, which by 1900 ranked third among the world's fleets, surpassed only by those of Britain and Germany.

No clearly defined overall foreign policy guided American expansion in the late nineteenth century; decisions were often opportunistic and politically motivated. Nevertheless, despite an erratic course, expansion continued during the three decades after the Civil War. The United States bought Alaska from Russia and established a naval coaling station on Samoa in the South Pacific. It signed trade agreements with countries in Latin America and the Far East. American forces helped wealthy white planters overthrow the native monarchy in Hawaii. Then, in 1895, the Cleveland administration warned Britain to arbitrate the boundary dispute between British Guiana and Venezuela or face the possibility of war with the United States. Active American intervention in international relations involving a major power marked a significant departure from traditional foreign policy, shocked the European nations, and led the British to back down.

The War with Spain

The Spanish-American War of 1898 continued the United States' rise to global activism. Like a crab scampering sideways across the sand, the country crawled hesitantly toward war. After the Cuban Revolution erupted in 1895 under José Martí and bogged down in a bloody stalemate as the Spanish military governors struck back with brutal counterguerrilla measures, Washington tried to persuade Madrid to grant the reforms, autonomy, and ultimate independence necessary to restore stability and commerce on the island. As the conflict dragged on, President McKinley came under increasing pressure for U.S. intervention from business interests that had invested in sugar plantations and other economic facilities on the island and from large numbers of Americans who sympathized with the Cuban fight for freedom. In a gesture of resolve, McKinley had dispatched the small battleship *Maine* to Havana harbor. On February 15, 1898, a series of explosions sank the ship, killing 260 of its crew. Although it still remains unresolved what caused the blasts—external mines or unstable internal powder magazines—the most belligerent American newspapers immediately blamed the deaths on Spanish saboteurs. "Remember the *Maine*" soon became the American war cry.

In New York the sensationalist Hearst and Pulitzer newspapers, vigorously competing for circulation, helped whip up war hysteria, but sentiment for American action to "free" Cuba was also strong in the agrarian Midwest. When important business interests reluctantly decided that even a potentially unsettling war was preferable to continued disruption of the American political and economic situation, McKinley obtained authority from Congress to use U.S. forces to drive the Spanish out of Cuba and end the war. Antiannexationists in Congress added the Teller Amendment (by Republican Senator Henry Teller of Colorado) stating that the United States had no desire for "sovereignty, jurisdiction, or control" over Cuba.

With the declaration of war in April 1898, prewar U.S. naval plans were put into operation, beginning with a swift attack by Commodore George Dewey's Asiatic squadron on the antiquated Spanish fleet in the Philippines, also a Spanish colony. Dewey's victory at Manila Bay led the McKinley administration to consider establishing an American colony there, close to Far Eastern markets. Later that summer U.S. troops occupied the city of Manila.

In the Caribbean the U.S. Navy established a blockade of Cuba, containing the Spanish Atlantic fleet in Santiago harbor. An expeditionary force of 17,000 American troops landed on the eastern end of the island and stormed a series of fortified positions leading to Santiago. The most publicized action was the taking of San Juan and Kettle hills by two dismounted cavalry regiments, one of regular troops, one of citizen-soldier volunteers. The so-called Rough Riders, a collection of eastern aristocrats and western cowboys organized by former assistant secretary of the Navy Theodore Roosevelt, was assisted in overcoming the withering fire from the top of the hill by the steady advance on their flank by the 10th U.S. Cavalry Regiment, a segregated unit of black regulars. With American artillery on the high ground, the seven warships of the Spanish squadron sought to break through the U.S. naval blockade; all seven were destroyed in the attempt. Cut off from reinforcements, the Spanish forces surrendered to the Americans.

In the three-month war the United States was victorious in Cuba and the Philippines and in the invasions of the Spanish colonies of Guam in the Pacific and Puerto Rico in the Caribbean. At the same time, Washington annexed the Hawaiian Islands as an American territory. Since 1891 the islands had been governed by a group of American sugar planters who had overthrown the native Hawaiian monarchy and sought incorporation into the United States. The war with Spain increased the importance of the U.S. Navy's facility at Pearl Harbor there and also overcame political divisions in Congress over annexation. The Hawaiian Islands were acquired for their strategic and economic value. America made the most of what Secretary of State John Hay called a "splendid little war."

An Island Empire

McKinley's decision to demand an island empire — Puerto Rico, Guam, and the Philippines — in the peace treaty with Spain triggered a major debate over the direction of American foreign policy. Both the shapers of foreign policy opinion — government officials, editors, former diplomats, international lawyers, peace activists, missionaries, and religious and business leaders — and the general public were divided over the issue of annexation.

Expansionists like Theodore Roosevelt and Senators Albert J. Beveridge and Henry Cabot Lodge supported annexation as the responsibility of a great power. If the United States did not guide, protect, and educate the native peoples toward self-government, they argued, they would be taken over by some other, more aggressive country like Germany or Japan. Advocates of a "large policy" also saw economic benefits for the United States. They viewed the Philippines as the "pickets of the Pacific, standing guard at the entrance to trade with the millions of China." Manila would become an American Hong Kong, an entrepôt for that market. Guam would be a naval coaling station.

Puerto Rico would provide a site for protecting the trade routes to a Panama Canal.

Anti-imperialists like William James, Andrew Carnegie, and Senator George F. Hoar of Massachusetts viewed the acquisition of colonies in far-flung underdeveloped lands as another dangerous threat posed to American traditions by industrialization. The taking of "vassal states" without the consent of their inhabitants, one senator declared, was "trampling . . . on our own great Charter which recognizes alike the liberty and dignity of individual manhood." Andrew Carnegie offered to write a personal check for $20 million to buy the independence of the Philippines.

Despite their efforts, the anti-imperialists failed to prevent the annexation of an American colonial empire. A few days before the Senate ratified the Treaty of Paris, which ended the Spanish-American War and provided for the annexation of Puerto Rico, Guam, and the Philippines, fighting broke out between American troops and Filipino nationalist forces under Emilio Aguinaldo who wished independence rather than American rule. It took more than two years and 125,000 U.S. soldiers to suppress the revolt. The Americans suffered more than 7,000 casualties, and more than 200,000 Philippine civilians died from privation, disease, and brutality during the fierce and ruthless guerrilla war that solidified American power in the Philippines.*

As a Pacific power, the United States began to participate actively in the momentous developments in China. With the decline in the power of the Manchu dynasty, Europeans and Japanese began to carve out spheres of influence in what Western diplomats called "the sick man of Asia." Attempting to enunciate a coherent and defensible American policy toward China, Secretary of State Hay circulated two "Open Door" notes among the great powers—Britain, France, Germany, Italy, Japan, and Russia—in 1899 and 1900. These defined American interest as maintaining the territorial integrity and sovereignty of China and keeping the spheres of influence, or leaseholds, of other powers there open to trade with other nations, such as the United States. The European nations acquiesced in this statement of policy because they feared that a scramble to divide China might lead to a world war. When Chinese nationalists staged the Boxer Rebellion, the United States added 2,500 troops to a multinational expedition that rescued the foreign legations besieged in Peking. Hay's notes were also designed to reassure Americans that the government did not intend to keep U.S. troops on the Asian mainland, as it had in the Philippines.

The acquisition of an empire and the recognition of great-power status had seemed so easy that many Americans were deceived into

---

*Spain went on to spend more money and lose more soldiers in an attempt to regain imperial status by conquering Morocco in North Africa.

believing that intervention in the name of moral idealism could be achieved without significant costs to the nation. But others were concerned about the effects of this new role on American ideals and traditions. As William Graham Sumner argued in an 1899 article titled "The Conquest of the United States by Spain," it might do much harm:

> We cannot govern dependencies consistently with our political system, and. . . if we try it, the state which our fathers founded will suffer a reaction which will transform it into another empire just after the fashion of all the old ones. That is what imperialism means.

The Challenge of Change

"My country in 1900," Henry Adams wrote, "is something totally different from my own country in 1860. I am wholly a stranger in it. Neither I, nor anyone else, understands it." Americans considered change to be part of the progress ordained for their nation, and many applauded the industrial growth that by the turn of the century had made the United States one of the most powerful nations on earth. But the developments of the end of the nineteenth century — the closing of the frontier, industrialization and the emergence of the trusts, massive new immigration, the rise of giant metropolises, and the conquest of a far-flung island empire — were so new and rapid that many people were not sure they represented progress. Indeed, Harvard art historian Charles Eliot Norton concluded that it was a "degenerate and unlovely age."

Cracks in the Victorian Order

The old order of thought was also disintegrating under changing social conditions and recent ferment in the intellectual world. America and the Western world were beginning the transition from an age of confidence to an age of doubt. The United States had been born in the Enlightenment and had grown to maturity in the Victorian period with its emphasis on an orderly, Newtonian universe of natural laws, fixed moral principles, the dignity of humanity, the omnipotence of God, and the benevolence of nature. Nature and experience had justified the optimism of Americans, who saw evidence of progress in the growth of their country's wealth and power. But this comfortable Victorian concept of life and the universe began to fall apart under the impact of industrialization and the blows of Darwinism.

One of the most influential concepts of the nineteenth century, Darwinism caused an intellectual revolution not only in biology but also in people's attitudes about the place of humankind in nature. In what he called the "struggle for existence," the English naturalist

Charles Darwin concluded that the organisms that were best equipped to get food and shelter would inherit whatever favorable variations occurred in their genetic makeup. Gradually, through a long process of "natural selection," higher, more developed species would evolve. The English sociologist Herbert Spencer applied Darwin's theories of evolution and "survival of the fittest" to society as well. His work was popularized in the United States by the sociologist William Graham Sumner and the philosopher John Fiske.

Evolution banished the absolute and knowable Newtonian universe and substituted one that was in constant flux, whose beginning and end were unknown. The process of natural selection relegated God and individual human beings to virtually passive roles. It also took away the moral authority of institutions and, by subjecting them to the law of evolution, required that they justify themselves. Evolution provided a scientific foundation for the march toward a better civilization, but since the process operated relentlessly through natural selection, there was little room for people as active agents. Thus the price of scientific determinism was submission and conformity. Americans could accept evolution because the notion of change and growth was part of their experience, but they could not accept determinism, which implied that individuals had little or no control over their destinies.

The New Social Criticism

In the late nineteenth century many writers, social scientists, and other intellectuals began to attack the assumptions of the Victorian order and such prevailing concepts as social Darwinism, unrestricted individualism, the unregulated marketplace, and laissez-faire. Investigative journalists such as Henry Demarest Lloyd in *Wealth against Commonwealth* (1894), an attack on Standard Oil, and Jacob Riis in *How the Other Half Lives* (1890), a study of poverty in New York City, stressed the brutality of contemporary life. The most important manifestoes awakening middle-class readers to the need for reform were Henry George's *Progress and Poverty* (1879) and Edward Bellamy's *Looking Backward* (1888). Although their solutions to the problems of industrialization differed — George suggested a single tax on rising land values, and Bellamy advocated nationalization of industry — both vividly portrayed the shocking contrast between vast wealth and extensive poverty in the emerging industrial society.

Probing and protesting much of the change that industrialism brought to American life, novelists challenged the genteel Victorian literary tradition. Mark Twain, in such later works as *The Man That Corrupted Hadleyburg* and *The Mysterious Stranger*, and William Dean Howells, in *A Hazard of New Fortunes* and *Traveler from Altruria*, had criticized the irresponsibility of acquisitive capitalism and industrialism and the disintegration of traditional standards of morality. But the gentle criticism of "realists" like Howells was supplemented in the 1890s with a harsher literature, "naturalism," which documented and confronted the dilemmas and problems of urban, industrial society. Stephen Crane dealt with subjects that were previously taboo for most American writers as he portrayed prostitution in *Maggie: A Girl of the Streets* (1893). Never before had American writers been so sharply estranged from contemporary society.

Relentless forces in nature and society frequently provided the context for "naturalist" novels, challenging a primary assumption of the classic literary realism of the Victorian era that characters were autonomous agents, generally responsible for their own behavior. Instead, a conception of pervasive economic or psychological determinism permeated the works of Frank Norris beginning with *McTeague* (1890) and later in *The Octopus* (1901), the first volume in his trilogy about the struggle between wheat growers and the Southern Pacific Railroad. The determinism of powerful forces fascinated Jack London, but so did a character's struggle for survival, even if determined ultimately by powers beyond one's control. His best-selling novel, *The Call of the Wild* (1903), told of a great dog who felt the pull of nature and escaped from civilization to lead a wolf pack in Alaska. In *Sister Carrie* (1900), Theodore Dreiser's first major work, men and women were portrayed as poor creatures driven to what society considered immoral acts by urgent desires that they neither create nor control in circumstances generally beyond their ability to change. As one of Dreiser's characters in *The Genius* (1915) concluded exhaustedly, "Life was nothing save dark forces moving aimlessly." Despite their pessimistic determinism, Dreiser and the other naturalist writers hoped, like their model, the French social critic Emile Zola, that people would be so repelled by the inhumanity they portrayed that they would somehow repudiate it and create a better world.

But even while naturalists pursued their mood of doubt, another group of writers represented tradition instead of change, reflecting the widespread concern about certain aspects of "progress." These "traditionalists" shared Victorian convictions that there were standards and that style was important. Henry James, sensitive and subtle, disdained the materialism of a pecuniary civilization in books like *The American* (1877). He stressed the need to preserve moral integrity and artistic values. Edith Wharton focused on ethical values in conflict with social or material values in her portraits of the changes in upper-class New York society. But she also reflected the sexual consciousness of the era of the "new woman." Indeed, Wharton made sexuality a crucial focus of her work, insisting that sexual drives were primary motives of self and society and that sex was central to power in relationships. Yet, like James, Wharton, although unhappy with contemporary life in America, did not adopt the position of outrage of the crusading naturalist writers.

Origins of Interventionism

Americans believed too strongly in the idea of progress and in their destiny as a chosen people to wish to bring the process of change and modernization to a halt. But the society was in such turmoil that Americans began an extensive struggle to gain some kind of control over the process. Few mechanisms existed for directing such widespread change. National institutions such as the federal government and the major political parties were hampered by timidity and traditional checks on the power of the central government. Traditionally, Americans had relied primarily not on government but rather on individuals and institutions in the private sector and the market system to determine the direction of society and the allocation of resources. But the developments accompanying industrialization—especially the shock of the depression of the 1890s—caused many people to fear undirected social change. In an increasingly complex, interrelated society, people began to turn to collective action. "We live in an atmosphere of organization," the leader of the organized charity movement in Baltimore wrote in the 1890s. "Men are learning the disadvantages of isolated action."

"We have to act," the philosopher John Dewey asserted, "in order to keep secure amid the moving flux of circumstances." Although they initially represented a minority in the late nineteenth century, some scholars began to revolt against abstract and formalistic determinist thought and advocated collective action, including expanded governmental power, to improve social conditions. They began to challenge laissez-faire and the idea of a self-regulating society. Beginning in the 1880s the sociologist Lester Frank Ward assailed the concept of inevitability in evolution as mindless and wasteful. Intervention could improve matters through purposeful manipulation.

The most active advocates of increased governmental action in the marketplace were a group of rebellious young economists who challenged Adam Smith and classical political economics. They did not think the self-interest of individuals necessarily coincided with the best interests of society. "Private self-interest," Henry Carter Adams declared in 1887, "is too powerful, or too ignorant, or too immoral to promote the common good without compulsion." Although they did not think government should intervene everywhere, the interventionist economists did believe, as Richard T. Ely declared in 1885, "that the conflict of labor and capital has brought to the front a vast number of social problems whose solution is impossible without the united efforts of church, state, and science." From his position at Johns Hopkins and, later, the University of Wisconsin, Ely urged a program of social reform and full publicity (along with personal responsibility on the part of the directors) about corporations in order to raise the level of competition to a higher moral plane. Simon Patten at the University of Pennsylvania urged the need for national planning to help Americans to adjust to the new industrial environment. But the neoclassical economist John Bates Clark argued that competition was the "social guarantor of progress," and he proposed to regulate and enforce competition by prohibiting unfair practices that had led to monopoly.

New-school economists and other social critics began to lay the groundwork for interventionism to curtail the harsh conditions of the marketplace. The dramatic changes of the late nineteenth century and the proposals of the interventionists created a brittle tension between modernizers and traditionalists and between those who followed different paths to modernization. Most of the problems of industrialization were clear by the end of the century: growing poverty, increasing class distinctions, maldistribution of wealth and opportunity, increased crime rates, violence, pollution of the environment, and corruption of American values. Ex-President Rutherford B. Hayes complained in his diary in 1890 about "the wrongs and evils of the money-piling tendency of our country," which were "giving all power to the rich and bringing in pauperism and its attendant crimes and wretchedness like a flood." Americans now looked into the twentieth century with a mixture of hope and fear.

CHAPTER 3

The Corporate Revolution

On a snowy evening as the new century opened, two men in tuxedos paced in front of a crackling fire in the library of a brownstone mansion in New York City. Shadows of dancing flames flickered on stained-glass windows and Renaissance masterpieces. Amid a collection of art treasures from the past, two modern titans helped shape the economic structure of the future as they put together the largest manufacturing company the world had ever seen, the United States Steel Corporation.

Sparring verbally, the two men stood in striking contrast: the vigorous young contender and the deliberate old warrior. Combining captivating warmth, optimism, and driving ambition, 38-year-old Charles Schwab, the son of a stablekeeper on Andrew Carnegie's estate, had scrambled up to become the manager of Carnegie's mills. His host, J. P. Morgan, had inherited his father's banking company and, through his own skill and awesome personal authority, expanded it into the most powerful investment banking house in the United States. At 64, "Old Jupiter," a gruff and towering figure with piercing eyes and a walrus mustache, was one of the world's leading bankers.

In his meeting with Morgan on that winter evening, Schwab thrust forward his proposal: consolidation of most of the major steel companies, with the giant Carnegie firm as the centerpiece. The combination could prevent a potentially destructive price war and might well stabilize both American and international markets. Cautiously, Morgan probed and tested Schwab's assertions. As dawn streamed through the stained-glass windows, the banker finally acquiesced. All that remained was the asking price for Carnegie's holdings. Without a word, Schwab handed Morgan a piece of paper with the figure $492,000,000 on it. Silently, Morgan scrutinized it, then tersely gave his answer: "I accept."

Within a year Morgan's banking syndicate created the United States Steel Corporation, a giant industrial combine that controlled iron- and steelworks, shipping and railroad lines, and ore and coal properties. The company owned 156 major factories and several hundred smaller plants in a dozen states. It employed 168,000 workers and was capitalized at $1.4 billion. When it was created in 1901, U.S. Steel controlled 60 percent of American steel production. With an annual gross income that soon exceeded that of the U.S. treasury, the new industrial behemoth was bigger and more powerful than many nations.

The creation of U.S. Steel—the world's first billion-dollar corporation—symbolized one aspect of a virtual corporate revolution. Before the turn of the century there were only a few supercorporations. Yet in only a half dozen years, from 1897 to 1903, a sudden wave of reorganization and consolidation created vast new empires in industry, railroads, and finance. This dramatic private intervention in the marketplace through the consolidation of economic power led to an oligopolistic pattern in which a small number of giant firms dominated the most important industries. Economic growth produced structural change, which led to new behavior, new attitudes, and new tensions as it reshaped traditional American society.

The Great Merger Movement

The combination movement resulted largely from the belief of financiers and corporate managers that some kind of consolidation and intervention was necessary to curb price competition and reduce the instability created by an unregulated marketplace. It was also induced by promoters' desires for immediate profit. A dramatic increase in the supply of gold-backed currency due largely to the discovery of gold fields in Canada and Alaska stimulated easy credit and economic recovery in the United States between 1897 and 1907. Indeed, the chief beneficiaries of the expansion of the U.S. currency supply from $2 billion to $3 billion in those years were the promoters of the industrial consolidation movement. Using successful consolidations like Standard Oil as a model, corporate reorganizers created a revolution in the structure of American industry as the new century began. The great merger movement saw more than 3,000 substantial manufacturing companies—many, like Carnegie Steel, already huge firms—combined through mergers or holding companies into a few hundred supercorporations. Like U.S. Steel, each dominated a particular industry: General Electric, National Biscuit Company (Nabisco), American Can Company, Eastman Kodak, U.S. Rubber (later Uniroyal), American Telephone and Telegraph, and many others. By 1904 the 300 largest industrial corporations owned $20 billion in assets, or more than 40 percent of the industrial wealth of the United States.

At the same time, Morgan and railroad entrepreneurs like Edward H. Harriman of the Union Pacific, James J. Hill of the Great Northern, the Vanderbilts of the New York Central, and the wealthy Philadelphians who controlled the Pennsylvania Railroad transformed the nation's rail system. During the depression of the 1890s at least one quarter of the trackage in the country went into the hands of bankruptcy receivers. In 1897, as economic recovery began, the half dozen reorganizers pumped new funds into the carriers and consolidated the railroad network from hundreds of independent and often competing lines into a few large, noncompetitive rail systems, each of which exercised virtual monopoly control in a particular region. In a reference to the trusts that applied to these new rail consolidations as well, James J. Hill wrote in 1901 that they "came into being as the result of an effort to obviate ruinous competition."

A favorable economic and legal climate spurred the consolidation movement. Although many businesses went bankrupt in the depression of 1893–1896, trusts such as Standard Oil, American Sugar, and American Tobacco kept making profits by limiting the decline of prices in their industries. When prosperity and investor confidence returned, reorganizers tried to emulate their achievement by consolidating other industries. With the endorsement of respected financiers like Morgan, a market developed for the stocks of the industrial corporations (the securities market had previously been limited primarily to railroad and government issues). Consolidators sold stock in the new supercorporations to banks, trust funds, insurance companies, and wealthy investors. By the late 1890s the legal framework seemed to ensure the legitimacy of the giant corporation. New Jersey, Delaware, and a few other states had authorized the corporate holding company device, and despite passage of the Sherman Antitrust Act, the Supreme Court had agreed with attorneys for the American Sugar Company and upheld the legality of that monopoly in the *E. C. Knight* case. "What looks like a stone wall to a layman," one critic declared, "is a triumphal arch to the corporation lawyer."

The creation of big business and the supercorporations also led to an internal revolution in management and the rise of substantial corporate bureaucracies, which in turn produced a new kind of corporate leadership. Managerially minded men succeeded the dynamic, individualistic capitalist entrepreneurs. Capitalists such as Carnegie and Vanderbilt had been rugged competitors with a zest for combat. The new managers were the servants of the corporation, salaried employees rather than owners, and they were more cautious and less willing to take extreme risks. They wanted to control, not exploit, ruthless price competition, and they were willing to intervene in the marketplace and to maintain a live-and-let-live philosophy. The new corporate managers were less flamboyant than their individualistic predecessors, but they were no less successful in accomplishing their aims. The aggressive competition of the open marketplace began to be brought under some control.

The attempts of the new interventionists to modify the operation of the marketplace were more successful in certain areas than in others. Control of price competition proved most effective in capital-intensive, technologically advanced industries like steel and petroleum, which obtained genuine economies of scale, and in those that built up consumer loyalty through extensive advertising of brand names. In these industries, prices were often "administered" rather than set entirely by market forces. A dominant firm became the "price leader," setting a profitable price, with the rest of the industry following suit.

But in many areas the marketplace proved unconquerable. Much of American industry remained highly competitive. Small and medium-sized firms, operating locally or regionally, battled each other vigorously in textiles, clothing, leather goods, furniture, lumber, and printing. At the retail level, price competition remained a major characteristic of small business, as contrasted to the administered prices of big business. To protect their own interests—but not administer prices—small businesses formed their own trade associations and joined local chambers of commerce, the latter uniting nationally in 1912 to form the U.S. Chamber of Commerce.

Even big business did not eliminate competition entirely. Indeed, during the Progressive Era many of the supercorporations lost some of their dominance of the market to newer, more aggressive competitors. U.S. Steel, for instance, proved slower than its rivals to convert to new technology and shift to the growing market for lighter, alloy steel products. Its share of the market dropped from 62 percent in 1901 to 40 percent in 1920. Similarly, Standard Oil, which from its oil fields in Pennsylvania and Ohio had refined 90 percent of the nation's petroleum at its peak in 1899, lost its monopolistic position. The discovery in 1901 of the great Spindletop oil field in Texas, one of the richest oil gushers in the world, led to large-scale petroleum exploration in Texas, Louisiana, Oklahoma, and California and marked the beginning of an unprecedented boom in oil production in the United States. New companies—Texaco, Gulf, and Union—rushed in to develop the new fields; they also led in exploiting the use of petroleum as gasoline and fuel for heating homes and running ships and automobiles. By 1907 they had cut Standard's share of the market to 84 percent; it eroded further to 80 percent in 1911 (the year the Supreme Court ordered its division into several lesser companies, among them the Standard Oil companies of New Jersey, Ohio, and California). By 1920 their combined share had dropped to 50 percent of the expanding market.

Oligopoly, in which a handful of large firms dominated the market, characterized American industry, not monopoly, control by a single firm. But the giants did mute price competition, replacing it with less destructive competition in such areas as sales promotion, advertising, cost reduction, and quality of goods and services. The fact that some competition remained reassured many Americans that the market system continued to operate. Yet many also became fearful of the concentration of power in another area—finance.

The Wall Street Connection

From the financial centers of the East, investment bankers emerged as powerful agents of industrial development and consolidation. With access to capital from investors in the United States and Europe, they underwrote the expansion and reorganization of American railroads and industry. Acting as intermediaries between investors and the corporations, they promoted and financed consolidations through massive issuances of stock. The underwriters received a handsome profit (the Morgan syndicate earned perhaps $60 million for organizing U.S. Steel), but they also saw themselves as financial statesmen, directing the flow of capital and credit to avoid ruinous competition and encourage orderly and sustained economic growth.

The most prestigious investment banking houses, located in New York, Boston, and Philadelphia, did not number more than a dozen firms. The majority—such as J. P. Morgan; Kidder, Peabody; and Lee Higginson—were run by a handful of old-line Anglo-Saxon Protestants who usually came from successful merchant or banking families. There were also a few German Jewish firms like J. & W. Seligman, Lehman Brothers, and Kuhn, Loeb, most of them built by self-made individuals.

Beginning in the 1890s, a number of bankers began to expand into new areas of investment. In addition to railroad and government securities, they started to finance the reorganization of the giant new companies in mining, refining, and manufacturing. They also began to demand a share in management in return for assisting the corporations in meeting their capital and credit needs. At the same time, Morgan and other investment bankers sought positions with institutions that were sources of funds—commercial banks, trust companies, and the rapidly growing life insurance companies. Investment bankers tried to limit the unpredictability of the money market by ensuring coordination of further economic development.

The Reaction to Consolidation

"If the carboniferous age returned and the earth repeopled itself with dinosaurs," one economist observed, "the change would scarcely seem greater than that made in the business world by these monster corporations." The sudden emergence of huge concentrations of economic power in industry and finance within a few years startled most Americans. Many feared that such combinations, if allowed to continue, would take on all the worst attributes of monopoly: prevention of competition, inefficiency, arrogance, destruction of the marketplace, and corruption of the political system.

The greatest fear was that the financiers had created a "money trust" that monopolized the credit resources of the country. When agrarian Democrats gained control of the House of Representatives, the Pujo Committee launched an investigation of this alleged "trust." The committee found a significant concentration of control over investment funds in the House of Morgan and the Rockefellers, whose profits from Standard Oil provided an enormous source of funds channeled into controlling interests in other companies. In 1913 the Pujo Committee report concluded that four allied financial institutions in New York City, representing primarily Morgan and the Rockefellers, held 341 directorships in 112 major banks, railroads, public utilities, and insurance companies, whose aggregate resources totaled $22 billion, an amount equal to half the gross national product of the United States at the time.

Although the Pujo Committee did not prove that a monopolistic money trust existed (there remained substantial competition in banking), it did demonstrate the high degree of concentration that had taken place in the preceding two decades. It also enshrined the "directing power" of New York investment bankers as part of American folklore and thus helped to increase support for some form of public, decentralized body in the banking system, a sentiment that contributed to the creation of the Federal Reserve System.

The Progressive Era was the time when Americans most fully debated what was called the "trust issue": the tendency toward consolidation or even monopoly in industry. Traditionally suspicious of centralized power, many Americans — particularly people in small and medium-sized businesses, workers, farmers, consumers, reformers, and radicals — assailed the trusts as "great engines of oppression." They feared that the giant corporations were closing out opportunities for people to become independent as artisans, mechanics, or owners of small businesses. Life within the corporate structure was very different from life in a small business, warned Hazen Pingree, governor of Michigan and a former businessman; the employees, he said,

> become a part of a vast industrial army. Their personal identity is lost. . . . There is no real advance for them. They may perhaps become larger cogs or larger wheels in the great complicated machine, but they can never look forward to a life of business freedom.

Critics also feared that the giant corporations were destroying the market system. They blamed administered prices for the inflation that began with the return of prosperity in 1897 and continued for the next two decades. The reformer Henry Demarest Lloyd listed some of the evils of the trusts in 1910:

Blowing up competitors, as the oil monopoly has done;

shutting up works and throwing men out of employment, as the sugar monopoly has done;

selling the machinery of rivals for junk, as the nail monopoly has done;

paying big bonuses to others not to run, as the steel monopoly has done;

restricting production, as the coal monopoly has done; and

buying up and suppressing new patents, as the telephone monopoly has done.

Defending big business against this onslaught, corporate leaders and many clergy, writers, economists, and political leaders argued that the giant firms were an inevitable and beneficial result of industrialization. Consolidation was also occurring in Europe, and American defenders of the supercorporation asserted that such a structure was necessary to compete effectively against European cartels in the international market. Furthermore, supporters of big business claimed that through mass production, efficiencies of scale, and the elimination of local monopolies, the giant corporations could provide more products at lower prices. Although some industrialists, such as Rockefeller, were reluctant to accept limitations on their power, some other corporate managers, such as George Perkins, the Morgan partner who headed International Harvester, the main manufacturer of agricultural equipment, accepted the notion that the mammoth corporations, funded as they were through the sale of stock to the public, were in fact quasi-public enterprises and not strictly private property. Perkins warned recalcitrant industrialists in 1911 that they would have to accept some kind of federal regulation and reform. "If we continue to fight against it much longer," he cautioned, "the incoming tide may sweep the question along either to Government ownership or socialism."

From different perspectives and interests, Americans in the Progressive Era generally clustered into five schools of thought regarding big business. Many continued to believe in laissez-faire and argued either that big business was inevitable and beneficial or, like William Graham Sumner, that the marketplace, which had temporarily produced monopoly, would restore competition by inviting new competitors if necessary. Others, such as economist John Bates Clark, believed that some governmental intervention was needed to restore the marketplace. Jeffersonian agrarians such as Bryan urged the use of antitrust suits and the taxing power to reduce corporations that exceeded a specified size. They also argued that patents and the protective tariff, which encouraged trusts, should be modified or eliminated. Some corporate managers and heads of industrial trade associations envisioned a new kind of self-regulation or associationalism, in which business would cooperate through private groups such as trade associations to reduce the problems of destructive price competition, waste, unemployment, and violence in labor relations.

Others, including Perkins, Theodore Roosevelt, and economists Richard Ely and Simon Patten, believed governmental regulation was required to ensure that the giant firms did not operate to the disadvantage of the public interest. Roosevelt eventually recommended federal charters and supervision of capitalization as well as wage and price policy. Still others argued for government ownership. A substantial number, including Ely, recommended it for what they considered natural monopolies such as railroads, streetcar lines, and utilities such as gas, water, electricity, and even the telegraph and telephone. A minority, mainly socialists and radical agrarians, urged that the government take over the giant manufacturing firms in steel production, petroleum refining, and other essential industries.

Much confusion existed in the early years of the twentieth century over what was happening in industry and what to do about the "trusts." People were confused about the shape of the emerging corporate economy, about whether it was characterized by monopoly or oligopoly, and whether that made a significant difference. The fact that some competition continued, though in a different manner, led many people to believe that the marketplace had survived despite the trusts. Furthermore, many feared that the complete breakup of big business would create chaos, jeopardize economic growth, and would restrict the flow of new material goods that were being produced in the developing mass consumption society.

The Mass Production, Mass Consumption Society

The organizational revolution that produced the supercorporations took place in an economy that was booming with the mass production of industrial and, increasingly, consumer goods. Mounting industrial output boosted real gross national product an average of 6 percent annually between 1897 and 1914. National income increased by nearly one-third. This economic growth was accompanied by the first sustained period of inflation since the Civil War. The cost of living went up 39 percent between 1897 and 1914, an average annual inflation rate of 3 percent. Although there was no sustained depression, the recessions of 1907 and 1914 were sharp despite their brevity. Nevertheless, the era was viewed by many as one of great economic growth in productivity and in the standard of living.

Economic growth came partly from a crackling new power source. Electricity was hailed by George Westinghouse, the developer of long-distance systems of transmitting alternating electrical current, as a modern Aladdin's genie that would relieve men and women of the burden of heavy toil in factory and home. It offered an efficient, convenient, and uniform source of energy, and it was cheaper than the steam-powered belts and pulleys that it replaced. In the first twenty years of the century, more than one-third of America's manufacturing plants converted to electrical power for their machines. Westinghouse's genie also began to turn the motors in the first mass-marketed electric fans, vacuum cleaners, and washing machines.

Production of consumer goods for the mass market, a process that had begun in the late nineteenth century, dramatically expanded in the early years of the new century. The birth of the mass consumption society was made possible by staggering leaps in productivity, which enabled manufacturers to reduce the prices of goods to a level within the purchasing power of millions of consumers. The boost in productivity came primarily from the increased use of machinery, either general multipurpose machines or, much more dramatically, the various single-purpose components of the assembly line. This American invention had been used in the nineteenth century for watches, sewing machines, typewriters, and bicycles, but in 1913 a lanky farmer and mechanic turned auto maker, Henry Ford, brought it to maturity by using it to make automobiles consisting of several thousand parts. America became the master of mass production and mass consumption, and Ford emerged as the presiding genius of the new flow technology, which Europeans labeled "Fordism." Interchangeable standardized parts and precise new automatic machines made the new technology possible. Putting these together in a moving assembly line, Ford converted the construction of automobiles from a jerky, unpredictable process to a smoothly flowing stream. To do this, he decided to make all cars alike. "The way to make automobiles," he explained, "is to make one automobile like another automobile . . . just as one pin is like another pin when it comes from a pin factory." In 1913, at his plant in Highland Park outside Detroit, Michigan, he subdivided the work of assembling the chassis of a Model T Ford and put the components on a moving line. Slicing assembly time from 12½ to 1½ hours, the Ford Motor Company cranked out 500,000 Model Ts a year and eventually chopped the base price from $950 to $290.

Ford proved tremendously successful at expanding the market. By cutting costs, he brought his cars down to what he called the "buying power." He sold 15 million of his "tin Lizzies" or "flivvers" before he changed to the Model A Ford in 1927. At the same time, he also expanded his market and amazed the nation by establishing the "five-dollar day" for his workers, a pay scale that was nearly double the average daily earnings of industrial workers. The pay hike not only increased workers' purchasing power but also reduced absenteeism and turnover on the assembly line and helped forestall unionization.

Henry Ford's success convinced many other industrialists of the efficacy of mass production techniques. They began a changeover that accelerated during World War I and the 1920s. The assembly line, like the supercorporation, became a symbol of the mass production and mass consumption economy and the new industrial America.

To absorb greatly increased production, American business needed to stimulate demand for consumer goods. Advertising was the key. During the Progressive Era, ad agencies developed slogans and jingles, made great use of syndicated display advertisements, and began to use psychological appeals to create mass consumer demand. Instead of merely advertising the curative or other functional aspects of products, the agencies began to associate happiness, attractiveness, and status with products ranging from soap to automobiles.

Mass production meant major changes in retailing to handle the new flood of consumer goods. Some manufacturers, like the automakers, established local dealerships that marketed, financed, and serviced the manufacturer's products. The oil companies erected service stations. Department stores, which had first been established at the time of the Civil War, grew into giant emporiums: Macy's, Lord & Taylor, Wanamaker's, and Marshall Field. Mail order houses such as Montgomery Ward, founded in 1872, and Sears, Roebuck, established in 1895, revolutionized rural retailing. Chain stores such as Woolworth's "five- and ten-cent" store, first opened in Utica, New York, in 1879, and J. C. Penney, founded in 1902, spread rapidly.

The materialism encouraged by the mass production and mass consumption economy proved almost as controversial as the giant corporations themselves. Like them, consumerism was both praised and pilloried. Some people thought that abundance of consumer goods might replace abundance of arable land as a frontier of economic growth. Some saw this growth as a sign not only of increased well-being but also of improved morality. "Material prosperity," asserted a Massachusetts bishop in 1901, "is helping to make the national character sweeter, more joyous, more unselfish, more Christlike."

Critics found much of the gospel of mass production and consumption appalling. Blanching at the excesses of advertising as it sought to stimulate mass demand, Walter Lippmann, a leading journalist and political commentator, warned how powerless the public was against such advertising: "the eastern sky ablaze with chewing gum, the northern with toothbrushes and underwear, the western with whiskey, and the southern with petticoats, the whole heavens brilliant with monstrously flirtatious women." More radical critics such as the economist Thorstein Veblen feared that the emphasis on consumption of material goods would divert discontented industrial workers from attacking the economic system and lead them to accept the wage system and seek satisfaction in immediate symbols of status and achievement.

Changes in Work and the Work Force

In the early years of the century, new immigrants from southern and eastern Europe filled the bottom ranks of heavy industry and construction and helped to produce significant changes in the nature of the work force and, consequently, of society itself. Although the foreign-born accounted for only 20 percent of the working population, they made up more than 60 percent of the wage workers in heavy industry. Much transition occurred in these years. Until the 1890s, most of the anthracite miners in Pennsylvania had been English-speaking men from Britain, Ireland, and Wales. By 1919, however, over 90 percent were Slavs, Italians, or Greeks. The steel mills of Pittsburgh and the textile factories of Lawrence, Massachusetts, presented a similar picture.

Increasing numbers of rural Americans also trekked to industrial jobs in towns and cities. Even the South, the most agrarian region of the country, began gradually to industrialize. Tens of thousands of impoverished tenant farmers and their families — men, women, and children —went to work in the new textile factories that sprang up in the mill towns of the piedmont region of the Carolinas. More than 90 percent of these mill hands were white. Work was stratified by gender and race, with women paid less than men and precluded from supervisory positions, and the few African Americans who were hired were confined largely to menial jobs. In the tobacco factories blacks composed a larger percentage of the work force but were rigidly segregated within the plant and assigned the more objectionable and lower-paying tasks.

One of the most significant population shifts in these years was the beginning of the mass migration of southern blacks into northern cities. When World War I caused a labor shortage, more than 330,000 blacks fled the poverty and discrimination of the South. "I should have been here 20 years ago," a black carpenter wrote home to Hattiesburg, Mississippi, from Chicago in 1917. "I just begin to feel like a man." The black exodus had an important impact on race relations in the North. Small, scattered settlements of blacks were consolidated into large ghettos, such as Harlem in New York and the south side of Chicago. Immigrants, blacks, and Spanish-speaking workers (in the Southwest) composed the bottom level of the industrial work force. Thus race and ethnicity increasingly became the basis for social class and stratification, to a degree unique among major industrial societies at the time.

Millions of women joined the work force at the turn of the century. One woman out of five had worked outside the home in 1890, but by 1910 one out of four did so. Before the 1920s most women who obtained gainful employment were working only temporarily, a stage between living with their parents and marrying. The idealized woman's role remained that of wife and mother. But a minority of women—predominantly black or foreign-born—were forced by economic necessity to perform as both homemaker and wage earner. As late as 1870 fully 50 percent of all working women (again primarily the black and foreign-born) had toiled as domestic servants and washerwomen, but as often as they could, most young women workers turned to jobs offering greater status and personal freedom. By 1920 only 16 percent of working women were paid household workers.

Black women, usually excluded from offices and factories and restricted to the lowest-paying jobs, generally worked as agricultural laborers or as daytime domestic servants, returning to their homes and families at night. Since both men and women in African-American families received lower incomes than whites, married black women worked in greater numbers than white women—26 percent in 1900, compared to 3 percent of married white women. Within the small black middle class, a number of women found positions as teachers at segregated public schools in both the South and the North.

Among whites, a small but growing number of college-educated women pursued careers as nurses, teachers, social workers, or physicians—and captured media attention as examples of the "new woman"—while the majority of working women toiled in blue-collar, clerical, and service occupations. The most visible workers were young single immigrants. Though previously many young Irish or Scandinavian women had been live-in domestic servants, now they, and other young immigrant women, were able to gain a somewhat greater measure of autonomy by working in factories—laundries, canneries, garment factories, and textile mills. The hours were long, sometimes ten hours a day, six days a week; working conditions were often dangerous; and the wages were low. Furthermore, most of their meager earnings went to help to sustain their families, the parents and siblings with whom they lived. In the urban North, among the native-born white women who went to work outside the home, the majority found so-called white-blouse jobs as salespersons in retail shops or department stores or as clerks, typists, telephone operators, or secretaries in the growing number of offices resulting from the bureaucratization of business.

Many poor and working-class children spent their days in mines and mills instead of in school, helping to augment inadequate family incomes. During the last decade of the nineteenth century, the percentage of boys and girls between the ages of 10 and 15 who worked for wages increased dramatically, especially in the South, where a threefold rise in the number of employed children led to widespread protest by trade unionists and other reformers. Opposition to the use of child labor helped to cut that percentage in half in the second decade of the twentieth century through prohibitive legislation.

Begrimed with coal dust, "breaker boys" in a coal mine stop work for some lunch. Hired to break lumps of coal into smaller pieces, many of the boys were even younger than the ones pictured here in a mine in Pittston, Pennsylvania in 1911. (*Lewis W. Hine/Hine Collection/New York Public Library*)

The Costs of Industrialism

America paid a high price for industrial supremacy. At the turn of the century industrial accidents killed 35,000 workers each year and maimed 500,000 others. Only when scores of workers perished in a single disaster did the public rise in indignation. The Triangle fire in New York City in 1911 was such a tragedy. The blaze broke out in the Triangle Shirtwaist Company factory atop a ten-story loft building just as some 500 young Jewish and Italian immigrant women were preparing to leave work on a Saturday afternoon. Swirling flames quickly turned the shop into a furnace. In panic and confusion, workers pressed toward the exits. But the fire doors had been locked from the outside for fear that the women would steal pieces of fabric. When firemen finally reached the factory rooms, they found the women's charred bodies piled up behind the locked doors. Other fleeing workers crammed into two freight elevators, but women who were still trapped on the top floors jumped into the elevator shafts to escape, and their bodies jammed the mechanism and halted the elevators' descent.

Dozens of women leaped from the roof of the building to their deaths on the streets below, many holding hands and jumping in groups. By the time firemen brought the blaze under control, 146 young women were dead. Investigation placed the blame on the owners, the insurance company, and the city's building and fire departments, although no one was convicted on criminal charges.

The public outrage that resulted from the Triangle fire and a series of deadly mining disasters led to the passage of a number of laws designed to increase factory safety standards and improve working conditions, especially for women and children. Together with workers' organizations and some employers' groups, reformers pressed state legislatures to enact mine and factory safety laws, new inspection requirements, and worker compensation legislation, which placed a larger share of the cost of accidents in the hands of employers. Nevertheless, America's industrial accident rate remained among the highest in the world.

Industrial violence was another cost of the harsh and rapid pace of industrialization. Wage cuts and layoffs frequently triggered massive resistance by workers. Violence often stemmed from workers' attempts to organize unions and management's attempts to destroy the unions. In the first decade of the new century, twice as many strikes erupted as in the last decade of the nineteenth century. Many were bitter and several were brutal, but the bloodiest was in the mining region of Ludlow, Colorado.

Few places exceeded the dismal exploitation of the feudalistic mining camps of southeastern Colorado. In the soft-coal fields of the foothills of the Rockies, some 30,000 Italians, Slavs, Greeks, and Mexicans scratched a living out of the earth in isolated canyon communities. Three corporations, one of them owned by the Rockefellers, controlled the lives of these people, not just employing them but owning the land on which their shacks were built, the schools, churches, saloons, and the company store where food, clothing, and supplies were sold at marked-up prices. The corporations censored movies, magazines, and books, proscribing the works of Marx and Darwin and Omar Khayyám's *Rubáiyát*. "We wish to protect our people from erroneous ideas," an official explained. Wages were lower than elsewhere, the disease rate was high, and the death rate in the mines was twice the national average. But the company maintained control through force and terrorism, employing spies and dominating the civil government and the police. Protesters found themselves ejected from their jobs, their homes, and the community. In short, the corporate tyranny deprived the workers and their families of their fundamental rights as citizens.

In a snowstorm in late September 1913, some 9,000 workers and their families went on strike, demanding an eight-hour day and recognition of their union. They moved out of company housing and into tent colonies in the canyons. The companies imported strikebreakers and constructed an armored machine gun vehicle called the "Death Special" to protect themselves and to terrorize the strikers. Fighting broke out between the two sides, and several persons were killed. Then, in an act of senseless violence, the militia, sent in by the governor, attacked the largest tent colony near Ludlow, firing into it and then burning it to the ground. Twenty-one residents of the tent community were killed in the melee, including three women and eleven children. In retaliation for what was called the Ludlow Massacre, the miners lashed out against the companies and the militia. Thirty persons died before President Wilson sent in the U.S. Cavalry and brought the open warfare to a halt. Despite much public castigation, the companies won the struggle, for after fifteen months the miners voted to go back to work with some improved conditions and a company union the only fruits of their long struggle.

The civil war in the Colorado mine fields was extreme but not unique in this period. Violence among strikers, police, militia, and strikebreakers erupted in a number of places. The old mill towns of Lawrence, Massachusetts, and Paterson, New Jersey, became battlefields as employers sought to cut wages and to crush strikes. Labor radicals retaliated against antiunion violence in Idaho by assassinating the governor of that state, Frank Steunenburg, in 1905. In 1911 other radicals blew up the antiunion *Los Angeles Times*, killing twenty persons.

In the wake of this violence Congress resorted to a relatively new device: it appointed the Commission on Industrial Relations, an ad hoc national committee of private citizens and officials to investigate, hold hearings, and try to discover the underlying causes of the strife and make policy recommendations to the federal government. The commission concluded that industrial violence stemmed primarily from industrial oppression and lack of adequate worker representation. Workers needed mechanisms to protect themselves, the commission's director of research concluded, or they would be "driven by necessity and oppression to the extreme of revolt."

Scientific Management

Industry realized the difficulties that worker resistance posed to its labor policies, which were designed to obtain maximum productivity from employees while keeping labor costs to a minimum. "Scientific management" was the system that engineers devised to improve the performance of the work force.

The enormous increase in productivity in the early years of the new century came with hardly any boost in the percentage of the labor force engaged in manufacturing. The gains in productivity came primarily from mechanization, as illustrated by the introduction of the assembly line. But corporate managers sought to bolster production even further by making the most efficient use of workers as well as machines. The process they employed to try to remold human activities so as to eliminate wasted motions was called Taylorism. The founder of modern scientific management, Frederick W. Taylor, a Philadelphia engineer, preached a gospel of efficiency in order to produce more goods more cheaply and effectively. His efficiency ethic subordinated individuals to the goal of expanded production, which Taylor hoped would lead to a higher standard of living. "In the past," he wrote in 1911, "the man has been first; in the future the system must be first."

Working-Class Culture

Management did not gain a complete victory in its attempts to gear workers to the pace of the machines and to obtain total control over the activities on the factory floor, nor, even in company-owned towns, did it establish complete control over their behavior outside of work. Industrial employers did increase the pace of production through a system of fines and other penalties and most effectively in the long run through the piecework system, under which pay was based on the number of items that a worker produced in a day. Nevertheless, recent studies have shown that American industrial workers in the late nineteenth and early twentieth centuries were able to retain some autonomy and self-esteem.

Even as waves of previously rural dwellers came to operate machines in the factories of the towns and cities of America, they were able to take advantage of niches and loopholes in what otherwise seemed to be all-powerful company systems. Through their ingenuity, the workers were able to find some human consolation and relief from a work regimen that aimed at forcing them into machinelike production. The initial absence of fences around factories might allow children to visit; gaps between production of batches of material might offer some time to socialize; shop supervisors who came from the same ethnic group or had relatives among the workers might treat them sympathetically. Skilled workers vigorously resisted attempts at "deskilling," the replacement, through mechanization, of skilled craftspeople with semiskilled or unskilled "machine tenders" or "operatives."

The shift from farm to factory jobs often contributed to a deep ambivalence in people's feelings about their work. A grim picture of low wages, long hours, and dangerous working conditions was ameliorated somewhat by the workers' success in forging, within the confines of their narrow world, links of mutual cooperation that substituted for the kinship ties of extended families. Belief in themselves and support from coworkers, family, and the local community sustained these

workers. On the job, resentment against subservient status was counterbalanced by pride in work skills and accomplishments. At home and
in public, the family and the local community, with its ethnic and
religious institutions and its places of recreation and leisure, offered
sustenance. A commitment to worker cooperation rather than competition, at least within each ethnic or racial group, was for many years an
abiding feature of the mill village culture. The habits and beliefs of
farm people, whether immigrant or American-born, who became a
first-generation manufacturing work force, were more than remnants
from a rural past. They were instruments of power and protection that
helped new factory workers survive and maintain their self-respect in
an industrial world.

When Workers Organize

Although only a minority of workers joined unions, labor made significant strides in organization at the turn of the century. Union membership leapt from less than 500,000 in 1897 to more than 2 million by
1904. The greatest growth came in the unions of the American Federation of Labor (AFL). Like the trusts, the AFL survived the depression
of the 1890s virtually intact, demonstrating a greater degree of stability
than any previous American labor organization. With the return of
prosperity, AFL membership soared. The growing economy created a
tighter labor market, giving workers more leverage. In addition, inflation spurred workers to seek wage boosts to compensate for rising
prices. Labor also benefited from widespread public criticism of deplorable working conditions. In the first fifteen years of the new century, the AFL grew from fifty-five unions, representing 60 percent of
organized labor, to more than a hundred unions, with 80 percent of
union members.

The growth of big labor increased the reputation and stature of
Samuel Gompers, the moderate leader of the AFL. Following the
model of the trusts, Gompers sought to combine and intervene to
eliminate or greatly reduce competition, in this case in the labor market. Much earlier he had renounced his youthful belief in socialism and
accepted capitalism and the wage system. Now he accepted the trusts:
"We welcome their organization. . . . When they assume a right for
themselves, they cannot deny that same right to us. They are organizing; organization is the order of the day."

Organized labor, like organized business, was a protest against the
destructive forces of the free marketplace. Unlike the socialists, who
advocated complete removal of competition from the labor market
through the elimination of capitalism, Gompers did not aim at completely eradicating the labor market; instead, he tried to limit competi-

tion in certain ways. Workers protested that labor was not a commodity, like grain or potatoes, whose price was to be determined by supply and demand. Such a view, they claimed, was repugnant to human dignity, a position validated by Congress in a section of the Clayton Antitrust Act of 1914, which upheld the right of workers to organize and declared flatly that "labor is not a commodity." To obtain higher wages, shorter hours, and better working conditions, the skilled craft unions of the AFL—carpenters, machinists, and others—used their economic power to withhold their labor, engaging in strikes or boycotts when necessary. To increase their leverage, the unions tried to include all the members of a particular craft. The growth of organized labor, like that of organized business, helped to modify the free-market system in the pursuit of other goals.

Gompers not only rejected the socialists' call for revolution but also argued against the creation of an independent labor party. Distrustful of government, which in the nineteenth century had usually acted against labor, Gompers emphasized "voluntarism," collective action by workers in the private sector. The conservative leaders of the AFL craft unions generally opposed minimum wage legislation (they thought it would be translated into maximum wages) and suggestions for government-run social security programs (they preferred their own pension programs). Gompers and the others sought to make gains through their economic strength in the marketplace. "Economic need and economic betterment," Gompers declared, "could best be served by mobilizing and controlling economic power." Nevertheless, the AFL increased its political activity, shifting in 1906 from purely lobbying tactics to electioneering for its friends and against its enemies.

In this era of organization, the AFL unions prospered, with growing membership rolls and swelling treasuries. They became large, stable, hierarchical, and business-oriented institutions. Union staffs moved out of rented rooms and into permanent headquarters. Union officers consolidated their power and began to serve for longer terms, sometimes for life (Gompers remained president of the AFL until his death in 1924). The collective bargaining agreement signed as a contract between union officials and management not only bound the employer to a specific schedule of wages and working conditions but restricted employees as well, requiring adherence by workers to minutely delineated formal work rules. It made the union a kind of mediating force in industrialization. By holding their members to the provisions of the contract, craft unions, in return for recognition as the bargaining agent for the workers and improved wages and conditions, helped accommodate skilled workers to the new corporate industrial system.

Ironically, just as the labor movement obtained dramatic success on the basis of stable trade unions and collective bargaining agreements, it was undermined by a drastic change in the nature of industrial conditions. The spread of mass production and scientific management increased management's opposition to collective bargaining and impeded the union strategy of controlling the labor market, for the greatest growth in the mass production industries was not in the skilled trades of the AFL but among the unskilled or semiskilled machine tenders, the operatives on the assembly lines, who were increasingly immigrants from southern or eastern Europe. To some extent the AFL was barred from the heart of the new mass production industries by its own trade union conservatism, its male chauvinism, and its Anglo-Saxon racism (AFL leaders considered women, blacks, and new immigrant workers transient and inferior). Even more important was an aversion to unions among many Americans and overt hostility on the part of many business interests and much of the judiciary.

Only in a few industries, such as coal and clothing, were AFL unions able to organize new workers successfully, and there they did it on an industrywide rather than a craft basis. In the hard-coal fields of Pennsylvania, the United Mine Workers (UMW), under the leadership of John Mitchell, built a union that numbered more than 100,000 members at the turn of the century. Through a major strike and governmental support, the UMW in 1902 obtained a substantial wage increase. Even more dramatic, however, was the mobilization of the garment workers in New York, which caught the city and the country by surprise. Their action was the first industrywide strike of immigrant workers in the nation's largest city. In several hundred small dress factories and sweatshops in Lower Manhattan, thousands of young Italian and Russian Jewish women toiled at sewing machines for fifty-six hours a week, Monday through Saturday, for wages as low as $6.00 a week. Worse still, some employers charged them for mistakes or deducted fees for "rental" of the machines and use of electricity. In 1909 many of these workers walked off their jobs in a strike called the "Uprising of the 20,000." Employers brought in unemployed blacks to break the effort, but several hundred of them joined the strikers. "It's a good thing, this strike is," one young black woman wrote in her diary. "It makes you feel like a real grown-up person."

Demonstrating unusual solidarity, the women workers marched in picket lines during the long winter months. They gained widespread public sympathy and support. Early in 1910 the International Ladies' Garment Workers' Union (ILGWU), aided by mediator Louis D. Brandeis, won a pay hike, a reduced workweek, a preferential union shop, and arbitration machinery composed of representatives of labor, management, and the public. ILGWU membership soared from only 400 to 65,000 as the victory demonstrated the potential power of female and ethnic workers and of collective action.

The Challenge of the Left

Labor groups with more extreme goals challenged the AFL's policy of exclusive trade unionism and accommodation with management. They advocated industrywide organization of workers and urged the overthrow, or at least a major overhaul, of the capitalist system of owner and managerial control in the pursuit of profits so as to distribute the benefits of mass production more equitably. The socialists urged national government ownership of all major industries, utilities, banks, and railroads. The more militant minority that made up the Socialist Labor party, founded by the theoretician Daniel DeLeon in 1877, demanded separate socialist unions and worker seizure of power. The majority of American socialists took a more moderate position. They tried to convert the AFL unions to socialism and, at the same time, work toward political power through the Socialist Party of America, which they founded in 1901.

Despite their factionalism, American socialists won significant strength in labor and politics. At their peak in 1912 they accounted for nearly one-third of the delegates to the AFL national convention, representing unions with more than 300,000 members. In that year the Socialist party candidate for president, Eugene V. Debs, garnered 900,000 votes, 6 percent of the total. The Socialists elected two members of Congress, fifty-six mayors (in cities like Milwaukee, Schenectady, and Berkeley), thirty-three state legislators (in seventeen states), and nearly 1,000 persons to town and city councils. Like the European socialist parties, the Socialist Party of America grew dramatically in the years before World War I, fed by popular dissatisfaction with the status quo.

Debs, a former railroad worker from Indiana, became the leading missionary of American socialism. He ran for president five times on the party ticket. A magnetic orator, the kindhearted Hoosier became an American folk hero, preaching in his broad midwestern accent the need for the workers to block exploitation by the capitalists. As a young man he had been deeply stirred by the writings of Edward Bellamy and Henry George, but not until he found himself in prison after the government's suppression of the Pullman strike of 1894 did he read Marx. Then, as he recalled, "my eyes opened—and in the gleam of every bayonet and the flash of every rifle the class struggle revealed itself."

The most aggressive force in the class struggle and industrial warfare was the tough, defiant Industrial Workers of the World (IWW), whose members were called "Wobblies." Sprouting up in 1905 among exploited miners, lumberjacks, and migrant field hands of the West, the IWW's membership never exceeded 100,000, but its radicalism and its successful participation in several important eastern strikes, such as those in Lawrence, Massachusetts, and Paterson, New Jersey, frightened many moderate and conservative Americans. IWW leaders believed in syndicalism, a position then in vogue in the French, Italian, and Scandinavian labor movements, which emphasized the takeover and operation of industries by autonomous workers' unions or syndicates. The organizers and martyrs of the IWW—especially William "Big Bill" Haywood, the 6-foot-tall hard-rock miner and symbolic proletarian leader of the Wobblies—became part of the legend of the American Left.

Employers' Counterattack

Seeing the growth of such radicalism and of organized labor in general as major challenges to the economic system, the marketplace ideal, and their own position, many employers joined forces to launch substantial counteroffensives. The most aggressive of these came not from the trusts but from small and medium-sized businesses. Branding the AFL as "un-American, illegal, and indecent," the National Association of Manufacturers (NAM) argued that "labor trusts" were "contrary to law and the rights of man." It helped drive unions out of a number of cities, many of them in the Midwest.

After the spurt of unionization at the turn of the century, labor's organizing drive lagged for almost a decade. Comparatively few American workers belonged to unions. A tradition of rugged individualism, a belief in opportunity, and a desire for self-improvement, and ultimately self-employment, led many Americans to dislike the idea of joining class-conscious unions. Unlike Europeans, American industrial workers did not have to band together to obtain the vote; suffrage came before industrialization. Moreover, many believed in their freedom to work when and where they wanted. The ethnic and racial diversit of the American work force also hampered unionization. So did t hiring policies of employers, who put together ethnic groups that w r traditionally suspicious of each other: Russians and Poles, Greeks and Turks, Irish and English, blacks and whites. In addition, many employers harassed union organizers, required prospective workers to sign agreements not to join unions (called "yellow-dog contracts"), and hired spies and private guards to identify and oust unionists. During strikes, employers obtained police, National Guard, and sometimes U.S. Army assistance in protecting company property and allowing strikebreakers to enter plants. The conservative attitude of the judiciary also hampered the labor movement. Courts issued injunctions against strikes, boycotts, and picketing on the ground that these actions deprived the employer of property without due process of law.

During the second decade of the twentieth century, as reform sentiment grew, the labor movement resumed its progress, so that by

1917 more than 3 million men and women, or 11 percent of the nonagricultural work force, held union cards. The federal government and some of the new, more liberal corporate leadership, particularly in oligopolistic industries, which could safely pass on wage increases to consumers through higher prices, began to provide some support for more moderate unions in the AFL and the railroad brotherhoods. However, radical labor organizations such as the socialist unions and the IWW were detested by business and feared by government. As the Progressive Era ended, organized labor, though a significant new force, exerted relatively little influence on most industrial workers or on the labor market as a whole. The limited number of workers in the skilled trades had been the primary beneficiaries of union activities. Not until the Great Depression, the New Deal, the founding of the Congress of Industrial Organizations (CIO), and the spread of unionization through the mass production industries in the 1930s and 1940s would organized labor achieve substantial influence in the industrial labor market.

Productivity and Pain in Agriculture

Industrialization contributed to fundamental changes in agriculture, helping to increase agricultural yields with fewer farmers. It was a painful process, this contraction of the number of small, independent farmers. These men and women were caught in the squeeze of economic forces beyond their control—declining commodity prices and farm income at the same time as rising costs of credit and crushing indebtedness. The number of farms, which had doubled in the last third of the nineteenth century to nearly 6 million, increased by only about 10 percent between 1900 and 1914. After World War I the total number of American farms slumped, for the first time in the nation's history, into a permanent decline. When the numbers of farms peaked, agricultural production had also reached a record high, increasing by one-third between 1897 and 1917. The use of new farm machinery and chemical fertilizers helped farmers who could afford them to grow more corn, wheat, oats, citrus fruits, cotton, and tobacco with fewer workers.

In the 1890s and 1900s declining farm income from falling commodity prices combined with heavy indebtedness to push several hundred thousand small farmers into bankruptcy. Many left the land; others became tenant farmers working for landowning planters, growers, corporations, or banks. Farm tenancy mounted steadily from 25 percent of total farms in 1890 to 35 percent in 1900 and 37 percent in 1910 and 38 percent in 1920. The most marked increases in the number of poor tenant farmers and sharecroppers came in the cotton states of the South and the wheat-growing states of the prairie West.

What was later hailed as a "golden age of agriculture," the pre–World War I decade when agricultural prices were stabilized, was in fact a period of relative prosperity only for larger farms. For the majority of America's farmers, seeking to eke out a living on small pieces of land, it was a period not only of continued relative privation but of the actual loss of land and the subsequent onset of landless tenantry and impoverishment.

As America became a nation of city dwellers, it not only expanded its food consumption but also began to change the commodities it consumed. Americans continued to buy large quantities of beef, pork, bread, and milk. But in response to changes in fashion, modern urbanites wanted more vitamins and less fattening foods. They consumed increasing amounts of protein in the form of dairy and poultry products. Less strenuous work and better-heated homes and offices also led to fewer requests for starchy, energy-producing foods and more calls for lighter fruits and vegetables. Improvements in irrigation opened up land for extensive citrus groves in California and Florida, and refrigerated cars enabled growers to send fresh oranges and grapefruit to the cities of the North. The tastes and lifestyles of urban residents also led to increased consumption of coffee and sugar. The urban, industrial tempo led to a growth in alcohol consumption and a dramatic increase in cigarette smoking.

Industrialism and mass production meant some product shifts and increased production by fewer farmers. The problem of overproduction plagued farmers and led ultimately, beginning in the 1920s, to government aid and intervention to modify the impact of the market system by dumping surpluses abroad and, in the 1930s, to restricting output.

Supplier to the World

Throughout much of its history, the United States had been an agricultural supplier in the world markets. Midwesterners shipped wheat and corn to European cities. Growers in Virginia and the Carolinas supplied tobacco. Southern planters had sent millions of bales of cotton to the textile mills of England and the Continent as well as to American mills. But early in the twentieth century the United States also became manufacturer and banker to the world. It exported capital and credit and a variety of manufactured goods ranging from sewing machines to locomotives. By the end of World War I, America would become the leading economic power in the international marketplace.

In the first two decades of the new century, American foreign trade expanded faster than at any time since the Civil War. As exports and imports doubled by 1914 and spurted again during the war years, manufactured goods became America's leading overseas shipments.

Longshoremen swung giant loads of crates aboard ships bound for Europe, Canada, Mexico, and sometimes the Far East. Like an enormous factory, the United States took in supplies for its machines and additional foodstuffs for its workers. Freighters unloaded copper, rubber, tin, manganese, nickel, and zinc for the metal factories, hides for shoes and leather goods, and sugar and coffee for American appetites.

Corporations and wealthy individuals transformed America's foreign investment pattern. Traditionally a debtor nation, the United States had obtained significant European capital for its development. Now, however, American investors placed large sums overseas in the construction of foreign railroads and industrial facilities. They also helped to underwrite the expenses of the Boer War in South Africa and the Russo-Japanese War in Asia. Between 1897 and 1914, American investment abroad multiplied fivefold, from $700 million to $3.5 billion.

The precursors of multinational U.S. enterprises emerged in the early years of the twentieth century. Following the depression of the 1890s, several of the new supercorporations expanded overseas. In a number of mass production industries, production outran immediate domestic demand. "Dependent solely upon local business," John D. Rockefeller explained in 1899, "we should have failed long ago. We were forced to extend our markets and to seek for export trade."

As they probed for new markets, the supercorporations established sales outlets and then manufacturing plants abroad. The first of these, the Singer Sewing Machine Company, set up sales offices in a half dozen countries. American Tobacco built a cigarette-rolling mill in China; Ford erected auto plants in Britain and France. Industrial and consumer goods companies such as these concentrated primarily in countries with high incomes, mainly in Europe and in Canada, but the extractive industries engaged in mining and transportation operations in income-poor underdeveloped nations. For instance, American Smelting and Refining owned mines, smelters, railroads, and port facilities in Mexico and Chile. Unlike the millions of competitive farmers, who could not individually affect world markets, the giant corporations could and did seek to limit international competition. American Tobacco signed agreements with British competitors to divide and share global markets rather than engage in unprofitable price competition. Similarly, many other American supercorporations split overseas markets with European cartels.

American foreign-policy makers encouraged the expansion of American business, believing that active foreign trade and investment would stimulate a prosperous, expanding domestic economy, which would in turn contribute to national power and prestige. "America has only just begun to assume that commanding position in the international business world which we believe will more and more be hers," President Theodore Roosevelt asserted in 1901.

The New Corporate Economy

Trusts, internationally active corporations, Wall Street, and, to a much lesser extent, national trade unions—these became the symbols of the organizational revolution that accompanied and helped to shape the mass production and mass consumption economy dominated in the United States by large-scale modern manufacturing corporations. The nature of business combinations and administered prices in major industrial markets was not part of an irresistible process of economic evolution. Corporate leaders and those in politics, the media, and the professions who supported the general framework of this new, evolving corporate economy tried to guide industrialization and to direct it.

It has been argued that in the period between 1890 and 1920, a new stage of capitalism—liberal corporate capitalism as contrasted to the previously dominant laissez-faire individual capitalism—evolved in America. As it emerged as the dominant philosophy in major sectors of the economy, liberal corporate capitalism meant that the ideal of unregulated market individualism was modified in many instances by partially administered markets (certain sectors in which price competition was constrained by administrative decisions within industry). Few Americans were willing to allow giant corporations to have complete control of even their own markets, let alone the national economy.

In an accommodation and restructuring that resulted from a broad process of reform and regulation in the Progressive Era, the United States emerged with a modified economy. In many of the major sectors of this new corporate economy, the markets were largely administered by private economic forces—primarily small groups of giant corporations. But they also became subject to at least some regulation by the government.

Industrialization posed similar problems in other countries. Although the nations of western Europe experienced the mechanization of industry, the rise of mass production, the growth of large-scale enterprise, the migration of the labor force from the farms to the cities, and the growth of unions, each nation responded somewhat differently because of its peculiar characteristics. In Germany the legal system and the banks encouraged the formation of cartels among large and medium-sized firms to reduce the otherwise chaotic price competition in the coal, steel, potash, electrical, and chemical industries. In France, where the development of mass production lagged, small-scale, family-owned enterprises that emphasized quality rather than quantity continued to characterize the economy, although there were some rather weak trade associations. Britain had a legal system most like that of the United States. Since cartels were illegal there, outright consolidation was more common, and amalgamation led to oligopoly.

In Europe the rapid rise of nationally organized industrial labor in the second half of the nineteenth century coincided with worker agitation for the vote and the prevalence of a class-conscious socialist philosophy. Militant unions organized millions of skilled and unskilled industrial workers. This set of circumstances helped politicize the European labor movements and led to socialist-oriented labor parties, which gained significant influence in Britain and Germany at the start of the twentieth century.

By the end of the first decade of the new century, several trends of industrialism had emerged in the United States, western Europe, and Japan. Accelerated economic growth and the development of mass production industries led to the creation of large new centers of economic power, encouraged massive shifts in population and the work force, and challenged old relationships, traditions, and ideals. The future remained uncertain. It was not fully known what impact these forces would have on society. Nor was it completely clear what would be the effect on the economy of the growth of organizations like trusts, trade associations, and labor unions, which sought to limit some aspects of the operation of the marketplace. The changes accompanying industrialization were affecting virtually every institution in society. The scope and pace of change and the pressure for collective intervention posed a major challenge to the American faith in a self-regulating society.

CHAPTER 4

A Changing Society and Culture

 "Never in the history of the world was society in so terrific flux as it is right now," the novelist Jack London wrote in 1907. "The swift changes in our industrial system are causing equally swift changes in our religious, political, and social structures. An unseen and fearful revolution is taking place in the fiber and structure of society. One can only dimly feel these things, but they are in the air, now, today."

The Progressive Era was a time of general awakening of social thought, a new spirit that had Americans thinking about their society in new ways, reexamining institutions, attitudes, and the culture itself. The pace of economic and demographic change put great strains on a society whose institutions were created for a land of agrarian settlements. Urbanization and industrialization pushed people toward more collective action. In larger groups they could better control the forces that affected their lives. The discipline of industrial life proved constraining for a people that prided itself on individuality and freedom. Yet mass production offered a higher material standard of living for Americans and reinforced their sense of abundance. From European thinkers—Ibsen, Bergson, Nietzsche, and others—came a new emphasis on the liberation of the individual and the importance of self-realization and fulfillment. Amid the new century's challenges to agrarian America and the Victorian order of the nineteenth century, Americans struggled to understand the changes that were occurring around them.

"There isn't a human relation, whether of parent and child, husband and wife, worker and employer, that doesn't move in a strange situation," commentator Walter Lippmann observed. "There are no precedents to guide us, no wisdom that wasn't made for a simpler age. We have changed our environment more quickly than we know how to change ourselves." In the Progressive Era, Americans tried actively to adjust their institutions to the conditions of a new age.

A Growing Nation

America experienced a virtual population explosion. The population leapt from 76 million to 106 million in the first two decades of the new century. The greatest part of this expansion came from a natural rate of increase due to better living conditions for many people resulting from higher income, more adequate food and shelter, and improvements in health care. The result was longer life expectancy. Medical science made great strides toward eliminating traditional causes of premature death. Following the acceptance of the germ theory of disease, bacterial enemies came under attack through improvements in antiseptic procedures, personal hygiene, and public sanitation. Physicians and public health workers helped to curb the infant mortality rate; reduced the number of deaths from tuberculosis, typhoid fever, pneumonia, and diphtheria; and practically eliminated smallpox and malaria. Consequently, life expectancy among white males, for example, grew almost 20 percent, from 46 to 55 years, between 1900 and 1920. Thus, despite a declining birthrate, the number of native-born Americans increased.

With life expectancy increasing and the birthrate falling, older people made up a larger proportion of the population. The percentage of people over 65 nearly doubled, rising from 3 to 5 percent between 1870 and 1920. Old age became a social problem in the Progressive Era. Like other "social problems" that had previously been private matters, the plight of the elderly came to be seen as a concern of the entire community, one that called for community action. The short but severe panic and recession of 1907–1908 dramatized the devastating economic problems of older people in an industrial society. The pace of factory work and the lack of security in the wage system forced older people out of the job market. Many retired in poverty. Although most European nations had compulsory old-age insurance programs, the United States did not. In 1909 the first public commission on aging, which studied the situation of the elderly in Massachusetts, found that 25 percent of people over 65 were on some form of dole. For a long while, however, attempts to deal with this problem were frustrated. The first state pension plan, adopted by Arizona in 1915, was declared unconstitutional. Not until 1935 was the federal social security system established.

Immigrants and Nativists

The most visible increase in the American population came from immigrants to the United States. Fifteen million entered between 1900 and 1915, as many as had arrived in the preceding forty years. They accounted for nearly a third of the nation's population growth. More than

70 percent were "new immigrants" from southern and eastern Europe. Typically, several young men from a village would set out together for America and find work in the same mill, factory, or mine. They would live in a boardinghouse or with friends or relatives who had preceded them. Many intended to live in America only long enough to save money and return home to buy land or redeem the family mortgage, but many remained in the United States.

Nativists saw the immigrants clustering in ethnic "ghettos" and warned of the "Balkanization" of the United States. The immigrants themselves drew much succor from the churches, schools, foreign-language newspapers, and social and cultural associations they created to sustain them in the different and often threatening American urban environment. Nevertheless, recent research indicates that contemporaries exaggerated the homogeneity of the so-called ghettos, which were actually composed of people from many different villages and provinces who had little in common. Immigrant neighborhoods contained a variety of nationalities. Only rarely did a single ethnic group dominate an area of several city blocks, and even then many immigrants soon moved out of such areas. The Lower East Side of Manhattan was known as the Jewish ghetto in 1892, when three out of four of New York's Jews lived there, but twenty-five years later the district contained less than one out of four of the city's Jews. Thousands had moved uptown in Manhattan or to the boroughs of the Bronx, Queens, Brooklyn, or Staten Island. Like those who had arrived before them, the new immigrants were a mobile people.

The immigration of Catholics and Jews from southern and eastern Europe in numbers reaching more than a million a year frightened many Americans, especially those who were already suspicious of the challenges to traditional American culture and values presented by the growth of industry and cities. The immigrants bore the brunt of the antiurban bias of rural Americans. They were also objects of disdain to racially obsessed social Darwinists, who argued that Mediterranean and Slavic peoples were genetically less fit than Anglo-Saxons. Nativists feared the diminution of American traditions, ideals, and standards of living.

Resistance to the direction of modern urban, industrial America, which numbers of traditionalists, particularly in rural areas, linked to urban growth and the new immigration from southern and eastern Europe, was sometimes accompanied by painful outbursts of anti-Catholicism and anti-Semitism. America's volatile anti-Catholic tradition had been temporarily checked by the prosperity and cosmopolitanism of the early Progressive Era, but anti-Catholicism resurfaced in the 1910s with the tirades of racist Georgia politician and editor Thomas E. ("Tom") Watson, the blatant fabrications (such as rumors of Catholic plots to establish papal tyranny in the United States) of hate magazines such as *The Menace* (1911), and the reemergence in 1915 of the Ku Klux Klan (KKK).

On a summer night in 1915, a group of white Georgians burned crosses atop Stone Mountain outside Atlanta and initiated a second KKK. Inspired in part by D. W. Griffith's feature film, *The Birth of a Nation* (1915), which depicted the Klan in the Reconstruction Era following the Civil War as a courageous defender of the white South against the blacks, the white-sheeted leaders of the new Klan reserved the majority of their hostility for contemporary "alien menaces." These were immigrants, modernists, Catholics, and Jews, and the Klan would build its efforts, legal and illegal, against them into a major crusade and into national political issues — prohibition, immigration restriction, and the issue of corruption and murder within the Klan itself — by the mid-1920s.

Anti-Catholicism and anti-Semitism were not limited to the South. Indeed, there was considerable hostility to Catholics and Jews in the North. The anti-Catholic Immigration Restriction League had its national headquarters in Boston. Anti-Semitism was increasing among the Protestant northern elites who, in the Progressive Era, began to exclude Jews from their clubs and social resorts and restrict the number accepted at Ivy League colleges. The most notorious example of increasingly virulent anti-Semitism of the period was the lynching of Leo M. Frank in Georgia. Superintendent of a factory and a prominent member of the small Jewish community in Atlanta, Frank was tried and convicted in 1914 of the murder of one of his employees, Mary Phagan, a 13-year-old Gentile. The governor was troubled by the evidence that suggested the guilt of a black workman, Jim Conley, rather than Frank, and he commuted Frank's sentence from death to life imprisonment. Subsequently in 1915, organized groups of men, stirred by the anti-Semitism that swept the state, attacked the governor's mansion and also broke into the state penitentiary and kidnapped Frank. The next morning Frank was lynched near Marietta, Georgia.*

The question of whether the United States should have a homogeneous or heterogeneous culture became a major national issue in the Progressive Era. Many people believed that society should resemble a "melting pot" (indeed, the term was first used in a play written at that time) in which all immigrants were blended into a new cultural type, the American. But a few intellectuals, including philosophers Horace Kallen and John Dewey, settlement house workers such as Jane Addams, and some representatives of the immigrants themselves put forward an alternative, cultural pluralism, in which each cultural group

---

*Students of the case long believed Frank to have been innocent, and in 1982, after an 83-year-old witness confessed that he had seen Jim Conley carrying Phagan's body on the day she was murdered, Georgia granted Frank a posthumous pardon.

would make its own contribution to the range, variety, and richness of what Kallen called the "orchestra of mankind."

Massive immigration challenged the faith of native-born Americans in the wisdom of the open marketplace as it applied to the flow of immigrant labor into the United States. Many began to question the tradition of open immigration. Under pressure from the Immigration Restriction League, the Daughters of the American Revolution, the American Federation of Labor, and other groups, Congress established the Dillingham Commission to investigate the impact of the new immigration. Its report confirmed some of the nativists' worst fears: that the new immigrants were largely unskilled, illiterate, and transient males from southern and eastern Europe and that the areas in which they lived had high crime and disease rates. (The commission correlated these social indexes with ethnic characteristics rather than with economic conditions.)

Although they were opposed by industry, which still desired a large pool of unskilled labor, nativists sought to limit the flow of immigrants and preserve the traditional ethnic mixture of the American population. In response to their pressure, Congress passed a literacy test requirement in 1896, 1913, and 1915, but it was successfully vetoed by Presidents Cleveland, Taft, and Wilson. Not until 1917, as a result of the intense nationalism of World War I, did Congress finally succeed in overriding a presidential veto and enacting a literacy test, thereby modifying the traditional policy of open immigration. Immigration restriction was placed on a new and more permanent basis in the 1920s.

An "Americanization" movement to acculturate the immigrants became powerful during the Progressive Era. Part of it was educational, as settlement houses, the YMCA, night school civics classes, and some large corporations taught the English language and American forms of dress, behavior, and ideals. In its most coercive form, the Americanization movement became an effort to get immigrants to change their culture — their religion, language, behavior, and patterns of thought and action. During World War I the movement for "one hundred percent Americanism," led by such groups as the National Americanization Committee and local vigilante bodies, became a national crusade involving schools, churches, patriotic societies, and civic organizations. Violence and harassment were used to force people of German birth or descent to give up their language, newspapers, clubs and associations, and parochial schools. Intervention for "Americanism" produced tensions in American society that were exacerbated in the 1920s.

Submerged Minorities

Like the new immigrants, African Americans suffered from the virulent racism of the time. In the South a drive to eliminate blacks from political and social life gained strength at the turn of the century, particularly after numbers of poor whites and blacks had joined dirt farmer organizations to vote in the early 1890s for some local populist candidates who denounced the wealthy. Within twenty years every southern state had disfranchised blacks through poll taxes and literacy tests and segregated them through Jim Crow laws. To keep the blacks subservient, white judges meted out long sentences on chain gangs for trivial offenses. Lynch mobs hanged or burned more than 1,100 blacks during the first dozen years of the twentieth century. The doctrine of white supremacy also prevailed in the North. Whites in Springfield, Illinois, sought to drive blacks out of town in 1908, destroying their homes and stores and burning three of them to death.

Confronted with such intense racism and repression, African Americans struggled to survive and to improve their situation. They listened to the opposing arguments of the two most nationally prominent black leaders. Booker T. Washington, who was born into slavery in Virginia, had been educated at Hampton Institute. Later he founded Tuskegee Institute in Alabama. After the death of the more militant Frederick Douglass in 1895, Washington became the main spokesperson for black Americans until his own death in 1915.* Washington recommended that blacks acquiesce temporarily in the loss of their political liberties and concentrate on becoming economically productive and self-sufficient. He urged them to become efficient farmers, merchants, teachers, and business people. His message to white southerners summarized his appeal. "In all things that are purely social," he declared, "we can be as separate as the fingers, yet one as the hand in all things essential to mutual progress." Tuskegeeism, with its conciliatory spirit and emphasis on gradual improvement, pleased white Americans and enabled Booker T. Washington to become the conduit for the funds of northern white philanthropists and the patronage of Republican presidents.

Opposition came from W. E. B. Du Bois, A Massachusetts-born, Harvard-educated black professor who advocated immediate direct action to obtain civil rights and economic equality for African Americans. He also predicted that the leadership of the black community by the clergy would be superseded by secular black elites. In 1905 Du Bois joined other black intellectuals, such as crusading journalists William Monroe Trotter and Ida Wells-Barnett, to form the Niagara Movement "to refuse to allow the impression to remain that the Negro-American assents to inferiority, is submissive under oppression, and apologetic before insults." In 1909, in reaction to the bloody race riot against blacks in Springfield, Illinois, Du Bois, Trotter, Wells-Barnett, Mary Church Terrell, and a number of other black leaders joined

*The year 1915 also marked the death of Henry McNeal Turner, bishop of the African Methodist Episcopal Church. An aggressive black nationalist with a wide audience among the African-American masses, Turner was probably the foremost black clergyman of his day.

with white reformers — including Jane Addams, John Dewey, and Oswald Garrison Villard, grandson of a leading abolitionist — to form the National Association for the Advancement of Colored People (NAACP), whose purpose was to work for the recognition of blacks' constitutional rights. Du Bois became editor of the organization's magazine, *The Crisis*. By the end of 1918 the NAACP had 165 local chapters, half of them in the South, and a membership of 44,000. The migration of blacks out of the South and into northern cities led to the creation in 1910 of the National League on Urban Conditions among Negroes (the Urban League), an interracial organization focusing on social and economic problems caused by the rapid influx of black migrants into New York, Philadelphia, Washington, Baltimore, Chicago, and other cities. Despite these efforts, however, the status of African Americans, like that of other nonwhites, grew worse during the intensive racism of the Progressive Era.

By the turn of the century many Mexican Americans in the Southwest were being forced into virtual peasantry. Giant commercial farms destroyed the old rancho system and drove the Chicano farmers from their land. The dislocation of native-born Hispanic Americans was aggravated by heavy immigration of Mexicans after the upheavals of the Mexican Revolution, which began in 1910. Chicanos provided much of the labor for American produce growers. In the cities, *barrios* (ghettos), or colonies of Spanish-speaking immigrants, developed. Whites tried to impose Anglo-conformity on the Chicanos, but at the same time they feared the influx of new workers and their preindustrial culture. Collective labor action by Mexican Americans began with strikes by California beet workers in 1903 and Arizona copper miners in 1915.

Anti-Chinese sentiment had led Congress in 1882 to prohibit additional immigration of Chinese laborers. Thereafter, tens of thousands of single male laborers returned to China — some voluntarily, many coerced. Between 1900 and 1920, however, Asian immigration to the West Coast resumed. Among the newcomers were some 40,000 Chinese, including skilled workers and entire families. Similarly, some Koreans and more than 200,000 Japanese arrived in the United States in the early 1900s. Some of the Japanese had settled first in Hawaii to work in the sugarcane fields. Many then moved on to the West Coast, where, joined by new immigrants from Japan, numbers of them labored as seasonal field hands, saved their money, and eventually leased land and grew vegetables for market. Rising anti-Asian sentiment on the West Coast in the early 1900s led to their segregation by the San Francisco School Board and the prohibition of Asians from buying land in California. After much tension, the so-called "Gentlemen's Agreement" between the United States and the imperial Japanese government in 1907 led the school board to rescind the order and Tokyo to withhold passports from Japanese laborers intending to emigrate to the United States.

Although the Japanese children were not formally segregated in the San Francisco schools, they and their parents were largely forced to live in certain areas of the western cities. As with the Chinese, the Japanese immigrants fell within the Immigration and Naturalization Service's ruling (upheld by the Supreme Court) that Asian immigrants were prohibited from becoming U.S. citizens. Consequently, foreign-born Japanese who remained in the United States (the *Issei*) were kept in a permanent-alien status and prohibited by most western states from purchasing farm land. Although their children (the *Nisei*), born in the United States, became U.S. citizens, it was not until after World War II that Americans of Japanese ancestry were able to settle voluntarily outside their segregated residential enclaves.

Class and Status in American Society

As the plight of the nation's submerged minorities indicated, American society remained significantly stratified. Nonwhites found themselves relegated to the lowest socioeconomic level. The religion and ethnicity of new immigrants also affected their status. Catholics and Jews from southern and eastern Europe were forced into low-paid menial employment.

Reformers helped to expose and document the conditions in which minorities were forced to live and the extent of poverty and suffering in the new urban, industrial America. The sociologist Robert Hunter, in his pioneering study *Poverty* (1904), presented statistical evidence to support his contention that 6 million people, or one-fifth of the population of the industrial states, lived in abject poverty. Because Hunter set his poverty line so low ($460 a year for a family of five), his estimate of the extent of poverty was in fact conservative. Father John Ryan, a Roman Catholic priest, scholar, and social activist who was a leading advocate of a "living wage" (a phrase he popularized, meaning the minimum wage necessary to live decently), thought that $600 was the minimum necessary for a family of five, $800 in some high-cost areas. Using an average of $700 for a family of five meant that somewhere between 30 and 50 million people, or 40 percent of the wage earners and clerical workers in America, were living in poverty in the first decade of the twentieth century. (This did not include the problem of rural poverty, neglected by urban-oriented reformers of the period, which included millions of sharecroppers, tenant farmers, and migrant workers who, particularly in the South, also suffered heavily from hookworm, pellagra, and malnutrition.)

One out of every ten persons who died in New York City did not have enough money for a funeral and was buried in potter's field. Investigators like Hunter challenged the traditional view that poverty stemmed from immorality. Instead, they concluded that it resulted from the failure of the economic system to meet the needs of all Americans. Plagued by unemployment, the poor were inadequately fed, clad, and sheltered. "My people do not live in America, they live underneath America," declared a Ruthenian priest in Yonkers, New York. "America does not begin till a man is a workingman, till he is earning two dollars a day. A laborer cannot afford to be an American."

The poor lived and died in misery. They skimped on food, substituting condensed or evaporated milk for fresh milk, leaf lard or beef suet for butter. Their children suffered from rickets. In general, health, like income, differed along class and racial lines. The life expectancy of a black man was ten years less than that of a white man, a result of inadequate health care and a greater incidence of malnutrition and disease. By vividly exposing the miseries of the poor, especially the immigrants in the cities, investigative journalists and other reformers helped convince hundreds of thousands of middle- and upper-class Americans that the causes of mass poverty were beyond the individual's control and that the poor were the responsibility of society at large.

Above the poor and the lowest-paid workers in the American social structure was a broad and heterogeneous middle class. Outside of the South, with its large numbers of poor white residents, the middle class included most native white Americans. Its members were descended from families who had come from western and central Europe. They included the old middle class of artisans, skilled workers, and self-employed shopkeepers, small entrepreneurs, farmers, and small manufacturers, as well as members of the professions—teachers, lawyers, and doctors. But these were joined by a growing new middle class—white-collar employees who worked in the proliferating urban shops and offices. They lived in homes that ranged from the row houses of the cities to the more spacious single-family houses of the suburbs and country towns or on prosperous farms.

At the apex of the socioeconomic hierarchy were the upper-class elite. Powerful and prestigious, they included old wealthy families who had inherited money earned in commerce and land speculation—the Cabots and Lodges of Boston, the Browns of Providence, the Roosevelts and Astors of New York, the Drexels and Biddles of Philadelphia—and the new industrial rich and their allies, the financiers, corporation lawyers, and managers—the Rockefellers, Vanderbilts, Carnegies, Dukes, Guggenheims, Seligmans, Lehmans, Morgans, Schwabs, Fricks, and Fords. They were mostly Protestants, along with a few Catholics and Jews; they or their ancestors came from Britain, Germany, Holland, or France. They lived in mansions in the cities or suburbs and had ornate summer "cottages" in Newport, Rhode Island, or Bar Harbor, Maine. They belonged to exclusive clubs and sent their children to eastern preparatory schools and then to the all-male colleges of the Ivy League or the women's colleges called the Seven Sisters.

The wealth of the superrich was enormous. The figures of Professor Willford J. King showed at the time that the rich, less than 2 percent of the population, owned 60 percent of the total wealth of the country. In contrast, the poor and very poor, 65 percent of the population, owned not more than 5 percent of the wealth. The middle class, 33 percent of the nation, owned 35 percent of the wealth. In 1910 it was estimated that the seventy richest Americans each had a fortune of at least $35 million and together owned one-sixteenth of the nation's wealth. Many millionaires spent their money lavishly. The sensationalist newspapers exposed the excesses of what Thorstein Veblen labeled "conspicuous consumption," the ivory and ebony bedsteads inlaid with gold, the $15,000 diamond-studded dog collars, and the parties at which the guests smoked cigarettes wrapped in $100 bills.

Despite the discrepancies in wealth and stratification, America remained a society in flux. Carnegie and Schwab, self-made millionaires, demonstrated the most extreme and rarest kind of success. But whites, both immigrant and native-born, often achieved some upward occupational mobility or saw the possibility of it. Amadeo Obici built a push-cart operation into the Planter's Peanut Company, and when A. P. Giannini discovered that California banks were refusing credit to Italian immigrants, he created the Bank of America chain in that state and made it one of the largest private banking systems in the world. Among the Italians and eastern European Jews who remained in Manhattan between 1905 and 1915, fully 32 percent moved from blue-collar to white-collar occupations. In addition, there was a large transient population, primarily poor, who moved from one city to another looking for work. A number of studies suggest the existence of a highly fluid society in white America. Modern industrialism may have increased the distance between the rich and the poor by creating a class of enormously wealthy families, but it also tremendously expanded the middle class through the creation of a wide range of new occupations.

Abject poverty nevertheless remained a major problem afflicting more than 40 percent of the population in the early twentieth century. Despite the middle class's "discovery" of the alarming poverty in the urban immigrant ghettos, the expansion of the middle class reinforced the persistent belief among many Americans that each individual, not the social or economic environment, was responsible for his or her own situation. The persistence of this belief contributed to the fact that the United States was the last advanced industrial nation to begin constructing a system of social welfare for its people—beginning with voluntary organizations and some state and local governments in the Progressive Era—and that it built such a system more slowly and more grudgingly than any comparable nation.

Women, the Family, and Sexuality

By the early twentieth century, it had become clear that the family was changing significantly: social, economic, and intellectual forces were reducing its size, modifying its functions, and individualizing and democratizing its structure. The same was true in other Western nations, possibly because they all were affected by the rise of an urban middle class, maturing industrial economies, and changing ideals about women and the family.

In a society as heterogeneous as America, wide variations existed among class, ethnoreligious, and racial groups in terms of the relations between husband and wife, the status of women, and the socialization of children. The new trends toward smaller families and more liberal divorce laws, along with expanded rights for women, first appeared in upper- and middle-class white Anglo-Saxon Protestant culture. Many other ethnic and religious groups retained a larger family size and a more patriarchal tradition for a longer period. Nevertheless, desertion was a common means of ending marriages, and by the 1920s the divorce rate in the working class equaled that of the middle class.

Within the family, reform began to redefine relationships between husband and wife. Beginning among the artistic and political radicals of Greenwich Village in New York City and then spreading haltingly in reform-minded families, a growing emphasis on individualistic and democratic values began to replace patriarchal authority, the dominant authority of the father or husband in the family, which had been legitimized in law and religion. The more egalitarian emphasis was also reinforced by new economic opportunities for middle-class women. Slowly, a new, alternative ideal began to emerge, one that emphasized a relationship among equals and shared decision making between husband and wife, though not yet joint responsibility for child care and housework. By 1909 the woman's pledge to obey her husband had been dropped from civil marriage vows, and many churches had also eliminated it. But the emerging ideal of equality faced much resistance, and probably most women continued to remain subordinated within the family structure.

Changing views, particularly among the upper and middle classes, also affected marriage and the divorce rate. A significant minority came to see marriage as based on romantic love and individual interests and thus as resting on mutual agreement and contract rather than entirely on sacrament. A mounting number of marriages ended when affection and respect disappeared. As mentioned earlier, the divorce rate soared from one in every 21 marriages in 1880 to one in every 12 by 1900; by 1916 it had reached an astonishing one in every 9. People spoke of the "divorce crisis" as a threat to the foundations of social order. Traditionalists, led by many of the clergy, tried to tighten legislation so as to restrict the spread of divorce. But feminists, social scientists, liberal members of the clergy, and other advocates of adjustment to modern trends urged the easing of divorce laws not only to allow people to escape from tyrannical marriages but also to permit greater freedom and equality in wedlock and thus to help strengthen the institution of marriage. The movement to restrict divorce by statute had failed by the end of the Progressive Era. As in other urbanizing Western countries, divorce laws were liberalized in the United States, an indication of increased toleration and acceptance of divorce and of the complex transformation of moral values and sexual customs that would become even more widespread in the 1920s.

The long-term trend toward fewer children in marriage, which had begun in the early eighteenth century, continued in the twentieth. Dwindling family size meant that by 1920 the average mother gave birth to two or three children, compared to three or four in 1900; and this represented a major drop from the average of five or six children in 1860 and seven or eight in 1800. The decline accompanied growing urbanization. In the cities, particularly with compulsory education and child labor laws, young people could not be put to work as quickly as on farms. Rather, additional children meant less room in crowded apartments and additional costs for food and clothing. Controlling the number of children was one way of improving a family's standard of living. Improved medical care may also have contributed to the declining birthrate. Due primarily to medical advances against infectious diseases and to the use of pasteurized milk, the number of babies who died in their first year dropped to one in ten. That was half the infant mortality rate of a century earlier. Since fewer children died at birth or in infancy, it became unnecessary to have large numbers of children to ensure that some would survive. Many women apparently also decided to have fewer children because they wanted greater personal freedom or at least some relief from the burdens of child rearing.

Within the upper and middle classes, particularly in non-Catholic families, the use of contraceptives to reduce the number of pregnancies became quite common. In 1906 one physician reported that "hardly a single middle-class family" did not expect him to help "prevent conception." By 1922 as many as 74 percent of the women questioned in one study reported that they practiced some form of contraception.

The birthrate was highest among the poorer classes, particularly among the new immigrants. To educate lower-income women — and many middle-income women as well — about reducing the number of births, Margaret Sanger, a visiting nurse in the tenement district in the Lower East Side of Manhattan, organized the modern movement for "birth control," a term she originated.* Concerned about women's health — she was particularly appalled by the deaths she had seen from self-induced abortions — and with women's freedom from continual pregnancies, Sanger declared that women "are determined to decide for themselves whether they shall become mothers, under what conditions, and when." In 1914 she began distributing contraception information, particularly among the poor. But state laws and the federal Comstock Act of 1873 banned such information as obscene, and many states forbade the sale of contraceptives. Sanger went to jail for opening the first birth control clinic in 1916 in the immigrant slums of Brooklyn. In the face of much opposition, it took her and her supporters twenty years to achieve legalization of the dissemination of birth control information and materials.

An Age of Adolescence

During the early years of the new century, the modern concept of adolescence was created by German and Austrian psychologists, including Sigmund Freud, and first popularized in the United States by psychologist G. Stanley Hall in his massive study, *Adolescence: Its Psychology and Its Relation to Physiology, Anthropology, Sociology, Sex, Crime, Religion, and Education* (1904). Applied to youth between 14 and 18 years of age, the concept emphasized that because of this age group's alleged instability and vulnerability, both it and society would benefit from treating these teenage years as a nurturing stage in life withdrawn from adult pursuits. The teenage children of the wealthy had been sheltered from the world of work for some time, but there had been grave doubts as to whether the economy could operate without the labor of youth of other classes. In the early twentieth century, however, in the United States and almost every Western industrial nation, the concept of adolescence was democratized and indeed often required of most teenagers.

Industrialization displaced many young people from the jobs they would have held on the farm or in the shop in an agrarian society. The decline in the birthrate and the wide spacing of children, together with the fact that adults lived longer, meant that families in which all children lived to be teenagers became common. Consequently, between 1890 and 1920 a host of urban reformers, educators, youth workers,

*After Sanger left the leadership of the movement, more conservative leaders changed the name of her American Birth Control League to the Planned Parenthood Federation of America, a change Sanger opposed as too moderate and equivocal about limiting births.

and psychologists reclassified young people as adolescents, in need not of advice but of adult manipulation of their environment to improve their personal growth and development. In a time of rapid social change, many people viewed children as instruments of modernization, more malleable than adults. At the very least, child rearing and the socialization of adolescents should equip boys and girls with the security, flexibility, knowledge, and skills to make choices and develop intellectually and emotionally in a changing social order.

To help prepare young people for the strains of modern life, parents, educators, and youth workers formed child study associations, nursery schools, and kindergartens for young children and a number of other institutions for adolescents to provide them with organized peer-group activities emphasizing healthy competition and social interaction. From boys' clubs sponsored by city churches and settlement houses to the playground movement, YMCA programs, 4-H clubs for farm youth, and the more authoritarian and disciplined Boy Scouts of America, these agencies attempted to prepare young people for membership in social and economic groups. Many of them also sought to control problems of hoodlumism, juvenile crime, and other aggressive forms of behavior characterized as "juvenile delinquency."

The proliferation of organizations for young people, the extension of compulsory school attendance up to junior high school, and legislated work restrictions on child labor that also flowed in part from the new concept of adolescence were not without opposition. Poor families in the cities and the rural areas were dependent on income from all members of the family, including young children and teenagers. Although some endured great sacrifices to educate their children, others sided with the employers of such inexpensive labor in opposing any movement to withdraw young people from the work force. In addition, many Roman Catholics saw the largely Protestant-directed youth organizations and the public schools as instruments to convert their children to Protestantism or at least to Protestant culture. Many fundamentalist Protestants, especially in rural areas, viewed some of the youth groups as secularizing agencies that distracted young people from issues of sin and salvation.

The Breakdown of Victorianism

Despite opposition from many of their elders, large numbers of adolescents and young adults in the first two decades of the twentieth century challenged long-standing restraints and taboos of the Victorian era. The growing link between romantic love and courtship helped to transform sexual customs and moral values in the new century. So did the crumbling of the old Victorian code that prescribed strict segregation of the sexes into separate spheres. A woman's place was no longer solely in

the home. The increasing appearance of women in public places—
schools, factories, and places of commerce and entertainment—
directly eroded older idealized images of the Victorian woman as pure,
dependent, submissive, and aloof from the rough and corrupting experiences of the world outside the sanctuary of the home.

The diminishing of the separate spheres began in the schools. The
former separation of boys and girls during adolescence receded like the
surf at low tide. Coeducation increased, particularly in public schools
and colleges. With compulsory education extended to higher grades,
particularly in urban states, young women joined young men in many of
the new public high schools. In addition, more women went to college.
By 1910 some 40 percent of college students were women—double
the number in 1870. Only 20 percent of the nation's colleges and
universities refused to accept the new "coeds." With middle- and
upper-class young people spending more of their time outside the
family and among people of their own age, a particular youth subculture began to emerge. In the 1920s this modern college-oriented "peer
culture," revolving around school and friends and featuring athletics,
clubs, dating, and formal dances (know as "promenades" or "proms"),
would be fully developed and would fascinate the national media.

In the first two decades of the century, in middle- and upper-class
rituals of courtship, young women could start "keeping company" with
young men at 14 to 16 years old. Going beyond the old-fashioned tea
party, adolescent and young adult couples could go bicycling or roller
skating or for buggy rides. These provided acceptable ways to hold
hands in public or be alone together. Some flirting was socially acceptable for girls and young women, but men had the responsibility of
proposing marriage. If accepted, the successful suitor then had to obtain approval from the woman's father, who would ask about the man's
prospects for sustaining his future family. Middle-class weddings, usually paid for by the father of the bride, often became lavish demonstrations of love and status. The "honeymoon," a brief interlude before the
onset of regular family life, was often taken at special resorts, the most
famous of the period being Niagara Falls, New York.

Economic scarcity among the poor and working classes precluded
such costly ceremonies. The majority of such families scrimped to get
by, lived in crowded quarters, and moved quite frequently. Although
practices varied among ethnic groups, children and adolescents went to
work for wages. Boys were more likely to be put to work than girls, but
in many immigrant families daughters were often sent into the job
market at an early age to help earn additional needed income for the
family or sometimes to allow the sons to continue their education and
increase their income-earning potential. Traditionally, one daughter
would remain at home to help care for younger children or elderly
parents. Among the working classes, young men and women often

worked for seven years or more before they had fulfilled their obligations to their parents and could then marry. Even then, given high costs
and low incomes, they often could not acquire their own apartments or
homes until they were in their early thirties.

Sexuality

In the early twentieth century in urban areas, men and women of all
classes began to appear in public places oriented toward pleasure and
consumption — dance halls, amusement parks, and theaters. In the
cities young people could often easily meet outside the supervision of
their families or neighborhoods, and their activities illustrated the new
century's sensual, pleasure-seeking culture, emphasized by mass consumerism on the one hand and individual fulfillment on the other.
Nineteenth-century euphemisms faded as, heralded by new fashions
and forms of entertainment and glorified by much of the media, sexuality became a major social concern.

The working classes — and the Greenwich Village radicals — led
the way. For some time young working-class women had been known
for their bold and showy dress and their eagerness for nightlife and
dancing. Rushing to urban dance halls after ten- to twelve-hour workdays, many of them would let young men treat them to drinks and
dance with them. Some of the new dances were considered highly
suggestive, particularly new "tough dancing," such as the bunny hug,
the grizzly bear, and "shaking the shimmy." Initially shocked by such
behavior, the urban middle classes began cautiously in the 1910s to
accept modified versions of some of these dances in more fashionable
cabarets.

By 1913 women's high fashions had replaced the hourglass figure
of the Gibson girl with a slender, smaller silhouette that was no longer
as pinched in at the waist by corsets and fluffed out and weighted down
at the skirt with petticoats. The new style not only allowed more
freedom of movement but also greater exposure, as skirts no longer
dragged on the ground. Facial makeup, previously forbidden by middle-class conventions, began to be used, as a few daring young women
daubed on rouge and eye shadow; by the 1920s its use would become
widespread.

The breakdown of Victorian sexual norms was a gradual process,
evolving first in certain urban areas and particularly among young
adults. Cultural attitudes continued to emphasize marriage and family
as the goals for women. To reject them required conscious rebellion as
well as the income to do so. Indeed, most of the young working-class
women who openly expressed their autonomy and sexuality at the
dance halls withdrew, after finding their mates, into a much circum-
scribed family life. Many of the second and third generations of col-

lege-educated "new women" maturing after 1900, however, had both the economic and intellectual resources to seek a new lifestyle.

Of the women who pursued careers in teaching, nursing, and other professions, many married later in life or not at all. Unmarried working women were no longer labeled "spinsters" or "women adrift" by the newspapers but rather "bachelor girls" or "working girls." Although a double standard of acceptable sexual behavior continued to exist, women's magazines and popular novels saw these single, wage-earning women as seeking autonomy and pleasure, like men.

Beginning in the mid-1910s the new motion picture industry featured two contrasting and stereotypical female characters, reflecting the ambivalence in America about the new sexuality. One popular image was the virginal child-woman, played to perfection and wide acclaim by Mary Pickford, born Gladys Smith in Canada in 1893. Looking pure and beautiful, with curling golden tresses, this talented and shrewd young actress portrayed a charming but impish adolescent on the verge of maturity in such 1917 films as *The Little Princess* and *Rebecca of Sunnybrook Farm*. On the silent screen Pickford, ever childlike, sweet, and demure, came to personify the nation's cherished innocence and youth and became known as "America's sweetheart." The other extreme was the openly sexual, dangerous, seductive temptress — the "vamp" — introduced by the vampirish, man-hungry screen personality portrayed by actress Theda Bara (born Theodosia Goodman, the daughter of a Cincinnati tailor) in the 1916 silent film *A Fool There Was*, with its provocative subtitle *Kiss Me, My Fool!* Bara was soon surpassed as the reigning seductive "sex queen" by Gloria Swanson (Josephine Swenson), whose stardom began in the 1919 film *Male and Female*. Before industrywide censorship was imposed in the 1920s, American motion pictures often endorsed women's new sexual freedom. Indeed, the "flapper," the convention-breaking young woman strongly identified with the 1920s, was already a powerful image by the mid-1910s.

The Women's Movement and the Origins of Modern Feminism

"I have an important piece of news to give you," the president-elect of the General Federation of Women's Clubs announced in 1904 to its more than half a million members. Previously the clubs had focused on discussions of literary classics, such as the allegorical account by the Italian poet Dante Alighieri of a descent into hell. Now, turning from cultural self-improvement to social improvement, the newly elected women's leader told the women's clubs, "Dante is dead. He has been dead for several centuries, and I think it is time we dropped the study of his *Inferno* and turned our attention to our own." In the Progressive

Era women joined in record numbers to improve their situation in a changing society and give support to each other.

Two broad and often conflicting strands of thought characterized the predominantly middle- and upper-class women's movement in the first two decades of the century. One major theme, inherited from the nineteenth century, focused on female solidarity in a male-dominated society. It accepted part of the Victorian conception that women were not only biologically different but also socially and morally different from, and superior to, men. Stressing a world divided by sex, this view emphasized the common positive and negative experiences of women as a group and sought both to protect women from exploitation and to apply their superior moral values to the improvement of society as a whole. The other theme—which gained major importance in the twentieth century—deemphasized inherent gender differences and focused instead on equal rights and opportunities for women. In contrast to commonality, the priority of its practitioners was individual self-expression and fulfillment. The tension between this view of women's heterogeneous and conflicting interests and the older conception of women's common cause provided a divisive ambivalence in the twentieth century.

With the dramatic increase in the number of women wageworkers at the turn of the century, many of those who saw women as a group emphasized the need for female solidarity to assist women condemned to harsh, dangerous, and low-paying jobs. Emphasizing part of the Victorian image of women as being in need of protection, middle- and working-class female activists fought for and got a number of state laws prohibiting long hours and hazardous working conditions for women and requiring that they be paid at least a minimum wage.

To counter the economic exploitation of wage-earning women, a number of working-class female activists went beyond these state-mandated minimum wage and maximum hour laws and encouraged women workers to join trade unions to achieve more than minimal protection. Both employers and male-dominated trade unions restricted women workers to the kinds of jobs that did not challenge predominant cultural views of women as temporary and inferior workers compared to men—unskilled or semiskilled tasks in laundries and canneries, garment, textile, or tobacco factories and in offices or retail stores. In addition, many employers also created another hierarchical job structure, with native-born workers given the better and higher-paying jobs, immigrant workers positioned below them, and nonwhite workers, male and female, restricted to the worst and lowest-paying jobs. Seeking to help wageworking women organize was the Women's Trade Union League, founded in 1903 by working-class organizers such as Leonora O'Reilly and Rose Schneiderman.

A number of educated upper-middle-class women formed organizations to benefit women and society. The leaders of these national and sometimes international organizations openly demonstrated the skills and judgment necessary to run large-scale organizations. While emphasizing women's moral superiority, they expanded the public role of women into new areas of concern to society—social work, public health, even international peace. In doing so, they obtained valuable sustenance from both public acclaim and their own private female support networks. In fact, they emphasized the importance of the solidarity of women. The majority of these leaders were unmarried career women such as Jane Addams, the founder of the settlement house movement; Lillian Wald, the originator of the visiting nurse system; and the divorced Florence Kelley, organizer of the National Consumers' League. The league, like the National Child Labor Committee and the Women's Trade Union League, in which working-class women joined forces with socialites, sought to eliminate.sweatshop wages and conditions through private organization and collective action, such as consumer boycotts and political lobbying.

Black women also became more active in forming economic self-help and political reform organizations in the early twentieth century. After they had founded the National Association of Colored Women (NACW) in 1896, middle-class, urban black women had responded as both a sexually and a racially subordinate group to the growth of general reform sentiment in the country. As educated, elite women, they actively supported the major women's reform movements for temperance, moral purity, self-improvement, and suffrage. However, most of the national women's organizations, such as the Women's Christian Temperance Organization, the General Federation of Women's Clubs, the Young Women's Christian Association, and the National American Woman Suffrage Association, were divided (when not totally opposed) over the issue of including and working with black women. Consequently, black women focused especially on the National Association of Colored Women and helped build it in the first decade of the twentieth century into a widespread, well-organized association for racial protection and advancement. Like most of their white counterparts, however, these elite black women also believed in the woman's sphere, which emphasized women's moral superiority, nurturance of children and social inferiors, and imposition of middle-class standards on the lower classes.

With the increased tempo of national reform in the second decade of the twentieth century, local black women joined with men in founding and maintaining a number of social welfare institutions in local black communities—day nurseries and kindergartens, settlement houses, orphan asylums, and homes for widows, the infirm, and the aged—as well as urban black hospitals created by African-American physicians and nurses as a result of increasingly discriminatory policies in white hospitals. Black women such as Mary Church Terrell, president of the NACW, and Ida Wells-Barnett, leader of the antilynching crusade, cooperated with black men and with whites in the formation of a number of interracial organizations, including the NAACP. Even though white suffrage organizations largely excluded them or equivocated about their participation, elite black women also vigorously supported the drive for votes for women.

Women's Suffrage

In the second decade of the twentieth century the drive for female suffrage became the primary focus of the largely white, middle-class women's movement, temporarily pushing broader social and economic aims into the background. Wyoming had given women the vote in 1869. There had been a brief flurry in the early 1890s when Colorado, Utah, and Idaho granted full suffrage to women, but then a long period ensued in which no state adopted this reform. Beginning after 1900, however, women's collective voice and strength grew as young college-educated women created new organizing methods for the suffrage movement. Emphasizing female solidarity as well as women's rights, these upper- and middle-class white suffragists reached out to build an alliance with working-class white women. Although some elite black women were included in these white-dominated suffrage organizations, most of the African-American women who fought for the vote did so in their own communities and organizations.

The white suffragist leaders took innovative action to achieve results. Ignoring internal disputes within existing suffrage organizations, they launched door-to-door campaigns in poor and working-class neighborhoods as well as middle- and upper-class suburbs. Some activists also took the unprecedented step — for women — of public speaking on street corners. Others won support from some farm, labor, business, and professional organizations. They lobbied state legislatures and ultimately the national government. These efforts gained suffragist victories beginning in the West. Washington state granted women the vote in 1910, and a half dozen other western states, including California and Oregon, followed soon afterward. In 1913, Illinois became the first state east of the Mississippi and the first industrial state to grant women the vote. Gaining momentum, the suffrage movement by 1914 consumed the energy of hundreds of thousands of women and their male allies. In a bid for men's support, many suffragists deemphasized some of the more radical goals of the nineteenth-century women's movement, such as equal rights and economic opportunity. Instead, they accepted elements of the Victorian image of womanhood and asserted that female voters would help male reformers to reduce political corruption.

Considerable opposition remained to the suffragists (critics often called them "suffragettes," a condescending and disparaging term). It came particularly from liquor interests that dreaded a female crusade to prohibit alcoholic beverages, urban political bosses fearing female anticorruption campaigns, businesses opposed to women's proposals for minimum wage laws and other economic reforms, and southern whites who feared the enfranchisement of African Americans. In addition, antisuffragists included many men and even some women who saw votes for women as a radical challenge to ideals and institutions built on the conception that woman's proper place was in the home, not the public arena, and that her primary role was the apolitical one of homemaker and mother.

Suffragists found encouragement in a more favorable political climate in the 1910s of widespread progressive reforms and of increasing numbers of states that had already enfranchised women. They rejuvenated the movement for a suffrage amendment to the U.S. Constitution.

A militant New Jersey Quaker and social worker, Alice Paul, had witnessed the transformation of the suffrage movement in England where, beginning in 1903, women held mass demonstrations, chained themselves to lampposts, physically attacked politicians, and went on hunger strikes when imprisoned. In 1913, Alice Paul led a counterdemonstration, a suffrage parade, at Woodrow Wilson's inauguration as president. She subsequently established the Congressional Union, which became the National Woman's Party in 1916, as the militant arm of the suffrage movement. In 1917 she began the first major picketing of the White House. When the women pickets were imprisoned, they went on a hunger strike to continue their protest.

The more conservative National American Woman's Suffrage Association (NAWSA) worked in less confrontational ways for a federal amendment. Carrie Chapman Catt, a longtime suffragist leader, became president of the revitalized organization in 1915. NAWSA grew to more than 2 million members, and Catt initiated its "winning plan," which coordinated local, state, and national efforts to achieve adoption of a national women's suffrage amendment within four years.

Success came to the largely middle-class women's effort in the wartime wave of democratization that also saw women enfranchised in Canada, Great Britain, and the Soviet Union. In 1917 suffragists won important victories in the first eastern industrial state, New York, and the first southern state, Arkansas. The need for women's support for the U.S. war effort against Germany in 1917 and 1918 contributed to President Wilson's endorsement of a federal suffrage amendment. The House of Representatives passed the amendment in 1918, the Senate in 1919. The Nineteenth Amendment was ratified, over dissent of the lower South, in time for the 1920 election. "Now at last, we can begin," Crystal Eastman, suffragist, labor lawyer, and feminist, declared; "what we must do is to create conditions of outward freedom in which a free woman's soul can be born and grow."

Equal access to all the rights and opportunities of modern life and the achievement of autonomy belonged to the other strand of the women's movement, one emphasizing individual self-expression and fulfillment. The tension between the path of individual liberty and equal opportunity for women, with its agenda of independence and self-respect through better jobs, and the path of female solidarity, with its emphasis on working together across class, ethnic, and racial lines to benefit women as a whole, became a major tension of twentieth-century feminism. Prominent in debates of the 1920s and 1970s over the proposed Equal Rights Amendment (ERA), this tension first emerged in the Progressive Era as women struggled to determine the political meaning of their experience and the appropriate goals of the governmental intervention they sought.

Feminism, a word and a concept that came into use in the United States in the 1910s, signaled a new phase in the debate and agitation about women's rights and freedoms that had been going on for hundreds of years. The militancy of the Congressional Union and National Woman's Party galvanized the political energies of radical young women who around 1912 had begun to call themselves "feminists." Among those founding the Heterodoxy discussion group in Greenwhich Village that year, a group that required that a member "not be orthodox in her opinions," were Crystal Eastman, journalists Mary Heaton Vorse and Rheta Childe Dorr, theorist Charlotte Perkins Gilman, and Elizabeth Gurley Flynn, an organizer for the radical labor organization, the Industrial Workers of the World (IWW). Feminists challenged previous generations' emphasis on female difference. As Dorr recalled in her 1924 memoir: "I wanted all the freedom, all the opportunity, all the equality there was in the world. I wanted to belong to the human race, not a ladies' aid society, to the human race."

The sudden appearance of feminism crystallized the cultural revolt of radical female intellectuals. Charlotte Perkins Gilman, a socialist and feminist who had written the classic work *Women and Economics* in 1898, wrote *Man-made World* in 1911 and lectured and edited her own monthly magazine, *The Forerunner,* from 1909 to 1916. A prolific writer, Gilman developed one of the first systematic analyses of the feminist position in the United States. In *The Home* in 1903 she called for communal and professionally staffed kitchens, cleaning services, and nurseries, which could give women the freedom to earn a living on an equal basis with men. A few radical feminists, such as Emma Goldman, a leading political anarchist who opposed all forms of governmental intervention and control, rejected marriage as an institution and advocated monogamous unions in which both partners preserved their freedom to have sexual relations with whomever they chose. Indeed, the centrality of sensual pleasures for women as well as men, as Goldman and many of the other "sex radicals" of the time proclaimed, was supported by the new "scientific" findings of European sexologists such as Havelock Ellis, English author of a multivolume work completed in 1910, *Studies in the Psychology of Sex.*

Modernism and Institutions: Schools, Hospitals, Places of Worship

Progressive Education

Schools, like homes, could be instruments of both conservation and change. The transformation of education in the Progressive Era put the school in the forefront of change, but it met with much resentment from traditionalists. Educators responded to new conditions by deemphasizing the classical tradition and reshaping the educational system to prepare increasing numbers of people for a continually changing urban, industrial society. To provide mass education, the number of public high schools doubled and the number of students there quadrupled. The percentage of high school graduates among 17-year-olds tripled between 1900 and 1920, reaching 16 percent.

Progressive education revolutionized teaching. Its leading advocate, the Columbia University philosopher John Dewey, stressed the child's own experience and the need to "learn by doing" rather than by rote memorization. Despite much resistance, the schools developed broader and more flexible curricula, less formality in the classrooms, the classification of students by intelligence and achievement tests, and the addition of gymnasiums, laboratories, manual arts shops, and rooms for art and music. Progressive education aimed at relevant education that would awaken children to human values and capabilities and instill good moral habits that would serve both them and a changing society.

Colleges and universities expanded their campuses and doubled their enrollment to 600,000 students. The universities, which had begun to emerge in the late nineteenth century, graduated thousands of technicians, managers, and professionals. Educators sought to inculcate the traditions and values of a liberal democratic culture. Many university presidents and professors saw the institution's role as including useful social research to help meet the challenges of change. But the alumni and the public seemed more concerned with the football and fraternity craze that swept the campuses.

Physical and Mental Health Care

The reexamination of established institutions that occurred during the Progressive Era led to major changes in the health care system, reflecting changes in medical knowledge and cultural values. Increased emphasis in American society on expertise and professionalization, coupled with many male physicians' desires to legitimate and control their profession and expand their practices contributed, not only to the positive restriction of untrained "quacks," but to the unwarranted curtailment of long-established female midwives as child deliverers and healers. Sexism and racism led many white male doctors to limit the number of and opportunities for women and black male physicians by curbing the number admitted to medical schools and by excluding all women, as well as black men, from the increasingly influential white male medical societies. (Washington, D.C., had only about 200 women physicians, black and white, between 1870 and 1900.) Increasingly, women healers were constrained to be nurses, a job involving caring in a dominant culture that defined caring as a female role not requiring either much expertise or much monetary compensation.

Part of the increased prestige of physicians came from developments in medical knowledge and new techniques for diagnosis and treatment, all linked by the profession to concepts of scientific and technological progress, including the use of X-rays, improved anesthetics, and the ability to provide blood transfusions. But part came from specific actions that enhanced medical knowledge and the profession itself. John D. Rockefeller, for example, established the Rockefeller Institute for Medical Research in New York City in 1901; six years later serum was discovered there for treating spinal meningitis. Andrew Carnegie established the Carnegie Foundation for the Advancement of Teaching in 1910, and one of its first activities was the study and exposure of abuses in medical education. A report by the Flexner Commission recommended significant reforms, especially the need to link medical education with the new universities and hospitals.

The modern general hospital emerged in the Progressive Era. In the past, hospitals had been refuges for the urban poor, institutions of charity and paternalism, stigmatized as houses of infection and contagion, or places where the poor went to die. When they became sick, most people fought back with home remedies, regimens of diet, sleep, and exercise, or—if they could afford it—travel to healthier climates. The middle and upper classes had received medical treatment—diagnosis, drugs, bone-setting, even surgery—in their own homes or the home of their physician, surgeon-apothecary, or healer. However, the use of antisepsis, the availability of costly new medical equipment and therapies, and a wide variety of medical specialists (among both doctors and nurses) allowed the hospital to take on its modern form as a center of medical science and expertise. In the fifty years between 1875 and 1925, hospitals proliferated in the United States and their numbers increased from 150 to 7,000.

Social and economic changes also helped to transform the hospital. Under the financial pressures of the depression of the 1890s, the old free-treatment philanthropic institutions gave way to business-oriented establishments that began to charge for health care. To encourage paying customers to use their facilities, they offered, for the first time, different classes of service within the hospital. The hospitals came to mirror the larger social and cultural realities of the world outside their walls, and these realities in turn influenced the medical care offered within the healing institutions. Although by the end of the Progressive Era the hospital had emerged as a center for advanced medical practice and a primary instrument in health care for all classes, that care was widely divergent according to class, race, and region, with the most inadequate health care in the region of the greatest rural poverty — the South.

Despite the development of patient payment as the basis for hospital care, the United States differed from most other industrial nations by not adopting a program of national health insurance to spread the increasing costs of medical care. Nevertheless by 1920 the hospital had moved from a peripheral role to a new position as an important and accepted part of the community.

Mental hospitals, whether to serve acute, short-term mental illness or to provide long-term care for the chronically ill, had been constructed in virtually every state during the nineteenth century as an institutional response to mental illness. At the turn of the century, however, a new mental health movement was inaugurated to improve the treatment of the mentally ill and to improve mental health. The nationwide movement began with the publication of a best-selling book, *A Mind That Found Itself* by Clifford W. Beers, a business executive who had suffered a nervous breakdown, attempted suicide, and was confined in a Connecticut mental hospital for three years before recovering. In 1909 the National Committee for Mental Hygiene was founded by Beers in conjunction with Adolf Meyer, a pioneering psychiatrist who was instrumental in discovering that serious mental disorders might yield to chemical and other treatments. American psychiatrists at the turn of the century had been trained mainly in clinical work in state mental hospitals; they ascribed mental illness to physical causes, such as lesions or other wounds on the brain. Initially, the mental hygiene movement deemphasized institutional reform in favor of a more sweeping vision of mental health that linked it to other movements against the spread of alcoholism and venereal disease. Beers and Meyer eventually quarreled over the issue of whether doctors or laypersons would control the association. After 1920 the emerging profession of psychiatry won, renaming the campaign the mental health movement and focusing less on institutional care than on scientific treatment modeled on general medicine.

By then the use of psychoanalysis had expanded considerably, encouraged in large part by the consulting work of psychiatrists to the wartime army and by the theories of European psychiatrists such as Sigmund Freud and Carl Jung, who had first gained wide recognition in the United States after giving guest lectures at Clark University in Massachusetts in 1909. Freud in particular had revolutionized psychiatry by providing it with a dynamic theory of personality and an effective means of treatment, called psychoanalysis. Freud's theories were designed to cope with the unconscious and overcome harmful repressions, whether neurotic or psychotic. Beginning in the 1920s, however, the oversimplification of Freud's complex ideas as they were transmitted to the general public would lead, inaccurately, to the impression that Freud asserted that sexuality was the key to a healthy and happy life.

Modernism, Traditionalism, and Organized Religion

Assurance provided by religious identity was important in this disorienting epoch of rapid change, and millions of Americans sought spiritual nourishment and social companionship at revival meetings and more traditional religious services in churches, synagogues, and other places of worship. Yet at the same time, organized religion was beset by the secular tendencies of modern life and the challenges that a strong new emphasis on science and rational thought posed to nonrationalistic systems of belief.

The tension between accommodation to change and reassertion of old religious traditions triggered debate during the Progressive Era that would intensify in the 1920s. The struggle is most familiarly identified as between "modernism" and what came to be called "fundamentalism," and it involved not simply specific issues of theology but also broader attitudes toward the modern world at large.

"Modernist" thinkers emerged in most of the major faiths in America. They emphasized liberal theological views, including social activism on behalf of the poor and the downtrodden, a greater toleration of other faiths, and a belief that human society was making progress on earth and moving toward the realization of the Kingdom of God. Influenced by the era's belief in rationality as well as the development of critical new methods of historical and textual analysis and a number of archaeological discoveries particularly in the Holy Land, modernists deemphasized literal reading of the Bible, particularly its reports of miracles. Instead, they favored a broader interpretation that emphasized the Bible's general moral and ethical teachings, and they accommodated some of its specific injunctions to prevailing secular humanist trends in modern society. Modernists were also persuaded by findings and theories in geology, paleontology (the study of fossil animals and plants), and biology, especially the Darwinian theory of human evolution. However, they refused to believe that these disciplines denied the divine origin of humankind, and instead modernist theologians tried to reconcile them with Scripture, largely through more metaphorical interpretation. Lyman Abbott, an influential Protestant minister and editor in Brooklyn, wrote in 1915 that evolutionary doctrine supported the view that "man is gradually emerging from an animal nature into a spiritual manhood." The Genesis account of creation was not the issue, Abbott asserted:

> For the question whether God made the animal man by a mechanical process in an hour or by a process of growth continuing through centuries is quite immaterial to one who believes that into man God breathes a divine life.

There were approximately 27 million Protestants in the United States in 1900. In most Protestant denominations, at least their northern branches (many Protestant churches had been split by region and by race since the period before the Civil War), modernists obtained major influence, although often at a cost of major dissension. Among the denominations in which modernism made significant inroads were the northern Congregationalists, the Episcopalians, the Unitarians, the Quakers, and, after deep controversy, the Methodists, Presbyterians, northern Baptists, and Disciples of Christ. Lutherans, still living primarily in ethnic German or Scandinavian enclaves, escaped the harshest aspect of the controversy until much later in the century.

In 1908, as part of the movement for social concerns, which was part of modernism, representatives from some thirty separate Protestant groups with a total of 12 million members founded the Federal Council (later the National Council) of Churches of Christ in America as the leading voice for amelioration of social and economic problems within a Christian context. The first major interdenominational organization, it became the main agency of the social gospel movement.

In opposition to modernism and such liberal, activist theology, traditionalists mustered significant support. Conservative theologians, opposing many of the secularizing trends of modern society as well as attacks on the absolute validity of the Bible (a key belief in Protestantism since the Reformation), sought to reinforce biblical and church authority. They opposed any departure from belief in the literal truth of Scripture, which was considered the bedrock of moral values and beliefs. *Fundamentalism* was the name given to the movement within American Protestantism that arose in the late nineteenth and early twentieth centuries in reaction against liberal religious beliefs and social gospel activism and indeed against many of the secular trends in urban America.

Fundamentalism stressed the infallibility of the Bible as a historical record and in all matters of faith and doctrine; it was particularly hostile to the theory of evolution. "Atheistic and absurd" is how T. De Witt Talmage, a popular Brooklyn preacher, described Darwinian theory. He claimed that the argument that humans came from beasts only made humans more bestial and that those evolutionists who argued against immortality jeopardized all foundation for morality and purpose in life. Similar denunciations were made by William Jennings Bryan of Nebraska, three-time Democratic presidential nominee and a leading champion of rural America and fundamentalism.

Perhaps the most important milestones in the early development of the fundamentalist movement were the publication of a series of booklets, *The Fundamentals: A Testimony to the Truth*, between 1910 and 1915 and the establishment in 1919 of the World's Christian Fundamentals Association by a group of anti-Darwinist ministers, led by J. Frank Norris, a southern Baptist minister from Fort Worth, Texas. One of the few early leaders of the fundamentalist movement from the South, Norris generated a stream of sensational attacks on liberalism, especially within his own denomination. The controversial founder of southern fundamentalism directly inspired a generation of young southern Baptist preachers, including ultimately Jerry Falwell, one of the leading post–World War II southern fundamentalists.

Although many fundamentalists sought to rebuild traditionalism and the authority of the churches, many revivalist preachers emphasized a different and individually focused fundamentalism known as *evangelicalism*, which stressed the importance of personal experience of guilt for sin and of reconciliation to God through Christ. In major revivalist (religious awakening) meetings in urban as well as rural areas, popular evangelists spread a message of religious zeal and the individual's ability to achieve salvation. Most of them also attacked modernism and religious leaders who tried to maintain a dialogue between theologians and scientists. One of the most popular evangelists of the early twentieth century, William A. ("Billy") Sunday, a colorful ex–baseball player turned preacher, declared that no reconciliation between science and religion was ever possible on biblical issues.

Although the struggles between modernists and fundamentalists took place primarily in the North, they influenced southern churches that also had fundamentalist-modernist controversies. The South's traditional religious life has been distinctive in ways that reflect the region's general distinctiveness. It is the only region where evangelical Protestantism is dominant, and that dominance has helped to give the South the reputation of being the country's most "religious region," where "old-time religion" is treated as an area of vital concern to individuals and the community. The preoccupation is with traditional morality, informal worship, the Bible as authority, and direct access to the Holy Spirit, with emphasis on baptism, communion, and spiritual rebirth.

The South was also home to 90 percent of African Americans in the early twentieth century, and religious life for the majority of them had originated in both the Anglo-Protestant evangelicalism that dominated the region and traditional African religions. In the nineteenth century, evangelicalism had been linked by abolitionist preachers with emancipation (slaves had actively participated and had connected their own history with the biblical story of the Exodus and the flight to freedom from bondage). The emotional behavior of southern revivalists had encouraged a kind of religious ecstasy similar to that of the danced religions of Africa.

In the early twentieth century, with the effective disfranchisement of black southerners, the church became the sole forum for black politics in the South, as well as the economic, social, and educational center of African-American communities across the nation. Black church membership was nearly 3 million out of a population of 8 million blacks at the turn of the century, the most numerous being the black Baptists and black Methodists; neither church was much affected by modernist theology.

In the great migration of southern blacks to the North in the twentieth century, ministers often traveled with the migrants and transplanted congregations from the South to northern storefront or house churches. The northern cities also offered a variety of new religious options for blacks. Two denominations, Holiness and Pentecostal churches (Pentecostalism is a religious movement among whites and blacks that spread out of the Southwest and focused on direct experiencing of the Holy Spirit and imminence of the second advent of Christ), emphasized experiential and ecstatic dimensions of worship. They also encouraged the development of gospel music by allowing the use of instruments and secular tunes in church services. Although criticized by some as accommodationist, the black church remained the most important and most effective public institution in the lives of most southern blacks and many northern blacks as well.

Churches and synagogues were also centers of religious and ethnic community life for Roman Catholic and Jewish minorities in America (there were 8 million Roman Catholics and 1 million Jews in the United States in 1890; 12 million and 1.5 million respectively in 1900). In both of these religions, divisions existed along ethnic grounds based on country of origin and time of immigration. There were also splits over issues of religious accommodation to modernism and to the dominant Anglo-Protestant American culture. Modernism existed in both religions but failed to become dominant as it had in the major denominations of northern Protestantism.

Within the Roman Catholic church, the new critical biblical analysis was denounced as "inept," and in 1907, Pope Pius X specifically condemned modernism for substituting subjective criteria for the authority of the church in matters of faith and morals. Officially branded as a heresy, modernism was ordered banished from Catholic seminaries, churches, and schools (by 1900, the Catholic church in America had become officially committed to a policy of separate educational facilities from the public schools, which Catholics and others saw as Protestant Christian, but that most Protestants saw as nonsectarian). The effect of the 1907 papal encyclical against modernism was to shift pressures for doctrinal unity within American Catholicism heavily in favor of theological and political conservatives such as James Cardinal Gibbons of Baltimore, as opposed to more liberal prelates such as Bishop John Ireland of Saint Paul, Minnesota. Gibbons, who had been named the second Roman Catholic cardinal in the United States in 1885, was the unofficial but acknowledged leader of the American Catholic hierarchy until his death in 1921.

Within Judaism, there were likewise concerns about the Bible (specifically the Torah, or Five Books of Moses), about attitudes toward history and tradition, modern civilization and the notion of progress, science, and the uneasy relationship between sacred and secular in the modern age. The Jewish community was sharply split on various grounds. The Jews who had arrived in America in the first part of the nineteenth century, mostly from Germany,* had brought with them the notion of reform (including vernacular worship, sermons, and hymns). They largely accommodated to the New World culture and emerging secular humanism and had established Reform Judaism. In what in other contexts would be called modernism, Reform Judaism adopted a platform in 1885 that rejected many old customs and beliefs that seemed outmoded in contemporary society. Four years later, Rabbi Isaac Mayer Wise of Cincinnati, Ohio, one of the leaders of Reform Judaism, established the Central Conference of American Rabbis. However, the majority of the hundreds of thousands of Jewish immigrants who arrived from eastern Europe in the late nineteenth and early twentieth centuries, maintained—at least to some degree—the rituals, customs, and beliefs of Orthodox Judaism.

In opposition to the accommodations by Reform Judaism, a number of Philadelphia rabbis headed a conservative movement in the mid-nineteenth century that led to the creation of Conservative Judaism

---

*The few thousand Jews who had arrived in the American colonies during the colonial period (the first group arrived in New Amsterdam in 1654) were mainly of Spanish, Portuguese, and Dutch origin.

and the founding of the Jewish Theological Seminary (JTS) in New York City in 1886. Attempting to reconcile tradition with change and Jewish history with prevailing American society, Conservative Judaism drew lines against what seemed too ready abandonment of biblical injunctions and rabbinate traditions. As a cultural compromise between Reform and Orthodox Judaism, it gained much strength in the Progressive Era. As Solomon Schecter, president of JTS, asserted in 1901:

> Our great claim to the gratitude of mankind is that we gave to the world the word of God, the Bible. We have stormed heaven to snatch down this heavenly gift . . . [and because this gift is so great, we have] allowed ourselves to be slain by the hundreds and thousands rather than become unfaithful to it.

In Protestantism, Judaism, and Roman Catholicism the tension between modernism and traditionalism remained a continuing source of controversy. (Among major religions in America in this period, only Christian Science,* Mormonism, Greek and Russian Orthodoxy, and Asian religions remained untouched by the controversy.) Most Americans probably stood somewhere in the middle. Nevertheless, the modernism-fundamentalism controversy intensified, becoming in the 1920s a significant national political issue involving legislation prohibiting a variety of actions, from the teaching of evolution to the sale of alcoholic beverages.

The Challenge of the City

The cities became the focus of the new America. In the second decade of the century, the United States passed a milestone similar to the closing of the frontier a generation earlier; it became a nation of cities. The 1920 census showed that for the first time a majority (51 percent) of the population lived in urban areas. These were years of growth for the cities. America developed more large urban areas than any other country. New York, Chicago, Pittsburgh, Detroit, and Cleveland doubled in size during this period. Smaller cities like Los Angeles, Seattle, Atlanta, and Birmingham were transformed. Boom towns skyrocketed with the opening of new oil fields in the Southwest; Dallas, Houston, Tulsa, and Oklahoma City were among them. "The city has become the central feature of modern civilization," the municipal reformer and

---

*The practice of Christian Science and the Church of Christian Scientists were founded by Mary Baker Eddy with the first church established in Boston in 1879. The religious association was reorganized in 1892, and its newspaper, the *Christian Science Monitor*, began publication in the first decade of the twentieth century.

social scientist Frederic C. Howe wrote in 1906. "Man has entered on an urban age."

The modern metropolis raised the specter of a new and dangerous America. Many people agreed with James Bryce when he said in 1912 that "a great city is a great evil." Many thought the metropolises, with their congestion, hectic pace, lack of adequate air and space, and crime, violence, and pollution, would destroy not only their residents but American civilization as well. "This life of great cities," Henry George warned in 1898, "is not the natural life of man. He must under such conditions deteriorate, physically, mentally, morally."

Despite such gloomy predictions, the Progressive Era was permeated with a spirit of hope and optimism that people working together could improve the environment and in turn create a better society. The problems of the cities, Frederic Howe argued, were not ethical or personal but economic, and they could be solved through planning and the assertion of public intervention and direction. As Howe wrote in 1912:

> The American city is inconvenient, dirty, lacking in charm and beauty because the individual land owner has been permitted to plan it, to build, to do as he willed with his land. There has been no community control, no sense of the public as opposed to private rights.

In the Progressive Era urban reformers began to challenge the nineteenth-century tradition of an unrestricted marketplace and unrestrained individualism.

Some attempts at planning the urban environment were initiated in the private sector. The 1893 World's Fair in Chicago presented the artificial but stunning "great white city" as a demonstration of the results of an entirely planned environment. It launched the City Beautiful movement, which resulted in the development in several cities of master plans, civic centers, tree-lined boulevards, public fountains and parks, underground electrical and telephone lines, and increased use of ornamentation. Influenced in part by the development in England of the garden city, a planned community, several companies created carefully laid out housing projects, the most famous being Forest Hills Gardens in New York City. A middle-class community of Tudor-style homes, spacious lawns, and a shopping center, this model of large-scale comprehensive planning was sponsored by the Russell Sage Foundation.

More influential in the Progressive Era was the expansion of governmental influence on urban growth. The response of the first generation of urban planners to the increasing problem of congestion was deconcentration through garden cities and zoning. Business people concerned with protecting their investment, especially in the downtown area, joined with reformers such as Lillian Wald, Florence Kelley, and Lawrence Veiller to argue the need for governmental intervention for humanitarian reasons. Together, they obtained the first major zoning law in American history. The New York City law of 1916 exerted public control over the use, height, and area of urban land and construction. With deference to existing private investments, the zoning law aroused interest throughout the nation, and more than 1,000 American cities adopted similar ordinances within the next decade. Like much of the legislation of the Progressive Era, zoning was primarily negative in its effects. It did not give government the power to encourage or provide adequate housing, nor did it provide a workable basis for coordinating housing and planning. But New York's zoning act did mark a major transition toward governmental intervention in the marketplace and the recognition that cities would continue to be a major aspect of America.

A New Mass Consumption Culture

The growth of cities — and the new mass market, consumer-oriented economy — also contributed to a transformation of American culture. Americans in the Progressive Era witnessed the rise of a new national mass culture midway between local or regional folk cultures and the more cosmopolitan culture of the national elites. The new, more standardized and mass consumption-oriented culture was based on the concentrated mass markets of the cities and on technological developments that provided new forms of mass communication and entertainment, including national advertising. Mass circulation newspapers and magazines and motion pictures helped break down localism and encourage a more national, cosmopolitan, and consumer-oriented outlook. Like other forces of industrialism, they served as instruments for weaving a previously scattered people into a more integrated national society. But they also challenged old values and ideals and led some groups to oppose them and other groups to try to ensure that mass entertainment served the public welfare.

The modern consumer culture began to emerge in America in the Progressive Era, which envisioned a society that, as T. J. Jackson Lears, a leading historian of the phenomenon, has written, would be "a world of goods produced in profusion, packaged and marketed by advertisers with subtle skills, avidly acquired on the installment plan by middle- and working-class Americans." Consumption became a cultural ideal in part because it was marketed by powerful individuals and institutions and accepted by millions of ordinary Americans.

Instrumental in this cultural transformation was the emergence of the new stratum of professionals and managers in a plethora of new, largely hierarchical organizations—corporations, government agencies, universities, professional associations, and the like—and the rise of a new gospel of physical and psychological "therapeutic release" preached by a host of writers, publishers, modernist ministers, social scientists, physicians, and advertisers. For masses of employees in the corporate economy who could no longer aspire to become their own bosses, consumption of new goods and services, it was argued, provided the promise of health and contentment.

The new cultural ideal also appealed to many of the old-line white, Anglo-Saxon Protestant upper and middle classes in the cities and suburbs of the industrializing North who had become increasingly alienated from what many of them saw as an "overcivilized" society of office workers and suburban dwellers. They felt cut off from experiencing "real life" by their own sense of physical atrophy and spiritual decay. Some embraced the "strenuous life" espoused by Theodore Roosevelt of rugged sports, hunting, and the martial arts to "reinvigorate" "manliness" in a postfrontier society. But more looked for a different sense of purpose in the face of the disintegration and decline, under the blows of Darwinism and the deflation of what many saw as an increasingly vapid, secularized Protestantism, of old religious sanctions for a moral life of sacrifice and toil.

Within the dominant culture an important shift occurred particularly as many upper- and middle-class northern Protestants seeking "real" firsthand experience and psychic and physical health turned from a morality that emphasized salvation in the next world to a hedonistic ethic that stressed immediate gratification and therapeutic self-fulfillment in this one. The values of perpetual work, compulsive saving, and self-denial were, it was widely believed, more suited to a production-oriented society of small entrepreneurs; the new culture epitomized a consumption-oriented society dominated by bureaucratic corporations.

It was the turn-of-the-century link between this ethic of individual hedonism and the Progressive Era idealization of efficient planning and administrative organization (of effective intervention and manipulation of attitudes and behavior) that marks the point of departure for modern American consumer culture because, as Jackson Lears has effectively contended, "the consumer culture is not only the value-system that underlies a society saturated by mass-produced and mass-marketed goods, but also a new set of sanctions for the elite control of that society." In addition to being a "leisure ethic" and an "American standard of living," the consumer culture was also the result of a new power structure and a new set of values. Earlier, people were urged to internalize ethical precepts of frugality and self-sacrifice. Twentieth-century corporate elites offered instead promises of the good life and personal physical and psychological fulfillment. These, it was asserted, would come through consumption of goods and services, shaped to an increasing degree by definitions of personality and images of the good life defined by advertisers and the mass media.

Between 1890 and 1920 the modern mass media and advertising grew into national institutions. The comparatively staid and simple newspapers of the nineteenth century vanished in the face of sensational new mass circulation dailies that provided not only information but also entertainment and advertising. New high-speed rotary presses, linotype machines, and the photoengraving process enabled publishers to create exciting mass appeal newspapers and national magazines. Some papers, such as Adolph S. Ochs's *New York Times*, won praise as generally reliable sources of news. But others, such as William Randolph Hearst's *New York Journal* and Joseph Pulitzer's *New York World*, deteriorated into "yellow journalism," excessive sensationalism and even fabrication to cultivate and satisfy the public taste for excitement and controversy. Within the expanding field of magazine publishing, a group of entrepreneurial editor-publishers, such as S. S. McClure, produced lively, colorful, even sensationalist new mass circulation magazines such as *Collier's, Cosmopolitan, Everybody's, The Ladies' Home Journal, McClure's, Munsey's,* and the *Saturday Evening Post.* The value of the press in raising public issues and exposing corruption was hailed, but many people condemned the more incendiary journals for inflaming public opinion and unsettling foreign affairs. Most important, critics blamed the press for contributing to American intervention in the Spanish-American War and exacerbating tense relations between the United States and Japan into a war scare in 1907.

Newspapers and magazines were private enterprises with public functions — informing the citizenry. But the free marketplace of ideas was eroded when publishers sought to limit the operation of the economic market by expanding their holdings and reducing competition. By the end of the Progressive Era a half dozen publishing chains, including those dominated by Hearst, Edward W. Scripps, and Frank A. Munsey, controlled more than eighty daily newspapers with a circulation of nearly 10 million, as well as numerous magazines. Like industry, the press had intervened in the marketplace and become big business.

Advertising was, of course, the main source of revenue for the expanding newspaper and magazine industry; it also became a major influence in the consumer culture. At the turn of the century, with the creation of a national, urban market and the increasing production of consumer goods, advertisers began to envision a buying public that was increasingly remote and hurried. To alert and arouse readers, advertising firms turned to the use of illustrations, brand names, trademarks, and slogans — more sensational tactics and visual as well as print techniques — to attract readers' attention. In the early 1900s the most successful advertising agents were also trying aggressively to shape consumers' desires, shifting from low-key statements to "salesmanship in print." Using psychological consultants as well as intuition, such firms moved advertising away from sober information about a product toward its alleged effects—not simply the direct results of use of a particular toothpaste, beverage, or patent medicine, but the way the client's product would transform the buyer's life. Advertising came to offer therapeutic promises of a richer, fuller existence.

America was at the turn of a century—a country whose new culture seemed to offer enormous possibilities for the future, enough to change some older patterns of behavior. The culture of consumption, despite much of its superficial and manipulative character, did imply a new freedom from self-denial and from repression. Despite the fact that it failed to live up to its fantastic promises, this consumer capitalism, as historian William Leach has suggested, attracted many people, especially the women who were the main targets of consumer advertising. Indeed, women as a group were pictured as the main purchasers of the variety of new consumer commodities for home and family.

The emporia of the new consumer goods were luxurious department stores that began to appear in the 1870s. They far outdistanced the drab dry goods houses of an earlier era by their size (up to a block long and several stories high) and by their dazzling displays. The widespread use of glass in the displays—curved or straight glass doors and shelves, counters, containers, and showcases—as well as artificial and natural lighting and color coordination of furnishings worked to lure consumers. All of this helped to create the magnificent emporia such as Bloomingdale's and R. H. Macy's department stores in New York, John Wanamaker's in Philadelphia, Marshall Field's in Chicago, and Gimbel Brothers in Milwaukee. These palaces of consumerism seemed to offer not only goods, but excitement and dreams. "[We] Got to Macy's Emporium," Sophie C. Hall, the wife of an Episcopalian minister in New York noted in her diary in 1879. "I saw so many beautiful things that we found it a trying matter to get out."

With the advent of relatively cheap plate glass in the mid-1890s, the "show window" became a central part of the department stores. By the 1910s the largest retailers were decorating windows much like miniature stage sets. Inside, the stores shimmered with exotic settings, such as Japanese gardens, and special programs ranging from a "carnival of nations" to a Paris fashion show. Everything was designed to create a new world of fantasy and the possibility of personal transformation—to encourage shoppers to buy the new goods and services. This was further enhanced by new liberal credit policies. By 1902, nearly every New York department store had adopted a liberal policy of charge accounts to encourage impulse buying.

The department stores were overwhelmingly oriented toward middle- and upper-income women. For many such women, shopping became a regular ritual. Indeed, by 1915, women were responsible for more than 80 percent of the consumer purchasing in the United States. William Leach's comparison of diaries of urban women in the 1840s with those of the 1900s indicates how the culture and institutions of consumption helped make the lives of many women more secular and public. They also contributed powerfully to drawing women into a new individualism and an equality with the male experience. But the female experience, this culture suggested, would be founded on consumption of commodities and services — an emphasis on desire and fulfillment, rather than production of goods or the ownership of property.

Yet, the new consumer culture also offered women new opportunities for employment. Beginning in the 1890s, many women worked as editors, writers, artists, and designers in the advertising and fashion industries. Although men owned and headed most of the department stores, women worked at nearly every other level, from sales clerk to buyer, the latter a prestigious position that included managing the budget for a particular department, traveling around the country and the world in search of new goods and styles, and a position that offered excellent salaries. Women also owned and directed a number of companies in the new and growing cosmetics industry.

Organized Leisure

Part of the new consumer culture was the consumption of leisure time activities, in part a result of the reduction of the workweek, a loosening of the work ethic in response to feelings of "overpressure," and a growing acceptance among the middle and working classes of what the philosopher William James called the "gospel of recreation." In preindustrial societies, leisure enjoyment for the masses had been provided through religious holidays and festivals. But in an increasingly industrial society with small but increasing amounts of leisure time (the average workweek in industry dropped from 66 hours in 1850 to 56 hours in 1900 and 41 hours by 1920), new forms of organized entertainment were developed for the urban masses.

Although some of these forms of entertainment arose spontaneously (community picnics and block parties, for example), many were conscientiously planned. Municipal governments, pressed by citizens' groups, built parks, playgrounds, and zoos and joined private groups in developing libraries and museums. Entrepreneurs such as P. T. Barnum had demonstrated the popularity of circuses. Also, in the late nineteenth century the availability of rail transportation permitted the development of seashore resorts such as Atlantic City and amusement parks such as Coney Island for urban dwellers.

Most dramatic, however, was the rise of urban spectator sports in the late nineteenth and early twentieth centuries. Professional baseball grew rapidly with urbanization after the 1860s and by the 1890s had become a major American institution as well as a lucrative industry. The most profitable teams, which drew crowds of more than 10,000, were from industrial cities with large working-class populations that provided the greatest numbers of spectators and players. Competition among cities drew enormous interest, with results telegraphed inning by inning and posted in saloons and other public establishments; upsets were reported in extra newspaper editions. By the Progressive Era two major leagues had been formed, the National League and the Western League, reorganized as the American League, and a World Series between them began in 1903 (first won by the Boston Red Sox).

Intercollegiate football began haltingly in 1869 in New Brunswick, New Jersey, with a game between Rutgers and Princeton (and a Rutgers victory). Four years later, Yale and Columbia joined them and established a series of regular intercollegiate matches. Coaching became professionalized by the 1890s, and from the beginning of the twentieth century, despite continual protests against its roughness, which took a death toll among players, football enjoyed tremendous popularity as a collegiate sport. The selection of an all-American team began in 1889, and in 1902 the first postseason Rose Bowl game was held (Michigan beating Stanford 49–0). Although professional football began in 1895, it did not begin to challenge the widely popular intercollegiate football until the 1920s. "Baseball and football matches," an English visitor observed in 1905, "excite an interest greater than any other public events except the Presidential election."

A Sac Indian from Oklahoma, James ("Jim") Thorpe (his Indian name was Bright Path), one of the greatest male athletes in the recorded history of American sports, rose to fame in this period. Like hundreds of other young Indian boys and girls whom the U.S. government sought to acculturate in the late nineteenth and early twentieth centuries, young Thorpe was sent to the government's Indian School at Carlisle, Pennsylvania. After four years, Thorpe, playing left halfback and coached by Glenn ("Pop") Warner, led Carlisle in 1911–1912 to startling upsets over such highly rated college teams as Harvard, Army, and the University of Pennsylvania. From football all-American, Thorpe went in 1912 to the newly revitalized Olympic Games held in Stockholm, Sweden, where he won a series of gold medals in the track and field events. Devastatingly, however, Thorpe was forced to return all his Olympic medals in 1913 when it was revealed that he had played semiprofessional baseball for a small team in a minor North Carolina league in 1909 and 1910, which technically disqualified him as an amateur athlete.

Boxing and horse racing drew substantial crowds. Races such as Louisville's Kentucky Derby, which began in 1913, were major social events, particularly for the wealthy; conversely, professional boxing drew audiences and fighters mainly from the working classes. John L. Sullivan, the son of Irish immigrants, was the last hard-slugging, bare-knuckles heavyweight champion. Bare-knuckles prize fights ended in 1889, but even with padded gloves, subsequent matches often proved bloody and grueling. "Gentleman Jim" Corbett, later credited with being the first "scientific" boxer, defeated Sullivan in 1892 with speed and a calculated style and held the title for nearly half a dozen years. The most controversial champion in the Progressive Era was Arthur John ("Jack") Johnson, an African American and former stevedore from Galveston, Texas, who in 1908 became the first black heavyweight champion. A masterful boxer with a strong punch, Johnson did not hesitate to proclaim his own abilities and insisted on treatment as a racial equal. In a period of increased segregation and discrimination, the white sporting press screamed for a "white hope" to take back the title from the black champion. In 1910, Johnson knocked out ex-champion James J. ("Jim") Jeffries, but angry whites attacked African Americans in a number of towns and cities. Johnson continued his victories in the ring, but the U.S. Justice Department obtained his conviction in 1913 for violating the Mann Act by taking a white lover across a state line. Johnson fled the country but agreed in 1915 to a match in Havana with the young giant Jess Willard. In the twenty-sixth round, Willard knocked out the 37-year-old, out-of-shape champion to the applause of most of the white press. In 1920, Johnson returned home to serve a year in federal prison. By then Willard had been knocked out of the championship in 1919 by Jack Dempsey.

Popular music also became a major entertainment industry. Mass production made pianos available to thousands of middle-class families. Beginning in the 1890s, New York's "Tin Pan Alley" publishing houses began turning out thousands of simple but catchy, sentimental songs to be sung around the piano. Some became all-time favorites: "Take Me Out to the Ball Game," "Daisy," "The Sidewalks of New York." By 1900, however, a powerful new challenger, the phonograph, had almost ruined the piano and sheet music business. Originally developed as a business recording machine, the phonograph was marketed in the Progressive Era for home entertainment. Millions bought the new phonograph records and danced to new, more suggestive lyrics such as the 1906 hit "You Can Go as Far as You Like with Me in My Merry Oldsmobile."

At the same time, black musicians were making their first real breakthrough into the realm of American popular culture. Beginning in the 1870s, the American high arts establishment "discovered" one aspect of southern black music, religious spirituals such as "Go Down, Moses," and "Swing Low, Sweet Chariot," and white entrepreneurs sent African-American choirs on the concert circuit in the cities of the North and of Europe. At the turn of the century another form of black music, ragtime, began to enter white commercial culture. Black musicians had long played on work gangs, in public settings, and at religious gatherings; now they moved into honky-tonks, juke joints, saloons, brothels, and minstrel shows, playing to black audiences in African-American churches and entertainment spots and to white or mixed audiences in the brothels of New Orleans and the clubs of Saint Louis. Black "barrelhouse" pianists, such as Ferdinand ("Jelly Roll") Morton, made the first big musical impact on American music, with their ragtime style created out of various folk music forms. Scott Joplin's "Maple Leaf Rag" became a national hit, and by 1900 ragtime was all the rage. White songwriters and musicians, such as Irving Berlin in "Alexander's Ragtime Band," appropriated the name, although not always the true style of ragtime. By the beginning of the 1920s, black musical styles, such as jazz and blues music (most popularly W. C. Handy's "Saint Louis Blues") were widely known and played by white as well as black musicians, and their commercialization in that decade made them a major influence on American culture.

Southern white folk music—"hillbilly" or "mountain music," as it was called at the time—had a long tradition in the rural regions of the South, at barn dances and camp meetings, but the balladry and folk songs of the Appalachian region and the cowboy ballads of the plains only began to be collected by folklorists at the turn of the century as the old culture began to disappear. The string bands, fiddlers, family gospel groups, and yodelers that made up the sounds of the hillbilly music would be put on southern radio stations as radio became a commercial reality in the 1920s, but it did not become a national phenomenon until after World War II, eventually as "bluegrass" and "country and western music," with Nashville as its commercial capital.

One of the major cultural influences of the Progressive Era was vaudeville, which had begun in the late nineteenth century as urban theatrical entertainment for working-class audiences. Rather boisterous live performances, shows consisted of two dozen individual acts, including singers, dancers, jugglers, comics, and skits. Reflecting and influencing urban and ethnic vitality and tastes, vaudeville reached its peak performance in the United States between 1890 and the mid-1920s. In that period, producers reached out to middle-class family audiences by cleaning up bawdier aspects of the shows (although some vaudeville houses continued the use of risqué humor and relatively scantily clad dancers such as those in impresario Florenz Ziegfeld's "Ziegfeld Follies"). With 20 percent of city residents going to at least one show a week, vaudeville was the main form of urban mass entertainment in the early twentieth century, surpassed by motion pictures only in the late 1920s with the advent of talking pictures. In their heyday, the acts and skits of vaudeville, with many of its talented stars coming from the ethnic working classes, helped to popularize new fashions in clothing, hairstyle, and makeup, as well as new styles of music, song, humor, and behavior, from the retention of many ethnic values to the acculturation of modern urban American life.

The first important challenge to vaudeville came from the "wireless"—radio. Lee De Forest developed the vacuum tube and the oscillating amplifier in Jersey City, New Jersey, in the first decade of the century. With a growing number of experimenters, ship operators, and amateurs building and using the new wireless transmitting sets and sending messages into the atmosphere to be received at will by others with receiving sets, the U.S. government intervened to maintain order and to allocate access to the limited range of frequencies on the radio spectrum, which was declared to be a public resource, although the radio broadcasters would be private commercial corporations rather than public or quasi-public broadcasting agencies as in most of Europe. The Radio Act of 1912 required operator's and radio station licenses to be awarded by the secretary of commerce, who had had power to assign time limits and wavelengths on the radio frequency spectrum.

First employed primarily by the navy for communications with ships at sea, the wireless was increasingly used by commercial stations that broadcast advertisements, musical performances, phonograph recordings, news bulletins, and, beginning in 1916, presidential election returns. The first major consolidation came in 1919, when Owen D. Young, general counsel for the General Electric Company, put together the Radio Corporation of America (RCA) from among GE and several other radio manufacturers and stations under the general direction of David Sarnoff, a talented young immigrant who headed the company from 1921 to 1971. Continuous regularly scheduled broadcasting began in 1920, and the number of both broadcasting stations and radio receivers in America skyrocketed during the 1920s, when the medium became a major part of the consumer culture.

Flickering Images on the Silent Screen

The greatest impact on entertainment and mass culture was that of the movies, the first of the modern mass entertainment media. Emerging in the 1890s, motion pictures established their dominance within two decades. They had come to America through Thomas Alva Edison's kinetoscope, a peephole viewing machine. The film used to produce the movies had been invented by George Eastman. Enterprising operators, including a number of immigrant fur workers and salesmen, used Edison's kinetoscope and later his large-screen motion picture projectors. They put them in amusement parks, penny arcades, and vacant stores, which were converted into "nickelodeon" theaters in working-class districts in the major cities. By 1910 some 26 million people, more than one quarter of the population, attended movies each week.

By 1920 an incredible 50 million Americans each week watched films in 15,000 movie theaters and a variety of documentaries and other films in 22,000 churches, halls, and schools.

From the beginning, American movie makers geared their product to mass audiences and to a fantasy of escape from the tedium and harshness of urban, industrial life. An early advertising jingle enticed potential customers thus:

If you're tired of life, go to the picture show.
You'll forget your unpaid bills, rheumatism and other ills,
If you'll stow away your pills, and go to the picture show.

Producers soon discovered that of the many one- and two-reel films they showed, subjects like *Taking a Bath* and *Who's in the Bedroom?* drew more audiences than *Otters at Play* or *Sleigh Riding in Central Park*. Sex and risqué skits were introduced almost from the beginning.

In the early years of the century, Edison and the immigrant entrepreneurs began to create longer narrative films. In 1903, Edison's cameraman Edwin S. Porter combined plot and characterization in *The Great Train Robbery*, reputedly the first motion picture in the modern sense. By 1913, after the industry had moved from New York and New Jersey to Hollywood, California, producers began to create so-called feature films, which ran for more than an hour and were designed to appeal to the huge middle-class market. Based on classic works and popular books and plays, these films featured stars such as comedians Harold Lloyd and Charlie Chaplin, western heroes such as Tom Mix and William S. Hart, swashbuckling Douglas Fairbanks, the glamorous Theda Bara and Gloria Swanson, and the ingénue Mary Pickford, billed as "America's sweetheart." In 1915 director D. W. Griffith set the style of the modern movie epic in his highly biased, antiblack Civil War saga *The Birth of a Nation*. Griffith included many of the techniques of modern filmmaking: the close-up, the long shot, crosscutting, and shadow and profile lighting.

As producers expanded from the tenement trade, they enticed the middle class with more sophisticated films and more attractive movie theaters. The nickelodeons were replaced by ornate palaces rivaling opera houses in grandeur. The Strand, which opened on New York City's Times Square in 1914, had thickly carpeted lounges, crystal chandeliers, original oil paintings, comfortable seats, an orchestra and an organ, and a corps of uniformed ushers. The program included a comedy, a newsreel, a travelog, and the feature film.

By the end of World War I, the motion picture industry had become big business. Hollywood had a payroll of $20 million a year and dominated both the American and world markets. In the 1920s the former nickelodeon managers, self-made men who had risen from the immigrant communities of New York and Chicago—men like Adolph Zukor, William Fox, Carl Laemmle, Samuel Goldwyn, and Louis Mayer — consolidated their holdings. They established giant companies — Paramount, Metro-Goldwyn-Mayer (MGM), Columbia, Radio-Keith-Orpheum (RKO), and Warner Brothers — which owned studios, distribution exchanges, and theater chains.

Americans quickly recognized the movies as a powerful new medium capable of influencing masses of people and manipulating thought and behavior. Traditional custodians of culture — educators, editors, clergy, publishers, critics — were divided in their assessment. Some hailed film as "authentic democratic art, straight from the hearts of the humble classes." Many, however, criticized the movies for sensationalism and creating dangerous emotions among the masses. *Good Housekeeping* in 1910 called films "a primary school for criminals . . . teaching obscenity, crime, murder, and debauchery for a nickel." Early critics of the movies often compared the storefront ghetto nickelodeons with saloons. Both attracted many of the same patrons and served as social and entertainment centers for the working classes. Middle-class conservatives and reformers condemned both as unseemly, germ-ridden places that jeopardized the health and morals of the people who went there.

Civic leaders were particularly concerned about the influence the movies had on young people. They were incensed at the vivid detail with which crime was portrayed in such films as *The Badger Game* (1905), in which a confidence man swindles the elderly. *The School Children's Strike* (1906), in which rebellious youngsters take revenge against the strict discipline of the principal by burning down the schoolhouse, also proved too provocative for the critics.

Various groups struggled to use newsreels, documentaries, educational and industrial films, and other kinds of motion pictures to espouse their views. Middle-class progressive reformers made a number of films supporting such causes as women's suffrage, child labor laws, sexual education, and political reform. Government agencies, industrialists, and labor and radical political organizations also sought to influence public opinion through film. By 1910 the antiunion drive by employers' associations included such films as *The Strikers* (1909) and *The Strike* (1912), which depicted strikes and mass movements as violent affairs led by corrupt union leaders and foreign-born "outside agitators," depicted on the screen with long, wild hair and pointy beards. Union- and radical-produced films included *A Martyr to His Cause* (1911), defending the McNamara brothers, John and James, who were "kidnapped" by authorities, taken back to California, and then indicted for the bombing of the antiunion *Los Angeles Times*. *From Dawn to Dusk* (1913), supported worker struggles from shop floor to political arena through the dramatization of the crusade of a young iron molder and his laundress woman friend. Many such prolabor, politically radical films were prohibited by local censors, and most of the small worker-producers who made them were driven out of business by these restrictions and by the cost of producing well-made films, which became prohibitively high in the 1920s.

Intervention to curb the direct influence of the movies in the Progressive Era took the form of attempts to limit the youthful audience through age restrictions for certain films, zoning requirements to keep theaters, like saloons, confined to specific areas, and censorship and outright suppression. Censorship — a form of cultural intervention — came through local government agencies or private voluntary review boards set up by citizens' groups, sometimes with the cooperation of the industry itself. Censorship was possible largely because the Supreme Court in 1915 found the movies to be a medium of entertainment rather than of information and opinion.

Typically, a coalition of community leaders — settlement house and youth workers, members of women's clubs, civic, religious, and business leaders who were concerned with young people and moral standards — either formed their own review boards or prodded the city into establishing censorship commissions. In Chicago, New York, and other cities, these censors banned parts or all of hundreds of movies. They excluded scenes that depicted criminals as heroes, ridiculed public authorities, or degraded women. Out came shots showing a ballerina smoking a cigarette or a policeman standing in his underwear. By 1922 the demands for stricter censorship had grown so strong that the studio heads formed their own national review board headed by Will Hays, who had been postmaster general during the Harding administration.

The custodians of culture hoped that the movies would convey middle-class values to lower-income groups. The producers' aim, however, was not to bring high culture to the masses but to entertain them. In the process the movies helped to teach new city dwellers the routines of urban, industrial life, in addition to which they also poked fun at the routines, making them more bearable through humor. Culturally, motion pictures assisted in bringing to the mass audience a sophistication in speech, dress, manners, and social attitudes unknown to the masses in the preceding generation.

Through the movies and other forms of mass entertainment and communication, information was conveyed to millions of people quickly and directly. These new tools helped to develop a new mass culture that in many ways supplemented or replaced the old folk culture and more personal transmission of culture. Mass communication, like mass production and mass consumption, helped to set the style of modern life.

Aviation and the Promise of Technology

Nothing in the early twentieth century fired the American imagination or symbolized the apparent promise of future progress more dramatically than the airplane. The "flying machine" seemed a miraculous achievement. Through mechanical flight, a pilot — like a bird — could soar aloft into the heavens. Conquest of the skies heralded a new age — the age of aviation. It began at 10:35 A.M. on December 17, 1903, at Kitty Hawk, North Carolina, when two bicycle mechanics from Dayton, Ohio, Wilbur and Orville Wright, held the first successful piloted, motor-powered flight in a heavier-than-air craft. Although individuals had ascended in gas balloons in the 1790s and soared in piloted gliders in the late nineteenth century, the Wright brothers engaged in *controlled* flight. They created the first effective control system by combining a rudder with primitive wing flaps that stabilized the tendency of previous motor-driven gliders to pitch or roll out of control. With Orville at the controls and a home-built gasoline-powered engine with two propellers sputtering along, the canvas and wood "Wright Flyer" stayed aloft for 12 seconds and covered a distance of 120 feet in the first of three flights that day before a gust of wind damaged the craft and ended the tests.

The historic event was not widely recognized or publicized. There were only a handful of witnesses, only one of whom took a picture of the plane leaving the ground. No newspaper reporters were present. Indeed, when some reports of the flight finally appeared, many readers thought it a hoax. Others, misled by the term "airship," concluded that it had been merely another flight by a lighter-than-air craft, a gas-filled flying machine invented in the late 1880s and known variously as an "airship" or a "dirigible."

Most people in those years had to see an airplane to understand that it was different from a lighter-than-air craft and to accept the fact that, unlike the large and unwieldy dirigibles, the relatively compact and fully maneuverable airplanes allowed their pilots to "conquer" the skies at will. After making further improvements, the Wrights held a major demonstration of their flying machine for the U.S. Army and the general public at Fort Myer military base in Virginia, near Washington, D.C. In September 1908, a crowd of up to 5,000 persons watched in awe as Orville Wright took the plane up into the air, turned and banked in the sky, clattered over their heads, and then swooped down for a landing on a grassy field.

The public flight trials in 1908 were widely reported by the press, but flight still seemed unbelievable to many people and, as historian Joseph J. Corn confirms, for years afterward crowds of people gathered to see for themselves whenever an airplane first appeared over their area. In 1909, while Orville Wright flew demonstrations in Europe,

Gently lifting into the air from a single-rail iron track, the Wright Brothers' twin-propellered biplane begins its brief, historic flight at Kitty Hawk, North Carolina, with Orville prone at the controls and Wilbur running alongside to time the flight. (*The Granger Collection*)

Wilbur drew a crowd estimated at more than a million persons as he flew along Manhattan island, out over New York Harbor, and around the Statue of Liberty. The next year an even larger number of spectators watched another pioneer airplane builder, Glenn H. Curtiss, a mechanic and former motorcycle racer from Hammondsport, New York, as he flew his own plane from Albany, New York, to New York City in two-and-a-half hours. Curtiss and the Wrights soon trained a number of pilots and promoted exhibitions of their aircraft at county fairs, racetracks, airplane races, or in simple country fields — almost anywhere a promoter could guarantee a crowd and an exhibition fee.

Although the Wrights did not admit women to their flight training school, several women were able to become pilots and exhibition fliers. Much of the aviation industry encouraged women because, as pilot Louise Thaden put it, "If a woman can handle a plane, the public thinks it must be 'duck soup' for men." One of the first American women to fly was Bessica Raiche who, with her aviator husband, built a Wright-type plane in their living room in Mineola, Long Island. Raiche made her first flight in 1910. Harriet Quimby, who left California to lead a career as an actress and then as a drama critic in New York, became an aviatrix in 1911. Quimby won international acclaim in 1912 as the first

woman to fly across the English Channel, but she was killed the following year when her plane crashed at a Boston air show. Despite such
tragedies, other women aviators continued to find a sense of liberation
in flying as would a subsequent generation of female pilots, including
Amelia Earhart, in the 1920s and 1930s. But as the deaths of Harriet
Quimby, Ralph Johnstone, Arch Hoxsey, and dozens of other exhibition
fliers (plus Earhart and many other long-distance pilots) indicated,
there were many martyrs in fledgling aviation. In the early decades of
the century, stunt flying, air racing, and the primitive state of aeronau-
tical design (wings collapsed under stress, and planes actually fell apart
in the sky) all contributed to a substantial death toll among fliers.

The public was captivated by the airplane and the aviation age.
Despite the numerous fatalities each new record-breaking event
seemed to confirm the pace of progress. Aviation stories were often
front-page news in the press: the first use of planes for commuting from
home to office (1913); the first regularly scheduled flights by a commercial airline (1914); the inauguration of government air mail service
(1918); and ultimately, of course, the first trans-Atlantic flight in 1927
by Charles A. Lindbergh.

Technological expertise and human daring seemed to have broken
the shackles that tied human beings to the earth for millenia. The
"miracle" of flight that led so many contemporaries to describe aviation as creating a "new era" or "epoch" in human history also produced some fantastic forecasts for the future. Alexander Graham Bell
predicted in 1909 that the "aerial motor car" was just around the
corner. The air was free—every family would have a plane—
everyone would fly. Many others believed that aviation would reorient
international relations and usher in an "age of peace," because, as one
commentator asserted in 1909, even a small nation equipped with
warplanes would be able to deter the armies of a powerful neighbor.
Still others believed that by breaking down the physical barriers that
divided the world, aviation would, in the words of Secretary of State
Philander Knox in 1910, "bring the nations much closer together." In
1917, in the midst of World War I, even the normally reticent Orville
Wright predicted that the airplane would soon make wars impossible.

That the airplane did not end wars, but actually helped make them
more costly in the loss of human lives, was not immediately apparent
amidst the optimism of early twentieth-century America. What was so
wondrous and even miraculous was that a technological breakthrough
had allowed human beings to scale the heavens. Millions marvelled at
this symbol of technological progress. In 1910, a million persons
watched the first airplane flight over Chicago. A minister wrote of his
fellow spectators in the streets, "Never have I seen such a look of
wonder in the faces of a multitude. From the gray-haired man to the
child, everyone seemed to feel that it was a new day in their lives." The

popular perception was indeed that airplanes augured a new day in human affairs and a new triumph for America.

Modernism in Thought and Art

"Nothing is done in this country as it was done twenty years ago," Woodrow Wilson declared in 1913. "We are in the presence of a new organization of society. . . . We have changed our economic conditions, absolutely, from top to bottom; and, with our economic society, the organization of our life." Despite the doubts of many critics, such as Walter Lippmann, about the nation's ability to adjust to the new conditions, Americans in the Progressive Era remade many of their institutions, redirected much of their behavior, and began to recast their ways of looking at the world.

While the entrepreneurs of the communication and entertainment industries worked to build a new mass culture based largely on the ethic of consumption and the pleasure principle, traditionalists resisted such a change. A sharp tension separated those who wanted to cling to tradition from those who emphasized the need for broad and rapid modernization. In the reform period of the Progressive Era, traditionalists — those in rural areas as well as urban dwellers who continued to assert the primacy of nineteenth-century standards of culture and morality — were on the defensive. Modernizers had the force of change behind them. But many of the social and cultural tensions of these years remained unresolved and in the 1920s were exacerbated into a national conflict over the direction of American society.

The Revolt against Formalism

The comfortable Victorian cosmos of middle-class mores and the tenets of scientific progress could not sustain the assaults of industrial change and the scientific discoveries of the twentieth century. On both sides of the Atlantic, artists, novelists, dramatists, social scientists, and philosophers revolted against the abstract, formalistic logic of the Victorian age. Abandoning the quest for a single "truth," they moved toward a more pluralistic acceptance of the possibility that there were many different apprehensions of truth. The emphasis on relativism and change placed the focus on the process of becoming rather than on the end itself.

Pragmatism was the most original American contribution to this relativism. Nicely suited to American optimism during a time of flux in which old certainties were being eroded and displaced, this vigorous and influential system of thought asserted that the meaning of any term and the reality of any object lay in what it could and would do. In short, the importance of ideas lay in their results. William James, a Harvard psychologist and philosopher and brother of the novelist Henry James, developed the philosophy that would dominate twentieth-century America. Actively positivistic, James declared that in a changing world people could often affect the course of change through bold, creative action. Pragmatism offered reassurance of individuality, free will, initiative, and human spontaneity in opposition to the seemingly helpless position of men and women in the deterministic framework of social Darwinism. "Believe that life is worth living," James wrote in books such as A Pluralistic Universe and The Meaning of Truth (both published in 1909), "and your belief will help create the fact."

John Dewey, a Columbia University educator and philosopher, went even further than James. In the concept of instrumentalism, Dewey held it proper to use the instrument of collective action, whether through private association or through the actions of government, to improve society. Guided by intelligence and employing scientific methods, people, Dewey believed, could intervene purposefully, modify their environment, and improve the quality of their lives and of society itself.

In Support of Intervention

Faith in the marketplace ideal and a self-regulating society was undermined by the rigors of industrialization, but the framework of thought that supported the status quo — natural law, unrestrained individualism, social Darwinism, and laissez-faire — was overturned by a new class of intellectuals, university-trained and often academically employed social scientists. They helped to overcome traditionalist thinkers who continued to defend the old concepts. Although William Graham Sumner lived until 1910, he and his disciples found it increasingly difficult to deal with the fact that giant businesses were not strictly private but were "affected with a public interest" and therefore presumably subject to regulation by the public. Their other problem was the inconsistency of business people who championed laissez-faire but wanted maintenance of the status quo — governmental protection in the form of tariffs, patents, aid against labor — for themselves but not for their adversaries.

Increasing numbers of individuals and groups became impatient at the helplessness of their position as it was reflected in the concept of inevitable, gradual evolution. Through its organization, business had shown how to influence the environment. Evolutionary determinism could be stood on its head. If the environment determined adaptation and other behavior, then by altering the environment for the better, people and society itself might be improved. This kind of "reform

Darwinism" gave hope of improvement through manipulation of the environment.

Abandoning mechanistic doctrines and abstract principles, the social scientists of the Progressive Era sought to understand how society really worked so that people could improve its operation. Many attacked the justifications for the status quo. The historian Charles Beard, in *An Economic Interpretation of the Constitution* (1913), undermined the sanctity of the Constitution and the Supreme Court's use of it to thwart reform by unveiling the property interests, and presumably the economic motivations, of the nation's founders. The radical economist Thorstein Veblen, in *The Theory of the Leisure Class* (1899) and later works, differentiated between engineers, who, he claimed, were responsible for mass production, and business people, who were more interested in profit than in production for society. The legal system's emphasis on the need to adhere to absolute principles, with highest priority to laissez-faire and the protection of private property, was challenged by Roscoe Pound of the Harvard Law School, who formulated a "sociological jurisprudence." Like pragmatism, it shifted from absolutes to relatives, arguing that the law was dynamic, was a product of experience and could thus be created, and was subject to continuous improvement in the interests of society. "The Fourteenth Amendment," Justice Holmes declared in a famous dissent from the Court's invalidation of a law limiting the working hours of New York bakers (*Lochner v. New York*, 1905), "does not enact Mr. Herbert Spencer's Social Statics."

Sociologists like Edward A. Ross also rejected Spencerian sociology and social Darwinism. Ross helped to develop the concept of social control, the use of collective action to control forces threatening to pull society apart. Ross rejected the concept of a self-regulating society in which individuals, following their own interests, contributed to social progress. Rather, in the view of Ross and many others, such individuals posed a social danger.

The Jeffersonian tradition of limited government was addressed directly in a widely read book, *The Promise of American Life* (1909), by Herbert Croly, one of the editors of the liberal *New Republic* magazine. Given the changing nature of society and the growth of industrialization and giant organizations, Croly argued, Jeffersonian, liberal democratic ideals could no longer be attained without governmental action. Croly, like Roosevelt and others, urged the use of strong, positive government to ensure continued progress toward its ideals, to use, in his memorable phrase, Hamiltonian means to achieve Jeffersonian ends.

The conceptualization and intellectual justification of private collective and governmental interference in the functioning of society accompanied the interventionism that was already taking place. The construction of the intellectual argument did not create intervention in the marketplace or cause the erosion of the idea of a self-regulating society. But once it had been formulated in intellectually respectable terms, it provided a powerful justification for these trends and helped to stimulate the widespread interventionism of the Progressive Era.

Social Criticism and Individualism

Writers challenged genteel literary strictures and emphasized instead the seamy side of modern society, the despair of the masses, and the impact of impersonal forces on people's lives. Influenced by Emile Zola and other European social critics, American naturalistic writers helped set the stage for social reform. Theodore Dreiser introduced naturalism with *Sister Carrie* (1900), which dealt with economic and sexual exploitation. He went on to attack big business in *The Financier* (1912) and *The Titan* (1914). Frank Norris exposed railroad monopoly in *The Octopus* (1901) and the commodities exchange in *The Pit* (1903). Upton Sinclair assailed the meatpacking industry and the capitalist system in *The Jungle* (1906). But though many of the naturalist writers were influenced by Darwinism and the belief in vast, impersonal forces that controlled human destinies, they also emphasized collective action or powerful individuals struggling to dominate the environment. Cowperwood, in *The Titan*, is a symbol of force in business and politics, and the larger-than-life protagonists of Jack London's novels, like Wolf Larsen in *The Sea Wolf*, resemble Nietzschean supermen.

In a time of increasing social organization, there was also a countermovement to emphasize the importance of the individual. The individual in mass society was a critical focus of a number of writers, including Ibsen, Bergson, and Nietzsche. Freud too, contributed to the intuitive probing of inner experience, providing a new appreciation of the need to come to terms with the irrational and the absurd and the importance of personal integrity, fulfillment, and freedom.

Some of this new individualism appeared in the transformation of art. Modern art, which moved from the social criticism of naturalism to highly individualistic expressionism, arrived in the United States in the first decade of the century. Like the new literature, it repudiated the genteel culture of the Victorian era. Influenced by romantic realism and French impressionism, such painters as George Luks, John Sloan, and George Bellows and the photographer Alfred Stieglitz portrayed the drabness and repressed violence in urban, industrial life so forcefully that after their New York exhibition in 1908, critics labeled them the "ashcan school."

At the New York Armory show of 1913, these artists introduced European modernism, including cubism, expressionism, and other avant-garde schools of painting. The works of Picasso, Matisse,

Cézanne, and others emphasized the unpredictable, the unmanageable, and the flux and formlessness of modern life. They challenged the positive optimism of many American intellectuals and progressives. Many traditionalist critics attacked the new movement. One described the cubist Duchamp's *Nude Descending a Staircase* as "an explosion in a shingle factory." Theodore Roosevelt denounced cubists and futurists as the "lunatic fringe."

Cultural Rebels

Emphasis on the creation of a freer, more fulfilling life and repudiation of oppressive, outdated institutions became the focus of a subculture of young cultural rebels who established Bohemian centers in New York and Chicago. To the little cafés of Greenwich Village came Max and Crystal Eastman and the other editors of the startlingly radical new journal *The Masses*; the poet Edna Saint Vincent Millay; the playwright Eugene O'Neill; John Reed, scion of a wealthy Oregon family, former Harvard cheerleader, and radical journalist; and many others. These young people felt keenly the gap between outdated ideas and institutions and new social and industrial conditions. Dissenting from conventional standards and values, outraged by the poverty, injustice, and oppression they saw all around them, they assailed the dead hand of tradition and conscienceless industrialism. "The old world was dying," wrote Floyd Dell, the literary chronicler of Greenwich Village. It could not survive the clash between "utopian ideals and machine-made fact." In one of the first documents of the countercultural tradition, a young Columbia College graduate, Randolph Bourne, published *Youth and Life* (1913), which juxtaposed the spontaneity and daring of youth with the arid conventionality of adulthood: "It is the young people who have all the really valuable experience. . . . Very few people get any really new experience after they are twenty-five."

"Everywhere new institutions were being founded — magazines, clubs, little theaters, art or free-love or single-tax colonies, experimental schools, picture galleries," the literary critic Malcolm Cowley recalled of the years just before World War I. "Everywhere was a sense of comradeship and immense possibilities for change." The mood of the nation encouraged Americans to assume responsibility for their fate as a people and to do so with an assertiveness that was virtually unprecedented in their history.

CHAPTER 5

The Progressive Impulse

The Great Light

"Slowly as the new century came into its first decade, I saw the Great Light," wrote America's most celebrated small-town newspaper editor, William Allen White. The Great Light he saw was progressivism, a collective effort of millions of Americans to "modernize" institutions at the beginning of the twentieth century. "Around me in that day," White recalled,

> scores of young leaders in American politics and public affairs were seeing what I saw, feeling what I felt. . . . All over the land in a score of states and more, young men in both parties were taking leadership by attacking things as they were in that day.

Progressivism was the name given at the time to a number of major efforts to reform society through the power of private groups and public agencies. As a nationwide movement, it began to influence events during the 1890s' depression and faded after World War I began. Although traces of it lasted nearly thirty years, progressivism became most influential between 1906 and 1916. During that decade millions of people sensed the increased tempo of reform. One progressive, a political scientist, claimed in 1913, with an overoptimism characteristic of the middle-class reformers, "one of the most inspiring movements in human history is now in progress."

The movement proved both inspiring and confusing because progressive leaders — nostalgic knights of reform — mixed new methods with old visions and often differed among themselves over their goals. Successful political leaders like Theodore Roosevelt and Woodrow Wilson tended to blur the differences among their followers. The tumultuous 1912 convention that gave birth to the short-lived Progressive party* illustrated how different reformers were pulled together by their faith in a progressive spirit and belief in "noble" leaders.

*The capitalized *Progressive* refers to the political party that existed from 1912 to 1916. The lowercase *progressive* refers to participants in the diverse social reform movement regardless of party affiliation.

132

Modern crusaders swelling with righteousness and hope, the delegates to the Progressive party convention set out to battle the forces of evil. Their champion, Theodore Roosevelt, appealed to them with the shrewdness of a politician and the moralistic fervor of an evangelist: "This new movement is a movement of truth, sincerity and wisdom, a movement which proposes to put at the service of all our people the collective power of the people, through their Governmental agencies." Roosevelt ended his "confession of faith" with a rousing declaration:

> Our cause is based on the eternal principles of righteousness; and even though we who now lead may for the time fail, in the end the cause itself shall triumph. . . . We stand at Armageddon, and we battle for the Lord.

Leaping to their feet, the delegates filled the great hall with applause and responded with choruses of "Onward, Christian Soldiers" and "The Battle Hymn of the Republic." With enthusiasm as their armor, the Progressives marched forth against their foes.

Such displays of mass enthusiasm concealed great differences within the Progressive party and within progressivism as a whole. Among the delegates cheering Roosevelt that day were people as diverse as George W. Perkins, a former Morgan partner and the head of International Harvester Corporation, and Amos Pinchot, a maverick millionaire and socialistic labor lawyer who favored breaking up trusts such as International Harvester. Progressives included militarists like Roosevelt, who thrilled to wartime combat, and pacifists like the Quaker settlement house worker Jane Addams, who founded the Women's International League for Peace and Freedom to help abolish war.

In diverse ways and with divergent goals, the progressives sought to modernize American institutions while attempting to recapture the ideals and sense of community that they believed had existed in the past. They battled conservatives, radicals, other reformers, and often each other. But despite their disagreements and difficulties, progressives played a major role in helping Americans to adjust to new conditions and create new institutions for coping with the challenges of the time. They took the lead in establishing a social agenda for modern America.

Progressives as Interventionists

Most historians have labeled the first two decades of the twentieth century the "Progressive Era," but they have not been able to agree on the nature of either progressivism or the era. Some, such as Richard Hofstadter in the 1950s, saw it as a movement led by declining gentry and professionals of the "old" middle class anxious about their loss of status and the threats to the social order posed by corporations and unions. Progressivism was, in Hofstadter's "status-revolution" theory, "the complaint of the unorganized against the consequences of organization." A different economic-determinist school of interpretation, led by Gabriel Kolko in the 1960s, asserted that the key agents of change were the new corporate leaders and financiers who, seeking to protect their immediate interests, gained at least partial control of the federal government and used it to aid particular industries in domestic and international markets. Kolko believed that the state did the bidding of big business; thus progressivism represented not the victory of reform but the "triumph of conservatism." Other historians, such as David Thelen, who looked primarily at the state and local levels, suggested that progressivism was radical in its potential for building coalitions of consumers across class and ethnic lines.

Examining both local and national levels, Samuel Hays and Robert Wiebe concluded that the progressives were members of the "new middle class," primarily professional and managerial people. In an influential "organizational synthesis," Hays and Wiebe asserted that functionally the progressive reformers continued the long-term trend toward rationalization, bureaucratization, and centralization in an industrializing society. Amid such a welter of interpretations, Peter Filene concluded in the 1970s that a coherent progressive movement had never existed and that the concept of progressivism should be abandoned as factually inaccurate and analytically useless.

Yet scholarly analysis of progressivism and the Progressive Era proceeded, continuing to generate considerable controversy. In the 1980s, in an interpretation that emphasized big business's predominant influence yet was more temperate and sophisticated than Kolko's, Martin Sklar suggested that the key development of the era was the effort of a number of corporate capitalists, professional politicians, economists, jurists, and government bureaucrats to guide industrialization by forging a new system of power relationships and public consciousness. The previously dominant ethos and structure of market individualism was modified by administered markets and a regulatory state. Most of the trade unions and the middle class were coopted by accommodation. However, the role of the expanded government was still overshadowed by that of private economic forces, including the corporations. Sklar and James Weinstein argued that this development represented a new stage of American capitalism, one they called "corporate liberalism."

Directly challenging the thesis of big business's domination of the state, Morton Keller in 1990 denied that economic power became concentrated in a small number of dominant corporations in the early twentieth century or that government was unduly influenced by the large corporations. Instead, he emphasized the continuation of pluralism (a wide number of competing interests, all of which Keller saw as influential) and the persistence of the existing structure of politics, government, and law and of continuing attitudes of skepticism toward government management of economic affairs and of belief in competition and the marketplace.

The Progressive Era has remained so controversial because of differences over the nature of progressivism and of the environment in which it operated. The debate also derives from differences over the kinds of changes that were possible and desirable in American society. Although the standards of the historical profession uphold an ideal of objective, critical inquiry and assessment of data, historians are, in varying degrees, influenced by their own times and beliefs as well as their training in historical methods of research and analysis.

In regard to the reforms of the Progressive Era, historians continue to differ over the identity of the primary agents of change, their motivations, and their accomplishments. Part of the problem has been a tendency by scholars to focus largely on those who called themselves progressives. In fact, those men and women were only part of the forces for innovation in the Progressive Era. Alliances in support of particular changes usually consisted of a variety of groups, often differing in attitudes and goals. Part of the problem confronting historians has been the frequent discrepancy between the idealistic rhetoric of leaders and the variety of motivations involved in particular coalitions and between the stated humanitarian goals and the actual results of specific reform movements. Arthur S. Link and Richard L. McCormick have wisely recommended distinguishing the goals of a group advocating a particular reform from its rhetoric and from the results achieved. They also believe that there were common characteristics in progressivism, and they have urged historians to study and identify them.

One recent trend in historical scholarship of the Progressive Era has been to go beyond specific questions about the nature of progressivism to study its context — the environment of politics, power, ideas, and values within which the rhetoric and reforms of the era occurred. Studies have shown that this environment included the decline of party loyalties and voter turnout and the rise of issue-oriented political pressure groups; the growth of occupational specializations, communication networks, and "functional organizations" binding the specialists together, as emphasized in the "organizational synthesis"; and of course, the emergence of powerful corporations and new attitudes toward a corporate and consumer-oriented economy.

Yet historians continue to try to understand the nature of progressivism within that context, and they remain in disagreement over the nature of both the reforms and progressive social thought. In an imaginative essay drawing on new concepts of the role of political rhetoric, Daniel Rodgers has contended that the glue that held together leaders who called themselves progressives and who built coalitions behind particular changes was not a common creed or a system of values. Rather such leaders drew on distinct clusters of ideas — Rodgers calls them distinct social languages — to articulate their discontents and social visions. Rodgers categorizes these clusters as antimonopoly, social efficiency, and community. The progressives are therefore best understood as users rather than shapers of ideas. To Rodgers there was no ideology of progressivism.

I have long contended that the concept of intervention helps to clarify the nature of many of the changes that occurred in the first two decades of the twentieth century. "Modernization" resulted not only from the actions of people who called themselves progressives but also from initiatives taken by other groups, including many radicals, nonprogressive reformers, and advocates of conservative reforms. (Some of the specific changes were opposed by traditionalists; others were opposed by conservatives who thought that they went too far in modifying existing power relationships or by activists on the left who saw developments increasing the power of the corporations.) The corporate reorganization movement, the labor movement, the women's movement, and the agrarian reform movement all contributed to change. All were willing to intervene in the economy and society, and sometimes world affairs, on an unprecedented scale. The new interventionists — progressives among them — challenged the dominant nineteenth-century belief in an autonomous and apolitical market system, the idea that the economy and society benefited when each individual was free to follow personal goals and self-interest with only a minimum of governmental interference. The concepts of laissez-faire, unrestricted individualism, and an open, competitive marketplace had been seen as encouraging the development of a vast continent. But the closing of the frontier, the depression of the 1890s, the transformation of America through massive immigration, rapid urbanization, and sweeping industrialization, and the public's "discovery," largely as a result of investigative journalism, that government was widely corrupted by business interests led many Americans to question the continued usefulness of these traditions without some modification on behalf of the public interest. The faith in natural development fostered by unrestrained individualism and an unregulated marketplace gave way to a fear that blind social forces and greedy individuals threatened to transform society without regard to social values and goals. Many feared the destruction of American society and ideals.

In the first two decades of the twentieth century, Americans first sought on a nationwide basis to bring industrial change under control. Those with influence modified the philosophies of laissez-faire, an unregulated marketplace, and unrestricted individualism and intervened to direct change in what they considered a purposeful and intelligent manner. The leaders of this transformation employed new methods of science and the techniques of modern business organization. The new interventionists formed voluntary associations and other private cooperative groups and, when necessary, expanded the power of government to achieve their ends. They understood that they faced conditions that demanded new responses, and they were willing to create new or reorganized institutions — trade associations, professional groups, chambers of commerce, consumers' leagues, unions, and government regulatory agencies — that would benefit their own particular group and at the same time be consistent with their vision of the national interest.

Some Americans remained anti-interventionists. They continued to believe in classical political economy, laissez-faire, the unregulated marketplace, and a mechanistic type of gradual progress through what John D. Rockefeller called "the working out of a law of nature." Progress could not be achieved by legislative fiat. "God Almighty made men and certain laws which are essential to their progress in civilization," the financier Henry Lee Higginson wrote to President William Howard Taft in 1911, "and Congressmen cannot break these natural laws without causing suffering." Progress was possible but painfully slow. In a 1912 speech, Elihu Root, a corporation lawyer and former secretary of state, saw progress as measured "not by days and years but by generations and centuries in the life of nations." The most conservative noninterventionists linked private property with a divine plan. They refused to believe that property rights should be restricted. In a famous declaration against unionization of coal miners, George F. Baer, a mine owner and president of the Philadelphia & Reading Railroad, asserted in 1902 that "the rights and interests of the laboring men will be looked after and cared for, not by the agitators, but by the Christian men to whom God in His infinite wisdom has given the control of the property interests of the country."

Such assertions in favor of complete freedom to use private property without concern for the immediate impact on society were heard less frequently in this interventionist age. Some of the leading nineteenth-century advocates of laissez-faire continued to expound it until their death; Sumner died in 1910 and Carnegie in 1919. During the Progressive Era, however, those who espoused such ideas were on the defensive. Even many conservatives realized the need for change. "Every one of us must recognize that the days of pure individualism are gone," Taft's secretary of commerce and labor, Charles Nagel, admitted. Nicolas Murray Butler, president of Columbia University and one of the leaders of the Republican old guard, asserted in 1912 that the "new development is cooperation, and cooperation as a substitute for unlimited, unrestricted, individual competition has come to stay as an economic fact, and legal institutions will have to be adjusted to it."

Despite the breadth of the forces for change—social, economic, cultural—in the early twentieth century and the scope of the new interventionism, the Progressive Era cannot be understood without understanding progressivism. It was a crucial part of the new interventionism. A multifaceted reform movement affecting nearly every aspect of American life, progressivism—like its successor, liberalism—was controversial and complex. Millions of people in both major political parties and several other parties and in every region of the country called themselves progressives. The progressive leadership came primarily from the urban and small-town middle and upper classes, particularly well-educated and socially secure white Anglo-Saxon Protestant or German Jewish men and women from the professions—lawyers, journalists, educators, scientists, physicians, social workers—and initially also from independent entrepreneurs from small and medium-sized businesses as well as from among managers at various levels in hierarchical organizations, from foundations to corporations. (However, conservative, antiprogressive leaders also generally came from the same social background and occupational categories, with the exception of social work, which produced few political conservatives.) But while the progressives all believed in some kind of reform, they differed over its substance and tempo. Progressivism was not a united movement but a broad and diverse effort for moderate social change within the American tradition.

Progressivism is best understood as a dynamic general reform effort composed of many specific social movements and shifting coalitions of self-interested groups uniting temporarily over different issues and behind different political leaders. The specific nature of the progressive coalition varied, depending on the issue, the region, and the political leadership. Among the important nonprogressive (in the sense that they did not call themselves progressives) constituencies that sometimes supported and sometimes opposed particular progressive reforms were big business, labor unions, urban immigrant groups, agrarian interests, and occasionally rural fundamentalists. Effective progressive political leaders such as Theodore Roosevelt and Woodrow Wilson often muted the differences among their followers. They sought to maintain their coalitions by avoiding conflict among their members as much as possible and by promoting conciliation and compromise when disagreements threatened to disrupt the alliance. The fact that so many different people and groups worked so hard for reform in these years gave the era much of its distinctive quality. Progressives established a national reform agenda, helped create widespread support for it, and obtained a significant amount of legislation based on its principles.

Progressives differed from their critics on both the left and the right. Moderate modernizers, they were optimistic about their ability to achieve important, but not radical, change in the social system within a short time. They used collective action, even dramatic governmental intervention, to achieve progress. Yet as reformers, not radicals, they supported only enough change to counteract the ills of what they considered a basically sound, liberal, democratic, capitalist system. "The world moves and we have got to move with it," one progressive editor wrote to a conservative friend in 1912. "So with all that is going on in politics today. . . . It is evolution, and not revolution."

Many conservatives and traditionalists saw such a position as a prelude to disaster. They feared that the progressives were going too far too fast, unduly interfering with liberty and property rights and raising dangerous expectations among the masses. Conservatives considered the social fabric to be a fragile web held together by the stability of institutions and morality under the watchful eye of the judiciary. They warned that the progressives jeopardized the social order. Senator Henry Cabot Lodge protested in 1910 that reformers sought "to bring in laws for everything, for everything that happens, to try and find a remedy by passing a statute, and to overlook the fact that laws are made by men and that laws do not make men."

Radical activists devoted themselves to more drastic change. Despite the differences among socialists, syndicalists, and anarchists, all radicals considered it impossible to achieve industrial democracy without major deviations from the prevailing capitalist order. Debs, Haywood, Goldman, and scores of other dissenters condemned capitalism and the wage system as inherently exploitative and oppressive.

The largest of the radical groups, the socialists, contained almost as many differences as the progressives. Marxists and non-Marxists, political gradualists and militant extremists, Christian socialists, atheists, and agnostics — all were disillusioned with current institutions. Some came to socialism from the labor movement or from the writings of Edward Bellamy. Many radical tenant farmers of the Midwest and the Southwest came to it from populism. To numbers of Jewish Russian and German workers and intellectuals in Chicago, New York, and Milwaukee and to Finnish miners in Minnesota, socialism provided an ethnic bond and an intellectual heritage. Socialists pointed out injustices and proposed alternatives ranging from improved working conditions to public ownership of utilities, transportation, and many basic industries. Their challenges to private property, limited government, and organized religion appealed to millions of Americans but frightened many more, including most progressives.

Averse to extreme solutions, progressives nonetheless recognized that solutions of some kind were urgently needed. Like other interventionists, progressives tried to rectify the problems accompanying industrialism and replace drift and indecision with positive, creative direction. But they differed from the others in possessing a unique progressive ethos, which combined the nineteenth-century sense of

Protestant evangelism with the new methods of science and large-scale organization. Evangelistic modernizers, progressive leaders wedded quasi-religious idealism and scientism in a movement that worked for specific reforms while seeking to restore a sense of community and common purpose to a nation they saw splintering into diverse ethnic and interest groups.

The leaders of progressivism grew up in the late Victorian era, a period of intense revivalism, evangelism, and affirmation of the cultural and moral values of small-town America: hard work, frugality, self-improvement, decency, and altruism. This moral idealism led younger members of the dominant American elite to try to impose their group's standards on an increasingly diverse society, using new methods learned from science and business. Fired with the passion of moral rectitude, the progressive leaders were also obsessed with efficiency, rationalization, and orderly procedure. "There are two gospels I always want to preach to reformers," Theodore Roosevelt told delegates to a conference on city improvement. "The first is the gospel of morality; the next is the gospel of efficiency. . . . I don't think I have to tell you to be upright, but I do think I have to tell you to be practical and efficient."

But the progressives, like other interventionists, also drew on science and the corporation. Imbued with faith in predictability and efficiency, they launched a search for systems through which to manage change in an orderly manner. Instead of relying on chance and ad hoc local responses to problems, reformers turned to the methods of the physical and social sciences. They employed scientific methods of investigation: extensive data gathering, analysis, prognosis, and prescription. Heirs of Darwin, they thought that by manipulating the environment and behavior, they could improve the human condition. They gathered extensive statistics to document problems and then sought to alleviate them by educating the public. To produce the desired results, progressives tried to alter attitudes, behavior, and even environmental conditions. In doing so, they were influenced by the model of the large-scale corporation, which showed how thousands of people could be organized and directed efficiently and how the organization's environment could be manipulated. Progressives emulated these organizational and management techniques, particularly specialization, bureaucratization, and expert professional direction. "The trust," Jane Addams explained, "is the educator of us all."

The Progressive Agenda

As they challenged established policies and officeholders, progressives became key leaders in public and private organizations: political parties, government, the media, and institutions and associations ranging from education to engineering. In these positions they translated the reform spirit into an ideal and clusters of American beliefs into a powerful reform rhetoric that could mobilize millions of citizens to participate in campaigns for "progress" portrayed as pitting "the people" against "the interests." Progressives helped establish a diffuse agenda for reform that gave some coherence to the myriad efforts for change and provided identifiable dimensions to progressivism in politics. That agenda included four broad categories of issues.

First, the business regulation movement represented an effort to make business more responsible to American values and the public interest. Rejecting the theory of laissez-faire and unrestricted individualism, Theodore Roosevelt declared:

> The man who wrongly holds that every human right is secondary to his profit must now give way to the advocate of human welfare, who rightly maintains that every man holds his property subject to the general right of the community to regulate its use to whatever degree the public welfare may require it.

Although all progressives agreed that there must be some public control of business, they disagreed over the amount of such control, especially with regard to the supercorporations. Some, such as William Jennings Bryan and Wisconsin Senator Robert La Follette, urged that the supercorporations be broken up into smaller companies to encourage competition and protect the public. They wanted to strengthen the antitrust laws. Others, such as Roosevelt and George Perkins, a partner at J. P. Morgan and Company and one of the major financial contributors to the Progressive party, argued for federal charters and regulations of the giant corporations to sustain them and yet ensure that they operated in the public interest. "Competition," Perkins declared, "has become too destructive to be tolerated. Cooperation must be the order of the day."

Second, the good-government or direct-democracy movement represented an effort by progressives to capture and reform the political system. "Give the government back to the people" became a rallying cry for progressives. They detested the so-called invisible government, a system in which nonelected and unaccountable political party bosses manipulated elected officials and ran city and state governments. Disdaining legislators as corrupt and captured by special interests, progressives sought to reduce the power of party bosses and legislators and masses of poorer voters by increasing the power of middle-class voters and members of the executive branch of government — mayors, governors, and the president — as well as nonpartisan experts like city managers and regulatory commissioners.

Third, the social justice movement sought to aid exploited workers and the urban poor. The major organizations in this movement were led by women, who demonstrated their concern as well as their administrative skills and leadership in efforts to abolish child labor, establish wage and hour laws for workers and ensure factory safety, alleviate poverty, and encourage respect for human rights. The women social workers who led this movement were assisted by social gospel clergy and a number of social scientists. Although they often failed to obtain the backing of more conservative interventionists, social justice progressives frequently formed a political coalition with labor and foreign-stock urban dwellers on these issues.

Fourth, the social control movement represented a coercive effort by old-stock Americans to impose a uniform culture based on their values. Distressed by increasing cultural and racial diversity, many progressives joined with large numbers of conservatives and fundamentalists to employ governmental power to impose homogeneous standards of behavior on the entire population. Directed especially against Catholic and Jewish immigrants and blacks, the movement took the form of compulsory education, mandatory Sunday closing of business and entertainment establishments, prohibition of alcoholic beverages, control of narcotics, restriction of immigration, and limitation of voting privileges.

Regional differences in progressivism reflected the sectional variations in American society; the common political culture of the nation was modified by distinctive conditions and attitudes. The South was particularly shaped by its predominantly rural and racially divided nature, its evangelical Protestant religious culture, and its political domination by one party — the Democratic party. The dispersed rural population sustained strong traditions of individualism and localism with popular suspicion of concentrated economic or political power and antagonism toward outside intrusion into local affairs. This, combined with the opposition of the wealthy and other property owners to taxation, helped to keep the role of government to a minimum. Although the southern economy was growing at the turn of the century — particularly in the lumber and textile industries and the emerging citrus cultivation in Florida and oil production in Texas — the region suffered fundamental problems: increasing farm tenancy, debilitating rural poverty and ill health, and the worsening plight of African Americans.

Because of the white South's emphasis on white supremacy, the reform movement that began in the 1890s espoused progressivism for whites only. Racism and reform were closely affiliated as southern progressives rapidly removed virtually all blacks, and a number of poor whites, from the electorate, using earlier established poll taxes and literacy tests. Beginning in the 1900s, southern states, responding to progressives' calls for more direct influence by the white electorate to eliminate "corrupt" party machines and also for disfranchisement of blacks, adopted statewide primary elections to determine political party nominees for office. Thereafter, state Democratic party officials found ways to exclude blacks from party membership and from voting in the Democratic primary elections. Since obtaining the Democratic party nomination was tantamount to election in the functionally one-party South, blacks were effectively excluded from the electorate.

Southern white reformers also employed rigid new statutes to segregate the now politically powerless blacks from white society. With the acquiescence of most northern whites and the support of the Supreme Court of the United States, official segregation (Jim Crow) spread throughout the South. State legislatures segregated all public transportation and depots; municipalities adopted ordinances segregating parks, beaches, auditoriums, jails, and neighborhoods; and businesses established their own Jim Crow policies. Little signs reading "whites only" and "colored" were put up in thousands of places, including on drinking fountains, ticket windows, and doors to restaurants and other places. Blacks challenged these actions; they held protest meetings, staged economic boycotts, took petitions to governmental authorities, and filed suits in state and federal courts. Although black activism sometimes delayed disfranchisement, it ultimately failed before the overwhelming power and determination of the whites. The judiciary upheld control of voting requirements by the states and by political parties (the white primary was not invalidated until 1944); the courts also sustained segregation under the "separate but equal" doctrine from the 1890s until the 1950s.

Some whites also turned to vigilante terrorism to keep blacks in a subordinate position or simply to vent their hostility toward African Americans. Lynchings had risen to more than 200 a year in the turbulent early 1890s. In the first two decades of the twentieth century, nearly eighty black men a year were hanged or burned to death by white mobs. Few whites were ever convicted of such crimes, and not one was executed.

The official segregation that would characterize the South for more than half a century developed in the Progressive Era because of the racial tensions exacerbated by the economic depression and the nascent cooperation of black and white populists in the 1890s, because of the race-baiting opportunism of political demagogues such as Benjamin ("Pitchfork Ben") Tillman and Coleman ("Cole") Blease of South Carolina, Tom Watson of Georgia, and James K. Vardaman and Theodore Bilbo of Mississippi, and because of the political helplessness of the newly disfranchised African Americans and the acquiescence of the North and the West, with their own growing ethnic and racial intolerance. As a result of the changes in the Progressive Era, white southerners expanded segregation from simply a legal code to a hallowed symbol of white supremacy and of the "southern way of life."

With the blacks, and not a few poor whites, excluded, southern reformers worked to improve conditions for the majority of whites in the South through expanded education and health care (particularly efforts to eliminate hookworm and pellagra), prohibition of alcohol, limitation of child labor, abolition of the convict lease system of labor, better resource conservation management and flood control measures, and the establishment of some government regulation of railroads and other large corporations. Southern progressives obtained their primary support from the urban middle class, including editors and other business and professional people who emphasized a "new South" philosophy of increased industrialization and reduced economic dependence on cotton, and other agricultural commodities.

But the nature of the South led to differences in the methods and programs of southern progressives. Because of the one-party dominance of the region, reformers worked solely within the Democratic party. To appeal to the localism and evangelistic Protestantism of rural southern whites, the progressives organized carefully planned open-air "tent meetings" to generate enthusiasm and educate the public about the need for new programs involving private organizations (such as the Rockefeller Foundation) or governmental intervention and increased taxation. In addition, southern reformers reflected progressives' faith in science and efficiency. The Southern Sociological Congress, organized in 1912 to serve as a regional focus for "social uplift forces in the South," promised to augment "pew religion" with the "'do religion' of twentieth-century efficiency."

Revivalistic reform, combined with scientific studies by charitable and reform organizations and the political efforts of progressive governors such as Hoke Smith of Georgia, Napoleon Bonaparte Broward of Florida, and James S. Hogg of Texas (who, as activist reform governor in Austin from 1891 to 1895, had been a forerunner of progressivism), helped to obtain considerable reform legislation in southern states. They ran into greater impediments in implementing these reforms. Laws compelling school attendance and the consolidation of rural schools into regional ones confronted considerable local opposition; so did many public health statutes. Business interests undermined much of the regulatory legislation. Laws outlawing child labor were largely ignored in the mills. Consequently, Alexander McKelway, a North Carolina minister and editor who became the most effective political strategist of the National Child Labor Committee, later helped to convert President Woodrow Wilson to supporting proposals for a national child labor law.

Prohibition (outlawing the manufacture and sale of alcoholic beverages) was an integral, if divisive, part of southern progressivism. Supported particularly by the Methodist and Baptist churches, the prohibition movement was portrayed as a moral issue, as a reaffirmation of particularly Protestant values. Some middle-class progressives endorsed it for various reasons: sobriety, family stability, social order, or economic efficiency. Through "local option" laws, which enabled local districts and counties to abolish bars and saloons, two-thirds of the counties (primarily rural ones) in the former Confederate states had become "dry" by 1907. Momentum for statewide prohibition began in the first decade of the twentieth century under the leadership of the militant Anti-Saloon League. Governor Hoke Smith linked progressivism and prohibition in Georgia, which adopted it in 1907. The same combination won in Alabama and Tennessee. But in Texas, although the crusade against liquor became synonymous with progressivism, it disrupted the Democratic party in the process and was rejected in a referendum in 1911. In Virginia, although the progressives allied with the dry forces, the reformers never made prohibition one of their main goals; nevertheless, it was adopted in 1914. Later the South voted disproportionately in favor of national prohibition under the Eighteenth Amendment, which went into effect in 1920.

Western progressivism took on a special cast because of the nature of the West. The railroads and extractive industries, which had initially been seen as vital to the economic growth of the region, came to be viewed as privileged and exploitative and in need of regulation in the larger public interest. Progressivism was also tied closely to the growing conservation movement for the protection or efficient use of natural resources. The importance of water in semiarid regions led to western progressive projects for irrigation and land reclamation.

In the West, as in the South, progressives deplored absentee corporate ownership of raw materials and the concentration of economic and political power in the urban, industrial North. Western states pioneered in the use of the initiative and the referendum (measures by which voters could initiate legislation or vote on proposed or existing laws) to implement political and economic reforms often designed to limit the influence of the railroads, private utilities, lumber and mining companies, and other corporations, particularly those controlled by eastern entrepreneurs or financiers. In 1903, Oregon became one of the leaders in the use of the initiative and the referendum, especially under progressive Democratic Governor George Chamberlain. Progressives came to power in California in 1910 with the election of insurgent Republican Governor Hiram Johnson, a crusading prosecutor from San Francisco. The progressive program there as elsewhere was antirailroad and anticorruption. In California it was directed particularly against the Southern Pacific Railroad, its domination of the legislature and local communities, and the special privileges that they extended to it. Initially the political base had been in southern California's middle-and upper-class business and professional groups. But by 1914 it had begun to shift to urban ethnic and labor groups, especially in the northern part of the state. A similar coalition of labor and farm organizations and urban reformers supported the progressive reform movement in Washington state, which elected Miles Poindexter to the U.S. Senate.

Women's suffrage was an important part of western progressivism (of all the regions, the South resisted it the most for cultural, racial, and political reasons). The West had a tradition of female enfranchisement as one way of encouraging women to immigrate to the sparsely settled and disproportionately male society on the frontier. Later it was endorsed by populist and then progressive reformers. Following Wyoming (1869) and Colorado, Idaho, and Utah in the 1890s, women suffragists won the vote at the city and state levels in Washington, California, Oregon, Arizona, and Kansas between 1907 and 1912.

The adoption of women's suffrage and other direct-democracy measures in the West occurred in a region in which the rights and opportunities of Hispanic and nonwhite minorities (Chinese, Japanese, and native American Indians) had been sharply restricted. The minority status of the Spanish-speaking people in the West and Southwest was apparent by 1900 because of the influx of new peoples and new industries replacing the old agrarian and pastoral pursuits. The Mexican-American community, while strong in its sense of familial identity and contributing in numerous ways—economic, social, cultural—to the larger society, remained divided by generational and local regionalism, and this facilitated the subordination of the Hispanics to the larger Anglo society. Registrars in the West and Southwest kept Hispanics from voting in many of the same ways that were used against African Americans in the South. Similarly, members of the Chinese and Japanese communities on the Pacific coast were segregated and restricted economically and politically. Immigration from China and Japan was curtailed, and Asian immigrants were prohibited from becoming U.S. citizens.* California and several other western states adopted laws limiting the right of Asian immigrants to own (1913) or even lease (1920) farmland, actions upheld by the Supreme Court of the United States in 1923.†

In regard to Native Americans, the majority of whom lived in the West, by the 1890s, Congress had abolished communal landholdings

---

*This prohibition had its roots in racial prejudice, cultural antagonism, and economic rivalry; legally, it resulted from a 1911 directive of the Bureau of Immigration and Naturalization based on an amendment to the 1870 naturalization law, which provided that only free whites and aliens of "African descent or African nativity" could apply for U.S. citizenship. After 1911, most East Asians who applied for citizenship were refused.

†The western states used the category of "aliens ineligible for citizenship" to establish local laws restricting certain people (in this case Asians) from acquiring or transferring real estate. The Supreme Court held that this did not violate the equal protection clause of the Fourteenth Amendment because it affected all persons placed by law in a special classification for a reasonable purpose.

and substituted individual allotments of land. In 1898 it abolished the tribal governments altogether and replaced them with superintendents from the Bureau of Indian Affairs. When whites became interested in Indian lands, they tried to dispossess the Indians by lowering them to a status similar to landless blacks in the South. As agriculture, timbering, and subsurface extraction of oil and minerals expanded, more Indians lost their lands and were forced to become sharecroppers or wage laborers. Their local subsistence economies were destroyed, and their standard of living declined even further as they entered the cash economy. In 1907, after an influx of white settlers, Oklahoma, the former Indian Territory, was admitted as a state. Although some acculturated Indians gained financially, many traditionalists lost control of their lands to whites through legal proceedings that declared them "incompetent" or through graft or intimidation. While many traditionalist Indians remained isolated in rural, economically marginal communities, their government-appointed "guardians" or white settlers reaped bonanzas from the discoveries of rich oil and gas fields in Oklahoma in the mid-1920s. It was not until the 1930s that the federal government admitted that coercive assimilation was a failure and reversed its policy.

In the highly urbanized states of the northeast and north central regions, progressivism took on an urban cast in its concern for the improvement of the cities. Despite such distinctive variations, progressivism was nationwide in scope, the first general national coalition of reform movements since abolitionism, temperance, women's rights, and a host of other issues fueled the ferment of the Jacksonian era.

The Development of Nationwide Reform

In the late nineteenth century two earlier sectional movements—mugwumpism and populism—had heralded the need for reform. The mugwumps, a group of upper-middle-class businessmen and professionals in the Northeast, had bolted from the Republican party in the 1880s over issues of partisanship and corruption. Although critics satirized them as indecisive fence sitters—with their mugs on one side and their wumps on the other—the mugwumps were more generally portrayed as independent civic reformers. Many of the good-government measures of the Progressive Era flowed from the mugwumps' advocacy of nonpartisanship, civil service, and independent voting.

Populism emerged from another side of society, the financially squeezed, discontented dirt farmers of the South and the Midwest. By the 1890s it had become a potent agrarian movement attacking high tariffs, deflationary currency, trusts, railroads, and big banks. The Populist party merged with the Democrats in William Jennings Bryan's unsuccessful bid for the presidency in 1896. Few populists became progressives, however. Indeed, most of the leaders of progressivism had been unsympathetic or actively hostile to populism. Nevertheless, agrarians from the South and the West, former populists as well as nonpopulists, later provided an important element in the progressive coalition. They supplied votes and issues such as tariff reduction, business reform, rural credits, and the income tax. As William Allen White put it, the progressives had "caught the Populists in swimming and stole all of their clothing except the frayed underdrawers of free silver."

Narrower movements also paved the way for progressivism. The social justice movement had its antecedents among the settlement house founders, social gospel clergy, labor leaders, and socialists of the late nineteenth century. Business regulation had been advocated by agrarians, shippers, some social scientists, and reformer-writers like Bellamy and George. Budding movements against vice, obscenity, alcohol, and immigration and against political participation by blacks and alien immigrants laid the foundations for the larger social control movement to follow. A new urban middle class, produced by the increasingly mass production and service-oriented economy, came to believe that rationality, efficient administration, and manipulation of the environment could be applied to public affairs as well as to business.

It took a cataclysmic event like the depression of the 1890s to disrupt society sufficiently so that reformers could begin to forge the separate elements of discontent left from previous decades into the broad-based nationwide movement known as progressivism. Formerly divided along regional, ethnic, or class lines, many disaffected groups were temporarily pulled together by local reformers. Progressive political leaders, especially on the local level, minimized differences among their constituents by stressing their common position as "exploited" consumers. "The people," as the reformers called them, were robbed by "selfish interests" in business and politics. The depression made people conscious of their role as consumers. It helped reformers expose the corporate arrogance by which monopolies like the privately owned gas and electric utilities and streetcar companies maintained or increased rates during the economic downturn without consequent improvements in service. Progressives showed that as local governments raised taxes to meet the higher costs resulting from massive unemployment, wealthy individuals and corporations often dodged taxes through favoritism purchased from governmental officials. Hard times and the exposure of exploitation led many consumers to support radical measures such as progressive taxation, recall of public officials, and public ownership of utilities and streetcar lines. Angered consumers and urban reformers took over some of the utilities and established a form of municipal socialism in more than 100 cities.

When the depression ended and prosperity began to return in the late 1890s, the reform movement continued. Although many of the temporary consumer alliances split apart, the pressure for reform was sustained among many consumers in middle- and lower-income groups by the new problem of inflation. The period was primarily one of economic growth, and Americans defined themselves less as exploited consumers and more as members of job-oriented groups. The identification of Americans with broad national functional groups—for example, the machinists' union, the engineers' association, the National Organization of Settlement House Workers, the National Association of Manufacturers—developed rapidly in the late nineteenth century as urbanization and industrialization uprooted people and replaced small-town loyalties with more segmented economic affiliations.

During the Progressive Era these production-oriented groups, national in scope and organization, continued to increase in number, size, and influence. They lobbied actively to promote their own interests, often identifying these with the public interest. Thus reform activity, which had begun on the local level to mobilize large numbers of people as consumers during the depression, moved during the subsequent period of economic growth to shifting alliances of organized, producer-oriented interest groups working especially on the state and national levels to protect their own interests. This resulted in the rise of a national political order dominated by an unprecedented variety of producer-oriented pressure groups vying for public protection and favor. Soon Washington was dotted with the headquarters of these groups: the Farmers Union, founded in 1902; the International Brotherhood of Teamsters, 1903; the American Federation of Teachers, 1905; the American Institute of Chemical Engineers, 1908; the United States Chamber of Commerce, 1912; and scores of others. But while these job-oriented interest groups helped to give substance to many of the Progressive Era's reforms, they were not responsible for the fervor or the breadth of progressivism.

The spirit of moral indignation and the sense of idealistic purpose came in part from the "muckrakers." Like later investigative journalists, these reporters exposed dishonesty, greed, corruption throughout American society and helped rouse Americans, especially middle-class readers of the muckraking magazines, to action for reform. The literature of exposure went back to Thomas Nast's cartoons and the press assault on the Tweed Ring in New York in the 1870s and Henry Demarest Lloyd's attack on Standard Oil in the 1890s. But in the first decade of the twentieth century, exposure journalism reached an unprecedented scale. In city after city the muckrakers demonstrated the corrupt interrelationships of business and political machines. They showed the American public that business corrupted politics, not merely in a few cities but throughout the nation.

The muckrakers alerted citizens to the national scope of political corruption. Beginning in 1902 with a series in *McClure's Magazine*, Lincoln Steffens documented municipal corruption linked to business interests in Saint Louis, Minneapolis, and a dozen other cities. His findings were republished as *Shame of the Cities* in 1904. In addition to municipal graft, reporters discovered gouging by oil companies and the railroads, poison dispensed by patent medicine companies, and fraud in high finance. Muckraker Ray Stannard Baker mused forty years later:

> I think I can understand now why these exposure articles took such a hold upon the American people. It was because the country, for years, had been swept by the agitation of soap-box orators, prophets crying in the wilderness, and political campaigns based upon charges of corruption and privilege which everyone believed or suspected had some basis of truth, but which were largely unsubstantiated.

The muckrakers provided the facts to substantiate these accusations. However, by 1906, when the exposure movement reached its peak, some reporters were ignoring the need for careful documentation.

Increasing stress on sensationalism weakened the muckrakers' reputation. Conservatives and even many progressives condemned them, and in 1906, President Roosevelt denounced the more sensationalistic journalists by comparing them with the man in Bunyan's *Pilgrim's Progress* who was so busy raking the filth from the floor that he neglected the beauty of the world. By 1912 the muckraking era had passed, terminated by hostile business, which withheld credit and advertising, and by public fatigue. Yet investigative journalism had done much to sustain and direct the reform impulse and, by demonstrating the national scope of corruption between business and politics, had helped to create the spirit of indignation necessary for a broad reform movement in favor of honesty, democracy, and accountability in American institutions.

Voluntarism as a Middle Way

Progressives and conservatives did not always turn directly to government to adjust institutions or gain control over the powerful forces of industrialism. Concerned with establishing the antecedents of the liberal activist state, many historians have oversimplified progressives' positions regarding the expansion of governmental power. Subsequent political figures like Franklin D. Roosevelt, seeking to legitimize the New Deal through historical continuity, also contributed to the conception of progressivism as a major step toward the welfare state. But the traditional focus on the progressives' proposals to expand the powers of government to deal with new problems, though partially warranted, distorts the greater complexity of the progressives. They generally acted first through private associations and saw voluntary cooperative effort as an essential part of the progressive impulse. This area is generally ignored by historians, who concentrate on advocates of governmental intervention like Roosevelt and Herbert Croly.

Traditional interpretations often neglect progressives like Jane Addams and Oswald Garrison Villard, who remained deeply suspicious of giving too much power to the government. Indeed, many progressives continued to fear that business would corrupt politics and bureaucracy as well and that big government under the control of big business would be a threat to American democracy. Large numbers of progressives, and other interventionists, believed primarily in collective action in the private sector as a means of directing change. "Our national idea is not a powerful state, famed and feared for bluster and appetite," the muckraker David Graham Phillips asserted in 1905, "but manhood and womanhood, a citizenship ever wiser and stronger and more civilized—alert, enlightened, self-reliant, free."

Voluntarism offered a device that could mediate between social demands and the American traditions of individual autonomy, privatism, and cooperative groups. Progressives sought to use voluntary associations as effective instruments of reform. To do that, they patterned their organizations to some degree after the corporation, with boards of directors, expert administrators, hierarchical chains of command, and multiple branches and field offices. Through carefully defined goals, precise rules and regulations, and adequate coordination, such organizations could function effectively on a national scale. Progressives believed that through intelligence, will, and proper organization and techniques they could manipulate society and the environment for the betterment of all.

The settlement house movement typified that optimistic belief. "Life in the Settlement discovers above all what has been called 'the extraordinary pliability of human nature,'" said Jane Addams, the founder of Hull House in Chicago, "and it seems impossible to set any bounds to the moral capabilities which might unfold under ideal civic and educational conditions." At Hull House and at other settlements in Boston, New York, and elsewhere, reformers established private, voluntary institutions to give advice, education, and care to the immigrant poor in the ghettos. The profession of social work, an outgrowth of the settlement house movement, departed from the nineteenth-century reform emphasis on saving individuals. It focused instead on changing the environment, which was seen as responsible for the plight of both the individual and the family.

The women's consumer movement also demonstrated the role of cooperative action in the private sector to ameliorate conditions. The National Consumers' League, organized in 1899, grew out of an effort by upper- and middle-class New York City women and a number of clergymen to improve the working conditions of saleswomen in the city's department stores and the women who toiled in the garment factories and sweatshops. The league, which within a decade had twenty-five chapters in nearly a dozen states, attempted to organize the power of women as consumers to improve working conditions for women and children. According to Florence Kelley, the head of the league, organized consumerism—through selective purchasing and, when necessary, boycotts—could protect both the workers and the consumers from exploitation. Increasingly, however, it was the mass production companies and advertising agencies that manipulated consumer tastes and habits. The National Consumers' League turned to programs of education and lobbying to ensure passage and enforcement of legislation regulating the wages, hours, and working conditions of women and children, a significant part of the social justice movement.

Like settlement house workers, many physicians encouraged efforts to improve the environment and the standard of living. Together with social workers they played leading roles in a number of reform movements. They participated prominently in the campaign against tuberculosis, the "white plague," which was a major killer, especially in tenement districts. The antituberculosis campaign offers a specific model of the organized reform movements of the Progressive Era. When medical researchers identified the tuberculosis bacillus and learned that, though communicable, it was not hereditary (as people had believed for years), reformers set out to educate the public in the proper treatment of the disease and to establish sanitary measures to combat its spread. To do so, they had to overcome a tradition that considered tuberculosis, like venereal disease, a forbidden subject. Through local and state antituberculosis societies and, after 1904, the National Tuberculosis Association, the reformers educated other physicians and the public in the new findings, helped to discourage public acceptance of spitting (spittoons began to disappear), began registering cases of TB, and increased the number of public sanitariums. Within fifteen years the mortality rate from tuberculosis had dropped 30 percent as a result of both the antituberculosis crusade and a higher standard of living. The movement's success, like that of many other reform movements, encouraged progressives to believe that they could manipulate society and the environment in beneficial ways and curtail many of the hazards of urban, industrial society.

During the Progressive Era the general concern with public issues led many professionals—physicians, lawyers, educators, and others—to examine the operation and organization of their professions in an attempt to gauge their responsiveness both to society's interests and to their own needs for standards and authority. For example, by the turn of the century the emergence of the new corporate law firms had transformed the legal profession. Small-town and country lawyers still constituted the majority of the practitioners of law, with the new immigrant solo practitioners at the bottom level in terms of income and prestige. Desiring cohesion and control within such a divided profession, prominent lawyers established bar associations in every state and major city and sought to standardize training and licensing requirements. To provide at least some legal services to the urban poor, attorneys and other reformers founded more than forty legal aid societies in the first two decades of the century.

Another important effort to defend the profession against charges that it was dominated by the corporate interests came from the professors at the law schools that were replacing the old system of "reading law" in the offices of practicing attorneys. Legal scholars like Roscoe Pound, Felix Frankfurter, and Thomas Reed Powell portrayed themselves as keepers of the professional conscience and as neutral social scientists who could evaluate data and produce legal solutions to social problems. In their sociological jurisprudence (which stressed social context and not just legal precedent), the law could be used as an instrument of social engineering and progressive reform in the public interest.

Engineers also transformed their conservative group of professional associations during the Progressive Era. Traditionally, the societies for civil, mechanical, electrical, and mining engineers had served as gentlemen's clubs for elite engineer-entrepreneurs like the Roeblings, who built the Brooklyn Bridge. They ignored the large numbers of engineer-technicians and showed virtually no interest in public policy. Consequently, progressives charged them with shirking their social responsibilities, noting especially their failure to do anything about the problem of air pollution in the cities, which had become even more serious after the massive switch to soft coal following the anthracite strike of 1902. Under pressure, the engineering societies abandoned their traditional laissez-faire attitude and began to establish codes and standards for boilers, electrical generators, and other devices. "The golden rule will be put in practice through the slide rule," the president of the American Society of Mechanical Engineers optimistically predicted in 1912.

Converting from elite clubs to mass membership bodies, the engineering societies democratized their organizations. By the end of the Progressive Era they included a majority of the engineers in America. By linking citizens living in different areas through their common occupational roles, the engineering societies, though still led by elites, took on new roles as modern functional associations.

Conservatives as well as progressives established professionally directed organizations in the private sector to help to guide change in appropriate directions. Andrew Carnegie and John D. Rockefeller, for example, created giant philanthropic foundations to work for the improvement of humankind. In the process they transformed the nature of philanthropy and produced a truly unique American contribution to modern social organization: the giant philanthropic foundation, a large autonomous body that used private wealth for public purposes. Andrew Carnegie, whose concept of the stewardship of wealth led him to consider it a disgrace to die wealthy, gave more than $330 million to funds for education, peace, pensions, libraries, and heroism. The largest, the Carnegie Corporation of New York, was established in 1911 with a grant of $135 million. Two years later John D. Rockefeller created the Rockefeller Foundation with a grant of $242 million "to promote the well-being of mankind throughout the world." Rockefeller's philanthropies, which totaled nearly $500 million, encouraged medical research, education, and a major program to combat hookworm, malaria, pellagra, tuberculosis, and other diseases in the rural South. As the United States lagged behind Europe in accepting the idea of a welfare state, philanthropists consciously created alternative private mechanisms for social improvement to help to deter the governmental planning of the socialistic state they feared. In so doing, they created the largest foundations the world had ever seen.

In the field of labor relations, conservative interventionists also established a private-sector mechanism for encouraging cooperation among contending groups. The National Civic Federation (NCF), organized in 1900, included representatives of the new supercorporations, labor leaders like Samuel Gompers, and public representatives such as ex-president Grover Cleveland. Opposed to both laissez-faire and governmental ownership and control, the NCF advocated a number of moderate social reforms, such as workers' compensation. It played an important role in educating many business people, professionals, labor leaders, journalists, and officials on the need for cooperation instead of conflict between management and labor.

The National Civic Federation was only one of many private voluntary associations through which interventionists—progressive and conservative—sought to reorient society, educate the public to new attitudes and modes of behavior, and provide mechanisms for managing relations in a new enlightened manner. It was part of the organizational revolution of the time, spurred by the belief in the ability of people to apply scientific knowledge to improve their environment and their lives. The list of organizations of this type founded in the Progressive Era includes chambers of commerce, community chests, the Boy Scouts of America, and the Institute for Government Research (now the Brookings Institution), a private association set up to promote efficiency and economy in government, as well as the Women's International League for Peace and Freedom, the American Civil Liberties Union, and hundreds of other groups. In this manner interventionists

employed cooperative effort to guide the direction of change and progress in industrial America.

Reform in the Cities

Despite the efforts of progressives in the private sector, it was in the
political arena that progressivism emerged as a most clearly identifiable
movement. There progressive reformers led a significant attempt to
oust incumbent politicians and restructure the political system to make
it more efficient and capable of managing the conflicting needs of
various groups while upholding the ideal of a single public interest for
the entire community. This difficult task began in the cities.

The depression of the 1890s struck the cities especially severely.
Local revenues plummeted and many urban social services failed to
meet the needs of millions of jobless residents. Many reformers blamed
the urban crisis on corrupt, inefficient boss government. Swayed by
nativist agrarian prejudices, many Americans were quick to view the
urban situation in terms of good and evil. "Sometimes, I think they'se
poison in th' life in a big city" the political satirist Peter Finley Dunne
had Mr. Dooley say. "The flowers won't grow there."

Critics often ignored the difficulties of controlling urban growth
and minimized the informal social services provided by the political
machines. Instead, they emphasized the "corruptible vote of the city."
This consisted of millions of immigrants, many of them recent arrivals
who were permitted to vote as soon as they officially declared their
intention of becoming American citizens. Reformers considered new-
stock residents ignorant of American ways and easily misled by dema-
gogic bosses. "Saloons and gambling houses and brothels," one Baltimore reformer charged, "are the nurseries of [urban] statesmen."

In the depression of the 1890s, progressives brought together the
separate elements of discontent from previous decades into a nationwide urban reform movement. Hard times led many people who had
formerly been separated by class or ethnic differences to unite behind
particular political leaders because of their common interests as "exploited" consumers. In addition, numerous citizens' and taxpayers'
associations demanded tax reduction through honest and efficient government. Reformers, often uniting upper- and middle-income old-stock
residents from the suburban wards with urban immigrant voters, led
this protest beyond mere tax cutting or economizing into a broader
movement for both structural reform and policy changes in the nation's
cities. The first step was to win control of city hall. This was done by
exposing municipal corruption, personal graft, protection peddling,
contract padding, and collusion between city officials and utilities,

streetcar companies, and other firms doing business with the city. Progressive mayors won office in New York, Chicago, Baltimore, and other cities and began reform programs.

While they controlled city hall, progressive reformers sought to end forever the potential for "machine politics" by restructuring municipal government. The structural reforms of the good-government movement drew on many of the administrative techniques used by business corporations, as suggested by the National Municipal League's model program, developed in 1894. Although they emphasized efficiency, honesty, and democracy, reformers often sought to take control of city government away from the alliance of companies doing business with the city and the representatives of lower-income immigrant groups who controlled the political machines. To lodge power in their own hands, reformers revised city charters to end the decentralized system in which each ward elected representatives to the city council. Reformers replaced this system with a strong mayor, city councils, and boards of education elected by the city as a whole. Urban reformers also expanded the use of appointed administrators and career civil servants in city hall and helped to bring modern methods of accounting and management to city government.

On a hot summer night in 1900, a giant tidal wave created by a hurricane in the Gulf of Mexico smashed down on the port city of Galveston, Texas. The flood waters killed one out of every six people in the city. When the municipal government proved unable to respond to the disaster, leading citizens replaced it with a special commission in which each commissioner headed a particular city department. So effective was the city commission plan of government that Galveston's ad hoc response to crisis was adopted in Houston, Des Moines, and a number of other cities. It was soon refined by the city manager plan, in which a single trained administrator, appointed by the city council, exercised all administrative authority. First adopted in Staunton, Virginia, in 1908, the city manager plan gained acceptance after Dayton, Ohio, adopted it in 1914. The idea of centralized planning by a unified board and efficient administration by a chief executive officer came directly from the corporate model. Indeed, the president of the National Cash Register Company, who helped establish the city manager system in Dayton, described the ideal city as "a great business enterprise whose stockholders are the people." Hundreds of small and medium-sized cities, especially in the South and the Midwest, adopted the new forms of city government during the Progressive Era.

It took more than efficiency to meet urban problems. "The challenge of the city," Cleveland reformer Frederic C. Howe explained in 1906, "has become one of decent human existence." Some reform mayors, such as Hazen Pingree of Detroit and Samuel ("Golden Rule") Jones in Toledo, tried to go beyond good government and structural reform to broad social programs that they hoped would retain the allegiance of the majority of urban voters, especially the working classes. Speaking for "the people" as consumers, they battled "the interests," particularly the privately owned utilities and transit companies, seeking reduced rates and improved services. They supported the construction of public parks, playgrounds, schools, and municipal hospitals to provide a better standard of living. They tried to provide some work relief during the depression. Pressed by angry taxpayers, they tried to redistribute the tax burden more equitably by reducing tax evasion. Bowing to indignant consumers, mayors and councils in more than 100 cities established municipally owned gas and water companies and in some cities public electric companies and city-owned transit companies as well.

Thousands of people joined in crusades for urban reform during the Progressive Era; yet for all their effort, they left a divided legacy. Reformers won elections and produced new forms of city government that consolidated upper- and middle-class rule. But although they captured city hall, they failed to reduce taxes, which increased at unprecedented rates during the period. Local governments met most of their increasing expenses through hikes in the general property tax (with the result that property taxes soared much more rapidly than property values). Property taxes also provided half of state government revenue at the turn of the century, but the statehouses turned more and more to a variety of new sources of revenue for their expanding services — motor vehicle registration fees, liquor licenses, sales and excise taxes, public utilities franchise taxes, inheritance taxes, and, beginning in Wisconsin in 1911, individual and corporate income taxes. These taxes were aimed at raising revenue, not redistributing it.

Rising municipal costs resulted less from inefficiency and waste than from inflation and the long-term trend of expanding urban services. Indeed, the municipally owned utilities slowed cost-of-living increases by keeping their rates lower than those of private utilities. They were one of the reformers' most lasting and most radical legacies, surviving various changes in government. Especially in the metropolises, the old bosses maintained or quickly regained power. For virtually a generation Charles Croker and Charles Murphy of Tammany Hall ran New York City's government. The Republican William Vare dominated Philadelphia, William Crump's Democratic machine presided over Memphis, and the Democratic Pendergast brothers ruled Kansas City.

Although they helped to make the cities cleaner and healthier, on the whole the reformers proved more successful at arousing indignation and protest than at maintaining effective government and substantially ameliorating urban problems. Many of the difficulties of the cities persisted, but the progressives and others had established an agenda of municipal reform—more efficient government, nonpartisan social services, zoning, planning, public ownership of some essential services, and improved standards of health and housing—that would influence urban politics for the next half century.

Progressivism in the States

"Whenever we try to do anything, we run up against the charter," the reform mayor of Schenectady complained. "It is an oak charter, fixed and immovable." Since the charters that spelled out the cities' powers were granted by the states, reformers soon discovered that they needed to capture the state governments to achieve their goals. Furthermore, the states set the requirements for suffrage, regulated business and labor conditions, and legislated to enforce morality. When they looked into the statehouse, reformers found as much corruption and intransigence as they had found in city hall. Muckrakers and progressive politicians exposed alliances between powerful business interests—especially the railroads—and state party bosses, who represented the big-city political machines or rural county courthouse rings and who actually ran the state governments.

Reform

Attacking collusion among the political bosses and the "special interests," progressive reformers overwhelmed many state machines in the first decade of the century and captured dozens of governorships. Robert La Follette, a small-town lawyer and former congressman, led the movement in Wisconsin. During his three terms as governor "Battling Bob" modernized the state government through what came to be known as the "Wisconsin idea." This state reform program included direct party primaries, an improved civil service, a graduated state income tax, a corrupt-practices act prohibiting direct corporate contributions to political parties, labor legislation, and a strengthened railroad regulatory commission. Other Republican reformers in the Midwest, such as Albert Cummins of Iowa, copied La Follette's program.

In the South the revolt occurred within the Democratic party. Progressives like James Vardaman of Mississippi and Hoke Smith of Georgia led white farmers against alliances of wealthy, conservative Democrats (who were called Bourbons), the railroads, timber companies, and other large corporations. Before adopting much of the Wisconsin idea, southern progressives disfranchised black voters, who they claimed were a source of Bourbon Democratic support. Using literacy tests, grandfather clauses, and sometimes terrorism, they purged blacks from the rolls. In Louisiana, for example, the number of registered black voters dropped from 130,000 in 1896 to 1,000 in 1904. Once in power, the insurgents adopted many of La Follette's programs. In addition, prohibition of alcohol was a strong component of southern progressivism, with its emphasis on rural Protestant morality and its antipathy toward the multiethnic, economically powerful urban Northeast.

The movement for progressivism in the states came late to the Northeast and the Far West. In the East it was largely a continuation of the urban reform movement, but many of La Follette's measures were also adopted. After exposing abuses in the life insurance field, the attorney Charles Evans Hughes became the progressive Republican governor of New York in 1906. He established stricter supervision of insurance companies and instituted a state public service commission to regulate utilities. Woodrow Wilson, president of Princeton University, won the governorship of New Jersey on the Democratic ticket in 1910 and began a program of progressive reforms similar to the Wisconsin idea. On the West Coast, attorney Hiram Johnson campaigned against the dominant position of the Southern Pacific Railroad and entered the governor's mansion in 1911 with a slate of reforms. Oregon, which had adopted the first maximum-hour law for women workers, elected the insurgent Republican William U'Ren to the governorship; he introduced a number of reform bills. Not since the burst of activity that had occurred in the 1830s had so many state governments been so strongly committed to reform.

Once in control of state governments, progressives in every region began far-reaching reforms by changing both electoral procedures and the scope of the electorate. Progressives wanted to create a political process that would break up the coalition between government and business and would make government responsive to the people and the new pressure groups. Progressives and others believed the problem was that the party system was hierarchical, dominated by bosses at the top. Many of the progressive political reforms were based on the idea that ways must be found to remove the bosses or limit their power. Through direct primaries the progressives took the nominating procedure away from party bosses, who had controlled it through their grip on local nominating conventions. They also sought to reduce the voting base of the machines. In the South this meant disfranchising blacks. In the North it meant eliminating alien voters through increased residency requirements, thereby restricting suffrage to native-born or fully naturalized citizens. Except in the South, which resisted vehemently in part because it might lead to enfranchisement of blacks, progressivism came to mean expanding the vote by including women, whose ballots were expected to aid the reform movement.

Having "purged" the electorate, progressives enacted a number of direct-democracy measures designed to increase the power of the remaining voters by allowing them to override legislators. By means of petitions voters could introduce legislation through the initiative, repeal legislation through the referendum, and call for a vote to remove elected officials through the recall process. Progressives also expanded home rule for the cities and, in state governments, helped to centralize administrative responsibility and modernize the budgetary process. Many of the progressive governors moved to the U.S. Senate near the end of the first decade of the century. But before they left for Washington, they helped reform groups to pass significant social and economic legislation in their states.

As a means of curtailing favoritism toward special interests and mediating conflicts among competing interest groups, most progressives and many conservative interventionists put their faith in the independent regulatory commission. Like the city managers, the commissioners were supposed to remove politics and special deals from administration and use the power of government to ensure that the economic system worked in the public interest. The regulatory commission was seen as a moderate alternative to both an unrestricted marketplace and government ownership and operation. Unfortunately, however, progressive legislators provided little guidance for the regulatory commissions on how to determine the public interest.

Not surprisingly, the legacy of the state regulatory commissions was ambiguous. For example, the railroad commission found itself confronting the contending interests of carriers and shippers rather than the public interests. The commissioners tried to derive compromises that were satisfactory to the major parties, that is, the railroads and the shippers. Citizens who had hoped that the railroad and other commissions would find that rates were inflated and would sharply reduce transportation costs and consumer prices were disappointed. They claimed, with much justification, that the commissions had become responsive to the interests of the industries they were supposed to regulate.

The Wisconsin Railroad Commission demonstrated the complexity of the situation. Created in 1905 as part of La Follette's campaign against "the interests," the commission failed to find the widespread injustices that the reformers claimed existed. By 1910, having dropped all pretense of battling the railroads, which originally opposed its creation, the commission sought instead what it called fair or "scientific" rates, a moderate program of piecemeal rate adjustments based on compromise. The regulatory commission worked primarily to reduce open conflict and remove the issue of railroad rates from popular politics. Two months before the first commissioners took office, the editor of the *Wisconsin State Journal* predicted such a result:

> The commission once in operation, its chief value will be in abating discontent. It is doubtful if the rank and file of us will know, by any marked reduction in prices of commodities, that anything has happened. But the distrust and suspicion born of secrecy and unqualified power will be relieved, for there is appeal to the commission.

As the editor prophesied, the state regulatory commissions proved a victory more for orderly management and adjustment to the new industrial system than for consumer interests, becoming one of the new mechanisms for managing change in twentieth-century society.

Under pressure from various private interventionist groups and from progressive governors and legislators, many states also adopted measures to reduce the harshness of industrial work. Workers' compensation was the most widespread of these reforms. Both workers and employers argued against the common-law assumption that employees willingly took on the risks of work and could collect compensation for accidents only if they could prove the employer negligent. Because of this assumption, most victims had received nothing while a few particularly grisly cases had won extremely high settlements. Maryland adopted the first workers' compensation law in the United States in 1902, and by 1916 most other states had adopted employer liability and workers' compensation laws. Workers' compensation, with its predictable but limited awards, conformed to the desire of conservative and most progressive interventionists for systematic and moderate solutions to social problems.

Social justice progressives and their organizations were less successful at obtaining and enforcing other legislation to assist industrial workers. The National Consumers' League led the drive for maximum hour and minimum wage legislation modeled on that of Australia and New Zealand. American judges proved willing to uphold such laws only as relating to women workers. They were impressed by arguments made by the league's attorney, Louis D. Brandeis, in *Muller* v. *Oregon* (1908) that long hours were dangerous to women's health and morality and hence to the future of society. Nearly two-thirds of the states adopted maximum hour laws, and a dozen states enacted minimum wage protection for women. In a more difficult battle the National Child Labor Committee obtained laws in most northern and western states prohibiting the employment of children under 14, but it failed to convince the legislators of southern states. On the whole, state labor legislation, though improved, left much of the progressive agenda unfulfilled. Even where progressives and their allies succeeded in obtaining satisfactory legislation, they often failed to secure provisions or appropriations for adequate enforcement.

Social Control

Under pressure from a variety of citizens' groups, the states also increased their powers of social control during the Progressive Era. Rising rates of violent crime, combined with the period's belief in human
malleability, led to a number of changes in the criminal justice and
penal systems beginning in the 1890s. Reformers attempted to make
these systems more effective and humane.

Many states converted from hanging to electrocution in the belief
that the new technology of the "electric chair" would reduce the
number of mishandled and prolonged executions and that the specter
of death by electric shock would deter potential criminals from com-
mitting capital crimes. For criminals who were convicted but not sent
to prison, the suspended sentence was generally replaced by supervised probation. In addition, legislatures authorized judges to hand
down indeterminate sentences, the ultimate decision on a convict's
release being relegated to newly formed parole boards acting on the
basis of their view of the convict's rehabilitation. Extensive systems of
probation and parole bureaucracies were established to monitor the
behavior of convicted criminals so as to ensure their readjustment to
society.

In addition, through the work of judges like Benjamin Lindsey of
Denver and Julian Mack of Chicago, a new system of juvenile courts
was set up to deal with youthful offenders on the basis of circumstances
and promise as well as guilt or innocence. A recent study of the origins
of the juvenile court and the industrial school for delinquent boys in
Pittsburgh shows that despite their creators' desire to encourage moral
reform and internalization of American middle-class values among the
convicted youths, the managers of the reform school emphasized control rather than reformation. By the end of the first decade of the
century, the institution had become primarily custodial and punitive.
To a great extent, the form of the criminal justice system for both
juveniles and adults in the twentieth century is a product of the Progressive Era.

State and local governments also intervened to regulate individual
freedom to drive the proliferating number of automobiles (from 8,000
in 1900 to 458,000 in 1910 and 8,131,000 in 1920) in a manner that
had not been used for vehicles pulled by animals, since the new motorcars were seen as considerably more dangerous than horses or mules.
Speeding or "scorching" was the first aspect to come under governmental regulation, with New York and Massachusetts adopting laws in
1902 that established absolute speed limits (generally 9 miles per hour
in "enclosed places"). Within four years, two dozen states mandated
registration and license plates for motorcars, and a number began to
require tests and licenses for automobile drivers as well. It was not until

the early 1920s that the modern structure of automobile regulation was well established.

One of the most widespread state attempts to control behavior and instill uniform social standards was the prohibition of the manufacture and sale of alcoholic beverages. Many progressive and conservative interventionists joined in this crusade to improve social conditions by dictating moral standards. In many ways prohibition was a cultural issue, for the saloons and the drinking habits of many urban immigrants appeared alien to nativist, evangelistic Protestant Americans, who were concerned with the transformation of America already under way. Sentiment for prohibition was strongest among evangelical Protestants in the rural areas of the country, especially the South and the West. It seems to have reflected in part these agrarians' antipathy to the growing dominance of the city. However, many members of the urban middle class also reacted to the changing nature of the city by supporting prohibition.

The issue of the "wets" versus the "drys" split the progressives. Many supported prohibition, but many others, especially those who identified with urban, labor, and immigrant elements, fought against it. The eastern-dominated Progressive party convention of 1912 opposed prohibition. So did labor, immigrants, Catholics, and many Episcopalians, Lutherans, and other Protestants.

The Anti-Saloon League, founded in 1893, mobilized the forces of evangelical Protestantism to promote abstinence and sobriety as public ideals and made prohibition a national issue. The league isolated itself from the broad social reform programs of the more established Women's Christian Temperance Union and the third-party tactics of the old Prohibition party. Instead, it focused on the eradication of the working-class saloon and used the new pressure-group politics on the two major parties. The campaign worked. Between 1906 and 1917, twenty-one states, mostly in the South and the West, passed prohibition laws. In 1913 the league obtained from Congress the Webb-Kenyon Act, which banned the transportation of intoxicating beverages into dry states. This was the movement's first major national legislative victory.

Prohibitionists pointed to the increase in the per capita consumption of alcohol, which had risen from 2 gallons per person in 1900 to 2.6 gallons by 1911, as a sign of the increasing danger to American society. They argued that the liquor interests demoralized and corrupted American politics and that alcoholism impeded workers, ruined increasing numbers of families, and filled taxpayer-supported poorhouses and prisons with its victims. When the United States entered World War I, the Anti-Saloon League associated prohibition with winning the war, and in 1917, Congress sent to the states the Eighteenth Amendment, which prohibited the "manufacture, sale, or transportation" of intoxicating liquors for beverage purposes. By the time the

Eighteenth Amendment was ratified in 1919, more than half the American population already lived in areas that had proclaimed themselves dry with the approval of their state legislatures. Prohibition was indeed one of the legacies of the Progressive Era.

Because narcotics addiction was not regarded as so great a threat to society as alcoholism, the movement for narcotics control was not as widespread as that for prohibition. Nevertheless, the narcotics control movement emerged in its modern form during the Progressive Era. The use of narcotics — primarily opium, morphine, and cocaine — increased steadily during the nineteenth century. By the turn of the century the United States had a comparatively large addict population of approximately 250,000 persons. Diluted quantities of opium were widely prescribed by physicians and were included in patent medicines like "Mrs. Winslow's Soothing Syrup" as analgesics for crying babies and others suffering from gastrointestinal illnesses. Cocaine was popular for treating sinusitis and hay fever and as a general tonic. Coca-Cola contained small doses until 1903. Only gradually did the medical profession agree that narcotics were too readily prescribed by physicians, that the inclusion of narcotics in patent medicines should be curtailed. and that addiction was a substantial and harmful possibility.

States began to enact narcotics legislation in the 1890s and continued to do so into the early twentieth century, but by the Progressive Era the major effort to curtail narcotics use had moved to the national level as a result of the interplay of both domestic and foreign forces. Progressive reformers exposed the dangers of improperly labeled patent medicines, many of which contained narcotics. As a result of lobbying by the General Federation of Women's Clubs, the American Medical Association, and the federal government's chief chemist, Dr. Harvey Wiley, the Pure Food and Drug Act, passed in 1906, banned mislabeled or adulterated drugs.

Other Americans became more concerned with the narcotics addicts, especially when addiction was identified with groups that were already feared and repressed. Opium smoking was associated with the Chinese on the West Coast and the use of cocaine with blacks in the South. Southern newspapers printed widespread but unsubstantiated rumors of "cocainomania" among blacks. Many white southerners feared that the euphoric properties of cocaine might stimulate a black rebellion against white society. Thus during the first decade of the century a significant body of opinion grew to support federal action to control the use of narcotics. This movement coincided with efforts to back the Chinese government's attempts at international narcotics control, and in 1909 the United States prohibited the importation of smoking-opium. Influenced also by reformers in the American Medical Association and the American Pharmaceutical Association, Congress adopted the Harrison Narcotics Control Act of 1914, which prohibited the dispensing and taking of narcotics for other than medicinal purposes. The belief that drug use threatened to disrupt American society led authorities to dismiss suggestions for wider toleration.

Prostitution

Perhaps because it seemed to strike simultaneously at society's moral and physical health, prostitution was widely seen as the greatest social evil of the Progressive Era. Certainly no other urban vice was of greater concern to reformers, who paled at such a challenge to Victorian notions of female purity and propriety and who also feared the spread of venereal disease (then mainly gonorrhea and syphilis). The number of prostitutes increased significantly in the late nineteenth century, accompanying the expansive growth of cities, whose populations were more anonymous and less subject to control than those of small towns and rural communities. Brothels and "streetwalkers" existed in virtually every city. In Muncie, Indiana, a small factory city of 11,000 persons, there were nearly 200 prostitutes in some two dozen brothels in the 1890s. By 1910 the Chicago Vice Commission estimated that there were 5,000 full-time and 10,000 occasional prostitutes in Chicago.

In true progressive fashion, journalists "discovered" the social problem, antiprostitution reformers set out to investigate and quantify it, and the public was mobilized in a great crusade to correct the social evil. In 1907, *McClure's Magazine* exposed widespread prostitution in Chicago, claiming that many of the women had been drugged, abducted, and forced into what was called "white slavery." In the resulting hysteria, Congress in 1910 passed the White Slave Traffic Act (the "Mann Act" introduced by Representative James R. Mann of Chicago), outlawing the transportation of women across state lines for immoral purposes. Much of the public wished to believe that prostitutes were innately immoral women or that they were moral women who had been abducted by a commercialized network of "white slave rings." However, although some women were held against their will in the brothels and there were 2,000 convictions in the following eight years, the explanation of the growth of prostitution proved far less simple than the theories of innate depravity or conspiracy suggested.

Investigation by social workers and public health officials indicated what many scientifically minded progressives already believed: that the social problem stemmed from economic and environmental causes. Most surveys indicated that economic need was the common factor. In these reports the majority of prostitutes came from the working class, primarily from among second-generation immigrant women in the eastern cities, from rural women of Anglo-Saxon stock who had recently moved to the cities in the Midwest, and from African-American women in the South. Many had turned to prostitution as a last resort, willing to take the risks of being exploited by pimps or harmed by their customers. As the Chicago Vice Commission concluded in its 1916 report, "Poverty causes prostitution."

In addition to curbing interstate prostitution through the Mann Act, progressives took a variety of approaches to the problem. The American Social Hygiene Association, created in 1914 and financed by John D. Rockefeller, Jr., sponsored medical research on venereal disease, underwrote vice investigations in numerous cities, and wrote model city codes against prostitution. In 1917, with the nation drafting millions of young men from their homes and putting them into army camps before sending them to France, reformers succeeded in forcing the closing of many previously tolerated red-light districts, among them Storyville in New Orleans and the Barbary Coast in San Francisco.

Women and the Origins of the Welfare State

Women played a major role in the progressive reform movement and in shaping the origins of the social welfare state. Even though women were excluded from or marginal to male-dominated political parties, trade unions, and fraternal organizations, women found other means of influencing public policy and of protecting themselves. They formed cross-class labor organizations, such as the Women's Trade Union League, to promote the growth of women's trade unionism and represent the interests of women workers. Poor and working-class women, using what Elizabeth Janeway has called the "powers of the weak," enlisted settlement house workers, reformers, and others as allies in efforts to protect themselves and their children. In their efforts on behalf of women and children, middle-class female reformers drew on society's dominant belief in the moral superiority of women, their wisdom, and their special responsibility for dealing with family issues and broadened it into a "maternalist" vision of women's gender-specific concerns in the public arena. They expanded the nineteenth-century cult of domesticity — the belief that a woman's proper sphere is in the home — to legitimize their expanding roles in influencing public policy, especially in areas commensurate with these social obligations (economic and health provisions protecting children, mothers, and working women and moral reforms such as combating prohibition and guarding the family against male alcoholism).

Organizationally, the women activists expanded their activities in the Progressive Era from the voluntarist moral reform associations of the nineteenth century to include the issue-oriented pressure groups of the early twentieth century, such as those seeking to end child labor, protect mothers and women workers, gain women the vote, and abolish arms races. During the height of the suffrage campaign in the 1910s,

Surrounded by a crowd of apparently bemused men and boys, Boston women hold an outdoor rally for female suffrage. (*Culver Pictures, Inc.*)

the women activists experimented with mass demonstrations, parades and pagentry, and even some bold direct-action techniques such as picketing the White House. As they moved further onto the political stage and demanded equal citizenship rights, most women activists continued to claim for themselves a kind of moral superiority based on their differences from men. As late as the end of the Progressive Era, Florence Kelley, former settlement house worker and the guiding force of the National Consumers' League, insisted that women had superior insight into issues of social justice and welfare and were, at the same time, entitled to special protection.

At the turn of the century, female maternalists used their private voluntary associations to develop social welfare programs for working-class women and their children in an industrializing society. Gradually, they transformed voluntary charity into the beginnings of a kind of "shadow" welfare state, what historian Sara Evans has called the "maternal commonwealth." Among the most important of these nationally organized women's benevolent groups were the Women's Christian Temperance Union, the General Federation of Women's Clubs, the National Federation of Day Nurseries, the National Association of Colored Women, and the National Congress of Mothers. Viewing needy women and children not as morally inferior but as victims of dislocations stemming from urban and industrial changes, such maternalist groups provided some services for these dependents, and they joined other women reformers in lobbying local, state, and national authorities for public funding for such social welfare.

These women, particularly college-educated, experienced, female social workers such as Jane Addams and Lillian Wald, gained great public respect as experts in social welfare policy. As numbers of such women became members of state boards of charity or served in local and state welfare agencies, they campaigned for maternalist policies with some success at the state level. Between 1900 and 1920 they obtained legislation for at least rudimentary mothers' and widows' pensions in forty states. They gained a base in Washington, D.C., in 1912 with the establishment in the Department of Commerce and Labor of the Children's Bureau, which also became the first federal agency headed by a woman, Julia Lathrop, a settlement house worker and social reformer from Illinois. The United States was one of the few Western countries not to have a system of national maternity assistance at the time. As a result of the enfranchisement of women in 1920, Congress the following year adopted the bureau-sponsored Sheppard-Towner bill, which funded public health nurses in offering maternal and infant health care information (but not direct services). However, the act was underfunded and not renewed in 1929; federal financial aid for dependent children did not really begin until the Social Security Act of 1935.

Without the maternalist politics of the women activists at the turn of the century, the gradually emerging welfare state would almost certainly have been less responsive to the needs of women and children, for male politicians tended to be more concerned with issues that affected male voters. Women activists also used the concept of maternalism as a vehicle into the public sphere; once there, they helped to expand the public agenda. Women activists demanded that the government take up the concerns of women and children as they also demanded the vote for women. However, although women obtained special protective and welfare legislation, the maternalist approach that they used also helped to perpetuate the concept of the cult of domesticity and women's morally superior but otherwise subordinate position in society. To offset their liability to marginalization, a younger generation of American activists in the Progressive Era — led by Julia Lathrop, Sophonisba Breckinridge, Edith and Grace Abbott, (the last, Lathrop's successor in the Children's Bureau, would write the aid-to-needy-children provisions of the Social Security Act of 1935) — consciously jettisoned maternalism, which they characterized as unsystematic and unscientific. The 1920s would see a major debate between those who advocated continued protective legislation for women based on their special needs and those who argued for female individualism and complete equality with men and who, beginning in 1923, championed an equal rights amendment to the U.S. Constitution.

The Progressive Impulse

Even before it dominated politics on the national level, progressivism emerged as the most pervasive political reform effort since the pre–Civil War period. Combining the efforts of various disaffected groups in the depression of the 1890s, it soon became a widespread movement for the reorganization and improvement of American life.

As part of the "new interventionism," private groups intruded into the marketplace or sought governmental intervention for their own benefit and presumably for society's as well. Outside of progressivism, corporate reorganizers, trade unions, and feminist groups sought to direct the marketplace. Radical interventionists wanted to expand government ownership and control of industry. Conservative interventionists, while balking at such a threat to private property, were often willing to have the government control labor or immigration or maintain dominant cultural standards through prohibition of alcohol, Sabbatarianism, or other forms of "Americanization." Different groups used interventionism in different ways. But all of them reflected widespread disillusionment with unrestricted individualism and an unregulated marketplace. These interventionists included many of the various groups that historians have identified as progressives—the anxious old middle class and gentry, the confident new professionals, the business and academic elites, the corporate managers and financiers, and the ethnic and working-class leaders. However, the members of each of these groups supported only part of the progressive reform agenda. Progressivism was a series of shifting coalitions of various interventionist groups coming together behind particular issues and political candidates.

Despite the diversity of its component groups, progressivism had qualities that made it distinct from other movements. Progressives combined religious fervor with an optimistic belief in the methods of science and organization. This made them particularly evangelistic modernizers. The combination of moralism and pragmatism also produced the progressive ethos, which characterized the leadership of the most readily identifiable progressives.

The progressive leaders who headed reform groups in various parts of the country in social work, philanthropy, medicine, public health, and other areas had good informal communication ties with one another. Although the specific reform movements were often backed by different sets of supporters, their leaders tended to use the same kinds of educational and political tactics and similar justifications on idealistic, practical, and social grounds.

In politics, progressive leaders throughout the country, like their opponents, came primarily from upper-middle-class or upper-class families. On the average, the progressive political leaders were substantially younger than the conservatives and other party regulars. In many ways progressivism represented a movement led by younger members of the American elite, whose sense of power to change the world was different from much of the pessimism or belief in automatic progress that characterized the last third of the nineteenth century.

Like many conservatives, progressives wanted to rid the country of the notion that there were different social classes. The hero of one of Harold Frederic's novels hoped that "the abominable word 'class' could be wiped out of the English language as it is spoken in America." Progressives insisted that there must be an organic community with common interests and values, with a single public interest. "We have come to the time," Harry Garfield, the president of Williams College, said in January 1917, shortly before joining the Wilson administration, "when the old individualistic principle of competition must be set aside and we must boldly embark upon the new principle of cooperation and combination." The progressives' refusal to accept the concept of conflicting and competing groups and classes was ironic, since they helped construct some of the most effective pressure groups. In their search for a larger public interest, progressives inadvertently contributed to the growth of the interest-group pluralism they bemoaned.

Their belief in private initiative led many progressive as well as many conservative interventionists to develop voluntary associations as alternatives to continued expansion of government power. The heritage from the Progressive Era includes scores of voluntary associations for civic improvement, social betterment, and economic advancement, many of which continue to play an important role in American society.

Despite their emphasis on private initiative and associationalism, progressives and other interventionists expanded the functions of government and laid the groundwork for the regulatory and administrative state. Progressives recognized the need for expanded governmental power in a nation of corporate and other private power centers. But they sought only enough state power to establish the public interest as a vital counterweight to more parochial private interests. They did not want to end the community's primary reliance on private, voluntary action and initiative. In government, progressives relied not on legislators but on strong executive leaders and expert nonpartisan administrators, authorities who could help the community avoid the pitfalls of lethargy and parochial selfishness. Progressives believed in leadership as an antidote to the tyranny of change.

For all their talk of "the people" and popular democracy, most progressive leaders, like many conservatives, believed that leadership was the province of an educated elite. Such a view clashed with the concepts of democracy and the distrust of experts and bureaucrats widely held by Americans, including many Jeffersonian agrarians and members of organized labor. In trying to balance the American ideal of democracy with their own belief in elite expertise, progressives suggested that the role of the people was to elect good leaders but that the leaders and their subordinates should then find and follow the general public interest unfettered by direct influence from the masses. "Our aim must be to give [wider] scope to the wise administrator," admonished the economist Richard Ely.

The progressives' faith in leadership for the entire community, their search for a general public interest, and their challenge to established power holders ultimately led them to Washington. In the nation's capital a new era began with a boisterous young politician who came to symbolize progressivism for millions of Americans. His name was Theodore Roosevelt.

CHAPTER 6

The Washington Whirligig

The Death of a President

In September 1901, President William McKinley took a few days' respite from his official duties in Washington to attend a public reception at the Pan-American Exposition in Buffalo, New York. As the president shook hands in a receiving line, moving toward him was a man with a bandaged hand. The white wrappings concealed a tiny pistol. As the president extended his hand in mechanical greeting, the assassin thrust his arm forward and pulled the trigger, firing two shots into McKinley's chest. The president staggered and slumped to the floor. McKinley's murderer was a 28-year-old unemployed laborer and anarchist from the slums of Pittsburgh and Cleveland. Embittered and alienated, Leon Czolgosz sometimes used the alias Fred Nieman—Fred Nobody. He had acted alone, but he had shot the president, he said, on behalf of the poor, the forgotten, and the exploited. "I didn't believe one man should have so much service, and another man should have none." McKinley died after lingering for eight days. Following a two-day trial, Czolgosz was sentenced to death. He was executed in the electric chair a month later.

In an era in which the forces of radicalism and reform gained strength throughout the country, the national government was led not by the lackluster McKinley but by one of the most colorful, dynamic political personalities of the century, Theodore Roosevelt. A former governor of New York, the aggressive young politician had felt stifled as vice-president. Now he responded candidly to McKinley's death: "It is a dreadful thing to come into the presidency this way; but it would be a far worse thing to be morbid about it." The youngest man to become president of the United States (he was 42),* Roosevelt set actively to work. Neither the Executive Mansion, which he officially renamed the White House, nor the country would ever be the same again.

---

*In 1960, at the age of 43, John F. Kennedy would become the youngest man to be *elected* president.

Theodore Roosevelt: The Warrior as President

For millions of Americans, Theodore Roosevelt has symbolized the Progressive Era. Personifying the vigorous, assertive leadership acclaimed by progressives, Roosevelt appeared a strong-minded hero to a generation of Americans. TR, as the press called him, acted the part well. He was constantly in motion, his face and gestures continually animated. When he spoke, his toothy grin, framed by his bushy mustache, stretched nearly into a grimace. He flailed about when driving home his points. Fists clenched, arms pumping up and down, he resembled a human windmill. "The President," journalist Ray Stannard Baker concluded, "ran full-speed on all the tracks at once."

Evangelist and Activist

As evangelistic as any progressive, Roosevelt summoned the country forward while seeking to rejuvenate traditional values. An active moralist, he lectured the American people on the proper code of life. In these secular sermons the president preached the need to maintain the virtues of hard work, self-control, duty, honesty, sobriety, and courage. Like many other eastern patricians, Roosevelt feared that changes in American life—the ending of the frontier, the influx of immigrants, and the urbanization of the country—were softening Americans and weakening their ability to compete as individuals and as a nation. Roosevelt's moralism came both from his desire to reinfuse direction and purpose in the American people and from his own peculiar personality.

From his youth, Roosevelt displayed the strenuous and flamboyant activism, intensive moralism, and desire for order that he exemplified as president. Born into a comfortable old New York mercantile family in 1858, he was sickly, asthmatic, and nearsighted. But under his father's tutelage he built up his strength through rigorous exercise and boxing lessons. He learned to master his emotions as he mastered his body. When his father died, the 13-year-old boy buried himself in his studies to avoid feelings that he considered weak and maudlin.

After attending Harvard College and Columbia Law School, Roosevelt entered politics as a New York state assemblyman from Manhattan. In 1884, when his wife perished in childbirth and his mother died on the same day, he insisted on rigid self-control. Three days after the double funeral, he returned to his seat in the Assembly. When the session ended, he headed west and spent the next two years running a ranch in the Dakota Territory, submerging his anguish in the hardships of the frontier. Although he eventually remarried, he never mentioned his dead wife again, not in his autobiography nor even to their daughter. Roosevelt had pushed himself beyond self-control to obsessive self-denial. Throughout his life he maintained his rigid determination to hold potential chaos in check in both private and social experience.

Roosevelt's insistence on order and his admiration for vigor, bold leadership, and martial virtues endeared him to many progressives and conservatives, but these qualities also led him to extremes. He viewed warfare as a test of character and a means of advancing civilization. During the Spanish-American War he thrilled to combat and bragged, "I killed a Spaniard with my own hand." By the outbreak of the war he had risen within the Republican party from U.S. civil service commissioner and New York City police commissioner to assistant secretary of the Navy. Resigning this last position, he had formed the 1st U.S. Volunteer Cavalry Regiment, that collection of eastern aristocrats and western cowboys known as the Rough Riders. A successful—and well-reported—charge up San Juan (actually Kettle) Hill in Cuba made him a war hero. When he returned home, the young colonel was elected governor of New York. Two years later he became the vice-presidential candidate, and the following year the "damned cowboy," as McKinley's campaign manager called him, was president.

Steward of the People

In the White House, Roosevelt initiated the modern presidency. Conceiving of the chief executive as a "steward of the people," he argued that the president had the right to do anything the nation needed unless it was specifically forbidden by law or the Constitution. "There adheres in the Presidency," he asserted, "more power than any other office in any great republic or constitutional monarchy of modern times." He broadened the power of the executive by greatly contributing to the modern roles of chief legislator, molder of public opinion, and world leader.

Previous presidents had outlined their goals through speeches to the country and messages to Congress. Roosevelt went beyond these methods by sending drafts of bills to Capitol Hill and lobbying for his legislation both privately and publicly. In dealing with Congress, Roosevelt moved boldly. He deliberately exceeded congressional authorization in withdrawing public lands for conservation purposes. He personally revived the Sherman Antitrust Act, thereby thrusting the executive branch into the corporate economy. In foreign policy he seldom waited for congressional approval before taking aggressive action. "I did not usurp power," Roosevelt explained later, "but I did greatly broaden the use of executive power."

Sensing the popular hunger for leadership and a sense of participation, Roosevelt fed the public's interest in the presidency. He encouraged people to expect the president to speak and act on matters of importance. From his "bully pulpit" he cultivated public opinion by

Beclad in a cowboy hat and a tightly buttoned duster coat, former President Theodore Roosevelt takes an automobile sight-seeing tour of western ranchland in 1911. (*Photo by Walter J. Lubken/The Bettman Archive*)

using the mass media. He gave information to selected reporters and provided the first White House press room. Together, TR and the press personalized the presidency. His active life made exciting copy. Roosevelt became the first president to play tennis, ride in an automobile, fly in an airplane, and dive in a submarine. Reporters scrambled after him as he hiked through Rock Creek Park in Washington and hunted bears in the mountains of the West. A news story of the president protecting an infant bear warmed the hearts of millions. It led an enterprising New York toy maker to create a stuffed honey-colored cub, which he promptly named the Teddy bear.

In his seven years as president, Roosevelt encouraged a positive role for the federal government in managing the direction of modernization. The president, he believed, should intervene in the economy when necessary to contain the most destructive aspects of assertive wealth and provide some protection for its victims. Without strong presidential leadership and some reforms, mounting discontent might explode into widespread militance and even class conflict. Roosevelt wanted to preserve American corporate capitalism as it was evolving by regulating it in the public interest. He had little patience with radicals, whom he called the "lunatic fringe," or with reactionaries who sought to block his reforms. "The friends of property," he told his attorney general, a wealthy corporation lawyer, "must realize that the surest way to provoke an explosion of wrong and injustice is to be short-sighted, narrow-minded, greedy and arrogant." Roosevelt was a reformer because he was basically a conservative.

The Square Deal, 1901 – 1909

Roosevelt had not been elected president, so his primary political aim during his first term was to build up the strength and reputation to win election in 1904. The task did not seem easy. None of the four previous vice-presidents who had succeeded to the presidency upon the death of the incumbent had ever won renomination.* The conservative Republican old guard, which dominated the party and Congress, distrusted Roosevelt as impetuous and unpredictable. "Go slow," the GOP national chairman advised him. "I shall," Roosevelt replied. Although he began by assuring Americans that he intended to continue McKinley's popular policies, Roosevelt quickly established his own program.

He started with the trusts. In his first inaugural address he picked up McKinley's theme, the need for publicity to expose any evils resulting from the recent corporate consolidation movement. Roosevelt went beyond his predecessor, however, when he insisted that the federal government should have the power to deal with big business:

> The great corporations which we have grown to speak of rather loosely as trusts are the creatures of the State, and the State not only has the right to control them, but it is in duty bound to control them wherever the need of such control is shown.

Roosevelt was not antibusiness. He thought the new supercorporations were inevitable and even beneficial. He believed that they could produce goods more cheaply and abundantly and could compete more effectively with the powerful European cartels. Nevertheless, he sought to apply his standards of moral conduct to them. He opposed rebates, watered stock, unfair competition, and the corruption of public officials. Thus he considered the behemoths to be "good trusts" or "bad trusts," depending on their practices rather than their size.

In Roosevelt's view, government should discover what the trusts were doing and then negotiate with the corporate managers to end improper practices. If the heads of the corporation proved recalcitrant, the president could, if necessary, expose them to adverse publicity and even antitrust prosecution. During his first administration, Roosevelt overcame opposition to active governmental intervention from conservatives like John D. Rockefeller and his son-in-law, Nelson Aldrich,

*They were John Tyler, Millard Fillmore, Andrew Johnson, and Chester Arthur.

the powerful old guard senator from Rhode Island, and forced Congress to establish the Bureau of Corporations with the power to investigate the giant interstate corporations. Despite Roosevelt's bellicose posturing, however, he took a relatively moderate position. As Mr. Dooley, the fictitious character created by satirist Peter Finley Dunne, recognized:

> Th' trusts, says he, are heejoous monsthers built up be th' enlightened intherprise iv th' men that have done so much to advance progress in our beloved country, he says. On wan hand I wud stamp thim undher fut; on th' other hand not so fast.

The early and somewhat misleading reputation Roosevelt acquired as a "trust buster" derived from the actions he took in 1902 against the Northern Securities Company, a projected railroad monopoly in the Northwest, and also against the beef trust. In a surprise move Roosevelt ordered the Justice Department to file suit to dissolve the enormous railroad holding company created by Morgan, Hill, Harriman, and Rockefeller. The government charged that the proposed consolidation was an illegal restraint of trade. It also contended that nearly one-third of the company's capital stock represented an unwarranted profit to the organizers and that it would lead to higher freight charges. While Wall Street gasped, most of the country cheered Roosevelt's resurrection of the moribund Sherman Antitrust Act. A few months later Roosevelt's suit against the big meatpackers of Chicago delighted eastern consumers and western farmers. Modifying its previous position, the Supreme Court supported the government in both cases.

Stunned, Morgan hurried to the White House. "If we have done anything wrong," Morgan reportedly told the chief executive, "send your man [meaning the attorney general] to my man [naming one of his lawyers] and they can fix it up." "That can't be done," Roosevelt replied. "We don't want to fix it up," the attorney general, Philander Knox, added. "We want to stop it." Although he considered the antitrust approach an antiquated idea, Roosevelt wanted to show that the supercorporations would have to reckon with the federal government. Although the Morgan-Hill railroad combination was barred from selling stock, the stock already issued was returned to the individuals who had conspired to restrain trade. Though the gambit was blocked, the individuals involved were not penalized. Most corporate leaders worked out "gentlemen's agreements" with Roosevelt under which they consented to provide the president with information about their companies and make whatever reasonable changes he suggested.

A few months after filing his first antitrust suits, Roosevelt intervened in a lengthy strike in the anthracite coal fields of Pennsylvania. Early in the winter of 1902 the strike threatened the Northeast with a critical fuel shortage. Roosevelt invited both sides to the White House, becoming the first president to try personal mediation rather than using federal troops to protect property and crush the strike. When the owners refused to meet with the union leaders, the irritated chief executive threatened to seize the mines and use soldiers to produce coal. Roosevelt may have been bluffing, but his ploy worked. J. P. Morgan and other financiers induced the mine owners to agree to arbitration by a presidential commission. The commission authorized both wage and price increases and averted the fuel crisis. Through his bold and unprecedented use of the presidency to help mediate industrial relations in the national interest, Roosevelt reinforced the idea that he would act to curb the excesses of big business while giving labor and capital a "square deal," as he called his program.

Election Strategy

By the 1904 election Roosevelt had strengthened both his personal position and that of the Republican party. Despite the animosity of some conservatives, the president received widespread popular acclaim for his forceful policies. Wooing recent immigrants with praise and some patronage, he had also tried to reduce the GOP's nativist image and expand its constituency among workers. He enlisted the support of southern blacks because they made up the majority of southern Republicans and the South elected nearly one quarter of the delegates to the Republican national convention. In fact, Roosevelt was the first president to invite a black man to the White House. Booker T. Washington joined him for lunch in 1901, evoking a howl of protest from much of the white South. Yet Roosevelt's southern strategy mixed expediency with principle. Like many other white Americans, he held a stereotypical view of African Americans. In 1906, for example, he dishonorably discharged three entire companies of black soldiers because a few unidentified soldiers had retaliated with violence against racial slurs in Brownsville, Texas.

Roosevelt's efforts to cultivate support within the Republican party proved successful, and in 1904 he won the nomination for president without serious challenge. Winning nomination was virtually tantamount to being elected, since the GOP remained the majority party and the dominant force in national politics for nearly forty years, from the depression of the 1890s to the Great Depression of the 1930s.* McKinley and Roosevelt had identified the GOP as the party of strong national leadership by actively promoting prosperity and national greatness. They had broadened its appeal to a wider range of ethnic groups than its traditional Protestant base.

---

*Woodrow Wilson, a Democrat, won the presidency in 1912 and 1916 largely because of divisions within the GOP.

The Democrats were still discordant and faction-ridden. They could not find a leader who could unite the party's two constituencies: the southern and western wing, which was composed of rural, prohibitionist, white Protestants, and the northern wing, which was made up of a few wealthy conservative business people and a number of city machines based on urban, antiprohibitionist, foreign-stock Catholics and Jews. The bastion of the Democratic party was the deep South. That region's racism and ruralism encouraged a program of states' rights and limited government and reinforced the party's notorious parochialism. The leader of the party's southern and western wing, William Jennings Bryan, ran for president in 1896, 1900, and 1908, but in 1904 the Democrats put forward a representative of the eastern conservatives: Alton Parker, a colorless New York judge.

Roosevelt whipped Parker in the most decisive victory since Andrew Jackson defeated Henry Clay in 1832. A personal triumph for Roosevelt, the election also indicated a popular demand for innovation. In addition, it raised the issue of campaign contributions by giant corporations, which, it was later confirmed, contributed 70 percent of the $2 million raised by the GOP National Committee that year. (Three years later Congress prohibited contributions by national banks and corporations—but not by their officers as individuals—to the election campaigns of federal officials.) In 1904, to the dismay of conservatives and many progressives, Eugene V. Debs, the nominee of the Socialist Party of America, multiplied his vote from 88,000 in 1900 to 400,000. Undeterred, Roosevelt basked in his personal victory. He was, he bragged to his wife, "no longer a political accident."

Roosevelt's Second Term

An astute politician, Roosevelt understood the increasing sentiment for new policies demonstrated by the growing success of progressive reformers on the local and state levels. During his second term he became more progressive. But recognizing the power of the conservative old guard Republicans in Congress and desirous of easing the growing split between progressive and conservative factions of the party, Roosevelt followed a middle path.

Moderate, not radical, reform was what Roosevelt favored, and his position on railroad regulation shows how he worked within the center of a debate to achieve a practical solution. The railroad problem was old and complex, but at the turn of the century new difficulties stemmed from the consolidation of hundreds of smaller lines into a half dozen major rail systems. Consolidation may have curtailed rate wars and brought stability to the carriers, but it also increased the railroads' indebtedness and contributed to higher freight rates, which were then passed on to consumers by shippers in the form of higher prices.

Southern and western shippers, especially, feared that Wall Street, once it controlled what had formerly been local or regional railroads, would neglect the needs of their commerce. Even the railroads themselves complained, since big shippers like Standard Oil often forced them to give major discounts or rebates. In 1903 the railroads, with Roosevelt's endorsement, therefore sponsored the Elkins Anti-rebate Act, which sought to prevent the loss of railroad revenues from such rebates by declaring them illegal. However, the problems of consolidation, collusion, monopolistic rate fixing, and other discriminatory practices continued and led to mounting public discontent. Concluding after the election that further action was inevitable, Roosevelt decided to lead the movement toward moderate goals.

Theoretically at least, a number of alternatives existed for dealing with railroad problems. Some conservative anti-interventionists wanted to end governmental regulation and return to laissez-faire and the free-market system. Radical antitrust advocates urged the government to break up the giant consolidations and go back to many smaller lines. Socialists and some progressives advocated government ownership of what they called natural monopolies, including the railroads. Most people probably supported increased governmental regulation, but they differed on its nature. Since the Interstate Commerce Commission was ineffective, radical progressives like Senator La Follette, who wanted strong national supervision, urged a new agency that could both prevent excessive rates and enforce adequate service. However, moderates like Roosevelt suggested only that the ICC be strengthened so that it could prevent discriminatory rates. Battling radicals, conservative senators, and railroad interests, who blocked such changes for two years, Roosevelt and congressional moderates finally won approval for a compromise measure through a combination of accommodation and coercion. The commission was given increased powers, but to satisfy conservatives it was left to the courts to determine how broad their review powers would be.

Despite its mild nature, the Hepburn Act of 1906 reinvigorated the ICC. For the first time the commission obtained authority to set rates. Soon its power expanded as the courts limited themselves to narrow procedural review and Congress, in the Mann-Elkins Act of 1910, authorized the ICC to act on its own initiative instead of waiting for a shipper to file a complaint.

During the Progressive Era the strengthened ICC acted against inflation and kept freight rates down by repeatedly denying railroad applications for increases. Despite greater traffic, the carriers found it harder to obtain capital investment from their cash flow or from the stock market. Instead, they increased their sale of bonds. Although railroad managers and some revisionist historians have blamed government regulation for this financial squeeze, the railroads themselves also bore major responsibility for their difficulties. Their reputation for financial manipulation and overcapitalization made many investors reluctant to buy their stock. As some reformers, like Brandeis, suggested, the railroads might have increased their cash flow through more efficient operation.

As a result of legislative action in the Progressive Era, the federal government greatly increased its intervention into the transportation sector of the economy. It moved beyond its old promotional role and acted as a negative regulator of the railroads, keeping down their rates in the larger public interest. Not until after World War I did it make a positive attempt to foster a sound, adequate national railroad system. That and a number of other efforts failed, however, and over the years the railroads became a "sick industry." By the 1970s the United States had evolved a mixed system of profitable private lines in the South and West and publicly owned unprofitable (but eventually profit-making) carriers in the Northeast.

In the area of consumer protection, Congress, under pressure from consumer groups and other associations, adopted two moderate reform measures to help to protect the public against unhealthy food and drugs. Muckrakers like Upton Sinclair, in *The Jungle* (1906), his exposé of the meatpacking industry, raised public fears about diseased meat. Although some conservatives opposed it, the Meat Inspection Act passed that year was shaped to a large degree by the big packers, who wanted to quiet public concern. Also, governmental inspection and certification would drive many of the smaller firms out of business. Roosevelt lacked enthusiasm for the second of the legislative enactments in this field, the Pure Food and Drug Act of 1906. Nevertheless, legislation forbidding adulterated or fraudulently labeled food and drugs was supported by the government's chief chemist, Dr. Harvey Wiley, physicians and consumer organizations, and large food and pharmaceutical firms, which sought to curtail patent medicine companies and the adverse publicity they generated. Although he did not initiate either of these pieces of legislation, Roosevelt characteristically received credit for both.

During his second term, Roosevelt applied the antitrust laws more vigorously than in his first term. Despite the fact that the Rockefeller and Morgan companies had contributed substantially to his election campaign, the president filed suits against American Tobacco, DuPont, Rockefeller's Standard Oil, and Morgan's New Haven Railroad. Roosevelt believed in regulation rather than antitrust action, but he relied on what he called the "foolish antitrust law" because Congress refused to enact his recommendations for federal licensing and regulation of interstate corporations.

The Wall Street panic of 1907 and the consequent short-lived but severe recession strained relations between the president and the business community even further. Although a temporary overextension of credit probably caused the recession, business blamed the uncertainty on Roosevelt's antitrust policy. In order to save one of the major brokerage houses and avoid a sharper market break and intensified economic contraction, the president subsequently gave tacit approval to U.S. Steel's acquisition of a competitor, Tennessee Coal & Iron Company. More significant, he had the treasury pump $150 million in bonds into the credit resources of the national banks, an action that helped to stem the decline. Angered by the attacks on him, Roosevelt lashed out against "certain malefactors of great wealth," who he charged had intensified the panic in order to discredit the government's policies. He named Standard Oil and the Santa Fe Railroad as examples of "predatory wealth." This most slashing assault on business by any president since Andrew Jackson showed Roosevelt's ability to direct public attention against "the interests." So did the conservation movement.

The Conservation Crusade

The modern conservation movement began during the Progressive Era, and Theodore Roosevelt came to symbolize it. Not as simple as Roosevelt often portrayed it, the movement demonstrated the tensions engendered by modernization. Industry's rapid consumption of natural resources and the Census Bureau's 1890 announcement that the frontier had come to an end caused Americans to worry that unbounded expansion had reached its limits. Economic growth had expanded opportunity and ameliorated social conditions. Now many Americans argued that it would be necessary to conserve resources in order to maintain that tradition. Progressives and many other interventionists asserted that the federal government should encourage rational, planned management through regulation to ensure wise and efficient use of resources.

In 1901, at the outset of his administration, Roosevelt announced that the conservation of forest and water resources was a national problem of vital importance, and through his leadership and that of the National Conservation Commission he appointed in 1908, Roosevelt helped to educate the country about the need for planned protection and development of natural resources. In one of the first major pieces of national progressive legislation, the Newlands Reclamation Act of 1902, Congress, with Roosevelt's support, provided that the proceeds of public-land sales in sixteen western and southwestern states would finance irrigation projects in the arid regions of those states.

Sensing a growing popular issue, Roosevelt took over the leadership of the movement and developed the comprehensive policy that gave conservation its particular character. He rejected as impractical the goals of aesthetic preservationists such as the Save-the-Redwoods League and the prominent naturalist John Muir, who wanted to maintain the forests untouched so that people could enrich their spirits through contact with the beauty of nature. In 1892, Muir had helped to organize the Sierra Club, which emerged as the leading aesthetic conservation organization, and served as its first president. But Roosevelt supported the programs of utilitarian conservationists such as Gifford Pinchot, chief of an expanded U.S. Forest Service, for federally regulated use of certain coal and mineral lands, forests, oil reserves, and water power sites. During his administration, Roosevelt quadrupled— to 200 million acres—the land taken out of the public domain and put into governmental reserves to be developed under federal supervision.

The most famous battle between the two wings—the utilitarian and the aesthetic—of what Pinchot called the "conservation movement" came in 1913 in California. The Hetch Hetchy valley controversy involved the question of whether that part of Yosemite National Park (established in 1906) should be used, as Pinchot agreed, as a water reservoir to supply the growing population of San Francisco or whether it should be preserved for its pristine natural beauty, as Muir insisted. The utilitarians won that political battle, and the Hetch Hetchy valley became a reservoir. In addition to splitting the conservation movement, the controversy led to the creation in 1916 of the National Park Service, supported by the aesthetic preservationists as a bureaucratic rival to the utilitarian U.S. Forest Service.

Progressives spoke of "conservation" (what would today be called the environmental or ecological movement) as a battle between the people and the interests, which the reformers identified as the big mining, timber, and oil companies that exploited the country's resources. In reality, conservation was less a grassroots popular movement than an attempt by eastern modernizers to make the federal government a mechanism to administer natural resource development. The majority of westerners—those who were or wanted to be ranchers, miners, or lumbermen—opposed this limitation on the tradition of exploiting the public domain, a tradition that had been one of the main avenues to wealth in the West.

In practice, conservation did maintain resources, but it also caused much hardship. It drove small operators from government land. Big companies continued to work there under lease, but they complained of bureaucratic interference. New federal conservation agencies were underfinanced and often relied on the companies to police themselves. Before long the companies and the agencies developed working relationships that limited the effectiveness of regulation.

The Roosevelt Legacy

Seven years in office left their mark on Roosevelt and the country. By the time he left office in 1909 to spend a year hunting big game in Africa, the president felt the strains of growing congressional discontent with his forceful actions and the widening breach between conservatives and progressives within the GOP. He had avoided prickly issues like currency and the tariff, the latter of which raised prices and cost consumers hundreds of millions of dollars each year. Nevertheless, Roosevelt had joined the growing movement for change. Putting the presidency behind the moderate reform wing of the GOP, he dramatized the progressive movement and helped to raise some of its issues to the national level.

Despite his rhetoric and activist image, however, Roosevelt was often less progressive than he sounded. More assertive reformers like Senator La Follette expressed disillusionment with the former Rough Rider:

> [Roosevelt's] cannonading filled the air with noise and smoke, which confused and obscured the line of action, but, when the battle cloud drifted by and the quiet was restored, it was always a matter of surprise that so little had really been accomplished.

Still, Roosevelt had achieved some results. He had pulled his party and the government along with him on the path toward moderate reform and interventionism, and he had strengthened the executive branch of government so that it might be a source of strong leadership.

Taft versus the Insurgents, 1909–1913

Inheriting a difficult situation, Roosevelt's handpicked successor, William Howard Taft, made the worst of it. Faced with mounting pressure for action, Taft sought to slow and consolidate change. The tide of reform overwhelmed him. Although historians were too quick to judge Taft a weak president, they correctly assessed him a failure. He failed to mobilize the people or keep his party intact. In the end the electorate repudiated him.

The Jurist as President

Taft was not the man for the presidency. He lacked the imagination and ability to manage contending political forces. He preferred the calm of the courtroom. Born into a moderately wealthy Cincinnati family, Taft had become a lawyer, then solicitor general and a federal judge before Roosevelt selected him as the first American governor general of the Philippines. He returned to the United States to become secretary of war. Taft did not want to be president so much as chief justice, a position he obtained in the 1920s. Sitting in the White House in 1909 after defeating Bryan and Debs, Taft said he felt "like a fish out of water."

Although he greatly admired Roosevelt, Taft proved incapable of imitating his predecessor. He did not have the personality for bantering with the press or the magnetism to rouse the public. In the White House he felt misunderstood by the people outside pressing for action. The kindly, 350-pound executive was slow-moving and somewhat indecisive. "The truth is," he wrote sadly to his wife, "it is not the height of my ambition to be popular." Despite his admiration for Roosevelt, Taft was too strict a constitutionalist to emulate TR's bold political ventures and too conservative to go along with continued sweeping reform. He could, however, be an activist president for conservative reasons — battling Congress to establish a budget for the federal government, vetoing actions of reformers in Congress, and dispatching Marines to Nicaragua without congressional consent. Trying to bring under strict control the movement for an expanded role for the federal government in social and economic areas, Taft believed his primary task was to integrate Roosevelt's reforms into the legal system and return society to stability.

In his first two years as president, Taft dissatisfied both progressives and conservatives within his party. Republican insurgents became angered by Taft's refusal to support their efforts to reduce the dominance of the powerful Speaker of the House, "Uncle Joe" Cannon. Taft also mishandled the tariff issue. True to his campaign pledge, he sought lower rates, thereby angering protectionists. But when conservatives maintained control of Congress and enacted the high Payne-Aldrich Tariff of 1909, Taft embittered insurgents by refusing to veto it. The measure did move toward flexible tariff schedules by authorizing maximum and minimum rates for each item, the rates to be determined by the administration. But Taft further alienated its opponents when he reportedly praised it as the "best tariff act" ever passed.

Hardly had the tariff row ended when Taft stumbled into an even more vehement conflict with progressives and eventually a battle with Roosevelt himself. The Ballinger-Pinchot controversy of 1909–1910 exploded from an administrative dispute into a cause célèbre. It raised serious questions about the administration's support of conservation and demonstrated widespread public suspicion that big business was corrupting the federal government.

The controversy began when a young special agent for the Interior Department, Louis Glavis, and Chief Forester Gifford Pinchot publicly accused Secretary of the Interior Richard Ballinger of weakening the conservation program in order to aid corporate interests. A Morgan-Guggenheim syndicate had been organized to mine government coal reserves in Alaska, and Ballinger was accused of aiding the giant combine. With tremendous lack of judgment, Taft took a narrow procedural view and decided that the matter was merely an interdepartmental squabble. He failed to recognize that the matter involved larger issues of conservation and public policy. Carefully examining the technical aspects of the case, he ruled in favor of his secretary of the interior and discharged Glavis and eventually Pinchot.

Progressives immediately raised a cry of outrage. A congressional investigating committee dominated by the old guard agreed with Taft and exonerated Ballinger of charges of fraud and corruption. Nevertheless, most Americans, including former President Roosevelt, continued to believe that Ballinger was guilty of working with giant corporations against conservation and the public interest. Convinced of Ballinger's innocence, Taft refused to sacrifice him for political gain. As the president complained to a friend in 1910:

> If I were to turn Ballinger out, in view of his innocence and in view of the conspiracy against him, I should be a white-livered skunk. I don't care . . . how it affected the administration before the people; if the people are so unjust as this, I don't propose to be one of them.

Long after Ballinger had become a political liability, Taft stood by him out of a sense of justice. Even the fact that Taft put more land into government reserves than Roosevelt had failed to win the support of progressives.

One major progressive interventionist issue with massive future potential that came of age during the Taft presidency was the federal income tax. Americans were traditionally adverse to taxation, and thanks to their limited government and comparatively small military establishment, they had one of the lowest tax rates in the industrial world. At the turn of the century, only 2.4 percent of gross national product was taken by federal levies (mainly customs duties and excise taxes on particular commodities) and 4 percent by state and local taxes levied mainly on real estate.

A desire to tap new sources of income and wealth generated by modern business, industry, and finance — corporate and individual profits, sales of stocks and bonds, inheritance — as well as a need for more federal revenues to fund growing expenditures (most dramatically in the first decade of the century the construction of a modern battleship navy that would rival the fleets of Germany, Great Britain, and Japan) led to the adoption of a federal income tax. The Spanish-American War had shown the need for additional sources of federal revenue, and the government adopted a graduated inheritance tax. Populists and other agrarians in the South and the West argued for a federal income tax to redress the sectional economic imbalance favoring the industrial Northeast. They were joined in the Northeast by organized labor, politicians with working-class constituencies, progressive reformers, socialists, a number of tax experts, and several mass circulation newspapers. The income tax was opposed by regular Republicans, conservative southern Democrats, and prominent industrialists and financiers.

Because the Supreme Court (in the *Pollock* case in 1895) had invalidated a short-lived federal income tax, a constitutional amendment was required. In 1909 the U.S. government faced an imminent $100 million deficit, the largest since the Civil War, and this plus the election of 1908 helped to create the crisis that would lead to the adoption of this major departure in American tax policy. In the election the Democrats under William Jennings Bryan advocated an income tax, and the next year a congressional coalition of Democrats and insurgent Republicans sent such an amendment to the states. Democratic victories in state legislatures in the elections of 1910 and 1912 enabled the Sixteenth Amendment to win ratification by early 1913.

Taft, unlike Roosevelt, proved unable to gain credit for legislation passed during his term in the White House. Although he had joined in defeating the provision for a federal income tax attached to the Payne-Aldrich Tariff and had sought to circumvent a federal income tax amendment by supporting a federal corporation tax instead, he finally concurred in sending the Sixteenth Amendment to the states. Characteristically, Taft received little praise from progressives, who disdained his attempts to restrict the legislation. Taft also disturbed many conservatives by supporting some progressive reforms during his first two years in office. The president helped to strengthen the ICC and supported the enactment of a postal savings bank system.

The election of 1910 made Taft's situation more difficult. Progressive insurgents unseated many conservatives and party regulars. Aided by divisions within the GOP, the Democrats won control of the House of Representatives for the first time since 1895. Confronted with a hostile and reform-minded Congress, Taft tried to appear as the leader of progressive forces and restore harmony to his party. He supported several kinds of factory safety legislation and endorsed the U.S. Children's Bureau. Despite these actions, Taft angered progressives by his vehement opposition to the recall of judges and by his lack of enthusiasm for another direct-democracy measure, the Seventeenth Amendment, which provided for the direct election of U.S. senators.

While alienating progressives, Taft also dissatisfied many conservatives by waging the most active antimonopoly campaign of the era. Taft filed more than seventy antitrust suits. Acting on his own belief that there was no halfway position (such as governmental regulation) between competitive capitalism and socialism, Taft sought to restrict major consolidations in order to restore the mechanism of the marketplace.

The Supreme Court, however, supported Roosevelt's more flexible approach, judging consolidation and monopoly not on the basis of its existence but rather by whether its behavior was acceptable or not. In the *Standard Oil* case (1911), for example, it ordered the dissolution of Rockefeller's giant holding company as an "unreasonable" restraint of trade. In enunciating this "rule of reason," a majority of the justices fundamentally altered the Sherman Antitrust Act. They implied that the Court would accept a reasonable restraint of trade, which it eventually did in 1920, when it upheld the dominant position of U.S. Steel.

The administration's antitrust suits failed to satisfy most progressives. The more extreme antitrust advocates, such as La Follette and Bryan, wanted to break up the big combines by outlawing specific actions, providing for criminal prosecution, and taxing them out of existence. Other progressives, business regulators like Roosevelt, favored giving the federal government the power to charter big business and regulate its behavior, even to the extent of regulating prices and wages. Taft's antitrust campaign challenged these progressives as well as conservatives who supported the regulatory system that Roosevelt envisioned.

The suit against U.S. Steel, filed by the Taft administration, had little impact on the structure of the steel industry, but it had a disastrous political effect on the GOP. A major part of the government's case rested on U.S. Steel's acquisition of Tennessee Coal & Iron, which had been approved by Roosevelt to help to stem the financial panic of 1907. In 1911 the Justice Department suggested that Roosevelt had been duped by the industrialists. The administration seemed blind to the implications of this action, which contributed directly to Roosevelt's decision to challenge his former friend for the Republican presidential nomination.

The Election of 1912

One of the most dramatic elections in American history, the political battle of 1912 temporarily split the Republican party and put a Democrat in the White House for the first time in twenty years. Although Roosevelt won most of the dozen state primaries, the incumbent president influenced the majority of state delegates, who had been elected without primaries, and easily won renomination. But it proved a hollow victory. Refusing to wait until 1916, Roosevelt decided to bolt the GOP and run at the head of the Progressive party, which was being organized by La Follette and other insurgents.

The election of 1912 dramatized the Progressive Era's emphasis on the politics of personality rather than party. All the major candidates stressed their own leadership styles and philosophies, a far different approach from that of nineteenth-century presidential candidates, who emphasized their party and often campaigned hardly at all. The main contenders, especially insurgents, appealed to voters through vigorous personal campaigns and the mass media, asking for support on the basis of their dedication and programs.

Voters listened to four different philosophies in 1912 as part of the issue-oriented politics of the age. Taft, the regular Republican candidate, expected to lose, but he hoped his defeat would discipline the insurgents and re-create a unified and conservative GOP. At the head of the Progressive party, Roosevelt wooed voters with a "New Nationalism." A program of broad social and economic reform, it included a call for national incorporation and regulation of interstate business, income and inheritance taxes, compulsory investigation of major labor disputes, limitation of labor injunctions, an eight-hour workday, and workers' compensation. The Progressive party program would thrust government directly into the economy to benefit business and industrial workers. After much wrangling, the Democrats nominated Woodrow Wilson, a southern-born educator who was the progressive governor of New Jersey. Attacking Roosevelt for catering to the trusts, Wilson called for a "New Freedom," encouraging the restoration of competition in the marketplace and opportunities for small entrepreneurs. The tariff needed to be reduced, Wilson said, and the antitrust laws and banking system improved in order to limit consolidation. In contrast, the Socialist candidate, Eugene V. Debs, summoned Americans to make drastic changes. He advocated restriction of capitalism through government ownership of railroads, grain elevators, mines, and banks. He called for unemployment insurance, old-age pensions, and a restructuring of government to include the elimination of the U.S. Senate, an end to judicial review by the Supreme Court, and limitation of the presidency to one term.

The Republican party split apart, thus enabling Wilson to win the presidency. More than one out of every ten GOP voters from 1908 sat out the 1912 election. The Republicans who voted were divided almost equally between Taft and TR, but Roosevelt and his program of business regulation and protection for workers proved particularly popular in the cities, where he drew the votes of large numbers of first- and second-generation immigrants. Of all 1912 voters, 27 percent cast their ballots for the Rough Rider. Taft received 23 percent of the popular vote, which, if combined with Roosevelt's, showed that the Republicans remained the majority party when united. Debs won 900,000 votes, which was 6 percent of the total and the highest number ever received by the Socialist ticket. Wilson won a plurality — 42 percent — of the popular vote by lining up the support of the South and the West. Aided by the division of the GOP, Wilson won a clear majority of the states. The electoral college gave him 435 votes to 88 for Roosevelt and 8 for Taft. Wilson thus became the first Democrat to sit in the White House since 1897.

Wilson's sectional victory meant that while the Democrats held power, southerners would dominate the executive and legislative branches of the federal government for the first time since before the Civil War. But this shift in control of the national government would be only temporary. In the long run the election of 1912 proved to be an aberration and failed to produce any fundamental realignment of voter allegiance. The GOP remained the majority party, the choice of most registered voters. It regained control of Congress in 1919 and of the White House in 1921, and it maintained that control until the Great Depression.

Identified as a symbol of standpattism, Taft was repudiated by the voters. An inept politician, he failed as a leader of the traditionalists, who tried to fight a rear-guard action against the mounting demands for reform. He never grasped the dynamics of pressure groups or understood how to balance reformers against reactionaries. He could not, like Roosevelt, play off interest groups, work one side and then the other, and gain credit by convincing a majority that he had obtained all that was politically possible. Taft failed to see the dangers in refusing to help unseat Speaker Cannon and in his positions on the Payne-Aldrich Tariff, the Ballinger-Pinchot controversy, and the suit against U.S. Steel.

Taft did expand executive power, however. He terminated private oil exploration on government oil reserves. He inaugurated a budget for the executive branch that temporarily brought business methods to the government before it was terminated by Congress, which was suspicious of centralized budget making (the concept of a unified federal budget was not adopted until 1921). He contributed to the dissolution of a number of corporate consolidations, including Edison's Motion Picture Patents Association, the "movie trust." He nullified treaties without asking Congress, and he sent Marines into Nicaragua without legislative approval. Nevertheless, Taft was a political failure. Trying to be a harmonizer when most people wanted a fighter, he alienated progressives, conservatives, interventionists, and traditionalists. In the end he retreated into a defense of conservative constitutionalism, spending most of his last year in office vetoing reform legislation passed by a hostile Congress.

Woodrow Wilson: The Scholar as Chief Executive

"I have no patience with the tedious world of what is known as 'research,'" a young Princeton professor once confided to a friend. "I should be complete if I could inspire a great movement of opinion." This young scholar, Woodrow Wilson, got his wish. He left the academic world to become one of the most important presidents in the nation's history and a leader of movements for progressivism and international peace. Working with a progressive-minded Congress, he signed more reform legislation into law than Roosevelt and Taft combined. He also pursued an active foreign policy. His response to the events of World War I made him one of the world's leading statesmen.

A forceful leader, Wilson nevertheless differed sharply from Roosevelt in personality and style. Slim and unbending, with a long, angular face and cold, steely eyes peering through pince-nez glasses, Wilson looked and acted like a schoolmaster to the nation. Reserved, aloof, and austere, he lacked TR's animation, exuberance, and camaraderie. "I have a sense of power in dealing with men collectively," he confessed, "which I do not feel always in dealing with them singly." He lectured the public and won its loyalty through this eloquent appeals to moral principles and ideals.

A longtime admirer of the parliamentary system, Wilson helped to transform the presidency into an instrument of party leadership and a vehicle for directing legislation. Acting like a prime minister, he boldly led Congress into enacting his proposals. He acted without hesitation. Upon taking office he summoned the lawmakers into special session and then drove to Capitol Hill, becoming the first chief executive to appear before Congress in more than a century. He and his advisers drafted reform legislation and worked closely with Democratic congressional leaders to get it enacted. Wilson coaxed, persuaded, threatened, and pressured. He appealed directly to the public when he thought it necessary. He also realized that he could help to define the issues for newspaper readers. Expanding on TR's use of the mass media, Wilson held the first general presidential press conference. In his substantive policies he understood that the country wanted reform and that the Democratic Congress was prepared to act. "We are greatly favored," he remarked early in his administration, "by the circumstances of our time."

Although he was an effective and courageous leader with great skill and inspiring strength and purpose, Wilson was in many ways his own nemesis. His character was that of the protagonist in a Greek tragedy, a heroic figure containing the seeds of his own destruction. The problem stemmed in part from his divided personality. "There are two natures combined in me," Wilson confided to his private secretary in 1912,

> that every day fight for supremacy and control. On the one side, there is the Irish in me, quick, generous, impulsive, passionate, anxious always to help and to sympathize with those in distress. . . . Then, on the other side, there is the Scotch—canny, tenacious, cold and perhaps a little exclusive. . . . When these two fellows get to quarreling among themselves, it is hard to act as umpire between them.

Compulsively ambitious, Wilson channeled his driving energy and rigid self-discipline into effective leadership. When he exerted it in behalf of worthy causes with widespread backing, he obtained significant results. But when his forceful leadership was applied to projects without such broad support, effective opposition triggered anxiety and ire and sometimes led him into dogmatic, self-defeating behavior. At those times the flaws in his temperament — pride, ambition, overconfidence, stubbornness, and intolerance — often changed differences over issues into bitter personal quarrels. This problem was exacerbated by a cerebrovascular disease that afflicted him with a number of strokes, including a particularly severe one in 1906 and a massive, crippling one in 1919. A combination of recurring physical disability, aggressive overconfidence, and impatience could lead this man, who could compromise on other issues at other times, to become petty, vindictive, intractable, and ultimately self-destructive.

The personality traits of political leaders like Wilson do not alone cause the outcomes of actions and events. Results also derive from the situation itself. Many of the difficulties Wilson faced would have confronted anyone who occupied the executive mansion at that time. Yet Wilson's personal values, motives, dispositions, and physical condition shaped his perception of a situation and his selection of a course of action from among the available alternatives.

Each of the three executive positions Wilson held during his long career produced a similar cycle: initial reform achievements were followed by insurmountable obstacles and intense personal frustration. It began at Princeton University. A circuitous path led Wilson there. The son of a leading Presbyterian minister, he had grown up in Virginia and Georgia during the Civil War and Reconstruction periods. Following a brief stint as a lawyer, he became a political scientist and historian, eventually teaching at Princeton. He became president of the university in 1902. A leading educator, he instituted a number of reforms but was defeated in his attempt to abolish elite eating clubs and integrate the graduate school into the college campus. Embittered, Wilson left to run for governor of New Jersey in 1910. Once in office he rammed through a progressive program until the Republicans regained control of the state legislature and brought his success to an end. Then he went to Washington. In the White House, Wilson would again accomplish significant reforms, but he would ultimately suffer a great defeat as his opponents blocked his proposal for American participation in the postwar League of Nations.

In his political thought, Wilson was a curious paradox, for he combined a conservative background with willingness to lead the country along progressive lines. Originally a conservative eastern Democrat, he publicly repudiated his early sponsors, embraced progressivism, and helped to make reform a moral crusade. Wilson began his presidency as a Jeffersonian states-rights Democrat favoring only enough expansion of national governmental power to prevent special privilege. Yet in the

White House he proved flexible enough to meet changing conditions and political needs. Realizing the widespread support for expanded governmental intervention, he adopted much of Roosevelt's New Nationalism and increased federal power far more than his predecessor had. His use of active intervention by the government both in the marketplace and in international affairs demonstrated that interventionism could stem from both conservative and progressive origins.

The New Freedom, 1913–1916

Wilson launched his administration with a sweeping series of reforms. This legislation resulted from the interaction of the president, Congress, and nationally organized pressure groups. However, Wilson skillfully maintained his leadership in managing the bills through the compromises of the legislature. Working with key congressional leaders and private advisers, the chief executive threw the weight of the presidency behind reform proposals that had been hammered out in Congress so that they would satisfy a wide range of interest groups and constituencies. Although it resented such a strong assertion of presidential power, Congress enacted a reform program that in most aspects conformed to Wilson's wishes, a legislative record unequaled at any time between the Civil War and the New Deal era.

In his first address to Congress, Wilson called for a general lowering of tariff duties. In doing so, he could count on support from farmers and consumers who wanted lower prices for manufactured goods. Many business people were willing to lower America's protective barriers in order to open up markets abroad through reciprocal tariff reductions. When protectionists opposed him, Wilson beat them down by publicly denouncing the "industrious and insidious" lobbyists of the trusts. The Underwood Tariff passed by Congress in 1913 was the first significant reduction in the protective tariff since before the Civil War. But despite the major political victory it represented, the Underwood Tariff had little effect on the economy. Within a year World War I interrupted normal trade patterns, and in the 1920s, Republicans restored protective barriers.

The new federal income tax had a greater impact. Empowered by the Sixteenth Amendment, ratified in February 1913, Congress adopted a graduated personal income tax, in part to compensate for the loss of federal customs revenue that would result from lower tariff duties. A moderate tax, it applied only to the 5 percent of the population who earned more than $4,000 a year, and its highest rate was only 7 percent. Nevertheless, the income tax of 1913 set an important precedent. It began to shift federal revenue from its nineteenth-century base — public lands and customs duties — to its twentieth-century foundation — personal and corporate income. Widely extended in future years, it would provide the basis for financing expanded social services and massive military costs.

Almost everyone agreed that the country needed banking and currency reform, but when Wilson turned to these issues, he found an array of conflicting proposals and interest groups. Inflation-minded farmers in the South and the West argued that currency based solely on gold and U.S. government bonds was too limited. After the panic of 1907, most of the business and financial community agreed that the money supply was too inelastic to respond to changing demand. Nevertheless, interest groups differed over an appropriate basis for the currency. The financial community was divided: urban bankers wanted to add commercial paper; rural bankers sought to use commodity notes as well.

Interested groups also differed over the best means of coordinating the reserves of America's 7,000 nationally chartered banks and 20,000 state-chartered banks and mobilizing them in a financial crisis. Unlike European nations, the United States had lacked a central bank since Andrew Jackson destroyed the Bank of the United States nearly a century earlier. Beginning in the 1890s, J. P. Morgan and other major New York bankers had provided limited private, centralized direction. Now they proposed a formalized, private central bank, controlled by them, that could issue currency and determine interest rates. This proposal was opposed by smaller local and regional bankers in the South and the West. They also wanted a privately owned and controlled system but not one dominated by Wall Street. Instead, they recommended a decentralized system of regional banks run by local bankers. In the most extreme proposal, left-wing progressives and Bryanite Democrats suggested that the government own and control both the banking system and the currency. Recognizing the lack of consensus, Wilson, assisted by Carter Glass of Virginia, the head of a House banking subcommittee, used the fragmentation of opinion over this complex issue to press successfully for a compromise that all the major interest groups could accept.

Overbilled as a democratic reform that curtailed the power of Wall Street, the Federal Reserve Act of 1913 aimed primarily at providing a more orderly, coordinated system to aid the banking and business communities and the nation's economy. It combined private direction with some public regulatory supervision. The Federal Reserve System contained twelve regional Federal Reserve banks — each a kind of regional clearinghouse — that held reserves for commercial banks. Each was privately controlled by a board of local business and financial people but was loosely supervised by a public body, the Federal Reserve Board in Washington. The system could regulate the credit supply by raising or lowering the rediscount rate it charged commercial banks to borrow from it or by buying or selling government bonds in the open market. The new currency, backed by at least 40 percent in gold, consisted of Federal Reserve notes based on government bonds and commercial paper. (Agricultural paper was added later.) Like the Interstate Commerce Commission, the Federal Reserve Board was designed to act as a nonpartisan mechanism to mediate among contending interest groups and manage a crucial section of the economy in the public interest while allowing initiative and responsibility to remain in private hands. New York banks continued to hold about one quarter of national bank resources; southern banks, in contrast, held less than 8 percent.

Wilson reversed himself on the trust issue. During the campaign he had emphasized the need to curtail monopolistic consolidations and to restore competition. But once in the White House he departed from his antitrust position. Bryanite agrarian Democrats introduced bills to break up supercorporations through punitive taxes, federal regulation of the stock exchanges, and a legal limit to the share of the market any one company could control. But Wilson gave only mild assistance to the Clayton bill, which in its first versions prohibited specific monopolistic practices. Many business people and a number of progressives had protested that such extensive government prohibitions would hamper all entrepreneurs and that monopolists would find new ways to achieve their goals. When the president lost interest in specific prohibitions, opponents were able to dilute the bill significantly. As enacted in 1914, the Clayton Antitrust Act outlawed price discrimination, exclusive selling agreements, holding companies, and interlocking directorates among competing firms only when the government could prove a tendency toward monopoly. It failed to declare these practices illegal in themselves. "When the Clayton bill was first written, it was a raging lion with a mouth full of teeth," one senator mused. "It has degenerated to a tabby cat with soft gums, a plaintive mew, and an anemic appearance."

Advised by Louis D. Brandeis, who had also reversed his position, Wilson turned instead to favor continuous federal regulation of big business. Some interest groups wanted a weak governmental commission empowered to investigate but not regulate business activities. Others, such as Morgan partner George Perkins, favored a strong commission authorized to advise corporations of acceptable behavior and then immunize them against antitrust proceedings. Taking a middle position, Wilson came out for a moderately strong Federal Trade Commission (FTC), which would oversee business activity and could prevent illegal suppression of competition. The FTC, created in 1914, had the power to investigate corporations and issue restraining orders to prevent "unfair trade practices." Antitrust sentiment was too strong to give the FTC authority to immunize business from governmental prosecution. But to assuage the doubts of those traditionalists and other conservatives who had opposed such a potentially powerful agency, the president agreed to support broad judicial review of FTC orders and appointed a number of business people as commissioners.

Having decided on federal regulation rather than active dissolution of the trusts, the Wilson administration made only modest gestures toward the antitrust tradition. Although it initiated some suits, it announced that corporations could seek advice from the Justice Department in assessing and rearranging their corporate structure. Beginning with American Telephone and Telegraph Company, the Wilson administration accepted consent decrees as a means of obtaining modification of monopolistic behavior. Under these court rulings — a kind of corporate plea bargaining — an indicted corporation could comply with government recommendations and thus avoid possible conviction for restraint of trade and the penalty of triple damages as well. In return for some corporate concessions, the Justice Department would drop its suit.

The most unfortunate aspect of the Wilson administration's record involved black Americans. Racial segregation was a part of the southern progressivism that the Democrats brought to Washington. In 1912, Wilson had appealed for black support, urging blacks to give up their historic allegiance to the Republican party. Some African Americans, like W. E. B. Du Bois, had campaigned for Wilson. Once in office, however, Wilson allowed southerners in Congress and his administration to dismiss many black civil servants and to initiate official segregation — Jim Crow — in federal offices, restrooms, and restaurants. Like many other southern whites, he argued that segregation was in the blacks' own best interests. Vigorously dissenting, northern newspapers like the *New York World*, which ardently supported Wilson's New Freedom program, labeled segregation "a reproach to his Administration and to the great political principles which he represented."

At the end of 1914, Wilson announced that his domestic program of reform had been adopted. But if Wilson seemed satisfied with his reform package, many Americans were not. The editors of *The New Republic*, a recently founded journal of progressive opinion, chided the president as follows:

> Any man of President Wilson's intellectual equipment who seriously asserts that the fundamental wrongs of a modern society can be easily and quickly righted as a consequence of a few laws . . . casts suspicion either upon his own sincerity or upon his grasp of the realities of modern social and industrial life.

A Second Burst of Reform

Wilson's original, limited aims gave evidence of the conservative nature of his brand of interventionism, but political realities eventually forced him to champion additional reforms. With the Republicans reunited, the Democrats fared poorly in the 1914 congressional elections. As the 1916 presidential contest approached, Wilson resumed his leadership of the progressive program and endorsed increased governmental activism and intervention in the economy. During the first three years of his administration, the president had been reluctant to support legislation benefiting specific interest groups as opposed to a wider national interest. In 1916, however, he modified this position and gave valuable support to groups of farmers, business people, and wage workers seeking beneficial legislation.

The president won over many workers and reformers with his increased activism in their behalf. He nominated Louis D. Brandeis, the "people's lawyer," to the Supreme Court in 1915. A campaign against Brandeis was mounted by conservatives and by anti-Semites, who were outraged by the first nomination of a Jew for the high tribunal. Wilson nevertheless obtained Senate confirmation of Brandeis's appointment. Also, despite his reluctance to aid particular interest groups, Wilson signed the La Follette Seamen's Act, which provided federally guaranteed rights and greatly improved living and working conditions for merchant seamen. Abandoning his earlier opposition, Wilson also helped to secure passage of the Keating-Owen Child Labor Act (later declared unconstitutional) and workers' compensation for federal employees. Just before the election he intervened to avert a threatened nationwide strike of railroad workers and, despite great personal reservations, signed the labor-supported Adamson Act, in which the government ordered that the regular workday on the nation's railroads be reduced to eight hours.

Business also benefited from the actions of the Wilson administration. The president appointed businesspeople to many federal regulatory boards. In 1916, as a result of wartime changes in trade patterns, Wilson abandoned his attachment to free trade and endorsed protection against postwar dumping of goods in the United States. In addition, he helped to establish a permanent U.S. Tariff Commission in an attempt to remove tariff rate making from politics and provide flexible schedules determined by experts. To aid American business abroad, he tried to amend the antitrust laws to allow manufacturers to form cartels for foreign sales, a proposal that Congress finally enacted in 1918.

Previously Wilson had blocked a movement to offer rural credits to farmers in the South and the West, arguing that the federal government should not aid special-interest groups. By 1916, however, he had changed his mind. His support proved decisive in securing the Federal

Farm Loan Act and the Warehouse Act, which provided farmers in
these credit-tight regions with long-term, federally supported, low-
interest loans based on the value of the farmer's land and crops. Agrarians also benefited disproportionately from the Federal Highway Act of
1916. This economic promotional legislation in the tradition of nineteenth-century governmental support for railroad construction was one
of the first examples of a "new federalism" in which the national
government gave substantial grants-in-aid to the states to spend for
specific developmental purposes. It marked the beginning of federal
intervention in support of an extensive highway network.

The Election of 1916

By the 1916 election Wilson and the Democratic Congress had enacted
much progressive and special-interest legislation. The president campaigned for reelection on a platform of peace, progressivism, and prosperity. Aided by his incumbency and the foreign policy issues raised by
World War I, Wilson effectively mobilized many new voters. The
Republicans had bypassed the rambunctious Roosevelt and nominated
an associate justice of the Supreme Court and former progressive governor of New York, the austere Charles Evans Hughes. Without Roosevelt, the Progressive party died.

Despite the GOP's reunification after the 1912 split, one out of ten
Republicans — especially social justice progressives and antiwar
Republicans — voted for Wilson. In the 1916 election Wilson added
many urban workers and social justice progressives and some socialists
to his original coalition of agrarians from the South and the West. The
president won reelection with 277 electoral votes and 49 percent of
the popular vote, compared to Hughes's 254 votes and 46 percent. The
Socialist candidate, A. L. Benson, won only 600,000 votes, 3.2 percent
of the turnout. Wilson had forged a coalition that combined several
urban eastern states with the agrarian South and West. More than any
previous Democratic candidate, he had been able to unite and expand
the two wings of the party. But the coalition was not held together. It
broke apart during World War I and was not fully resurrected until the
1930s.

Political Modernization

Progressivism was the most important new force in American politics in
the early twentieth century. It helped change the nature of politics and
the relationship between political leaders and government on the one
hand and the public on the other. It infused a new spirit into the
national government, rekindling public faith in Washington's ability to

respond to national problems. "Democracy is now setting out on her real mission," William Allen White wrote in 1910, "to define the rights of the owner and the user of private property according to the dictates of an enlightened public conscience." Progressive leaders like Roosevelt and Wilson encouraged capable, idealistic people to go to work in Washington. They helped to dispel the late-nineteenth-century view of government as corrupt and ineffective and replace it with a new belief that a responsible and expert, democratically based government could be an effective instrument of continued progress.

In little more than a dozen years, progressives and other interventionists greatly strengthened the role of government. They began to create regulatory machinery and, unwittingly, the broker state. The progressives' belief in a common public interest prevented most of them from acknowledging the emerging role of the federal government as a mediator or broker among various interest groups. But with the nationalization of issues many new pressure groups emerged on the national level. Bodies like the U.S. Chamber of Commerce, the National Consumers' League, the National Civic Federation, and a host of others lobbied actively for governmental action to protect and improve their position, and the various agencies of government responded to them. New political leaders like Roosevelt also recognized that they had to show some of the people who had been hurt by the forces of industrialism that government could be responsive to them. Despite their aversion to parochialism and interest-group politics and their search for a larger public interest, progressives found themselves pressured into creating a broker state as a replacement for the self-regulating marketplace. As Herbert Croly asserted in 1909:

Reform is both meaningless and powerless unless the Jeffersonian principle of non-interference is abandoned. The experience of the last generation plainly shows that the American economic and social system cannot be allowed to take care of itself, and that the automatic harmony of the individual and the public interest, which is the essence of the Jeffersonian democratic creed, has proved to be an illusion.

It was not only progressives who pressed for government action. Conservative interventionists also played major roles in the enactment of legislation dealing with railroad regulation, currency and banking reform, and consumer protection through meat and drug inspection and labeling. They were the most important force in achieving social control legislation involving alcohol prohibition, narcotics control, and immigration restriction and in expanding the armed forces. Organized labor supported governmental intervention to benefit unions and direct federal guarantees of workers' rights, including pay raises, for seamen and railroaders. Agrarian interventionists obtained a system of federal extension agents from land grant colleges to provide advice and, more important, a federally supported system of rural credit.

The new interventionists established a major role for the federal government in the economy and society. They created a regulatory state and established the federal income tax to pay for it. The new system emphasized executive, nonpartisan, expert mediation by government bureaucracies whose role was to balance the demands of contending interest groups in the larger public interest. Congress authorized, and the Supreme Court upheld, most of the new departures, which were designed to provide mechanisms for government to regulate important areas of the economic system while keeping primary initiative and responsibility in the hands of individuals and groups in the private sector.

The single most important innovation of the Progressive Era was the creation of the modern presidency. Activist and reform-minded, Roosevelt and Wilson drew on constitutional and latent powers of the office to serve as effective national leaders. To an extent unheard of in the late nineteenth century, they outlined major programs, mobilized public opinion, lobbied bills through Congress, and took bold executive action in support of labor when industrial disputes threatened to jeopardize the public welfare. Most important, they portrayed the chief executive as the only political leader who represented the American people as a whole. Thus the Progressive Era presidents reached for and often obtained new power to deal with national domestic problems and, increasingly, to assert actively American interests abroad.

CHAPTER 7

Taking the Flag Overseas

The Road to Interventionism

 Like a young giant flexing newfound muscles, the United States swaggered onto the center of the world stage in the early years of the twentieth century. The rapidly industrializing nation expanded its economic interests and began a policy of diplomatic and military intervention abroad. This new international activism moved beyond America's traditional foreign policy of reacting to events. Policymakers now sought to exert some control over external forces of change. They began to use American power to shape the international environment, protect American interests, and encourage progress in international relations.

Throughout most of its existence, the American republic had been sheltered from the need to engage in extensive diplomacy and substantial military defense. It enjoyed what one historian has called an "era of free security." During most of the nineteenth century the country benefited from a stable balance of power in Europe and the significant obstacle to invasion presented by the breadth of the Atlantic and Pacific oceans.

Although Americans had for generations sent their commodities and ideas overseas, the government maintained a policy of neutrality toward wars outside the Western Hemisphere and of isolationism from many events abroad. The United States had pictured itself as a moral exemplar to the world. American expansion had been primarily across its own continent. Although the Monroe Doctrine proclaimed U.S. opposition to new European colonies in the Western Hemisphere, it was seldom invoked in the nineteenth century.

The growth of American economic and military power, burgeoning national pride, and new international developments challenged this self-imposed curtailment. A limited number of Americans interested in foreign policy sought to establish new mechanisms to control developments and create an international order favorable to the United States. They wanted to influence events rather than merely react to them; they wanted to have the nation act as a world power. As one expansionist senator asserted at the outbreak of the Spanish-American War, "There is no such thing as isolation in the world today."

The world changed quickly. Industrialism stimulated competition among the great powers. It also provided new weapons: steel warships, airplanes, long-range cannons, and rapid-fire artillery and machine guns. Armed with these, the imperialist nations—Britain, France, Italy, Russia, Japan—plunged across the globe in search of markets, raw materials, enhanced security, and greater national glory. By 1900 they had conquered and carved up Africa and much of Asia, squashing local resistance and occasionally skirmishing among themselves.

Great Britain had already entered a period of long-term decline, and Germany, Russia, and Japan had begun to challenge the nineteenth-century world order. World War I, which lasted from 1914 until 1918, was the first general European war in a century. It ended nineteenth-century diplomacy and the balance of power. In doing so, it began the military challenges between conflicting alliances that dominated the first half of the twentieth century, although the devastation that resulted shifted the locus of international power away from Europe.

Until the outbreak of World War I, the U.S. government focused primarily on the Caribbean and to a lesser extent on the Far East. American interests and involvement in these areas were intensified by the acquisition of colonies and protectorates following the Spanish-American War. By 1900 the United States had acquired the territories of the Philippine Islands, Samoa, Guam, Hawaii, and Puerto Rico. It dominated Cuba as a protectorate through financial control and occasional military intervention. In the early years of the century the United States established protectorates in Haiti, the Dominican Republic, Nicaragua, and Panama. In Panama, Americans built a major interoceanic canal that transformed the Caribbean from a drowsy backwater into an international crossroads. In the Caribbean and the Far East, the conflicting aims of many of the big powers affected American economic, political, and strategic interests. The U.S. government saw America as both a beneficiary and a protector, and it began to try to influence events there in favor of the United States.

During the Progressive Era, American economic interests expanded dramatically. The United States had always been a major exporting nation, but in the two decades before World War I, U.S. exports doubled. More important, in 1905, for the first time in American history, manufactured goods surpassed agricultural commodities as the major items being shipped abroad. Crates filled with tractors, typewriters, automobiles, phonographs, and similar products illustrated the nation's industrial progress. The United States had also been a major importer, especially of investment funds from Europe. But Americans' growing wealth enabled them to quadruple their own investment in

Europe and elsewhere; this figure reached $3.5 billion in the two decades before 1914. During World War I the United States replaced Britain as the world's leading creditor.

Spurred by the depression of the 1890s, many American corporations turned to foreign markets and sources of raw materials to supplement their domestic activities, and some began to establish sales offices, plants, and other facilities abroad. Their names became familiar overseas: Singer, American Tobacco, Armour, Eastman Kodak, General Electric, Ford, Standard Oil, and eventually the ubiquitous Coca-Cola. Although some corporations sought raw materials, especially in Latin America, most engaged in selling American manufactured goods in more prosperous consumer nations such as Canada and the countries of western Europe.

Through such expansion U.S. corporations began to shape the economic development not only of smaller countries in Latin America but also of major nations such as Canada and Britain. By 1907 the British claimed that some 2,000 American firms in London dominated many of their industries and were reshaping aspects of life in Britain. Europeans, like others, were ambivalent about this process. They wanted American goods and investment funds but not American influence and control. The turn of the century saw them warning of the "American menace" and the "Americanization" of Europe.

Except in the Caribbean and the Far East, U.S. governmental policies and actions had only a small impact on this pattern of economic growth. The corporations took the initiative in expanding into foreign markets and sources of raw materials. They negotiated concessions from foreign governments or individuals. They established mines and smelters, railroads and port facilities. They opened sales outlets and constructed factories. When they encountered problems abroad, they often dealt with them by admitting local elites into the management or financing of the operation or by hiring foreign nationals as workers. Sometimes they joined with European companies in international cartels that fixed prices and divided world markets. The protective tariff had been the U.S. government's primary instrument for assisting business in the international marketplace. But in the early twentieth century the government began to negotiate reciprocal tariff reductions with other nations to open up markets for American goods.

The early twentieth century was also a time of increased communications as Americans made contact in a number of ways with peoples in other lands. The revolution in communications produced by the creation of a worldwide telegraph cable network led to increased news coverage of foreign events by American newspapers and magazines. Much of what Americans learned was filtered through their perceptions, also partly shaped by the media, about the ideologies and value systems of peoples and nations. These were assessed in the context of

Americans' own core values of themselves and their nation and of current ways of looking at the world—for example, in terms of racism, economic imperialism, humanitarian internationalism, religious evangelism, or geopolitical theories of growth or decline. Americans' sense of superiority, race consciousness, and eagerness to promote democratization and other aspects of American culture underlay their attitudes toward other countries.

In the history of U.S. foreign relations, nothing is more striking than the private initiatives of individual Americans to reach across national boundaries to engage in commercial, religious, educational, and other activities. The accounts of traders, missionaries, physicians, nurses, teachers, scientists, sailors, and travelers helped to shape American attitudes about other countries. These visitors also helped to acquaint other peoples—often at the price of a considerable clash of cultures—with American ideas about social reform, gender, child care, religion, morality, and peace, as well as efficiency, business rationalism, and capitalist internationalism. Beginning in the 1890s officials in Washington took considerable interest in Americans' activities overseas and sought to guide these so as to promote national political and economic interests, especially the extension of American trade and investment.

In the early stages of U.S. industry's leap overseas, many Americans believed that economic expansion abroad also took with it the best of Americanism, the values of industriousness, honesty, morality, and private initiative. Sales of Singer sewing machines and Standard Oil kerosene (for illumination) in China, for example, were seen by most middle-class Americans not simply as making profits but also as advancing Western civilization. This sense of the superiority of American institutions and culture also contributed directly to the establishment of overseas educational enterprises and the sweeping religious missionary movement of the turn of the century. Making profits, educating people, improving their health, and saving their souls were not seen as incompatible goals of America's mission overseas.

Missionary work had long been an important part of American Protestantism, but it became particularly energized during the nation's outward thrust and internal reform at the turn of the century. In 1895, with the financial support of industrialists John D. Rockefeller, Jr., and Cyrus McCormick, John R. Mott, a Methodist missionary director, created the World's Student Christian Federation to harness the energies of dedicated youth. In its first twenty years, during the peak of the social gospel movement, the organization sent out more than 5,000 young people on foreign missions. Mott's work and writing, including his popular book *The Evangelization of the World in This Generation* (1900), received praise in Europe and America. The Young Men's Christian Association (YMCA), with Mott as general secretary of the

International Committee in 1915, planted dozens of American-style YMCA branches overseas, particularly in China and India. Women Baptists, Congregationalists, Methodists, and Presbyterians had organized their own foreign missionary societies in the late nineteenth century, and more than 3 million American women were involved by 1914, raising consciousness and money at home or serving overseas as doctors, nurses, teachers, or spouses of ordained clergymen (women were excluded from the clergy at that time). By 1920 in China alone Protestant missionaries operated more than 1,300 schools, plus numerous colleges, seminaries, medical schools, orphanages, hospitals, leper colonies, and institutions for the deaf and blind; and the American Bible Society had sent nearly 20,000 Bibles and 2 million other publications to China. Although China was the major focus, other Protestant missionary efforts were made in Korea, Japan, Thailand, and Burma, throughout the South Pacific, and in much of Africa.

American Roman Catholics became active missionaries after the Vatican in 1908 declared the church in the United States to be no longer missionary-dependent. Founded three years later, the Catholic Foreign Missionary Society of America, headquartered in Maryknoll, New York, sent thousands of missionaries overseas, especially to Central and Latin America. As with the Protestants, the Maryknoll priests and nuns interpreted their roles broadly to meet human as well as spiritual needs; they developed schools, hospitals, and orphanages as well as churches and seminaries for native-born clergy. Helping to launch the process, Boston's archbishop, William H. O'Connell, sounding very much like John R. Mott, declared in 1908, "The providential hour of opportunity has struck. We must be up and doing. All indications point to our vocation as a great missionary nation." Through the independent efforts of U.S. Protestants and Catholics, Americans surpassed the previously dominant British in financing and creating foreign missions.

American Attitudes

As the United States became increasingly involved overseas through economic, diplomatic, cultural, and strategic interests, many Americans reexamined their attitudes toward world affairs. They wanted the government to pursue a foreign policy that would protect the nation's interests in a changing world and also reflect its traditions. Not surprisingly, they differed over what was the best solution.

Traditionalists continued to accept basic policies that the U.S. government had employed for decades. They believed in political isolationism, supported a policy of staying out of foreign quarrels in Europe or Asia, and endorsed the Monroe Doctrine. To protect American security they relied on barriers provided by the great oceans, reinforced by coastal fortifications, mines, and a defense-oriented navy composed of submarines, gunboats, and destroyers. Isolationists supported a small regular army, which could be augmented in an emergency by the National Guard and citizens who would enlist in regiments of the U.S. Volunteers. This policy emphasized America's natural security and its role as an exemplar to the world. Support was strongest in the rural South and Midwest, especially among followers of William Jennings Bryan.

Modernizers in foreign policy considered many of the nation's traditions inadequate for the new international circumstances. Those who sought new directions concurred on the necessity for greater activism, but they disagreed on the form it should take. *Militant expansionists* such as Theodore Roosevelt, Admiral Alfred Thayer Mahan, and General Leonard Wood, military governor of Cuba and later army chief of staff, wanted to commit the United States to active use of diplomatic, economic, military, and naval power in pursuit of broadened goals. They argued that the United States should secure a dominant position in the Western Hemisphere to prevent the incursion of expanding European nations, especially Germany. In addition, the United States should vigorously pursue prestige and commercial opportunities abroad. Militant expansionists emphasized *Realpolitik*, the use of force and the balance of power to achieve the nation's aims. They advocated a large, modern high-seas fleet and an efficient, expandable army with large numbers of trained reservists. Believers in a kind of international Darwinism, militant expansionists saw international competition and war as inevitable and sometimes beneficial.

Reform internationalists were also modernizers who wanted to change American foreign policy. But they placed greater emphasis on the improvement of international relations. Seeing war as anachronistic, they hoped to curtail or even eliminate the use of armed force. Among them, the *legalists*, such as William Howard Taft, Woodrow Wilson, and Elihu Root, Roosevelt's secretary of state, advocated arbitration, mediation, adjudication, and the use of a world court or international parliament. *Pacifists* or *communalists* such as Jane Addams and Oswald Garrison Villard agreed, but in addition they emphasized the need to eliminate the causes of war by actively working toward equity, justice, and a nonviolent community for humankind.

There was considerable overlap among traditionalists, militant expansionists, and reform internationalists as they sought appropriate foreign and defense policies. Although progressives tended to be modernizers in foreign policy, they could be found among both militant expansionists and reform internationalists. All three groups included conservatives, moderates, and radicals, Republicans and Democrats. Such diversity confirmed the lack of consensus on the proper course for America.

Within this broad spectrum the president and his chief advisers played the most important role in determining foreign policy and the manner in which the United States responded to specific events. But there were limitations on the president's power in foreign affairs. He was constrained in part by the growth of national interest groups concerned with events abroad. Business associations, ethnic groups, and ideological societies, such as peace groups and the Army and Navy Leagues, kept track of foreign developments and sought to influence U.S. policy. Presidents also found themselves restrained by political realities and the continued widespread popularity of political isolationism. Furthermore, the United States' role abroad was limited by the activities of other powerful nations.

Despite these limitations, the chief executives in the Progressive Era helped to modernize American foreign and defense policy. They greatly expanded the power of the president as an international manager and promulgated doctrines that defined national interest and policy. Expanded activity in foreign affairs proved to be one of the foundations of the modern presidency.

Roosevelt's Big-Stick Diplomacy

As an apostle of *Realpolitik*, Theodore Roosevelt sought to protect the United States' national interests. Admiral Mahan and others taught him to think of those interests not only in racial and geographic terms but in strategic and commercial terms as well. Roosevelt became convinced that the United States had to be strong and purposeful to protect itself and its areas of prime concern, such as the Caribbean. Fearing that Germany would challenge U.S. interests in Central and South America and that Japan would threaten the Open Door policy in China and the security of the Philippines, he worked to protect American interests in those areas. Roosevelt also knew how to capture the public imagination through personal deeds or colorful phrases. When asked about his foreign policy, he liked to quote an old African proverb: "Speak softly and carry a big stick."

In relations among nations, as among individuals, Roosevelt was convinced that power commanded respect and that, as a rich and expanding country, the United States needed force to protect its interests. He launched America into the naval arms race that was developing among Britain, Germany, and Japan. During his two terms as president he doubled the size of the navy. U.S. naval expenditures grew from $56 million in 1900 to $118 million in 1905 – leaping from 11 to 21 percent of total federal expenditures and remaining close to that percentage until World War I. Although Congress reacted to the high cost of navalism and curtailed an even more ambitious battleship-building program in 1907, it had already authorized an expanded, modern high-seas fleet second only to that of Great Britain.

It was in the Caribbean that Roosevelt intervened most boldly. The centerpiece of his policy and of U.S. national interest was a canal between the Atlantic and Pacific oceans. Like many other Americans, he considered an interoceanic waterway essential to increased trade and to more effective protection of the U.S. coastline and sea lanes. Roosevelt obtained the canal site in Panama and established American hegemony in the Caribbean.

Because Colombia controlled Panama, the United States negotiated with the Bogotá government to build and operate the canal. However, the Colombian senate rejected the Hay-Herran Convention of 1903, which provided a payment of $10 million and an annual rental fee of $250,000 for the canal zone. Recklessly, Roosevelt considered seizing Panama. Instead, his purposes were served by a revolt instigated by foreign promoters and native elites led by the former chief engineer of the French Panama Canal Company, Philippe Bunau-Varilla. He had met with Roosevelt in the White House less than a month earlier and had learned that the president was dispatching U.S. warships to the area. On the day the U.S.S. *Nashville* arrived, the Panamanian revolt began. The presence of the U.S. Navy prevented Colombia from landing forces to suppress the revolt, and three days later Roosevelt recognized the new Republic of Panama.

Within two weeks Bunau-Varilla arrived in Washington to sign the Hay–Bunau-Varilla Treaty. It gave Panama the sums rejected by Colombia. In return the United States received, in perpetuity, the use and control of a canal zone 10 miles wide and the right to intervene in Panama if its independence was threatened by Colombia or by any other country. The treaty was ratified in 1904, and the Panama Canal opened in 1914 after a decade of construction.

Roosevelt's actions represented an extreme form of the new American interventionism overseas. They were controversial from the start. Acting precipitously, with little regard for law or morality, he had encouraged revolution and infringed on Colombian sovereignty. He justified his high-handed action by claiming that immediate construction of the canal was vital to the United States and in "the interests of civilization." Later he boasted, "I took the Canal Zone and let Congress debate; and while the debate goes on, the Canal does also." Roosevelt's nationalism proved popular with many Americans, but others abhorred it as disreputable and unnecessary. In 1921, after Roosevelt's death, the United States paid $25 million to Colombia to make amends and obtain oil concessions there. Half a century later, Panamanians forced the United States to renegotiate the treaty and provide, in 1979, for increased annual payments and for transfer of the Canal Zone to Panama in the year 2000.

Throughout the Caribbean, Roosevelt extended American power and hegemony. Partly to prevent possible German expansion, the United States annexed Puerto Rico as a territory in 1898. Cuba, governed by the American military from 1898 to 1902, remained a protectorate under the Platt Amendment, which authorized U.S. military intervention when necessary "for the preservation of Cuban independence" and "the maintenance of a government adequate for the protection of life, property, and individual liberty." American economic investment in Cuba grew from $50 million in 1898 to $500 million in 1920.

Roosevelt's Caribbean policy was most forcefully stated in his 1904 pronouncement known as the Roosevelt Corollary to the Monroe Doctrine. The Corollary grew out of the attempts of European governments to force debt-ridden Latin American nations to pay their creditors. In Africa and Asia this kind of action had often led to European occupation and colonization. To prevent such incursion into the Caribbean, after European warships had been dispatched to Venezuela and the Dominican Republic to obtain payments for creditors, Roosevelt decided in 1904 that the United States should intervene. He unilaterally expanded the Monroe Doctrine from a prohibition against additional European colonization in the Western Hemisphere to an authorization for preemptive U.S. intervention. The United States would police the Carribean. With American warships in Santo Domingo harbor, the president's representative obtained an executive agreement with the government of the Dominican Republic authorizing the reorganization of the nation's debt and shifting it from European to American creditors. The United States also took over management of the customs house through which the nation's exports flowed and its revenues returned. Thus through the use of American economic and military power, Roosevelt launched a policy that his successors have pursued in varying degrees.

Roosevelt also pursued his active diplomacy in East Asia, where it proved neither as decisive nor as successful as it was in the Caribbean. In the Far East the United States faced the great powers competing for spoils from the impending collapse of the Manchu dynasty and central authority in China. The United States was in a weak position to achieve its Far Eastern goals, which Roosevelt defined as protection of the Philippines and maintenance of the Open Door in China. The president tried to balance Russia and Japan against each other as the two major Asian powers clashed in the iron- and coal-rich Chinese province of Manchuria. In the Russo-Japanese War of 1904–1905, both sides accepted Roosevelt's offer to mediate, and the president sought a compromise that would keep each in a position to check the other. The Treaty of Portsmouth, New Hampshire, recognized Japan's dominant rights in Korea and split both Sakhalin Island and the railroad rights in

Manchuria between the two powers. The first American president to play such a significant mediating role in world affairs, Roosevelt won the Nobel Peace Prize for his efforts.

Next Roosevelt conciliated Japan, which emerged from the war as the strongest naval power in the Pacific. When the Japanese public grew incensed over a San Francisco School Board order segregating Asian children, the president fumed at the "infernal fools in California" and finally persuaded the school authorities to rescind the order. In the following year, 1907, he reached the Gentlemen's Agreement with the Japanese government, which promised to prevent agricultural laborers from emigrating and competing with American workers. In the Root-Takahira Agreement of 1908, Roosevelt placated the Japanese by recognizing their hegemony over Korea and Formosa, which they had captured in the Sino-Japanese War of 1895. In exchange, the emperor's government renounced any interest in the Philippines and affirmed the Open Door policy in China.

The United States' new role in world affairs led to increased involvement in the shifting power relationships of Europe. While in the White House, Roosevelt encouraged the growth of Anglo-American friendship, one of the most important diplomatic developments of the period. Despite the traditional hostility of many Americans toward Britain, elites in both countries brought about a *rapprochement* in the two decades between the war scare with Britain over the Venezuelan border dispute in 1895 and the American entry into World War I on the British side in 1917. In the meantime, the United States joined its new power to Britain's in the face of aggressive challenges from Germany, Japan, and Russia. The British, in turn, acquiesced in American dominance of the Western Hemisphere.

An alternative to Roosevelt's *Realpolitik* was put forward by the peace movement, which contributed greatly to the effort to improve international relations. After years of relative lethargy, the American peace movement grew dramatically during the first decade and a half of the new century. Since its inception during the reform outburst of the 1830s, the movement had been composed primarily of Quakers and other religious pacifists and a handful of New England reformers. Beginning around 1905, under the pressure of events and changing attitudes, an influx of new members transformed the traditional peace movement. Many believed that war had become an anachronistic and inefficient way of settling disputes. At the same time, concern over the naval arms race between Britain and Germany and the bloodiness of the Russo-Japanese War intensified the search for new forms of international relations by demonstrating the costs of modern war. Under pressure from a number of peace advocates, including several members of Congress, President Roosevelt called, during the 1904 election campaign, for a second international disarmament conference, to be held at The Hague in 1907.

Plans for that conference helped to expand the peace movement, which swelled in the following decade. The expansion of traditional peace groups was matched by the creation of new organizations to curtail war. The steelmaker Andrew Carnegie gave $10 million to establish the Carnegie Endowment for International Peace. As a result of attending the Hague Disarmament Conferences of 1899 and 1907, the United States agreed to participate in the Permanent Court of International Arbitration, the so-called Hague Tribunal. Peace advocates urged further steps: a world court, the development of international common law, arbitration of disputes between nations, multinational disarmament conferences or unilateral abolition of armaments, and even a world parliament. Jane Addams, the social worker and founder of the Women's International League for Peace and Freedom, proposed the creation of an international welfare community as a substitute for war. As early as 1904 she suggested that the labor movement, with its ideal of human solidarity, and the social reform movement, with its trust of the masses, could serve as moral substitutes for international conflict. So popular was the idea of arbitration that Roosevelt sponsored several treaties requiring the United States to arbitrate certain limited kinds of international disputes. This was only a gesture, however, and Roosevelt is accurately remembered for his bellicosity.

Taft's Dollar Diplomacy

Roosevelt expected his handpicked successor, William Howard Taft, to stick closely to his policies, but in foreign affairs as in domestic politics, the two presidents differed significantly, though on methods rather than goals. Taft wished to avoid Roosevelt's bellicose posturing and bold assertion of power. Seeking to abandon strident rhetoric, exaggerated executive action, and the use of force, the former jurist looked for more orderly, cooperative, and constitutional means of pursuing U.S. interests.

"Dollar diplomacy" (the expression coined by the Taft administration) stressed economic policy as a means of influencing international affairs in the interest of the United States. Taft encouraged active private economic intervention to maintain stable, pro-American governments in the Caribbean and China. His aim was avoiding military incursion, "substituting dollars for bullets." Nevertheless, when economic solutions failed, the Taft administration did not rule out the use of military force. In fact, Taft sent the Marines into more Caribbean countries than Roosevelt had. In Nicaragua, for example, from 1909 until they left in 1925, the Marines kept a minority party in power. Military control, not social and economic improvement, kept Nicaragua stable and pro-American, an ironic finale to the diplomacy of an administration that sought to demilitarize American foreign policy.

The primary aim of dollar diplomacy was to maintain American hegemony in the Caribbean. It did expand U.S. power there and, like foreign aid after World War II, it linked underdeveloped nations to the United States both economically and strategically. But there was not enough private investment to accomplish major changes, and the haughty use of dollar diplomacy proved highly unpopular in Latin America.

Financial diplomacy succeeded in extending American control in the Caribbean, but it failed in China. There Taft tried to use American capital to build up a counterweight to Russian and Japanese expansion. The former consul general in Manchuria, Willard Straight, a New York banker, called dollar diplomacy the financial expression of the Open Door. He predicted that it would help to protect and guide China along its road to modernization. Reversing Roosevelt's strategy, Taft decided to strengthen China rather than conciliate Japan.

Taft's attempt to apply financial leverage in the Far East encountered major obstacles. Russia and Japan resisted it, and Britain proved unwilling to alienate the two countries, which had become its allies. American financiers did not respond enthusiastically to their government's invitation to invest heavily in China. They considered the situation there uncertain and risky; they could earn higher returns investing at home. Thus financial diplomacy in the Far East backfired. The timidity of American bankers hampered Taft's policy, and the determined opposition of other major powers halted it. The United States did not increase its influence in China. Rather, it alienated Japan and Russia and heightened suspicion of American motives among all the powers.

An Illusory Transition

Witnessing the new international interventionism of Presidents McKinley, Roosevelt, and Taft, most Americans thought the country could enlarge its global role without wholly rejecting its traditional foreign policy. Expansion in Latin America and the Far East had come at such little cost that many Americans believed that moral rectitude was sufficient to ensure the triumph of U.S. policy. Yet others tried to establish a realistic relationship between aims and commitments and the means to obtain them.

Instead of the old policies of reacting to events or merely offering a moral example to the world, the U.S. government and private groups like those in the peace movement attempted to devise new mechanisms to shape the international environment. Corporations and business associations moved beyond the old policy of trade expansion through limited commercial arrangements to active industrial and financial penetration of other countries. Despite these developments, public debate was often couched in moralistic terms frequently unrelated to the immediate concerns of national interest and power relations.

In the first decade and a half of the twentieth century, Americans found it possible to possess overseas colonies and protectorates and still adhere to their traditional principles of isolationism and neutrality and to the Monroe Doctrine. The costs of expansionism seemed small because in the main area of American concern, the Caribbean, the only major competing power, Great Britain, decided not to challenge U.S. actions. Thus the United States could expand at relatively little immediate cost to itself and little distraction from its primary concern with domestic issues. Traditional American parochialism counterbalanced the new outward thrust. Not until the outbreak of World War I did the United States confront the first real test — as well as the major costs — of its new international position.

Wilson's Missionary Diplomacy

Placing greater emphasis on idealism than his predecessors, Woodrow Wilson encouraged Americans to view foreign policy in terms of morality and mission. He grafted the new interventionism onto Americans' traditional sense of national rectitude and their evangelistic mission to improve humanity, thereby enabling many previously skeptical Americans to endorse the departures in foreign affairs as consistent with the country's traditions. "We created this Nation," Wilson asserted, "not to serve ourselves, but to serve mankind."

In his emphasis on American morality and mission, Wilson was not utopian. He understood the country's strategic and economic needs and the realities of international relations. He accepted the widely held theory that the closing of the western frontier meant that America would have to find a new frontier of expanding exports and investments abroad.

The Wilson administration laid the foundations of modern American international economic policy. In doing so it emphasized that a humane, reformist capitalism could serve as the economic arm of an expanding democracy that would benefit entrepreneurs, workers, and consumers at home and abroad. The U.S. government encouraged American expansion and competition in an open world marketplace and opposed the traditional European systems of colonial control or exclusive foreign concessions in which investors were virtually sovereign. As a result of this activist economic policy and the dislocation of European trade and finance during World War I, the United States achieved economic predominance in Latin America.

Wilson's idealistic, reformist diplomacy blended with the progressive interventionist impulse. The successes of reform at home suggested that a combination of moralistic fervor and pragmatic activism might be applied abroad. The urge to replace drift and mere response to events with mastery and direction led modernizers to seek new policies and institutions and attempt to create a more favorable environment for American interests. In a world of great international change, Wilson offered a middle path between oppressive colonial imperialism and violent revolution and radical change. He urged the promotion of international peace and orderly development through democracy and liberal capitalism.

Like many Americans, Wilson adopted a universalistic approach, believing that American standards and values of stability, democracy, and liberal capitalism could be applied to countries with divergent cultural traditions and national aspirations. He tried to impose democratic solutions in Latin America and later in Russia, where liberal democratic, capitalistic concepts were not widely accepted and could not be imposed from the outside. Wilson sought an Americanized world order, and his self-righteousness and periodic rigidity sometimes led him to oversimplify issues and act too hastily.

In his policy toward Latin America and the Far East, Wilson publicly dissociated himself from his Republican predecessors. He denounced Roosevelt's aggressive use of force and Taft's dollar diplomacy. Despite his original hopes, Wilson came to adopt "moral imperialism," which led him to use more military force in the Caribbean countries than either Roosevelt or Taft. Nevertheless, because of Wilson's stress on educative and uplifting goals and his stated desire to encourage "the development of constitutional liberty in the world," his policy became known as "missionary diplomacy."

Missionary diplomacy often led to military intervention. When an unpopular Haitian president was murdered in 1915, Wilson sent in the Marines to suppress revolution. The leathernecks easily put down the rebellion, but in 1918 they killed more than 2,000 Haitians to crush a second revolt. For nearly twenty years the Marines remained in Haiti maintaining stability and U.S. control. By the end of the Wilson administration, the United States had a firm hold on the Caribbean, with territories in Puerto Rico, Panama, and the Virgin Islands (purchased from Denmark in 1917) and troops in Nicaragua, Haiti, and the Dominican Republic. Cuba remained an American protectorate.

Revolution in Mexico

In Mexico, Wilson's combination of missionary diplomacy and military force led him into a morass. American meddling in the Mexican Revolution, which broke out in 1910, demonstrated what could happen when moral diplomacy collided with political realities, indigenous nationalism, and intractable local problems. Wilson found that he could neither easily shape events abroad nor readily remove the United States from such situations once committed.

Mexico began nearly a decade of intensive revolution and civil war when a rebellion led by an aristocratic liberal, Francisco Madero, overthrew the aging dictator Porfirio Díaz in 1910. U.S. corporations had invested $1 billion in Mexican mining, railroad, and other facilities, and they soon became distressed by Madero's reform program, which was directed against the government, the army, the Roman Catholic church, and foreign economic involvement. In 1913, Victoriano Huerta, one of Madero's generals, had the new president assassinated. Many foreign investors supported the would-be dictator as a conservative strongman, and most European nations recognized Huerta's regime. Wilson, however, refused to do so, despite pressure from business, arguing that Huerta had seized power illegally and did not represent the Mexican people. "I will not recognize a government of butchers," he declared.

In refusing to recognize a government in power, Wilson broke a century-old American tradition, but he did so in the name of constitutional principles and human rights, raising his action to a high moral plane. Wilson thus became the first president to use nonrecognition as a diplomatic tactic. But he went beyond nonrecognition to achieve his purpose; he engaged in active interventionism in Mexico.

During the civil war that followed Huerta's *coup d'état*, Wilson used American power to depose the general and replace his regime with a liberal, pro-American, constitutionalist government. The president began by establishing an embargo of American arms and credit. Then he blockaded foreign munitions. Finally, he authorized outright military intervention. In 1914 a petty incident involving alleged disrespect for the U.S. flag served as a pretext for Wilson to order American sailors and Marines to capture Mexico's main port, Vera Cruz, to prevent a shipload of German weapons and ammunition from being delivered to Huerta. Although Wilson had anticipated a bloodless occupation, 19 Americans and 126 Mexicans were killed in the fighting. But the gambit succeeded. Cut off from his sources of military supplies and besieged by the troops of the Constitutionalist party leader, Venustiano Carranza, Huerta fled the country. Then, in a major blunder, Wilson chose to back not Carranza, who had condemned the American occupation of Vera Cruz, but Francisco ("Pancho") Villa, a dashing, peasant-born general who had broken with Carranza. Not until the fall of 1915 did Wilson reverse himself and give *de facto* recognition to the Carranza government. But this alienated Villa, who then turned against Wilson as well as Carranza.

To embarrass and discredit the Carranza government, Villa recklessly sought to force U.S. intervention in Mexico. In 1916, *Villistas* raided border towns in Texas and New Mexico, burning buildings and killing nearly two dozen Americans. Posting the National Guard to protect the border, Wilson ordered a "punitive expedition" into Mexico to try to capture Villa. Led by General John J. Pershing, some 12,000 U.S. Army troops trekked more than 400 miles into northern Mexico following the elusive Villa. But the Americans' advance roused Mexican nationalism. A skirmish at Carrizal between Pershing's and Carranza's troops almost led to a full-scale conflict between the two countries. War was averted through peace organizations, which bolstered Wilson's reluctance to fight. Facing the prospect of entering the European war, the president withdrew the expeditionary force early in 1917, and later that year, after the Mexican constitution was proclaimed and Carranza was formally elected president, he finally extended *de jure* recognition to the Carranza government.

The Rising Sun in the Pacific

In the Far East, Wilson found that he could not influence events as he could in the Caribbean. In his first year in office he recognized the new republican government in China that had overthrown the crumbling Manchu dynasty. He protested when Japan, taking advantage of the international situation during World War I, gobbled up Germany's Pacific colonies in the Mariana, Caroline, and Marshall islands and the German leasehold on China's Shantung peninsula, and when Tokyo issued the "Twenty-one Demands," which would have made China virtually a Japanese client state. In response to American and British complaints, Tokyo modified its ultimatum, at least temporarily. Wilson then sought to prevent the new Chinese republic from becoming dependent on Japan for investment funds. Reversing his earlier policy, he encouraged the formation of an international consortium of bankers to finance modernization in China.

The events of World War I, however, forced Wilson to return at least partially to Roosevelt's policy of conciliating Japan. When the Japanese threatened to make a separate peace with Germany in fall of 1917, the Wilson administration concluded the Lansing-Ishii Agreement. In return for Japan's endorsement of the Open Door and a pledge not to take advantage of the war to infringe on the rights of other powers in China, the United States recognized Japan's "special [although not "paramount," as the Japanese had wanted] interests" in China. Wilson viewed the ambiguous document as a stopgap measure designed to prevent full recognition of Japan's expanding position in Asia.

Wilson sought to maintain the Open Door and the integrity of China without the use of military force. To do so, he first repudiated and later encouraged investment there. Like Roosevelt, he recognized Japan's growing power and tried, through executive agreements, to integrate the Japanese into a structure of power that would maintain at least some opportunities for Americans in China and some protection for the Philippines.

World War I: U.S. Neutrality, 1914–1916

The greatest test to active internationalism and American attempts to improve the world order during the Progressive Era came in World War I. In August 1914, millions of men marched onto the battlefields in the giant struggle between the Central Powers — Germany Austria-Hungary, and Turkey — and the Allies — Britain, France, Russia, and eventually Italy. Americans initially looked on the carnage with disbelief and disdain. Wilson declared the United States legally neutral, but the president went beyond tradition and asked Americans to be "impartial in thought as well as in action." That proved impossible. The heterogeneous American population included nearly 8 million people from German or Austrian ethnic backgrounds, as well as several hundred thousand Russian Jews who despised the anti-Semitic czarist regime. Nearly 5 million Irish Americans hated the British government. The South and West had long viewed Britain with suspicion as the center of the gold standard and the world's moneyed interests. Despite this sizable opposition, however, the majority of Americans probably sympathized with the Allies. The British had strong ethnic and cultural ties to the Americans, and the French drew on American gratitude for France's assistance during the American Revolution.

Both sides competed for support from the American public, especially the foreign policy elites; the British and French won. London dominated the transatlantic channels of communication. Its propaganda agency disseminated reports of German illegalities and atrocities. The official report of Lord Bryce's Commission, for example, certified rumors that German troops had been guilty of rape and pillage, had stabbed babies with bayonets, and had crucified Canadian soldiers on crosses. The Germans were stereotyped as "Huns." Only after the war did Americans learn that the Bryce Report had been based on unsubstantiated rumor and secondhand testimony. The Germans' own propaganda emphasized British violations of international law: seizing neutral ships, landing troops in Greece despite Greek protests, and blocking shipments of food to Germany. Many Americans came to view Germany as the aggressor and as a threat to world order. The callous manner in which the kaiser's government dismissed the treaty guaranteeing Belgium's neutrality as merely "a scrap of paper" and the German armies' brutal conquest of Belgium alienated many Americans.

Even more important than propaganda in influencing the United States was the growth of American economic ties with the Allies. With its control of the sea, Britain drew on American resources—food, fiber, arms, munitions. Total U.S. trade with the Allies more than tripled, from $800 million to $3 billion, between 1914 and 1916. At the same time, the British blockade of Germany helped to reduce American commerce with the Central Powers from $170 million to practically nothing. The Allied war trade helped to pull the United States out of a recession and into a boom.

Expanding trade led to one of the key decisions of the war. In the early days of the fighting, the French government sought to float a $100 million loan in the United States, but Secretary of State Bryan refused to endorse the proposal. He told American bankers that such loans would violate "the true spirit of neutrality." "Money is the worst of all contrabands," Bryan declared, "because it commands everything else." A few months later, in October 1914, Bryan and Wilson approved "short-term credits" from the bankers to the Allies. These proved inadequate, however, and by August 1915, Allied war trade had grown so large that the bankers asked permission for Britain and France to float a $500 million bond issue among American investors. This time several cabinet officers joined them. They argued that the bond issue was necessary to continue commerce and avert a depression in the United States. Wilson agreed not to prohibit the loans, thereby in effect repealing the old ban. Led by J. P. Morgan & Co., a nationwide banking syndicate floated this and other Allied loans totaling more than $2.3 billion. Although these loans did not violate international law, they and the commerce they financed made real neutrality virtually meaningless. Almost from the beginning of the conflict, the United States was the major supplier to the Allied war effort.

Within the context of widespread sympathy for the Allies, the growing war trade, and a strong American belief in freedom to travel, Wilson's strict definition of American neutral rights led to confrontation and eventually to war with Germany. In effect, the administration insisted on America's right to supply the Allies. The U.S. government's attempt to define and obtain British and German acceptance of the American definition of neutral rights followed a long and arduous route in the first three years of the war. Pursuing his policy in the face of substantial criticism at home and abroad, Wilson nevertheless succeeded in maintaining control of the nation's foreign policy.

When the European armies bogged down on the western front in a bloody war of attrition, the belligerents sought to throttle each other through naval blockades that quickly affected the United States as the world's leading neutral. In November 1914 the British threw a ring of mines and ships around the sea approaches to Germany and the neutral Netherlands and the Scandinavian countries, which might transship goods to the Germans. Gradually, Britain broadened the definition of contraband beyond arms and munitions to include foodstuffs and "strategic" raw materials such as cotton, which was used to make uniforms. The British navy seized neutral ships and confiscated contraband materials. Since international law gave neutrals the right to trade with all belligerents, such high-handed action provoked much criticism in the United States. Nevertheless, in 1916, London announced that American firms found trading with Germany would be "blacklisted" and British subjects would be forbidden to deal with them.

Although he protested British violations of neutral rights, Wilson agreed to postpone the settlement of American claims until after the war. The problem was that Britain was a maritime power and Germany a land power. If pushed to extremes by Washington, Britain would perhaps have loosened the blockade, since the supply of American goods and money was essential to it. In 1916, angered by British infringements, Wilson considered asking Congress for authorization to prohibit loans and exports to the Allies. However, he never took the drastic step of using America's economic leverage through an embargo or a severance of diplomatic relations.

Wilson established a much stronger position against the blockade that Berlin declared around Britain and France in February 1915. The Germans relied initially on two dozen submarines to interdict enemy merchant ships. But the *Unterseeboot*, or U-boat, did not operate according to the rules of cruiser warfare. These rules required raiders to stop their target, examine the manifest and cargo, and allow the crew to escape in lifeboats before sinking the vessel. But British officials encouraged merchant skippers to install and use deck guns and to ram surfaced submarines. Consequently, Berlin announced that within the war zone, its submarines would torpedo enemy ships without warning.

In response, Wilson held the Germans to "strict accountability" for the loss of American ships that might be sunk and the lives of Americans traveling on Allied vessels. Viewing submarine warfare as barbaric, he distinguished between the loss of lives caused by the U-boat raiders and the loss of property stemming from the actions of the surface cruisers in the British blockade. The tragic potential of submarine warfare was made clear by the sinking of one of the world's largest and most prestigious passenger ships, the *Lusitania*, a British Cunard liner.

On the morning of May 7, 1915, on its way from New York to Southampton, the 30,000-ton *Lusitania* steamed out of a fog bank off the southern coast of Ireland directly in front of a submerged U-boat. The submarine fired a torpedo into the ship's hull. The *Lusitania* stopped dead in the water, shuddered, and within eighteen minutes had slid bow first beneath the waves. Nearly 1,200 men, women, and children, 128 of them Americans, went down with her. The ship's death plunge, a survivor recalled, "sounded like a terrible moan."

The *Lusitania* disaster brought home to many Americans the brutality of modern war. Although ex-president Roosevelt and a few others urged America to enter the war immediately, the public reacted more with shock than with anger. Refusing to listen to jingoes like Roosevelt, Wilson kept his head. He decided to respond to the German action with diplomatic protests rather than with threats of force. He demanded that Germany disavow the sinking, indemnify the victims, and agree to stop attacking passenger liners. When the Germans debated his points, Wilson continued to negotiate. This was a wise decision, because the matter was not as clear-cut as it seemed. Before the *Lusitania* sailed, the German consul had published warnings in New York newspapers indicating that the German government considered the vessel subject to attack because it had carried munitions on past voyages. The rapidity with which the *Lusitania* sank suggested that it was indeed carrying a deadly cargo. The manifest, released fifty years later, confirmed that the holds contained shrapnel, fuses, and 4.2 million rounds of ammunition.

Secretary of State Bryan resigned in May 1915 to protest what he considered the president's unneutral position on the *Lusitania* incident. He told Wilson that ships carrying munitions should not be allowed to carry passengers. "Germany has a right to prevent contraband going to the Allies," Bryan argued, "and a ship carrying contraband should not rely upon passengers to protect her from attack." The secretary recommended that the U.S. government protest both the German and the British blockades, and he wanted to prohibit Americans from sailing on ships carrying munitions. The president, however, refused to consider the two blockades together. He insisted that Germany repudiate its submarine tactics. Wilson accepted Bryan's resignation and replaced him with the State Department's legal counselor, Robert Lansing, an international lawyer and a supporter of Great Britain.

Presidential persistence forced the Germans to comply for a time. In August 1915, Wilson resumed his protests when two Americans died in the torpedoing of the British steamer *Arabic*. In the so-called *Arabic* pledge Berlin agreed not to sink passenger liners without warning. For the next six months the Germans maintained this limitation on their U-boat campaign. The German government also eventually apologized for the deaths of Americans on the *Lusitania* and paid an indemnity.

Torpedoed by a German submarine, a merchant ship heads for the bottom as surviving crew members flee to the lifeboats. (*National Archives*)

The Peace Movement

As the European war continued, the American peace movement splintered into conservative and radical wings, pursuing different strategies. Many conservative peace advocates worked for a postwar league of nations that could use force if necessary to maintain peace and order. The Association for a League to Enforce Peace, headed by former president Taft and A. Lawrence Lowell, president of Harvard University, shunned discussion of proposals to end the present war through compromise and emphasized the postwar nature of its program.

In contrast, new (post-1914) peace organizations sought to conclude the bloody conflict as quickly and as fairly as possible. This spectrum of groups virtually reconstituted the peace movement. Some, like the League to Limit Armaments and the Emergency Peace Federation, were short-lived. But others were more enduring, notably the Woman's Peace Party founded by Jane Addams, Charlotte Perkins Gilman, and others, which later became the Women's International League for Peace and Freedom, and the American Union against Militarism (AUAM) headed by Lillian Wald, Crystal Eastman, and Oswald Garrison Villard, which became the American Civil Liberties Union. The new activist coalition was composed of action-oriented peace advocates, many of whom were social justice progressives. Among them were feminists, social workers, journalists, labor lawyers, and social gospel clergy. They saw the war as caused by militarists, munitions makers, and imperialists, and they warned that it sacrificed social progress to archaic means of settling disputes.

Drawing on liberal thought in Europe and America, the pacifist progressives urged that the United States play an active but peaceful role in ending the war and preventing future international conflagrations. They called on the Wilson administration to summon a conference of neutral nations that might mediate among belligerents. They also advocated terms that they believed would ensure a just and lasting peace. The liberal peace proposals provided for no annexations or indemnities, an end to secret treaties and entangling alliances, elimination of trade barriers and colonial empires, and the reduction of large armies and navies. In their place the liberal pacifists urged disarmament, neutralization of major waterways, self-determination for all peoples, democratic governments, open diplomacy, and international machinery for the judicial settlement of disputes between nations.

Wilson had been influenced for some time by the growth of the peace movement and by ideas of international organization and world law. In the White House he continued to listen to the proposals of the peace advocates, but he pursued his own policies. Initially he hoped for an early compromise peace that would maintain the balance of power and protect American security. Anxious to avoid U.S. intervention in the war, he attempted several times in 1915 and 1916 to mediate a conclusion to the hostilities, but without a convention of neutral nations. However, during the first two years of the war neither side was interested in mediation. Still hoping for victory, each rejected Wilson's proposals.

Many Americans feared that the president's policy of strict accountability would draw the United States into the war. In February and March 1916, congressional Democrats from the South and the West rebelled and tried to modify Wilson's position. The Gore-McLemore resolutions attempted to prohibit Americans from traveling on armed belligerent ships. The president crushed this challenge to his leadership, and Congress tabled the resolutions. But the vote of 276 to 142 in the House indicated that there was considerable opposition to Wilson's policy.

The Sussex Pledge

Wilson also won a major victory in diplomacy in the spring of 1916. A German submarine commander, carelessly mistaking the unarmed British steamer *Sussex* for a mine layer, torpedoed the vessel as it carried passengers and freight across the English Channel. The stricken craft limped to port, but several European passengers were killed and a number of Americans were injured. Secretary of State Lansing urged Wilson to break diplomatic relations, but instead the president presented Germany with an ultimatum. If Germany did not stop sinking nonmilitary vessels — freighters or passenger liners — without warning, the United States would sever formal relations. To avoid American entry into the war, and also because the German navy had only fifty-two submarines, of which only about eighteen could be at sea at any one time, Berlin agreed to Wilson's demand in May 1916 and issued the *Sussex* pledge, thereby essentially abandoning its submarine blockade.

For the moment, Wilson had weathered the crisis. At home, he had beaten down domestic opposition to his claim that Americans had the right to travel into the naval war zone, even on armed ships of belligerent nations. Abroad, he had forced the Germans to suspend submarine warfare. But in his dealings with the kaiser's government he had put the determination of relations between the two countries into the Germans' hands. If Berlin resumed unrestricted submarine warfare, the United States, under Wilson's policy, would be forced to break relations and would probably enter the conflict. It seemed an ominous possibility. As Wilson told his cabinet, "any little German [U-boat] lieutenant can put us into the war at any time by some calculated outrage."

The Road to Belligerency, 1916–1917

The "Preparedness" Controversy

In the two years before the United States went to war against Germany in the spring of 1917, the state of the nation's armed forces became a major political issue for the first time since the Spanish-American War. Led by former President Roosevelt, many corporation heads, most of them Republicans, founded organizations, such as the National Security League, advocating what they called preparedness. The United States, they claimed, was woefully unprepared for war with a major power. The regular army contained only 80,000 men, and the navy, with thirty-seven battleships and only a few of the new dreadnaughts or superbattleships, might not be able to protect both coasts simultaneously. Preparedness advocates did not suggest that the United States should get ready to enter World War I; isolationist sentiment precluded that. Rather, most of those urging increased armament warned that, as the world's richest nation, the United States would be a tempting target after the war and therefore must be ready to defend its interests. Emphasizing international uncertainty and potential danger, they attempted to discredit the Wilson administration and to modernize and expand the armed forces.

Preparedness advocates wanted the United States to build a navy larger than Britain's and recommended that land forces be completely reorganized. The militia should be eliminated and the dual military system abolished. The regular army would be maintained, but it would be slashed in both size and cost. It would act primarily as a constabulary and a cadre to train millions of reservists, who would be conscripted for six to eighteen months of military training before being passed into the reserves. Such a system would provide the United States with a large, trained, mass conscript reservist army much like those of the continental European nations and Japan. Universal military training among young American men, Roosevelt and the others asserted, would enhance the country's defense, and would also improve the health, self-discipline, and national spirit of America's male citizens.

Opponents of conscription and expansion of the armed forces fought what they called a radical and dangerous departure from American tradition. The National Guard, a powerful political force in the states and in Congress, lobbied to block attempts to merge it into the regular army. Led by groups like the AUAM, pacifists and other antimilitarists argued that a large and expensive army and navy were unnecessary. The United States was not threatened by any major power, they claimed, and no matter which side won, the nations of Europe would be exhausted after the war. Even if a threat should materialize, the country could continue its traditional reliance on citizen volunteers in locally raised regiments to meet future needs. Furthermore, many of the antimilitarists—social progressives, farmers, workers, and socialists—were suspicious of big business's support of preparedness. They warned that a large navy and conscript army could be used to help corporations to control labor and dissident groups at home and to expand abroad. Instead of enlarging the armed forces, the AUAM asserted that the United States should call a conference of neutral nations to mediate among the belligerents.

Declaring that he did not intend to "turn America into a military camp," Wilson initially resisted the movement for increased preparedness. But he soon came to believe that some Republicans were building national defense into a major issue for the 1916 election; in addition, he realized that he might need expanded military power to enforce his strict policy toward Germany. In late summer of 1915 the president came out for expanded national defense, and after several months of debate, Congress enacted a compromise measure. The lawmakers rejected proposals to eliminate the state militia or establish universal military training but approved an expansion of land forces. The National Defense Act of 1916 authorized an increase in the size of the regular army to 223,000 men—double the previous number. It also authorized the National Guard to expand to 450,000 men within five years if necessary. It empowered the president to federalize the militia in emergencies, making it part of the national armed forces and eliminating state control in such cases. It also created the Reserve Officers Training Corps (ROTC). The Naval Act of 1916 provided for the construction within three years of ten battleships, six battle cruisers, ten cruisers, fifty destroyers, and sixty-seven submarines, which with the existing fleet was designed to give the United States the largest navy in the world.

Viewing these changes in the armed forces as having been achieved by wealthy conservatives, the progressives and agrarians in Congress decided to make rich individuals and corporations pay the costs of expanding the army and building the enormous fleet. The Revenue Act of 1916 — which sharply increased income, estate, and corporation taxes — represented the first major victory for advocates of a progressive tax, that is, one that taxed larger incomes at higher rates.

Reelection and a Call for Peace

Foreign policy, not defense, was a main issue in the 1916 presidential campaign. Emphasizing the themes of peace, progressivism, and prosperity, the Democrats campaigned for Wilson on the slogan, "He kept us out of war." Although the GOP candidate, Charles Evans Hughes, ran much better than Taft had in 1912, he lost the votes of many progressives and other Americans who, though Republican, opposed the bellicose, interventionist speeches of ex-President Roosevelt. Wilson won the race by a narrow margin, and the Democrats retained control of Congress. The confused international situation helped the Democrats temporarily overcome their minority status and upset the largely reunited Republican party.

After his reelection, Wilson made a major effort to mediate an end to the war. Privately, he began to draft a call for a peace conference, and to get the British to agree he suggested that the Federal Reserve Board tighten short-term credits to the Allies. At the beginning of December 1916, just as Wilson was prepared to call for a peace conference, Berlin outraged American public opinion by deporting several thousand Belgians for forced labor in German industries. A few days later Berlin announced its willingness to discuss peace terms. Smarting after a failed offensive at Verdun and facing mounting discontent at home, Germany's military leaders believed they faced ultimate defeat if they could not soon obtain peace through negotiations, or, if the Allies remained adamant, by a desperate all-out submarine offensive.

Seeking to avoid any appearance of collusion with the German government, Wilson decided against issuing a call for a peace conference. Instead, on December 18 he made an impassioned plea to both sides, noting that their stated objectives were "virtually the same" in seeking security and prosperity in a stable world order and asking them to state their terms for an end to the war. There was a double purpose in Wilson's phraseology: to undercut the Allies' secret agreements for dividing the Central Powers' assets and to pressure both sides to state their goals in such a way as to maximize chances for agreement. However, the president had misjudged British opinion, which was bitterly hostile to being put on the same moral plane as Germany and which still hoped for victory. Surprisingly, Wilson was also undermined by Secretary of State Lansing, whose ardent pro-British sentiments led him deliberately and erroneously to suggest to the press that the president's note was intended to prepare the way for American entry into the war. Lansing also privately recommended to the Allied ambassadors that they demand harsh terms — including the return of Alsace-Lorraine to France; payment of a sizable indemnity to France, Belgium, and Serbia; settlement of the Balkan disputes by an international commission; and most important, replacement of the imperial German regime by a democratic government — terms that could be achieved only by a dramatic Allied victory.

Even without Lansing's sabotage of his policy, Wilson's proposals had no chance of being accepted in Britain or France and little chance in Germany. Berlin thanked Wilson but declared that terms could best be worked out by direct negotiations among the belligerents. The Germans avoided publicly stating their terms; secretly, they wanted most of the territory occupied by their military forces — Lithuania and Poland, Belgium — and the Belgian Congo. London and Paris followed Lansing's advice in responding to Wilson. Although the Allies did not mention it, their secret treaties also called for dismemberment of the Austro-Hungarian and Ottoman empires and Germany's relinquishment of its colonies. In their response to Berlin, the Allies effectively forestalled any peace conference by stating that they would not begin any negotiations without a statement of terms by Germany.

Frustrated, Wilson announced a program of his own based on proposals by the liberal peace movement. In a speech to Congress in January 1917, he called for a "peace without victory." A just rather than a vengeful peace, he said, needed to be based on principles of equality and self-determination of nations, freedom of the seas, universal disarmament, and an international organization to preserve world peace. Critics belittled Wilson's proposal. Roosevelt, for example, urged a complete Allied victory over Germany and an Anglo-American military alliance to maintain the postwar order. But liberals and war-weary people throughout the world applauded Wilson and increased his standing as an international peacemaker.

A Fateful Meeting at Pless Castle

In Germany, failure to achieve victory and the growing frustration and privation caused by food shortages eroded support for moderates like

Chancellor Theobald von Bethmann-Hollweg, who had made the *Sussex* pledge to end unrestricted submarine warfare. By the end of 1916 the right wing and the military had gained strength in the Reichstag, the German parliament. Kaiser Wilhelm II equivocated, but he had by that time lost a good deal of his power and prestige. Field Marshal Paul von Hindenburg, the popular hero of the eastern front, joined the admirals who claimed that the enlarged submarine fleet — now more than 100 strong and growing each month — could starve Britain into submission and win the war within five months.

In response to the Allied rejection of Berlin's peace offer, top German military and civilian leaders met with the kaiser at Pless Castle in the province of Silesia. On January 9, 1917, they voted to resume unrestricted submarine warfare. The military realized that this would bring the Americans into the war, but as the naval chief of staff had said, "The United States can scarcely engage in more hostile activities than she has already done up to this time." The Germans counted on defeating the Allies before the Americans could alter the situation by raising and training an army and sending it to Europe. Germany's Secretary of the Treasury Karl Helferrich cautioned that the navy had not considered the possibility of effective antisubmarine measures being developed by the Allies; he also warned that the American Civil War showed that once aroused, the Americans would continue fighting until they won. But such dissent was ignored; the kaiser approved the military's recommendations. On January 31 the German government announced it would resume unrestricted submarine warfare the following day. It was a risky gamble. "The U-boat is the last card," Bethmann-Hollweg commented ominously.

Events of the next two months led almost inexorably to war. Despite Berlin's announcement, Wilson tried to resist the Germans' violations of America's neutral rights. He also sought to avoid mobilization and other actions that he considered precipitous. He wanted the imperial government to reconsider its decision. He also wished to assure both himself and noninterventionists in the United States that he had sincerely tried to avert armed conflict. Although interventionists urged an immediate declaration of war, Wilson proceeded cautiously.

On February 3 the president severed diplomatic relations with Germany. With the blockade reinstituted, submarines soon frightened most neutral shipping from the seas, and goods piled up on the docks and in the warehouses of the East Coast. On February 26, Wilson asked Congress for authority to place weapons and naval gun crews on American merchant ships. He also solicited an open-ended endorsement to conduct limited naval warfare if necessary while Congress was adjourned for its summer recess. When the legislators resisted, Wilson applied pressure by releasing the Zimmermann telegram to the press. Intercepted by British intelligence, this message from the German foreign secretary to the kaiser's ambassador in Mexico City proposed that in the event of war, the German diplomat should offer money and weapons to encourage Mexico to attack the United States in order to obtain its "lost territory in Texas, New Mexico, and Arizona." The Americans responded with great indignation. Yet many still did not want war. When a dozen noninterventionists in the Senate filibustered against Wilson's proposals, the president excoriated them as "a little group of willful men." After Congress had adjourned, he armed the merchant ships by executive order.

Events in mid-March 1917 led Wilson to decide to enter the war. On March 18, U-boats sank three American merchant ships, killing more than two dozen crew members. In the same week, the beginning of the Russian Revolution led to the end of the czarist government and the abdication of Nicholas II. The establishment of a provisional government under the liberal Prince Lvov reduced the autocratic image of the Russian government and enhanced the Allies' argument that they were fighting for democracy. Still, Wilson found himself in a dilemma. American ships had been sunk and some Americans killed, and interventionists clamored for war. But many Americans remained unconvinced that the situation had changed sufficiently to threaten vital U.S. interests or justify American entry into the European conflict.

The Decision for War

Some noninterventionists suggested alternatives to full-scale belligerency. Bryan urged the president to prohibit American ships from sailing into the war zone and to submit the submarine dispute to a joint high commission for investigation and adjudication after the war. Others argued that the United States should form a league of armed neutrals and keep the sea lanes open to trade by means of a naval neutrality patrol.

Although Wilson knew of these proposals, he chose to ask Congress for a full declaration of war. The chief executive did not think a policy of armed neutrality would give the government adequate authority to mobilize public opinion, the economy, and the armed forces. He decided on full belligerency partly because he considered it the only proper course given the German assault on American shipping and the U.S. definition of neutral rights. He also believed it was essential for him to have a seat at the peace table. Only as a participating power could the United States work actively to reform international relations and create a progressive world order based on liberal, democratic, capitalist institutions and a league of nations.

Accompanied by armed cavalry, the president rode down Pennsylvania Avenue on April 2, strode up the steps of the Capitol, and delivered an inspiring war message. The kaiser's government, he said, had thrust war upon the United States: "The present German submarine warfare against commerce is a warfare against mankind." "The world," Wilson declared in what would become a historic phrase, "must be made safe for democracy."

Congress adopted the declaration of war, but only after vigorous debate. Anti-interventionists from the rural South and Midwest warned that the country was entering the conflict to protect the investments of American bankers and munitions makers in the Allied cause. "We are going to war upon the command of gold," declared George Norris, a progressive Republican congressman from Nebraska. Jeannette Rankin, a Montana suffragist who was the first woman elected to Congress, cast her first vote in the House against U.S. entry into the war only four days after taking her seat in Congress. Nevertheless, an overwhelming majority of the legislators supported the president, and the war resolution passed by a vote of 82 to 6 in the Senate and 373 to 50 in the House. On April 6, 1917, the United States officially entered World War I.

Wilson justified American entry into the war in terms of idealism and mission, rather than mundane self-interest. He thereby established war objectives that were so unrealistic that virtually no future peace conference could attain them. His grand vision led the American people to war, but it also doomed them to postwar disillusionment.

The Debate over American Entry

As with other great historical events, the causes of the United States' entry into World War I were complex. Historians have little difficulty identifying the precipitating cause as Germany's resumption of unrestricted submarine warfare. But there is much less unanimity on the role of Wilson's policies or the influence of underlying strategic and economic forces.

Although the president emphasized German violation of neutral rights, neither American tradition nor law nor economic necessity required him to guarantee the right of Americans to travel on armed belligerent ships. Though he couched his policies in terms of international law and principle, Wilson was responsible for defining the growth of trade with Britain as a legitimate and profitable expression of neutral rights. He rejected definitions by other neutrals—Spain, the Netherlands, and the Scandinavian countries—that banned such passenger travel and embargoed guns and ammunition. In addition, he refused to consider the German and British blockades similarly or to hold Germany to a postwar accounting, as he did in the case of Britain. Thus by 1917 Wilson found himself constrained by the framework created by his earlier decisions about American rights.

During the 1930s—a time of worldwide economic depression, growing fascism and militarism, and disillusionment with the results of

World War I—revisionist critics of U.S. entry into the war, such as Walter Millis and Charles Tansill, asserted that America had become a belligerent in 1917 primarily to protect its loans to the Allies and its trade in arms and munitions. Little evidence exists that the bankers or munitions makers had much immediate influence on Wilson's decision for war. The Nye Committee of Congress, which subpoenaed corporate records, proved only that these corporations had made enormous profits throughout the war. Rather, the bankers influenced the administration most directly in 1915, when they persuaded Wilson to agree to the provision of loans to the Allies to avert a depression in the United States. That decision facilitated the growth of the American economy by rejecting governmental interference with the expanding war trade.

Some scholars, such as George Kennan, have argued the importance of strategic realism in explaining the American entry into the war. The United States went to war, they suggest, to preserve a favorable balance of power in Europe and maintain Anglo-American control of the sea lanes. This argument proved particularly popular during the height of the Cold War, from the late 1940s to the mid-1960s, as the United States linked its defense to that of western Europe against the Soviet Union. Although a few of Wilson's private comments support the assertion that he understood American security to be involved in the European war, this was not his primary concern, and he did not try to educate the public about it.

Since the 1960s, New Left critics of American foreign policy such as William A. Williams have offered a broader economic argument. With considerable justification, they claim that the United States went to war partly to establish an international Open Door for expanding American capitalism. Although Wilson thought primarily in terms of universal principles of law and morality, his world view included the need to open markets to American business. He sought to generate American prosperity and opportunity as well as to reform international relations. Wilson's economic policy, as the historian N. Gordon Levin has shown, was part of his foreign policy, whose goal was to encourage the development of a liberal, democratic, capitalist world order that he believed would benefit all nations.

It is probably most accurate to see Wilson's policy toward Germany and his decision to take the United States into World War I as part of the development of international activism and interventionism by policymakers in the Progressive Era. His immediate predecessors—McKinley, Roosevelt, and Taft—had emphasized the United States' growing role in world affairs and the nation's responsibility to shape and improve its environment. As the world's richest and most powerful neutral, the United States could not be unaffected by a war for dominance in Europe and, consequently, in other areas as well. Given the prevailing legal, strategic, economic, and idealistic forces, it is likely that any president would eventually have taken the country into World War I.

Wilson's policies reflected the traditional American belief that the ideals of America were the ideals of all humankind and that other nations must conform to American prescriptions and ideals. But he now applied these to a major nation outside the Western Hemisphere. This global interventionism was new, but it drew on an attitude of superiority that had much earlier become a part of American culture. Germany had to be restrained because it had broken America's rules, disputed its ideals, threatened the rights and property of American citizens, and even challenged its security and hegemony through the proposed military alliance with Mexico.

In taking the United States into the war, Wilson protected both humane principles and commercial interests. His emphasis on freedom of the seas and the extensive rights of neutrals reflected not only his views but those of many others at the time, and it indicated that American economic, strategic, and moral concerns in world affairs were greatly intertwined. In the end, Wilson entered the war because he believed that the Germans had forced him to do so and because such action also offered him the opportunity to play a leading role at the subsequent peace conference. He promised and believed that the United States could help to remake the world in the American image by creating a new world order that would promote human rights, democracy, self-determination, and open-market economic growth and would restrain violent revolution and aggression. The United States entered World War I not simply because German submarines attacked its shipping but because the new interventionist foreign policy view in America became politically predominant. American leaders were willing to commit the nation to fight across the seas in defense of high principles and economic and strategic national interests.

Within the limits set by national interests at the time, by public opinion and pressure groups, and by tradition and recent developments in foreign policy, Wilson gave U.S. policy his own particular stamp. Another president might have entered the war earlier and justified it on different grounds. Or he might have joined it later or prolonged armed neutrality. Wilson's neutrality policy achieved its basic goal of avoiding American belligerency and preserving with honor trade and travel until early 1917, when the Germans decided to end their policy of restraint. By that time the United States had missed the bloodiest years of the war. Not until the closing six months of the conflict, in 1918, would large numbers of American soldiers arrive in France.

Although progressives were divided over American entry in 1917, Wilson employed the rhetoric of reform—idealistic fervor, national purpose, and governmental activism—to justify his policy. Thus he tried to link the progressive crusades at home and abroad into a war for progressive aims, even though both the war and U.S. entry meant the failure of pacifist progressives' attempts to reform international relations so as to eliminate war. In what historian Lloyd C. Gardner has called the liberal covenant with power, Wilson and the interventionist progressives sought to harness illiberal means—the massive use of military force—to achieve liberal goals—the creation of a world without war and with freedom and economic and political democracy.

CHAPTER 8

World War I and the Search for a New World Order

1917–1920

 "The American is undoubtedly an idealist," a cynical British diplomat observed in 1918. "He was never afraid of Germany, or jealous of her. American troops go to Europe with a rather vague idea that they are going to democratize Europe, and put the Kaiser in particular, and all autocrats generally, out of business; an ingenuous notion that they want to make the rest of the world as democratic as they believe their own country to be."

Yet Americans combined practicality with their missionary impulse, the diplomat, William Wiseman, reminded his government, noting that Woodrow Wilson personified this dualism. "He is by turns a great idealist and a shrewd politician."

In taking the United States into what he called "this war of redemption," Wilson sought to adjust and control forces in the international arena and to create a more stable, predictable, and prosperous world order. Yet with its extraordinary demands on a people and a nation, large-scale warfare had enormous impact, much of it unanticipated, on society. Even though the United States was at war for only nineteen months in 1917 and 1918, the war experience was intense, affecting virtually all aspects of the economy, society, and culture.

Wartime mobilization, postwar demobilization, and the American role in world affairs expanded and contracted opportunities and also exacerbated conflicting tensions within American society. Clad in progressive rhetoric — "a people's war," Wilson called it — the crusade to make the world safe for democracy ended in the disillusionment of postwar discrimination and repression at home and refusal to join the League of Nations abroad. Like the earlier reforms of the Progressive

233

Era, wartime mobilization and the reaction of the immediate postwar period also helped to shape the nature and direction of modern America.

America Goes to War

Most Americans initially thought that the U.S. contribution to the war would be economic and naval, with a stream of merchant ships carrying food, munitions, and other supplies to the Allies. Such an American effort, it was widely believed, even by Wilson himself, would cause the Germans' desperate submarine campaign to fail, and Berlin would be forced to accept peace with the United States and the Allies.

The naval effort was vitally important, for the U-boat campaign initially proved devastating to the British economy. The sizable German submarine fleet sank one out of every four merchant ships that left England. The British were able to replace only one ship for every ten sunk. U-boats sunk 881,000 tons of shipping in April 1917, and the British Admiralty estimated that the merchant marine would be completely destroyed by November. Although London kept it a secret, the country was near economic strangulation; in May barely a few weeks' supply of food remained. Only under great prodding from Wilson and some of his naval advisers did conservative British admirals adopt a system of grouping merchant ships into escorted convoys instead of scattering vessels on individual routes across the Atlantic. The experiment proved an enormous success. The convoy system, together with aggressive antisubmarine warfare, including the use of submarine-spotting aircraft and destroyers and smaller escort ships (many of them built by Americans), equipped with new underwater detection devices (primitive sonar) and explosives ("depth charges"), defeated the German submarine blockade. By November, British shipping losses were down to 289,000 tons a month, and production of new ships began to surpass the number being sunk. Less than 1 percent of ships in escorted convoys were lost; almost by itself the convoy system turned the war against the submarine.

Increasingly, Americans provided escort vessels to protect the convoys; Wilson forced reluctant naval officials to shift from building battleships to rapid construction of escort vessels (building time for a destroyer was cut from twelve months to less than two months). By the end of the war, the United States had 248 destroyers and 176 submarine chasers. Although the breaking of the German submarine threat and the continued imposition of an Allied surface vessel naval blockade of Germany were important, they were not militarily decisive. Victory or defeat would be decided by ground warfare among gargantuan armies on the European continent.

Bloody Stalemate on the Western Front

Technology had made the stalemated war in Europe a vast slaughter-house. By increasing the range and rate of fire, the new weaponry gave defensive forces tremendous advantages over troops on the offensive. Machine guns spewing 600 bullets a minute and high-powered rifles created a "killing zone" 2 miles wide. Long-range artillery fired high-explosive shells even beyond the horizon. After the initial German offensive in 1914 had been stopped at the Marne River northeast of Paris, the armies of both sides dug extensive earthworks composed of trenches approximately 7 feet deep and 5 feet wide and underground shelters to protect the troops from direct enemy fire. The front lines became a maze of trenches stretching from Switzerland to the English Channel. Soldiers served for the duration of the war, unless they became casualties or prisoners. In the muddy and rat-infested world of the trenches, many soldiers became incapacitated by tuberculosis and other ailments. The armies lost more soldiers to disease than to enemy fire.

The battle casualties were enormous. Massive offensives against entrenched enemy positions involved hundreds of thousands of troops and were preceded by weeks of massed artillery bombardments. Sixty percent of the battle casualties in the war were caused by artillery. Millions of soldiers were killed by exploding shells, and many of their comrades suffered nervous breakdowns under prolonged bombard-ments (this new mental disorder was known as "shell shock"). In an attack, soldiers clamored "over the top" of their trenches. Those who were not killed or wounded in the initial outpouring of enemy fire rushed across the scarred and shell-marked "no-man's land" separating the opposing trenches, crawled through barbed-wire entanglements, and finally sought to engage the enemy with rifle and bayonet. Such frontal assaults and artillery bombardments produced enormous losses but few gains. During 1916, nearly 700,000 soldiers died in the unsuc-cessful ten-month German siege of the French position at Verdun. Also that year, an unsuccessful, four-month-long British-led offensive in the valley of the Somme River resulted in nearly 1.3 million casualties, including 420,000 British, 195,000 French, and 650,000 Germans (19,000 British soldiers were killed and 41,000 wounded on the first day of the attack, the worst one-day loss in the history of the British Army). For almost four years, despite repeated assaults and the deaths of millions of soldiers, neither side advanced more than a few miles on the "Western Front." By the end of the war, of the 65 million men mobilized, some 8 million had been killed and 21 million wounded.

By the time the United States entered the conflict in the spring of 1917, the war had become one of attrition, and both sides were search-ing desperately for means to break the stalemate before a collapse of morale at home and at the front. In 1915 the Germans began using barrages of poison gas to disorient or incapacitate the enemy. They first introduced artillery shells containing chlorine, a choking agent; in 1917 they began using mustard gas, which could severely blister lungs or exposed skin. By 1918, both sides were using chemical weapons on a large scale. These did not prove decisive, because of rapid dissipation in the air and widespread use of protective clothing and gas masks. Nevertheless, among the Allies, poison gas caused 79,000 deaths and more than 1 million casualties, with many of the victims permanently scarred by terrible burns or painfully seared lungs.

Although both sides sought to employ aircraft in pursuit of victory, air weapons merely continued the deadlock and increased the casualties. From the beginning of the war, aerial reconnaissance behind enemy lines by rickety, fabric-covered biplanes had reduced the element of surprise by alerting defensive commanders to the massing of enemy forces for offensives. The battle for control of the skies by lone aviators in their pursuit planes above the infantrymen in their grimy trenches captured public attention as the press emphasized the daring "aces"—Manfred von Richthofen, the "Red Baron" of Germany, Eddie Rickenbacker of the United States, and others—and the number of "kills" these pilots achieved in aerial "dogfights." The planes used machine guns, grenades, and sometimes bombs against enemy lines as well. Again the Germans initiated the use of indiscriminate warfare that failed to distinguish between combatants and others. Seeking to undermine civilian morale through terror bombing, they attacked London beginning in 1915, first using long-range dirigibles called Zeppelins (lighter-than-air craft lifted by hydrogen gas) and subsequently two-engine Gotha bombers. In more than 100 air raids they killed 1,400 civilians but failed to affect the course of the war.

Most promising of the new weaponry was the tank, an armed and armored vehicle powered by an internal combustion engine that moved on continuous metal treads. The British invented it to break through enemy lines and end the stalemate of trench warfare. The first tanks were used in 1916 at the Battle of the Somme, but small numbers and mechanical failures—not even a dozen reached the battlefront—limited their impact. This remained true for the next two years, as the British and French experimented with tank development. The Germans built only a few tanks at the end of the war.

The Allied military situation deteriorated rapidly in the spring of 1917 just as the Americans entered the war. On the Eastern Front, the Russian army had suffered more than a million casualties in 1916 in a massive offensive that was ultimately blocked by a German counter-offensive. Those staggering losses contributed to the Russian Revolution in March 1917 when mutiny at the garrison in the capital city of Petrograd was followed by the abdication of the czar and the establishment of a provisional government.* Fearing suppression, the Soviet (Council of Workers' and Soldiers' Deputies), dominated by the radical Bolsheviks, asserted that military officers no longer had disciplinary authority. (The Bolsheviks were a faction of the Marxist social revolutionary party that urged the violent overthrow of capitalism by workers and soldiers under the leadership of the Communist party as the road to a socialist society.) Despite counterorders from the provisional government, the Soviet's directive and the war-weariness of the Russian forces caused the officer corps to disintegrate. Many officers were killed by mutinous soldiers and sailors; others were deposed by military councils. By mid-April half the corps was gone. To undermine the war effort further, the Germans smuggled the Bolshevik leader, Vladimir I. Lenin, back into Russia from exile in Switzerland, and he challenged the provisional government with the slogan "Peace, bread, and land [for the masses]."

On the Western Front, the Nivelle offensive, a giant French assault directed by General Robert Nivelle, proved an unmitigated disaster. The French lost nearly 120,000 men in five days, and whole divisions refused to continue the attack. The full extent of the mutiny was kept secret for more than a decade, but even after Nivelle was replaced and the revolt was quelled, the high command realized that morale was too low for another French offensive that year. Reflecting the views of most of the army, a French commander declared: "We will wait for the tanks and the Americans." In fact, the configuration of the front did not change until 1918.

Raising an American Army

The Allies sought not merely economic and naval assistance from America but also troops. In May 1917, nearly a month after the congressional declaration of war, the British and French asked that a contingent of the U.S. Army go to France as soon as possible and requested further a promise of many more American reinforcements on the Western Front in the future to bolster sagging French morale. The president agreed to this despite his original plans. In March and April Wilson and his military planners had envisaged building a wartime army of 1 to 1.5 million men over the next year or two and then sending part of that trained force to Europe at the decisive moment to help force the Germans to negotiate and to ensure an American role in the peace conference. Only after the United States entered the war did Wilson and the American generals learn something of the Allies' desperate situation, much of which had been kept secret.

---

*Petrograd was originally called Saint Petersburg. In 1924 it was named Leningrad, and in 1991 was renamed Saint Petersburg.

In May, Wilson authorized an initially small American Expeditionary Force (AEF), composed of regular troops and National Guardsmen and commanded by General John J. ("Black Jack") Pershing, who had led the punitive Mexican expedition in 1916. Ramrod-straight and steely-eyed, with a trim mustache, Pershing was an able, if aloof, commander. After losing his wife and children in a fire, he had adopted a stoic demeanor that he retained for the rest of his life. Arriving in Paris in June 1917, Pershing resisted Allied desires to use American soldiers as replacements in the British and French armies. Instead, with Wilson's full support, Pershing insisted on maintaining an integral American army with its own sector on the Western Front. In July 1917, Pershing asked for an AEF of 1 million men by 1918 and 3 million by 1919. At the end of the war in November 1918, there were 2 million American troops in France and nearly another 2 million being trained in the United States.

The creation of a modern mass army and an effective fighting force in eighteen months was an administrative miracle. The U.S. Army that entered the war had been molded by the Civil War, the Plains Indian Wars, and the Spanish-American War. The last veteran of the Union Army had retired from active duty in 1915, and the U.S. Army chief of staff in 1917 had begun his career by replacing an officer killed at Custer's Last Stand in 1876.

America raised its 4-million-man army through the modern military draft, another innovation of the Progressive Era. In previous American wars, the vast majority of troops had been raised through local volunteer units — the so-called U.S. Volunteers. This twentieth-century army consisted mostly of conscripts: fully 72 percent of the "doughboys" were draftees. Although the preparedness movement of 1915–1917 had failed to obtain a national reserve force based on a permanent system of universal military training, it had helped to convince many Americans of the efficacy of a selective draft over a purely voluntary system for raising large wartime armies equitably and with minimal disruption of the economy. Although Wilson accepted this idea, the hostility of the agrarian South and West toward both the war and the draft led him initially to believe that a trial of the volunteer system would be required before any resort to conscription.

At the end of March 1917, former President Theodore Roosevelt insisted on being allowed to raise and command one or two divisions of U.S. Volunteers and take them to France. It was at least in part this potential challenge to Wilson's wartime leadership by his old Republican nemesis that led the president to eliminate the U.S. Volunteers and turn directly to conscription. Considerable opposition erupted in Congress. Democratic House Speaker James B. ("Champ") Clark of Missouri declared that "there is precious little difference between a conscript and a convict." Nevertheless, in a vote largely split along urban-rural lines, Congress adopted the Selective Draft Act in May 1917.

The Selective Service System, an organization of "supervised decentralization," was devised and headed by the army's chief legal officer, Brigadier General Enoch H. Crowder. Some 4,000 local draft boards, composed of civilian members of the community, used guidelines established by Congress, the administration, and military officials in Crowder's office to decide who would be drafted. During the war the Selective Service registered nearly 24 million Americans and drafted nearly 3 million, most between 21 and 30 years of age. Another 2 million Americans volunteered for service, many in the navy. Deemed inefficient, voluntary enlistment was prohibited after August 1918.

Many volunteers viewed the war as a righteous crusade. This romantic view was reflected in the popular poetry of Alan Seeger, a young Harvard graduate who enlisted early to fight for France and who died there in 1916. The "sense of being the instrument of Destiny," Seeger had written, was the "supreme experience" of combat.

Unlike the generally well-educated volunteers, the typical soldier was a draftee between 21 and 23 years old, single, with little or no high school education. Some 13 percent were black, and 18 percent were foreign-born. Many of the draftees simply accepted their lot. Although some soldiers concurred in Wilson's idealistic war aims, large numbers were ignorant of the reasons the nation went to war. As a result the War Department held special "Americanization" classes, particularly for the foreign-born; it also directed that every soldier in the army be given a copy of the president's war message.

Opposition to the Draft and the War

Perhaps as many as half the American people continued to oppose U.S. entry into the war, including people who had ethnic ties to the Central Powers or, like Irish Catholics and Russian Jews, had bitter memories of persecution and bloody repression by Allied Powers.

Most socialists argued against the conflict as a capitalists' war. Pacifists saw it as an unnecessary war and continued to believe that negotiation and mediation (such as offered by Pope Benedict XV in 1917) was preferable to continued bloodshed. Agrarian isolationists opposed involving the United States in a foreign war, especially sending Americans to fight and die in Europe. Because of the widespread opposition, many Americans feared a repetition of the bloody draft riots that had accompanied America's first experiment with national conscription during the Civil War. Authorities broke up antidraft meetings and arrested and imprisoned Emma Goldman, Eugene V. Debs, and other antiwar activists who continued to speak out. The Supreme

Court sustained such a limitation on freedom of speech in wartime, and in the *Arver* case (1917) it upheld the constitutionality of national conscription.

Draft protests continued in a few isolated rural areas; some two dozen persons were killed in skirmishes between draft resisters and local police. In the largest protest, the so-called Green Corn Rebellion in eastern Oklahoma, more than 500 impoverished tenant farmers and migrant workers gathered to march to Washington, but a local posse arrested them, without injury, and the protest demonstration never even began.

More extensive was overt evasion. Although 24 million men registered for the draft, officials estimated privately that perhaps 3 million more may have successfully avoided registration. Most were never discovered. Some 338,000 registrants (12 percent of those actually drafted) failed to report or deserted after arrival at training camp. Fragmentary evidence suggests that these so-called "deserters," like the nonregistrants, were disproportionately from alienated, lower-income groups — ethnic immigrants in the North, poor whites, and impoverished blacks or Hispanics in the rural South and Southwest. About half of these were caught, some in the controversial "slacker" raids in which soldiers and sailors, local police, and federal agents swept through major cities demanding draft registration cards from all adult males of military age.

Many men, particularly in skilled trades and occupations, legally escaped conscription through work-related deferments. One of the most controversial was the deferment of Henry Ford's unmarried son, Edsel; the sons of the wealthy were supposed to be equally subject to conscription as anyone else. The most infamous "draft dodger," Grover Cleveland Bergdoll, son of a wealthy German-American brewing family in Philadelphia, was captured after the war when he returned home to visit his mother. He later spent five years in military prison.

The draft law allowed traditional religious pacifists, such as Quakers and Mennonites, to serve in noncombatant roles in the armed forces, and others applied for the same consideration. During the war some 65,000 registrants claimed conscientious objector status on religious or, in the case of socialists and anarchists, political grounds. Of the 21,000 objectors who were drafted, 80 percent were persuaded or coerced by the army into abandoning their objections. The most famous of these was Alvin C. York, a Tennessee mountaineer and religious fundamentalist who subsequently shot and killed twenty-five German soldiers in a single day and captured 132 more, becoming, as "Sergeant York," the most renowned doughboy hero of World War I.

Around 4,000 young men continued to maintain their conscientious objection even in the army. Some of these accepted duty in the medical corps; most were eventually furloughed for agricultural and relief work, and 450 were incarcerated in military prisons, where perhaps as many as 17 died of pneumonia or other ailments as a result of physical abuse and deprivation. Included among them were two religious pacifist Hutterite brothers from South Dakota whose corpses were sent home clad in the military uniforms they had refused to wear while alive.

Equity and Purity for a Progressive Army

The wartime army was the largest military force the United States had ever raised. The nature of the army reflected American culture in the Progressive Era. Because the wartime army was composed primarily of temporary citizen-soldiers, popular sentiment demanded that the federal government ensure a degree of equity, efficiency, and even purity in such a force. Despite objections by fiscal conservatives, Congress doubled the pay for soldiers, established an insurance program, and provided domestic allotments to be sent directly to needy dependents. As a result of lobbying by prohibition groups and youth and moral reform organizations, lawmakers sought to protect citizen-soldiers from alcohol and prostitution. The Selective Draft Act made it illegal to sell liquor to soldiers in uniform and empowered the administration to exclude saloons, taverns, and "houses of ill fame, brothels, or bawdy houses" from the vicinity of any army base.

Among the armies at war, only the American had such an extensive official program to prevent "corruption" and maintain the moral welfare of its soldiers. Coordinated by the Commission on Training Camp Activities, volunteer organizations such as the YMCA and the Jewish Welfare Board offered "wholesome" middle-class entertainment and recreation to the troops. This program undoubtedly reduced the loneliness of many men away from home for the first time in their lives. It certainly held the rates of alcoholism and venereal disease far below those that had plagued the regular peacetime army. The War Department's purity campaign had other, longer-range effects. For example, the closing of the brothels in New Orleans and other southern cities contributed to the national discovery of jazz music as unemployed black musicians moved to northern cities such as Chicago and New York. The prohibition of alcohol from the wartime army became an important step toward postwar national prohibition, put into effect in 1920 with the Eighteenth Amendment.

Racism and Sexism in the Armed Forces

The wartime forces also reflected ethnic, racial, and gender attitudes of the time. Although 11,000 women served in the navy, as a result of a decision by Secretary of the Navy Josephus Daniels, a former progressive newspaper editor from North Carolina, they were recruited only for the duration of the war and were confined largely to clerical, typing, or nursing assignments. The army had its female Nurse Corps, which had been in existence for some time, but the men of the War Department refused to accept any other role for women in the army. The military experience, seen as masculine and as linking military obligations to the political rights of full citizenship, was overwhelmingly male. Outside the services, women helped soldiers through the YMCA, the Red Cross, the Salvation Army, and other volunteer organizations.

Racism and ethnic stereotypes also prevailed in the military. Psychologists administered intelligence tests to all recruits in an attempt to make service assignments on a scientific basis. However, these primitive tests were skewed by class and cultural bias (questions asked, for example, "Who wrote 'The Raven?'" and "Is 'mauve' a drink, a food, a fabric, or a color?"). Although the answers revealed background rather than innate intelligence, they were widely interpreted as confirming popular prejudices labeling recent immigrants and native-born African Americans as "inferior."

Despite racism and discrimination, the military seemed to offer blacks a rare opportunity. Although African Americans had served in all the nation's wars, they had, since the end of the Civil War, been restricted to a limited number of racially segregated units in the regular army and the National Guard. Despite concerns about the southern influence in the Democratic administration and Congress, a number of black leaders, including W. E. B. Du Bois, called on African Americans to support the war and demonstrate their right to equal citizenship. For this and for the attractive wages offered to soldiers, blacks volunteered in disproportionately large numbers, but the army stopped accepting them once the traditional black units were filled. Many southern whites had opposed conscription of black men; in practice, however, blacks were drafted disproportionately. White draft board members were more liberal in granting deferments to whites than to blacks, a result of whites' prejudice and blacks' poverty and lack of industrial jobs. The Selective Service drafted one in three black registrants but only one in four whites.

Ultimately nearly 400,000 African Americans served in the war, 200,000 in France. The navy assigned them to menial positions; the Marines excluded them entirely; the army used most of them as food handlers, dockworkers, grave diggers, and laborers. Only 42,000 were assigned to serve in combat. Training camps were segregated and "white only" signs posted. Except for some 600 junior officers from the black middle class trained at Fort Des Moines, all the African American units were led by white officers (the army's senior black officer, Colonel Charles Young, was unjustly forced into retirement early in 1917).

In French helmets and with rifles, bayonets, and grenade launcher ready for action, African-American soldiers of the 369th U.S. Infantry Regiment (the "Harlem Hellfighters") guard a hastily constructed trench in the French section of the western front in May 1918, where they helped stop a major German offensive. (*U.S. Army Signal Corps/National Archives*)

Under pressure, the War Department created a black combat division, the 92nd, which saw action in 1918, as did four black American regiments serving under French command (one of these, the 369th "Harlem Hellfighters," received France's highest citation for valor, the *Croix de guerre*).

The experience of military training, of combat, and of greater acceptance in France than in America gave many black men a new attitude toward themselves and toward racial discrimination in America, but the attitudes of most American whites toward blacks did not change. In the summer of 1917 some black regulars, harassed by local whites in Houston, Texas, rioted. In the gunfire, seventeen white civilians and two black soldiers died. In a travesty of justice, the entire battalion was arrested, more than 100 soldiers were court-martialed, and thirteen were executed within three days after the sentence before an appeal could even get underway. As a result of this tragedy, the War Department changed its appellate procedures regarding death sentences, but its basic racial policy continued to be not to challenge segregation and its accompanying customs either in the military or in civilian society.

Mobilizing the Home Front

"It is not an army we must shape and train for war," Woodrow Wilson declared as the war began. "It is a nation." Since millions of Americans still opposed U.S. entry in the war in the spring of 1917, the Wilson administration and state and local authorities used a combination of persuasion and coercion to unite the country behind the war effort. To mobilize public opinion Wilson created the Committee on Public Information, headed by George Creel, a former crusading journalist for newspapers in Kansas City and Denver. In what he called "a fight for the *minds* of men," Creel built a nationwide publicity apparatus that included newspaper reporters, authors, academics, actors, orators, screenwriters, songwriters, and artists (one of them, James Montgomery Flagg, in 1917 produced the famous recruiting poster of a white-bearded "Uncle Sam" pointing and declaring, "I Want *You* for the U.S. Army"). Using modern advertising and public relations techniques, the Creel Committee and the mass media sold the war to America.

The government's propaganda campaign and the war effort itself were supported by the majority of the nation's clergy, educators, editors, filmmakers, and others who helped to shape the national culture. Adopting the British and French explanation of the nature of the conflict and the Creel Committee's propaganda, most portrayed the war as a struggle between good and evil, a battle to uphold values and standards that were threatened by German militarism. Most progressive intellectuals, such as the philosopher John Dewey and the editors of the influential magazine *The New Republic*, gave important public support to the war effort, arguing that it offered an opportunity domestically to achieve economic and social reform goals through a spirit of community and internationally to turn the war into a liberal crusade to "make the world safe for democracy."

Largely ignored were the voices of critics, such as Randolph Bourne, a young journalist and one of Dewey's former students, who argued against the prowar intellectuals' belief that they could mold war to their reformist goals. Rather, Bourne argued in a series of articles in 1917–1918, the intellectuals had become mesmerized by power, and the "fierce urgencies" of war were not so easily manipulated for positive democratic ends. "If the war is too strong for you to prevent," Bourne asked somewhat disingenuously, "how is it going to be weak enough for you to control and mold to your liberal purposes?" Rather Bourne believed that in a repressive and totalitarian sense, war was "the health of the state."

Although Bourne and other pacifist critics were dismissed as short-sighted and naive in 1917, John Dewey, Walter Lippmann, and a number of other liberal, prowar intellectuals eventually came to accept many of their critiques. Within two years after the end of the war, Dewey and many others had concluded that instead of aiding progressive reform, the war had encouraged reactionary and intolerant forces at home and abroad.

Wartime Hysteria and Vigilantism

The intensity of the propaganda in support of the war and against Germany and the inflammatory statements of ultranationalist groups fanned ethnic hatreds to near-hysterical levels by 1918. Hostility was directed against virtually anyone of German ancestry, and anything German became suspect. Schools stopped teaching the German language; cities prohibited music by German composers, sauerkraut was renamed "liberty cabbage," and hamburger became "Salisbury steak." Fired particularly by ultrachauvinistic organizations, incidents became increasingly ugly. Many German Americans and others were stopped on the street and publicly forced by angry gangs to kiss the American flag and recite the Pledge of Allegiance. In April 1918, near Saint Louis, an anti-German mob of nearly 500 persons seized Robert Praeger, and despite his pleas that he was a naturalized American citizen who had tried to enlist in the U.S. Navy, wrapped him in an American flag and hanged him. A local jury acquitted the ringleaders on the grounds that the lynching had been a "patriotic murder."

The impetus for such vigilantism and much of the widespread repression against people of German ancestry and also of other Americans who questioned the rectitude of the nation's cause or the nation's institutions — pacifists, socialists, and anarchists, for example — was encouraged by a variety of private and public sources, particularly on the state and local levels. Such quasi-official bodies as the wartime state councils of public safety and the American Protective League were in many areas little better than vigilante groups. These drew on existing strains of xenophobia and antiradicalism and inflamed them with intense wartime nationalism. Ultrachauvinists such as former President Theodore Roosevelt used examples of some German espionage and sabotage in the United States before 1917 to exaggerate the danger of internal subversion. They also used wartime hysteria to demand complete conformity, what people like Roosevelt called "100 percent Americanism." Such assertions contributed to the violence, often supported by local elites, against those who opposed U.S. entry into the war — for ethnic, economic, or political reasons — and who were consequently labeled German sympathizers or traitors. A pacifist clergyman in Cincinnati, Rev. Herbert S. Bigelow, was taken outside of town by a mob and horsewhipped. A veteran labor organizer for the Industrial Workers of the World (IWW), Frank Little, was tortured and then lynched from a railroad trestle in Butte, Montana. In a massive and illegal deportation, the sheriff and a posse of 2,000 men in Bisbee, Arizona, rounded up 1,200 striking miners — half of them members of the IWW, one-third of them Mexican Americans — locked them in railroad boxcars without food or water, and shipped them into the desert in New Mexico.

Government Suppression of Civil Liberties

Two federal laws, the Espionage Act of June 1917 and the Sedition Act of May 1918, as well as antisedition laws adopted by many states, gave authorities the legal right to repress dissenters. In sweeping language the Espionage Act provided penalties of up to twenty years' imprisonment for persons convicted of aiding the enemy, obstructing recruiting, or causing insubordination or disloyalty in the armed forces. It also authorized the postmaster general to withhold from the mail publications that he judged to be seditious or treasonable. The Sedition Act went even further by providing severe penalties for anyone convicted of using "any disloyal, profane, scurrilous, or abusive language" about the government, the Constitution, the flag, or the armed forces or urging curtailed production of necessary war materials.

While Postmaster General Albert S. Burleson vigorously suppressed a number of socialist newspapers and magazines, Attorney General Thomas W. Gregory, under pressure from ultranationalists, declared that opponents of the war could expect no mercy "from an outraged people and an avenging government." Zealous U.S. attorneys prosecuted 2,200 persons under the Espionage Act for actions that ranged from criticizing war taxes to opposing the draft and the war. Many more were prosecuted under state sedition laws, and thousands were persecuted and harassed.

Formal prosecution was directed primarily at economically radical groups — particularly socialists, anarchists, and the Industrial Workers of the World — that opposed capitalism, denouncing it as the cause of the war as well as the source of exploitation of wage workers. Ricardo Flores Magon, a radical, Mexican-American labor organizer in the Southwest, was sentenced to twenty years in prison for criticizing Wilson's foreign policy. For making antiwar statements, federal agents arrested 113 leaders of the IWW; the conviction of most of them under the Espionage Act destroyed the union. The government also arrested a number of prominent leaders of the Socialist party, including Kate Richards O'Hare, a labor organizer; Victor Berger, the first Socialist elected to Congress and editor of a daily socialist newspaper in Milwaukee; and Eugene V. Debs, the party's presidential candidate. By the end of the war almost a third of the party's national executive committee was in prison. Although the national leadership of the party was repressed, the Socialists, as the only political party opposing the war and many of the wartime measures, made a strong showing in several local government elections in 1917. In New York City they garnered 22 percent of the mayoral vote and elected ten assemblymen and seven aldermen. In 1919 the Supreme Court upheld the repression of speech that might be legal in peacetime but posed what Justice Oliver Wendell Holmes, Jr., declared in *Schenck* v. *United States* "a clear and present danger" to national security in wartime.

The wartime repression of freedom of speech was not unprecedented: European governments were more repressive; so was Lincoln in the Civil War. However, it was subsequently considered unnecessary by many Americans, particularly since there had been no real threat to security within the country. It had been unduly harmful to individuals, institutions, and the ideals of the nation. Justices Holmes and Brandeis sought in *Abrams* v. *United States* later in 1919 to narrow the government's authority to curtail free speech, warning, "we should be eternally vigilant against attempts to check the expression of opinions that we loathe . . . ." Although they were outvoted then, their position would later be adopted. Out of the wartime experience, the modern civil liberties movement emerged, encouraged by changing attitudes and by the founding of the American Civil Liberties Union (ACLU) in 1919.

Coordinating the Economy

The economic contribution of the United States to the war was vital to both the Allied and American military efforts. Consequently, there was an unprecedented expansion of the role of the federal government in the economy, one that drew on precedents and ideas from the Progressive Era and also provided the basis for many developments in the growth of the national government in later years. The government's aim was to maintain industrial and agricultural production required in an interdependent economy, as well as to supply additional demands of the war. The method was the establishment of a substantial wartime regulatory bureaucracy that used a combination of financial incentives, persuasion, and threats of coercion in attempts to achieve the government's goals in various sectors of the economy.

In the mobilization and coordination of industry, agriculture, and the transportation system, the Wilson administration, Congress, and powerful corporate leaders felt their way along to a wartime relationship acceptable to both business and government. At first Wilson attempted some coordination, through the advisory Council of National Defense, in establishing voluntary cooperation. But the president soon realized that strictly voluntary action was inadequate.

To combat soaring food prices Wilson established the Food Administration, headed by Herbert C. Hoover, a young Iowa Quaker and self-made-millionaire engineer who had successfully directed international relief efforts to occupied Belgium. Under the Lever Food and Fuel Control Act, the administration was given unprecedented control over the production and distribution of fertilizers, farm implements, and foodstuffs — especially wheat, meat, and sugar — and more limited control over prices. Rather than resorting primarily to price controls and rationing of commodities, Hoover's policy was to encourage increased production and diminished domestic consumption. Hoover, with one of his key assistants, Harriot Stanton Blatch, suffragist and daughter of pioneer feminist Elizabeth Cady Stanton, produced a massive consumer education program aimed primarily at the women who did the grocery shopping and cooking, advocating "wheatless" and "meatless" days to free more commodities for the American and Allied armies. The Food Administration became the most successful regulatory agency. U.S. exports of foodstuffs tripled between 1916 and 1918, and the efficient, if humorless, Hoover emerged as one of the most respected figures of the war effort. Farm owners' income soared as commodity prices more than doubled between 1913 and 1918, and cotton prices, protected from price controls by a southern-dominated Democratic Congress, almost tripled. Such artificially high prices collapsed after the war, however, and the wartime expansion of agriculture proved an exception to the long-term contraction in the number of farms and farmers.

Centralized coordination had increased wartime agricultural production, and in the winter of 1917–1918, the president applied variations of the Food Administration to other sectors of the economy. Under the Lever Act, and ultimately the even more sweeping Overman Act of 1918, Wilson created the temporary governmental agencies that in cooperation with business associations directed the wartime economy, not always with success. The War Shipping Board, for example, failed to build a merchant fleet, and the Aircraft Production Board was unable to deliver a single one of the 20,000 proposed airplanes before the end of the war. For airplanes and merchant ships, the United States was forced to rely primarily on those of the Allies. Particularly after a disastrous fuel shortage during the frigid winter of 1917–1918, the Fuel Administration sought to expand the production of coal, the major fuel for home and industry, through allocation and, most important, by raising coal prices to artificially high levels. As a war measure Washington also mandated "daylight savings time" to expand the workday and also save on fuel. After major railroad tie-ups that winter, the Railroad

War Board brought order to the nation's transportation network by taking temporary control in December 1917 of the extensive and diverse network run by some 3,000 railroad companies. Owners were guaranteed a profit and workers received wage hikes; but despite pleas by some reformers to maintain nationalization of the carriers, the railroads were quickly returned to private ownership after the war, a symbol of the determination by most business leaders to view wartime governmental controls as temporary.

The central mechanism of control over the industrial sector was the War Industries Board (WIB). Originally designed to coordinate military purchasing and industrial production and allocation, it had not functioned well in 1917. But in 1918 Wilson expanded its role and powers and named as its new head Bernard M. Baruch, an independent and urbane Wall Street speculator. Under the leadership of the energetic and knowledgeable Baruch ("Dr. Facts," Wilson called him), the revitalized WIB used its expanded authority to conserve and allocate resources, standardize procedures and products, set prices for all governmental purchases, and determine priorities of production and distribution in industry. During the war the antitrust laws were suspended, and WIB encouraged even former competitors to cooperate in order to save on steel, rubber, and other commodities in scarce supply. Although the agency occasionally threatened coercion, industry implemented most of its recommendations voluntarily. Baruch was not the dictatorial "czar" of American industry that the media proclaimed him. He and most of his subordinates viewed themselves as part of a government-business partnership to win the war. WIB decisions were usually determined in consultation with business, and the heads of the various departments within WIB were not career civil servants but business or professional people on leave from their companies and often still on their payrolls. Not coercion but financial incentive lured most businesses into compliance with WIB directives. On military contracts, WIB guaranteed payment for all costs plus a predetermined profit ("cost-plus" profit contracts). Corporate profits soared during the war, on the whole tripling between 1914 and 1917, then leveling off at an annual increase of 30 percent. Net (after-tax) corporate earnings grew from $4 billion in 1913 to $7 billion in 1917, and even after the increased wartime taxes, they came to $4.5 billion in 1918.

Financing the War

Buying everything from weapons to foodstuffs for the armed forces, the federal government became temporarily the major purchaser in the economy. It also lent billions of dollars to the Allies to enable them to continue to purchase food and war supplies from America. War output in the economy, which had made up 1 percent of GNP from 1914 to

1916, grew to 9 percent in 1917 and 23 percent in 1918. Ultimately, the monetary cost of the war to the U.S. government reached $32 billion. Wilson and William G. McAdoo, his secretary of the treasury who had also married one of his daughters, had initially favored raising half of the war costs by borrowing and half by taxation in order to limit the inflation that vast loans would provoke. The enormous sums involved and the unwillingness of Congress to throw half the burden on the taxpayers resulted ultimately in two-thirds of the government's revenue being raised by borrowing and only one-third by taxation (which was still far more than all the major European nations, which relied almost entirely on massive borrowing to finance their war efforts). In a series of highly emotional "liberty loan" drives, the government, aided by celebrities such as movie stars Douglas Fairbanks and Mary Pickford, sold more than $22 billion worth of war bonds to the public, increasing political as well as economic support for the war. Using the new Federal Reserve System, Washington also expanded the money supply, making it easier to borrow. The federal debt soared from $1 billion in 1915 to $20 billion in 1920 and never returned to prewar levels.

Many business leaders and other fiscal conservatives favored financing a large part of the cost of the war through taxes on most consumer goods (a federal sales tax) and extending the income tax to the middle and working classes, which, they argued, would have had the simultaneous effect of raising revenue and reducing inflationary pressures from consumers. Agrarians and progressives wanted the wealthy classes, whose income was increasing the fastest, to bear most of the cost through extraordinary taxes on income, estates, and wartime corporate returns in excess of normal profits. In the Revenue Act of 1917, Wilson and McAdoo obtained a compromise that applied new and expanded excise taxes on a number of consumer goods and services and also dramatically increased taxes on incomes, estates, and excess profits; it ultimately raised more than $10 billion. Equally important, the pattern of national taxation in America changed during the war, as the main source of federal revenue shifted from customs duties and excise taxes on luxury goods to taxes on incomes and profits. Congress had adopted a progressive income tax structure featuring higher tax rates for higher incomes. Although it would be cut back drastically in the 1920s and again in the 1980s, the progressive income tax remained the centerpiece of the federal revenue system from this time onward.

Inflation rather than taxation proved the more politically attractive way of paying for the war. Massive governmental borrowing and the expansion of the money supply contributed to soaring prices, although the greatest inflation had come between 1915 and 1917 when the Wholesale Price Index had climbed 65 percent. During 1917 and 1918 prices increased by a comparatively low 12 percent. Nevertheless, the

Consumer Price Index had nearly doubled during the four years of war—food prices alone nearly doubled between 1917 and 1919— putting particular strain on the poor and lower-paid working classes.

Workers and War: Organized Labor, Women, and Minorities

Many working-class men and women benefited from the changed conditions, although not nearly as much as employers, farmers, and investors. An increased demand for labor resulted from expanded production, which was accompanied by a wartime curtailment of immigrant labor from Europe (although immigration continued from some other countries such as Mexico, which sent 100,000 people into the United States between 1917 and 1920) and the rapid withdrawal from the civilian work force of more than 16 percent of its men into the armed forces. With government contracts mounting and labor in short supply, American industry adopted some of the techniques that would characterize the "welfare capitalism" of the 1920s, including more effective management of personnel, company unions, cost-of-living increases, and some profit sharing to forestall worker discontent. Most important, wages increased. The average annual income of a garment worker in New York City, for example, nearly tripled between 1914 and 1919, enabling many people to move out of the ghettos. For some workers, the increased wages barely kept ahead of rising prices. But there were real economic gains. Average real wages (purchasing power adjusted for price inflation) for manual labor, which was in great demand in war-related industries such as shipbuilding, munitions, steel, and textiles, increased by nearly 20 percent between 1914 and 1918.

These gains did not come without strife. In 1917 there were 4,500 strikes, more than ever before in the nation's history. Employers generally sought to prevent wage increases and outside unionization. The Wilson administration worked to prevent disruption of production, whether through worker unrest or management exploitation. Neither Wilson nor Samuel Gompers, head of the American Federation of Labor (AFL), was sympathetic to radical labor organizations, such as the socialists or the IWW. In return for federal support for cooperative unions such as those of the AFL and the Railroad Brotherhoods, Gompers, despite substantial opposition within the AFL, supported the draft and the war and agreed to a no-strike rule for the duration.

In response to continued strikes by maverick AFL locals and the IWW, Wilson in 1918 created the National War Labor Board (NWLB), a kind of supreme court for labor disputes, cochaired by a distinguished labor lawyer, Frank P. Walsh, and former President William Howard Taft. In return for no-strike pledges, the board guaranteed the rights of unions to organize and to engage in collective bargaining. Because the board lacked any statutory authority, it generally relied on the force of persuasion and publicity to convince labor or management to accept its decisions. It was generally able to aid workers only where unions were willing and strong enough to organize them—primarily among skilled workers. Although the AFL expanded from 2.7 to 4 million between 1916 and 1919, the majority of American workers still remained beyond union or governmental protection.

New Jobs, New Tensions for Women and Minorities

Wartime labor shortages led temporarily to increased economic opportunities for members of groups that had previously been restricted largely to marginal jobs—African Americans, Hispanic Americans, women. As orders flowed into factories, employers searched the country for new sources of labor. Newspaper accounts, letters, and oral reports encouraged people to move to where the jobs were. Some Mexican Americans from the Southwest took advantage of industrial opportunities in the Midwest, especially in the steel mills of Indiana and Ohio and the meatpacking plants of Illinois. By 1920, for example, there were 4,000 Mexicans in Chicago.

The most dramatic internal migration, however, was by the 400,000 African Americans who moved from the largely rural South into the northern industrial cities. Driven out by poverty and discrimination, they were lured by the promise of what black newspapers such as the Chicago *Defender* called the "land of hope." Employers' agents actively recruited them; Henry Ford sent special trains to bring them to Detroit. In northern industry formerly impoverished field hands could earn $3 or $5 a day, and many of them felt a new sense of freedom. "I just begin to feel like a man," one new arrival explained in a letter back to a friend in Mississippi. "I don't have to humble to no one. I have registered. Will vote in the next election." Although wages were higher than in the South, blacks in the North still received lower wages and more dangerous and disagreeable jobs than whites and were confined to particular urban areas where they paid high rents for crowded, dilapidated housing. They received some assistance from other blacks in the Urban League and from middle-class African-American women, such as Mary Church Terrell, who helped to organize community centers known as Phyllis Wheatley Clubs.* Eager young migrants, most of them in their early twenties, surged northward, swelling the black populations of the northern cities—Cleveland's rose from 8,000 to

*Phyllis Wheatley was a slave from Senegal who was brought to Boston, learned to read and write English from her mistress, and became the first black woman poet of note in the United States. She died at the age of 31 in 1784.

34,000, Chicago's from 44,000 to 110,000 — and establishing the origins of the twentieth century's urban black ghettos.

The changes accompanying the war seemed to exacerbate racial tensions. In the South ninety-six blacks were lynched in 1917 and 1918, and seventy more in 1919, some in Georgia and Mississippi still in their military uniforms. The most brutal lynchings captured national attention, such as one in Waco, Texas, where a mentally retarded black youth was tortured and burned before a crowd of thousands, and in Lowndes County, Georgia, where, after a mass lynching, the pregnant wife of one of the victims was burned alive for continuing to profess her husband's innocence.

In urban, industrial areas, competition for jobs and scarce housing, combined with the increased pseudo-scientific racism of the era, contributed to violence against African Americans. White workers did not generally welcome blacks into unions, and blacks were sometimes recruited to break strikes, making racial tensions more explosive. In July 1917 in East Saint Louis, Illinois, where some 10,000 blacks had recently arrived from the South to work in defense plants, an organized group of white citizens, unobstructed by local police, burned down the homes of many blacks and shot at those who tried to escape. At least thirty-nine black men, women, and children died in a locally sanctioned antiblack riot that a Russian immigrant observer compared to a czarist pogrom against the Jews.

Blacks protested and fought back against the increased discrimination and violence. Initially, W. E. B. Du Bois and a number of other African-American leaders responded to Wilson's call to arms by urging black Americans to "forget our special grievances and close our ranks shoulder to shoulder with our own white fellow citizens." They believed that service in the nation's cause would lead to full citizenship. However, the continued discrimination and stark inequities in punishments for racial violence — white leaders of lynch mobs acquitted or given light sentences, black soldiers summarily executed — increased black militancy. Black women in Atlanta officially protested to President Wilson and other public officials against an attempt to "reenslave" the race, declaring emphatically, "We will be heard." An article by Du Bois titled "The New Negro" in the November 1918 issue of *The Crisis*, published by the NAACP, reported a "growing determination on the part of the Negro to claim his rights at any cost." Angrily the author declared: "We return. We return from fighting. We return fighting."

The northward migration continued, and by 1920 some 1.5 million American blacks were working in northern cities. They had developed sizable communities there. Churches served as one focus of the community in these northern ghettos, and the clergy provided a major source of leadership. So did the middle-class membership of the

NAACP, which doubled during the war. But the most dynamic activist organization was the Universal Negro Improvement Association (UNIA), a black nationalist body emphasizing pride in the African heritage. Established in New York City in 1916 by Marcus Garvey, a charismatic Jamaican, it had branches in most northern cities by 1919 and appealed to increasing numbers of poor, discouraged ghetto residents.

Women workers also found temporarily increased employment opportunities during World War I. As men went to war, women were hired to replace them in numerous jobs previously defined as men's work. The number of women in the paid work force increased by only about 5 percent (400,000 women joined 8 million women already working for wages). But new opportunities opened for many women already working outside the home. Although the majority remained in sex-segregated "women's jobs" — typist, clerk, nurse, or teacher for white women, servant or laundress for black women — significant numbers were able to move to better jobs than in normal times. Businesswomen and social workers sometimes became war agency administrators. Twenty women lawyers in New York were appointed temporary judges. Women clerks became bank tellers; tellers became bank managers. Some white women who had worked as semiskilled operatives in textile mills or canneries, for example, could temporarily take jobs as skilled construction workers, drill press operators, or factory machinists. Department store clerks sometimes became streetcar or railroad conductors, mail carriers, or police officers. As these white women moved to more lucrative jobs, their former places were taken by black women.

Although most black women wage earners continued to be employed in domestic work, as maids, cooks, scrubwomen, and washerwomen, the war opened employment for them in the South in lumberyards and brickyards and in the North as laborers in railroad yards and factory workers in the clothing, packing, and electrical supply industries. For the first time department stores hired black women to serve the predominantly white customers as cafeteria waitresses and elevator operators. In virtually every industry employers paid women less than men had received, sometimes only half a man's wages. Black women usually received lower wages than white women. Unlike the predominantly young, single white women wage earners, most black women worked for wages even after they were married and had children, because of the restricted economic opportunities for black men. Although black and white women sometimes went on strike, the conservative AFL unions generally exhibited little interest in organizing them or ending racial and gender discrimination in wage rates.

When the men returned after the armistice in November 1918, women were rapidly displaced. For the most part, neither unions nor the government had much interest in maintaining women's wartime gains. Society returned to its contention that men were the breadwinners and women's proper sphere was in the home. The number of women in the paid work force remained at about 8 million in 1920, the same as in 1910 — in both cases women represented about 21 percent of the work force, and about 24 percent of women worked for wages. However, their economic position declined dramatically from what it had been during the war. As Chicago settlement house worker Mary McDowell put it bitterly, "During the war they called us heroines, but they throw us on the scrapheap now."

Women and Reform during the War: Suffrage and Prohibition

The leadership of the women's movement split over the proper reaction to the United States' participation in the war, but most women activists agreed on the need for female suffrage. Complete pacifist-suffragists, such as the New Jersey Quaker Alice Paul, continued to oppose the war and advocate a negotiated peace. Paul and more than 200 members of her Congressional Union organization were arrested for picketing the White House in a demand for votes for women. Moderate and conservative suffragists such as Carrie Chapman Catt and Dr. Anna Howard Shaw, physician and the first woman minister ordained by the Methodist Protestant church, led the National American Women's Suffrage Association (NAWSA) and its 2 million members in support of Wilson's call for a war for democracy. While encouraging women to perform patriotic work, they also pressed Congress and the president to ensure that democracy included votes for women.

Millions of mainly middle-class American women, white and black, engaged in volunteer work in support of the war, making clothing for refugees and rolling bandages for soldiers, tending "victory gardens" to conserve food, helping to sell war bonds, and tending to the service personnel through the Red Cross, YMCA, Salvation Army, and other support organizations.

Women's wartime contributions — as well as the militant tactics of the Congressional Union and the more traditional lobbying of the NAWSA — helped to achieve women's suffrage. Wilson finally endorsed a constitutional amendment for it in 1918. Antisuffragist forces — the South, liquor interests, urban machine politicians — were able to block the amendment in the Senate that year. But Congress passed the measure in 1919 and by August 1920, three-quarters of the states had given the Nineteenth Amendment the approval necessary for ratification. The presidential election of November 1920 marked the first time in the nation's history that women were legally able to vote throughout the nation.

Nationwide prohibition of the manufacture, transportation, and sale of alcoholic beverages was also expedited by World War I. By 1916 twenty-three states, mostly in the South and the West, were legally dry, and Congress had prohibited the shipment of liquor from wet states to dry ones. The war undermined the opposition, located primarily in the urban, ethnic North, in a number of ways: many of the breweries bore German names, such as Anheuser-Busch, Pabst, and Schlitz; alcoholism impeded war production; and grain was needed for food for U.S. soldiers and the Allies. Primarily as a conservation measure, therefore, a temporary ban on brewing and distilling was adopted by Congress in the summer of 1917. Building on this achievement and emphasizing patriotic idealism, the Anti-Saloon League, the Women's Christian Temperance Union, and the prohibitionist forces of rural and small-town Protestant America obtained congressional passage in December 1917 of a constitutional amendment for permanent nationwide prohibition, a "noble experiment," as they called it. Ratification was completed in January 1919, and the Eighteenth Amendment took effect in January 1920. (Prohibition was repealed by the Twenty-first Amendment in 1933.)

Victory in France, Defeat in the Soviet Union

During the summer and fall of 1917, the Allies had resumed the offensive — in part to prevent the Germans from taking advantage of the weakness of the mutinous French army. The results had been inconclusive, if not disastrous. On the western border of Belgium and France, the British gained 5 miles at Passchendaele at a cost of 300,000 casualties. On the Italo-Austrian front, the Italians lost 170,000 men in an attempt to smash the Austrian army. Bolstered by Berlin, an Austro-German counteroffensive in November broke through the Italian lines at Caporetto, inflicting 40,000 casualties and taking 275,000 prisoners.

On the Eastern Front, Russia collapsed under the pressures of war and revolution. Pushed by the British and the French, who threatened to withhold loans and credits, the provisional Russian government led by Alexander Kerensky, a social democrat, reluctantly resumed the offensive in the summer of 1917 with the few troops still willing and capable of combat. These Russian forces soon crumbled under strong German counterattack. Alarmed by growing Bolshevik influence in the government, the commander of the Russian army marched against Petrograd but was defeated by his own defecting troops and armed workers. The Kerensky government fled Petrograd for Moscow. On November 7, 1917 (October 24 in the unadjusted calendar that Russia used at that time), the Bolsheviks under Lenin seized power and began negotiations that led in December to an armistice on the Eastern Front.

In March 1918, Berlin forced the Bolshevik leaders, Lenin and Leon Trotsky, to sign the peace treaty of Brest-Litovsk, surrendering to German control the territory of Poland, the Baltic provinces, and the Ukraine. An exhausted and revolution-torn Russia, now called the Soviet Union, was out of the war.

The Struggle for France

Shifting most of their forces from the eastern to the western front, the Germans under General Erich F. W. Ludendorff launched a massive offensive in March 1918 in a desperate attempt to achieve a decisive victory before the weight of the growing American army could have a significant effect. Lundendorff sought to drive a wedge between the British and French armies and then destroy the British Expeditionary Force in subsequent assaults while the French concentrated on protecting Paris. The Germans began shelling the French capital with their seven amazing new long-range "Paris guns," rail-borne artillery pieces with barrels 117 feet long that fired 9-inch shells up to 80 miles. Nearly 900 Parisians were killed or wounded, and the city was badly demoralized. At the same time, behind gas attacks the Germans launched the Ludendorff offensives along a nearly 50-mile front and punched a hole in the thinly stretched British lines. The Allies screamed for American reinforcements, and Wilson dispatched doughboys as rapidly as shipping could be found for them. Draft calls were raised from under 30,000 to nearly 400,000 a month.

The German shock troops quickly advanced 40 miles, but despite this initial tactical success, the first offensive failed within two weeks (at a cost of more than 250,000 casualties on each side), in part because the Germans rapidly outdistanced their supply lines and in part because the British and French rushed reserves into the gap. Two more offensives in April and May repeated this pattern. After the Germans advanced to within 40 miles of Paris, they were stopped by French forces and by the first Americans fighting in significant numbers. Nearly 30,000 U.S. troops—mainly regular army, National Guardsmen, and a few thousand Marines—helped to blunt the German advance at Cantigny and hold the line along the Marne River at Château-Thierry and in June launched local counterattacks that drove the Germans back at several places, including Belleau Wood. A final German drive at the ancient cathedral city of Rheims was stopped in mid-July by French and British imperial troops with the help of some 85,000 Americans. There were now 1 million American troops in France. Five months after their spring offensive had begun, the Germans had lost half a million soldiers, and Ludendorff, admitting that the offensive had failed, prepared to withdraw and establish new defensive positions.

In mid-July the Allies, now under the overall direction of French Field Marshal Ferdinand Foch, quickly launched a series of counterattacks, rolling the enemy back all along the line. In early August they achieved a complete rout of defending German divisions for the first time in the war. Ludendorff called August 8 "a black day" for the German army and warned Berlin: "The war must be ended!" Some 270,000 American troops joined the initial counteroffensive. In September the first distinctly American offensive eliminated the important German salient around the town of Saint-Mihiel on the Meuse River. In four days the Americans suffered 7,000 casualties and captured 16,000 German soldiers. It was the largest American military operation since the Civil War, involving 550,000 American troops and 100,000 French colonial forces.

What proved to be the final offensive of the war in late September 1918 involved a British attack in the north of France, a French assault in the southern part of the center, and an American offensive, the Meuse-Argonne, in the south. Some 1.2 million Americans, many of whom had been rushed to France with only a few months' training, assailed heavily fortified German trenches in the dense, ravine-filled Argonne Forest north of Verdun. In frontal attacks against intense resistance, including converging machine gun and artillery fire, the Americans, many of them inexperienced soldiers and junior officers, made mistakes and suffered casualties. The most famous blunder involved the "lost battalion," which advanced beyond its support, was cut off and surrounded, and lost 70 percent of its men before being rescued. The Americans gained more success by turning to night attacks, which took the Germans by surprise. Finally, in early November the Americans broke through the last German lines and into the open country of the Meuse River valley and severed a key railroad line to Sedan. In just over six weeks 10 percent of the American force — 120,000 men — had been killed or wounded.

With the combined successes of the Allied forces, the German lines began to crack. German generals said that they could no longer protect the nation from invasion from the west. The other Central Powers were collapsing. The Bulgarians were being overwhelmed by a drive through the Balkans by British, French, Italian, Czech, and Serbian forces. Sofia signed an armistice on September 29. In the Middle East, British imperial troops and Arab guerrillas broke through the Turkish lines, crossed the Jordan valley and the desert, and seized Damascus and Beirut; another British force seized the oil fields north of Baghdad. Constantinople signed an armistice on October 30. The Austrian army was collapsing under an Anglo-French and Italian offensive in Italy and through the Balkans; Vienna signed an armistice on November 3.

In October, Prince Max of Baden, the new German chancellor, asked Woodrow Wilson for an armistice along the lines of the president's "Fourteen Points" speech of January 1918. In that eloquent declaration of America's war aims, Wilson summarized the hopes of western liberals. His Fourteen Points included open diplomacy, free trade and freedom of the seas, disarmament, national self-rule, and an "association of nations" that would act collectively to maintain peace. Wilson's declaration stirred liberals in all the warring nations and had encouraged German liberals to seek negotiation to end the war. Wilson refused to negotiate with the existing military autocracy in Germany. Ludendorff was forced to resign his command; sailors of the high-seas fleet mutinied, and other refusals, disorders, and revolts spread throughout the country. The kaiser fled to the neutral Netherlands, and a new socialist government took power and proclaimed Germany a republic. Its representatives agreed to an armistice, in effect a German surrender, on November 11, 1918.

The Americans had entered the war late but still saw 50,000 killed in combat and 230,000 wounded, most of them in the final three months of the war. These casualties, although the largest Americans had experienced since the Civil War, were dwarfed by those of the European powers, who had suffered 8 million killed and 21 million wounded out of 65 million mobilized in the armed forces. In addition, nearly 7 million civilians died (the majority of them Russians, Poles, Serbs, and residents of the Ottoman Empire), most from malnutrition or epidemic disease, except in the case of more than a million Christian Armenians slaughtered by the Turkish army in 1915 ostensibly to prevent any uprising within the Ottoman Empire. In 1918–1919 a worldwide influenza pandemic — and the bacterial pneumonia that often accompanied it in the era before sulfa drugs and antibiotics — claimed the lives of another 10 million persons, including 500,000 Americans.

The Americans made a vital contribution to victory. Their economic support of the Allies had been essential. On the seas they had helped to defeat the submarine blockade. On the Western Front, with their optimism and their increasing numbers of troops, the doughboys had achieved important, though costly, military successes. From a larger perspective they had permitted the more sizable and experienced Allied armies to achieve significant successes and by their combined effort to force the Germans to end the war.

Failure in the USSR

American and Allied efforts had not been successful in Russia. Like most other governmental leaders, Wilson was hostile toward the Bolsheviks. Although he had welcomed the overthrow of the czarist autocracy and encouraged the democratic experiment in Russia, he disliked the methods and goals of the anticapitalist Bolsheviks at home and abroad. He considered their peace treaty with Germany a betrayal of the Allies, and he feared their vow to spread the communist revolution around the world. A number of Americans of various political persuasions argued that the Russians should be allowed to work out their own destiny without U.S. intervention, and Wilson made a number of statements in support of that idea. Although the president resisted Allied calls for more direct and extensive U.S. military intervention in Russia, he did join Britain, France, and other Allied Powers in seeking to undermine and destroy Lenin's government, which Wilson refused to recognize. (The United States did not establish formal relations with the USSR until 1933.) The administration also withheld economic assistance from Soviet Russia while channeling economic aid and shipments of arms and ammunition to anti-Bolshevik elements. Covertly, some American diplomats and military attachés in Russia organized intelligence-gathering networks and even collaborated with British, French, and anticommunist Russian agents plotting to overthrow the Bolshevik government.

Reluctant to intervene openly and directly, Wilson hesitated for several months until, under British and French prodding, he finally sent two expeditions of U.S. troops to Russia in August 1918. He did not, however, reveal his hope that military intervention would help to cripple the Bolshevik Red Army. In the smaller expedition, 5,000 American soldiers were stationed in Archangel and Murmansk in northern Russia. Although their orders were to avoid military action in the Russian civil war, they joined British troops there fighting Bolshevik soldiers. Some 139 American soldiers died before they were withdrawn in June 1919, long after the armistice. In a second expedition, also dispatched in August 1918, another 10,000 doughboys were sent to Siberia, where they restricted Japanese expansion, guarded military supplies, patrolled the Trans-Siberian Railroad, and assisted the anti-Bolshevik Czech Legion in Russia—all tasks that assisted those fighting the Red Army. Three dozen American soldiers died there. The Czech soldiers remained in Russia until an offensive by counterrevolutionary "White" armies had been defeated in the fall of 1919. In March 1920, remnants of the White armies, including the 100,000-member Czech Legion, were evacuated from Vladivostok and other ports by British ships. Although the Japanese did not evacuate Vladivostok until 1922, the Russian civil war was largely over by 1920; the Red Army had successfully protected the Bolshevik government. With the departure of the Czech Legion, the American Siberian Expedition returned home in April 1920.

Historians disagree on Wilson's motives in sending 15,000 U.S. troops into Russia between 1918 and 1920 as part of larger Allied military expeditions there. Some accept the official reasons given to the public: saving the Czech Legion fleeing from the Bolsheviks and, in northern Russia, guarding military supplies against seizure by the German army. Although not officially announced as such, the Siberian expedition, as Wilson indicated privately, served to restrict Japanese military expansion in Asia. Stressing that the situation in Russia was constantly changing and that conflicting reports made it impossible to know what was going on, Arthur S. Link, Wilson's magisterial biographer, portrayed an anti-interventionist president drawn reluctantly into the Allied military efforts there. "I have been sweating blood over the question of what is right and feasible to do in Russia," Wilson wrote to his confidant, Colonel Edward House, on July 8, 1918. "It goes to pieces like quicksilver under my touch, but I hope I see and can report some progress presently along the double line of economic assistance and aid to the Czecho-Slovaks." Indeed, Link has argued that Wilson prevented large-scale Allied military intervention in Russia, foiling almost single-handedly Marshal Foch's proposal for a major military campaign against Bolshevism, an idea that had some support in Britain. "In my opinion," Wilson said at the Paris peace conference in 1919, "trying to stop a revolutionary movement by troops in the field is like using a broom to hold back a great ocean."

The majority of historians, however, emphasize Wilson's anti-Bolshevism, expressed in numerous private comments, such as his complaints about the "poison of Bolshevism" as he traveled to the Paris peace conference. While supporting liberal reform movements throughout the world, Wilson opposed anticapitalist revolutionaries in Mexico, China, and Russia. Wilson wanted to reform capitalism; Lenin wanted to destroy it. The Wilson administration used a variety of means — diplomatic, economic, and military — to undermine Lenin and the Bolsheviks and to contain communism. Some American critics, such as Senator Robert M. La Follette of Wisconsin, advocated recognizing Lenin's government and including it in the peace conference and the emerging world order. Others, such as Walter Lippmann, recommended that the Russians be left alone to settle their own affairs without any outside interference.

However, the Bolshevik government was excluded from the Paris peace conference. Instead, the victorious Allied leaders, including Wilson, sought to contain the revolutionary movement. The Allies imposed an economic blockade on the Soviet government, aided the counterrevolutionary White forces there, and at the peace conference granted territory to Russia's neighbors, Poland, Romania, and Czechoslovakia (the latter created after the breakup of the Austro-Hungarian Empire, which also resulted in the formation of another new multiethnic state, Yugoslavia), and recognized the new nations of Finland, Latvia, Lithuania, and Estonia in an attempt to build a *cordon sanitaire* ("sanitary zone") to stop the communist contagion by means of a belt of anti-Russian states in eastern Europe. Whatever Wilson's motives may have been, U.S. military intervention in the Russian civil war of 1918–1920 was too restricted to have any significant military effect but large enough to be interpreted by communists then and for decades thereafter as overtly hostile to the government of the Soviet Union.

The Diplomacy of Peacemaking and the Rejection of the League

"Without ever being represented at Paris at all, the Bolsheviki and Bolshevism were powerful elements at every turn," wrote Ray Stannard Baker, Wilson's press secretary at the peace conference. Although the delegates were constantly aware of Russia and communism, they also dealt with other major issues raised by the conclusion of the world war: the fate of the defeated Central Powers (Germany, Austria-Hungary, Bulgaria, the Ottoman Empire), rewards for the victors, and the prevention of a recurrence of such a conflagration. Vengeful Allied nations sought the spoils of victory that they had promised one another in secret treaties. These included Germany's overseas colonies in Africa and Asia and the former Middle East provinces of the Ottoman Empire, which was formally dissolved and reduced to Turkey in 1920.

Never a party to the secret treaties, Wilson had renounced any territorial goals for the United States. Instead, his primary aim, reflecting his own views and those of liberal internationalists in most countries, was a nonvindictive, nonimperialistic peace and, to maintain a peaceful and prosperous world order, an international organization (a "league of nations") that would work toward arms reduction, freedom of the seas, free trade, international law, and collective security. This was the predominant liberal vision of a reformed, democratic, capitalist world order, an alternative to a world dominated by aggressive, belligerent imperialist nations (the system that had produced World War I) but also an alternative to Lenin's vision of a radical communist world order in which capitalism and nation-states would be replaced by worldwide socialism.

Wilson had seized the initiative by deciding to attend the peace conference himself. The first American president to go to Europe while in office, Wilson maintained his personal direction of foreign policy; in a large sense, his journey symbolized the active new U.S. role outside the Western Hemisphere. Three dozen nations were represented at the Paris peace conference (actually held at the palace of Versailles just outside the city) from January to June 1919, but Germany and Bolshevik Russia were excluded. Despite Wilson's promises of "open covenants, openly arrived at" all the major discussions and decisions at the conference were made, at the Allies' insistence, behind closed doors. They were made by the "Big Four," Wilson and the heads of the primary Allied governments: Georges Clemenceau, aged, angry, nicknamed "Le Tigre" (the tiger), who demanded revenge and security for France (and $200 billion and several provinces from Germany); David Lloyd George, maverick Welsh prime minister of Great Britain, supporting a strong France and a punished Germany; and Vittorio Orlando, a vigorous Italian nationalist. London and Paris in particular wanted to make Germany pay the financial costs of the war ("reparations") to ease the burden on their taxpayers and divide up its colonies. France also wanted the German provinces on the west bank of the Rhine. Italy wanted Trieste from Austria.

Cheering European crowds greeted Wilson as a savior. Two million people lined the boulevard des Champs-Elysées to scream his name and throw flowers in his path; similar throngs hailed his visits to England and Italy. But Wilson's ability to achieve the liberals' goals in Paris was undermined by some of his own failures and other developments in America. He had failed to sound out public or congressional opinion before leaving. He had neglected to build bipartisan support for his program: the delegation he handpicked included only one Republican, who had little influence in the GOP. Despite Wilson's plea in the November 1918 election to continue the Democratic majority in Congress, voters, disaffected by wartime controls, taxes, and inflation, gave the Republicans control of both houses of Congress.

At the peace conference Wilson proved to be a tough bargainer, even threatening to walk out at one point, but with the defeat of Germany, the United States had lost its most powerful lever on the Allies, their need for American reinforcements. The resulting Treaty of Versailles, written by the Allies and signed by the Germans in June 1919, represented a compromise between Wilson's vision and the demands of the Allied leaders. The treaty departed significantly from the hopes of most liberal internationalists. It was not a peace without victory but rather a vindictive settlement. Germany was forced to accept sole guilt for the war, to pay reparations initially set at $56 billion (eventually scaled down to $33 billion), and to disarm unilaterally. In the German Rhineland the peace treaty demilitarized the right bank of the Rhine, put the left bank under Paris's control for fifteen years, and authorized the French to occupy the coal-rich Saar region for a similar period. It also returned to France the province of Alsace-Lorraine taken by Germany in 1871. It cut eastern Germany into two parts by giving the newly independent Poland a corridor to the Baltic Sea through former German territory. The treaty stripped Germany of one-eighth of its territory, one-tenth of its population, and all of its colonies and saddled it with an enormous debt, humiliating and enraging the Germans without crushing them and thereby contributing to their desire for revenge.

The Allies grabbed the spoils of war that they had promised each other in the secret treaties. Italy received the South Tyrol and Trieste from Austria. The other major powers divided up the former German and Turkish colonies, allocating them to the countries that had conquered them. Britain obtained Palestine, Trans-Jordan and oil-rich Mesopotamia (Iraq) in the Middle East, and Germany's former colonies in Africa. France received Syria and Lebanon. Japan acquired Germany's island colonies in the Pacific and its concession in China's Shantung province. The treaty departed in other ways from many of Wilson's Fourteen Points. It said nothing about freedom of the seas or reduction of tariffs. Under pressure from European leaders, Wilson had sacrificed these to prevent an even more severe treaty such as Clemenceau proposed, one that would have permanently removed the Rhineland from Germany.

In accepting such departures from the liberal peace program, Wilson hoped that ultimately the settlement would be ameliorated through the work of the League of Nations. He insisted that the League be made a part of the peace treaty. The covenant (charter) of the new international organization provided for a small but powerful executive council including the major Allied powers (Britain, France, Italy, Japan) and the United States, a large assembly in which each nation would have one vote, and a permanent secretariat in the neutral capital of Geneva, Switzerland. In the controversial Article 10 of the covenant, member nations accepted the principle of collective security, pledging to preserve each other's independence and territorial integrity against external attacks and to use economic and military sanctions against aggressor nations. In an attempt to avoid future wars, members agreed to submit to the League all disputes that could lead to war. They also agreed to work toward the reduction of armaments and to establish a permanent court of international justice, popularly known as the World Court. In a bow to the idea of self-determination, the peace conference established a mandate system under which the British, French, and Japanese would govern the former colonies of the Central Powers as trustees and would have to report to the League on the steps they were taking to prepare the indigenous populations for self-government.

Wilson believed that the flaws in the Versailles treaty would ultimately be rectified by the League of Nations. The League was the world's best hope, he exclaimed when he presented the treaty to the Senate in July 1919 for ratification:

> The stage is set, the destiny disclosed. It has come about by no plan of our conceiving, but by the hand of God who led us into this way. We cannot turn back. . . . America shall in truth show the way.

Battle over the Treaty of Versailles

Although the majority of Americans favored the League of Nations, there was much dissatisfaction with various aspects of it and with the peace settlement. Discontent grew during the public debate in the summer of 1919, but even the following winter a majority of the public apparently continued to support ratification.

Much of the liberal critique was first put forward by prominent women from the United States and the Allied and Central Powers who, angered by the exclusion of women from the peace conference, held their own concurrent meeting in Zurich, Switzerland. At the International Congress of Women in the spring of 1919, these pacifist-feminist women lawyers, social workers, physicians, and writers formed the Women's International League for Peace and Freedom (WILPF) as an ongoing female peace organization and elected Jane Addams of the United States as its first president. In a series of resolutions, the women's congress denounced the Versailles treaty as vindictive and as planting the seeds for future wars. Though gratified by the League, the women criticized many of its aspects. They also urged immediate disarmament by all nations, not simply Germany; the abandonment of military action as a means of enforcing decisions by the League; freedom of trade and travel; and League commitment to worldwide guarantees for the rights of minorities, full equality for women, and the abolition of child labor.

Other critiques came from a variety of sources. Southerners wanted race relations excluded from the jurisdiction of the League. Some industrialists wanted similar protection for tariffs. Many believed that the Monroe Doctrine, limiting European intervention in the Western Hemisphere, should be specifically exempted from League intervention. There was dissatisfaction within various ethnic groups in America over lines drawn or not drawn in the peace treaty. Many German Americans were appalled that Germany was saddled with sole guilt for the war and burdened with such a vindictive peace. Italian Americans sputtered over Wilson's giving the port city of Fiume to Yugoslavia instead of to Italy. Polish Americans praised the president for helping to obtain an independent Poland, and the American Jewish community, though divided, included many who applauded Wilson's support for a homeland in Palestine for persecuted Jews that the British Foreign Secretary Arthur J. Balfour had promised in 1917 in the Balfour Declaration. But Irish Americans jeered Wilson for not demanding independence for Ireland. African American leaders also expressed resentment that the fate of thousands of Africans living in former German colonies had been decided without any representation at the peace conference.

In response to pro-League Republicans such as former President William Howard Taft, Wilson had agreed to restraints on League interference in matters such as tariffs and immigration controls, and had removed the Monroe Doctrine from the jurisdiction of the League. Such concessions to conservatives, however, together with the problems of the peace treaty itself, increasingly alienated progressive internationalists. The peace movement did not play a major role in the national debate over the treaty, primarily because of its failure to coalesce behind a single position.

Determined opposition to the treaty and the League came from several different groups. Some progressive journals such as *The Nation* and *The New Republic* concluded that the treaty was an "inhuman monster" and the League "not powerful enough to redeem the treaty." Some locally oriented business and labor associations feared that the League, by centralized control, would reduce popular influence on foreign policy and would benefit large corporate interests at the expense of small business and ordinary workers. Corporate industrialists Andrew Mellon and Henry C. Frick financed a nationwide propaganda campaign against the League. Isolationists, particularly strong in rural areas of the South and West, opposed any involvement in an international organization.

"Dare we reject [the League] and break the heart of the world?" Wilson asked as he presented the treaty to the Senate. Since a two-thirds vote in the upper house was necessary for ratification, indeed, a minority could do just that. Leading the fight against ratification was Henry Cabot Lodge of Massachusetts, Republican head of the Senate Foreign Relations Committee. Lodge personally detested Wilson; he also sought to curtail the gains of the Democratic party. Even more, like many other Americans, Lodge was an ardent, independent nationalist, believing that the United States should continue to maintain its freedom of action in foreign affairs and not commit itself in advance to policies that might be determined by an international organization. Lodge's tactic for defeating the treaty and American membership in the League of Nations was to delay ratification and to amend the treaty to death with numerous "reservations," appealing to various groups disillusioned with it. The most important reservation sought to limit the effect of Article 10 by indicating specifically that the United States retained freedom of action in foreign affairs and that only Congress had the constitutional right to declare war. In the Senate, Lodge and some two dozen "strong reservationists" were joined by a dozen "irreconcilables," Republican and Democratic isolationists vehemently opposed to any U.S. role in a League of Nations.

From July to November 1919, the Treaty of Versailles was bottled up in the Senate Foreign Relations Committee. Wilson met with the committee in August, to no avail. In September, against medical advice, the 63-year-old president took the case for ratification to the people in a 10,000-mile railroad speaking tour of the West.

Wilson's medical records, obtained in 1990 by Professor Arthur S. Link, indicate that the president was already suffering from a disease of the carotid arteries that hindered blood flow to the brain and from hypertension that worsened the condition. The stroke Wilson had suffered in 1906 apparently triggered periodic episodes of internal bleeding. While in Paris in April, 1919, he had "stomach flu" and a minor stroke. On July 19, he suffered a severe "small" stroke. Link concluded that by mid-August the disease had eroded Wilson's mental abilities and altered his behavior, making him confused, erratic, and unwilling to compromise.

On his tour of the West, Wilson spoke to crowds once or twice a day from his train. After three weeks he suffered increasing headaches and collapsed, exhausted and in pain, in Pueblo, Colorado, on the night of September 25, 1919. After returning to Washington, Wilson suffered a massive paralytic stroke on October 2 that almost killed him. The White House withheld details of the seriousness of his condition; virtually no one saw him for a month except his doctor, his secretary, and his family. Cary Grayson, his personal physician, and Edith Bolling Galt Wilson, whom Wilson had married in 1915 after the death of his first wife, determined who saw the president. Edith Wilson also thwarted suggestions that her husband resign or delegate his authority to his vice-president, Thomas R. Marshall, former governor of Indiana, who averted a constitutional crisis by refusing to seek the president's powers. Instead, the government was run by department heads. The president was completely incapacitated for four months. Not until early February, 1920 was he able to work, and then not for more than five or ten minutes at a time. He never fully recovered. The stroke permanently paralyzed his left side, impaired his speech, impeded his vision and his power of concentration, and weakened his emotional control. Wilson remained a semi-invalid for the rest of his term and until his death in 1924.

The stroke almost certainly precluded any chance Wilson had of gaining even a partial victory in the treaty fight; his illness put an end to his public campaign. At the same time, it made him increasingly dogmatic, unable to distinguish detail from principle and unwilling to accept any compromise. Instead, he viewed the situation in stark terms of good versus evil. Crucially, he would not let pro-League Democrats in the Senate offer limited interpretive reservations that might have attracted mild reservationists, allowed Republican internationalists to claim some credit for the League, and obtained ratification of the treaty.

Caught between Lodge and Wilson and a divided public increasingly concerned with pressing domestic issues, the Senate failed on two separate occasions to ratify the Versailles treaty. On November 19, 1919, the version with the Lodge reservations was defeated; then the version without any reservations was voted down. In a final reconsideration on March 19, 1920, the treaty with the Lodge reservations was defeated once again, this time only seven votes shy of ratification. Consequently, although four-fifths of the senators said they favored the treaty in some form, the United States did not become a member of the League of Nations. Not until after the Wilson administration left office did Congress pass a joint resolution in 1921 officially ending the war. In recognition of Woodrow Wilson's efforts, however, he was awarded the Nobel Peace Prize for 1919.

Domestic Discord and Repression

"If [Wilson] loses his great fight for humanity," the left-wing magazine *The Nation* charged in 1919, "it will be because he was deliberately silent when freedom of speech and the right of conscience were struck down in America." How could he expect to win support for a grand liberal vision, *The Dial*, a liberal journal, asked in June 1919, when his administration assisted conservatives in creating "that state of mind, which blocks his own endeavors"? The defeat of the League reflected not simply a deadlock in the Senate but a failure to mobilize a shattered and dispirited progressive coalition. Until 1917, Wilson had, historian Thomas J. Knock has written, built his sponsorship of a liberal league of nations on the same political left and center coalition as supported his 1916 domestic policies and reelection campaign. But during the war and after, Wilson had been unwilling or unable to take the lead in uniting this progressive coalition. He seems to have lost his political bearings as the administration turned its attention to mobilization policies, curtailment of dissent, and a growing antiradicalism that divided and alienated many people in the political center and on the liberal left who might otherwise have been molded into a strong constituency behind U.S. membership in the League of Nations. This failure was reflected in Wilson's simultaneous inability to move forward on the domestic front. That the American people failed to protest the defeat of the grand vision of the League was a symptom of the reactionary, repressive political climate of 1919 and 1920.

Racism and Race Riots

The bloody repression of the postwar period was nowhere more evident than in the widespread onslaughts against black Americans. Race relations deteriorated rapidly. In the South, lynchings, some of them advertised in newspapers in advance, thus providing almost official sanction, leapt from thirty-six in 1917 to seventy-six in 1919. In more than two dozen northern cities, racial violence broke out in the summer of 1919, the "red summer," red with blood, as one black leader called it; 120 persons were killed, most of them black. The worst race riot in American history occurred in Chicago in July 1919. While a police officer stood by, whites stoned to death a black youth who had swum or drifted into an area of a lakeshore beach normally reserved for whites.

Blacks mobbed the police officer, and gangs of whites, some with machine guns, attacked the black ghetto, killing indiscriminately. Blacks fought back, and the riot raged for five days, leaving more than 500 injured by beating or gunfire and thirty-eight people dead. But African Americans had armed themselves and fought back — evidence, hailed by the black press, of the "New Negro."

Labor, Radicals, and the Red Scare

While Wilson focused on peacemaking and the treaty and then fell to a massive stroke, the country was being torn by internal tensions and strife. Workers had made many gains during the war, but following the armistice, government protection was curtailed, war orders ended, and many employers resumed their traditional hostility toward unions. Postwar inflation threatened to wipe out the purchasing power of wartime wage increases. Consequently, more than 4 million workers went on strike in 1919.

Labor-management conflict spread throughout the country, causing 3,300 strikes that year. This was accompanied by a growing fear of radicalism, ironically at a time when American radicalism had lost many of its members and much of its political power. Wartime repression had eliminated the IWW and, together with internal dissention, had reduced the Socialist party to no more than 30,000 members. The Left continued to fragment. In the summer of 1919 the Communist Labor party was founded by a number of native-born former socialists, including Harvard-educated journalist John Reed and Benjamin Gitlow. That fall the rival Communist Party of the United States was founded, largely by foreign-born Americans. Together the two communist factions counted fewer than 70,000 members. Nevertheless, business, the press, and patriotic organizations warned that communists ("Reds") were everywhere. In Seattle a strike by shipyard workers turned into a general strike that crippled the entire city. Wilson's press secretary had overreacted by stating that the country was poised between "organization and anarchy." A newspaper headline warned "Reds Directing Seattle Strike — To Test Chance for Revolution."

In the largest strike of 1919, more than 350,000 steelworkers walked out in September. The AFL had changed strategy and sought to organize all the steelworkers regardless of their particular trades and skills into one large, industrywide union. The union had sought reduction of the twelve-hour workday and seven-day workweek, but U.S. Steel, headed by Elbert H. Gary, refused to meet with representatives of the union and instead hired Hispanic and black strikebreakers. The company maintained sufficient production to break the strike, particularly when national opinion failed to support the strikers, in part because of consumer opposition to inflationary wage increases and in part because the company and much of the press had focused on the radical background of one of the union organizers, William Z. Foster, the secretary of the organizing committee. The presence of Foster, a former member of the IWW who would later join the Communist party, enabled the press to depict the steel strike as a first step in foreign-inspired revolution rather than what it was, an attempt by a moderate AFL to bring normal working conditions to a recalcitrant industry. By January 1920 the steel strike had failed.

In the coal industry, when 450,000 striking miners in the fall of 1919 refused to heed a court order to return to work, the Wilson administration imposed the wartime Lever Act to force them back to work. The union agreed, but many miners defied their leaders and the government. Coal shortages forced schools and factories to shut down, and public pressure mounted for a settlement. Although a special commission ultimately awarded the miners a raise, much of the public saw the strikers as opposing the public interest.

Most symbolic of the fear of chaos and disorder was the Boston police strike in the fall of 1919. Without a wage increase since 1913, the police had been hit hard by soaring prices; they were now working 80 hours a week and earning less than manual laborers. After several unsuccessful attempts to obtain a cost-of-living increase, more than two-thirds of the city's 1,500 police walked off their jobs. Many people were outraged as criminals attacked individuals and looted stores in broad daylight. Refusing Samuel Gompers' offer to help settle the strike, the governor of Massachusetts, Calvin Coolidge, denied that public employees had the right to strike or form a union. "There is no right to strike against the public safety by anybody, anywhere, any time," Coolidge proclaimed in a statement that earned him national recognition and helped him to win reelection later that year and the Republican vice-presidential nomination in 1920. The strikers were all fired. A Philadelphia newspaper had warned, "Bolshevism in the United States is no longer a specter. Boston in chaos reveals its sinister substance."

The Palmer Raids

A series of widely scattered terrorist bombings throughout 1919 added to the tension and fear. On International Labor Day, May 1, 1919, three dozen mail bombs addressed to leading officials in the U.S. government were discovered and dismantled by postal workers. A month later a bomb exploded outside the home of the new attorney general of the United States, A. Mitchell Palmer of Pennsylvania. Although the perpetrators were never identified, the press speculated that they were communists, adding fuel to the "Red scare."

Hoping for the Democratic presidential nomination in 1920, Palmer linked the Wilson administration to the widespread fear that the United States was threatened by a communist revolution. He set up an antiradical division (soon to be known as the Federal Bureau of Investigation) under a young government attorney named J. Edgar Hoover and then launched a campaign to arrest and deport alien communists and other radicals. In November 1919 the first of a series of "Palmer raids" netted thousands of aliens, most of whom had committed no crime but were under suspicion because of their beliefs or immigrant backgrounds. In December 1919 some 300 alien radicals were deported by ship to the Soviet Union, among them the famous anarchist-feminist Emma Goldman; another 300 were deported later. In January federal agents swept down on private homes, union headquarters, and pool halls in three dozen cities and took more than 2,000 alleged communists into custody without arrest warrants. Many were beaten and held incommunicado without hearings. Arrests continued at a reduced rate through March, ultimately numbering more than 4,000.

Many states adopted antiradical statutes, and local vigilance organizations, including the American Legion and the Ku Klux Klan, screened the loyalty of workers, schoolteachers and others. In New York, the state legislature expelled five legally elected Socialists; Congress expelled Milwaukee Socialist Victor Berger and refused to seat him despite his having twice won election. The ailing 65-year-old Eugene V. Debs, four-time Socialist presidential candidate, remained in federal prison, serving a ten-year sentence for speaking against the draft and the war; Wilson personally refused to pardon or parole him.

The wholesale abuse of civil liberties involved in the Red scare eventually produced a backlash. In a revolt against Palmer, Assistant Secretary of Labor Louis Post and Immigration Commissioner Frederick Howe blocked Palmer's wholesale deportations and accused him of gross violations of human rights. The courts released most of the victims of the government arrests, but the hundreds who had already been deported were not readmitted. Palmer predicted a revolutionary uprising for May 1, 1920. The nation went on alert, but when the day went by without a single incident, Palmer was discredited. In the absence of major strikes and bombings, antiradicalism abated in the summer of 1920. In September, when a wagonload of bombs exploded at lunchtime at the corner of Board and Wall streets in the heart of New York's financial district, killing three dozen workers, the general reaction was appropriately one of horror and revulsion at the work of a fanatic, not fear of an incipient communist revolution. The Red scare was over, but the suppression of civil liberties during and after the war remained a major blot on the record of the Wilson administration.

The Election of 1920

Voters went to the polls in 1920 in a recession that had begun to throw millions out of work. Prohibition had been initiated in January 1920. The Nineteenth Amendment, ratified just before the election, enabled women to vote; many did cast their ballots, although Old World customs restrained most immigrant women, and racial disfranchisement kept southern black women, like black men, from the polls.

The choices for president were hardly exciting. Although some states had adopted presidential primaries, the party's candidates were still chosen largely at presidential nominating conventions. The infirm Woodrow Wilson would have run again to make the League an issue, but the Democrats dissuaded him; they also bypassed two of his cabinet members, Attorney General Palmer and Treasury Secretary McAdoo, who yearned for the nomination. Instead, at San Francisco they chose for president someone unconnected with the administration, James M. Cox, the moderately progressive governor of Ohio, and for vice-president, Wilson's young assistant secretary of the navy, Franklin D. Roosevelt of New York, a Democratic cousin of the late Theodore Roosevelt.

Anticipating victory, Republicans deadlocked in Chicago over two forceful foes of radicals and unions, General Leonard Wood and Governor Frank Lowden of Illinois. After nearly a dozen ballots, party leaders met in a "smoke-filled room" and decided to put forward a compromise candidate, Senator Warren G. Harding, a small-town newspaper publisher from Ohio, who had little glamour but also few enemies. The convention quickly chose him and selected Governor Calvin Coolidge of Massachusetts as his running mate. The candidates of both major parties largely avoided making the League of Nations an issue. Recognizing the widespread desire for calm, Harding engaged in a low-key, nostalgic campaign from his back porch in Marion, Ohio, and reassuringly stressed the need for tranquillity and harmony.

In November 1920 the Republicans restored the majority in the electorate that they had held since the mid-1890s and would hold until the Great Depression of the 1930s, broken only by Wilson in 1912 and again in 1916. In a repudiation of the Wilson administration, voters gave the Republicans one of the biggest landslide victories in American presidential elections. Harding won 16 million votes to 9 million for Cox; 60 percent of the popular vote to 34 percent, 404 electoral votes to 127. More than 900,000 persons, or 3 percent of the popular vote, cast ballots for the Socialist candidate, Eugene V. Debs, still in the federal penitentiary in Atlanta (his sentence was finally commuted by Harding, who released him at Christmas in 1921).

In many ways the America that emerged from the war years was an unsettled mix of the old and the new. Wartime and postwar tensions had accentuated racial, ethnic, gender, and class divisions in American society. Ideological schisms tore at the social fabric: conservatives versus radicals and progressives, modernists versus traditionalists, wets versus drys, pluralists against "Americanizers," pacifists against interventionists, nationalists against internationalists. After more than a decade of intensive crusades for reform at home and abroad and of bloody repression of blacks, radicals, unionists, and others, and after the loss of 50,000 soldiers in battle and 60,000 from disease, it was little wonder that after 1920, millions of Americans would desire an escape from what John Dewey called the "cult of irrationality" and accept relief in what Warren Harding described as "normalcy."

CHAPTER 9

The Meaning of the
Progressive Era

"Those who are young today," Walter Lippmann wrote in 1914, "are born into a world in which the foundations of the old order survive only as habits or by default. Scientific invention and blind social currents have made the old authority impossible. . . . Our time believes in change." Lippmann was right. The Progressive Era proved to be a time of extraordinary change — for good and ill. In many ways it marked the birth of modern America.

A generation earlier, people had debated national political issues that today seem archaic: reconstruction policies toward the defeated South, pensions for Union veterans, tariff levels, whether the currency should be backed by gold alone or by silver as well. But industrialization, immigration, urbanization, and a spirit of reform transformed America and the nature of political debate. In the Progressive Era national parties clashed over big business, antitrust policy, federal regulation, women's rights, the government's role in determining working conditions, the conservation of natural resources, and the extent of U.S. intervention overseas. These issues would dominate politics for the rest of the twentieth century.

The change in issues reflected basic alterations in the way Americans lived, worked, and thought. Industrialization was accompanied by the spread of factories and congested, unhealthy cities. It contributed to widespread poverty and labor violence, while concentrating great power in the hands of new industrial and financial elites. Yet industrialization also brought many benefits, including new jobs and goods, and much greater national wealth and power. The anxiety with which America viewed industrialization was a mixture of conflicting sentiments: admiration and anger, awe and outrage.

Problems confronting America at the turn of the century demanded attention. The business cycle had become increasingly traumatic; the depression of the 1890s had triggered thousands of business failures and massive unemployment. In the countryside, farm tenancy increased dramatically, and rural poverty and malnutrition became widespread. With the simultaneous emergence of an ostentatious class of newly rich "plutocrats" and a poverty-stricken urban underclass, class divisions became painfully apparent. Uncontrolled industrialism was polluting a fragile environment, draining finite natural resources, and endangering a largely unprotected work force. Industrial accidents, disease, alcoholism, and narcotics addiction threatened the health and safety of millions of Americans.

Centered in the cities of the Northeast, the emergence of big business challenged American suspicions of concentrated economic and political power. And there were other problems. Entrenched political organizations seemed stagnant or corrupt. Minorities were repressed and racial and ethnic divisions exacerbated. Women were subjugated and exploited. These problems and the changes suggested to alleviate them generated powerful tensions between traditionalists and modernizers of various kinds. Most of these tensions involved domestic concerns, but they also included America's relationship with other nations in a rapidly changing world.

The Interventionist Impulse

In the Progressive Era, large numbers of Americans concluded that the problems accompanying industrialization meant that they could no longer rely solely on Providence or evolution for automatic progress. They lost their faith in the long-held utilitarian concept of a natural harmony of self-interests and in the functioning of a self-regulating society. Given the dangers that were evident by the turn of the century, many Americans questioned whether the economy and society benefited from allowing decisions that affected everyone to be determined entirely by individuals and by market forces. With the optimism and the sense of power that came from developments in science, technology, and organization theory, the new interventionists decided that it was necessary to modify the concept of unrestricted individualism and the marketplace. They thought that intervention and intelligent direction could ensure continued growth and progress that would be consistent with the ideal of an efficient and liberal democratic society.

The new interventionists did not eliminate individualism, laissez-faire, or the market system or even make them secondary. These beliefs remained powerful and primary long after the Progressive Era. Rather, Americans in the early years of the new century made the first successful national attempt since the mercantilist system of the 1700s to place significant limitations on the market system. This shift to a mood that supported intervention and purposeful direction was probably the most important change of the Progressive Era.

The number of collective decisions to limit the self-regulating marketplace increased substantially. Officials in a somewhat expanded government made a few of these decisions. But many more were made by people in organizations in the private sector — supercorporations (themselves often conglomerations of formerly independent companies), trade associations, labor unions, farmers' groups, professional bodies, or other voluntary associations. Interventionists created new mechanisms for dealing with the problems caused by blind social forces or powerful, self-interested individuals or groups. Using the example of the supercorporations, which could greatly influence their environment, interventionists employed organization and intervention as tools for achieving their goals and imposing conscious direction on society. Writing in 1914, Lippmann noted the dramatic change:

> We can no longer treat life as something that has trickled down to us. We have to deal with it deliberately, devise its social organization, alter its tools, formulate its method, educate and control it. . . . The scientific spirit is the discipline of democracy, the escape from drift. . . . Men have to substitute purpose for tradition; and that is, I believe, the profoundest change that has ever taken place in human history.

By focusing on the progressives and on the expansion of governmental power, historians have until recently neglected the broader basis of change in the era, the context in which the progressives operated. They have concentrated on the transient nature of the shifting coalitions that formed around specific issues. In doing so, they have often misunderstood the widespread dissatisfaction with many of the results of unrestricted individualism, the unregulated marketplace, and the self-regulating society. The dominant development of the era was the emergence of an interventionist mood on a national scale. The need for some kind of purposeful, collective intervention, for what Lippmann called "mastery over drift," became apparent not only to radicals and moderate reformers like the progressives but to many conservatives as well.

Many conservatives, for example, supported some degree of intervention in the marketplace because of new industrial conditions. As Thomas A. Edison wrote to his friend Henry Ford in 1912,

> This is a pretty raw, crude civilization of ours — pretty wasteful, pretty cruel. . . . Our production, our factory laws, our charities, our relations between capital and labor, our distribution — all wrong, out of gear. We've stumbled along for a while, trying to run a new civilization in old ways, but we've got to start to make this world over.

Conservatives created instruments for collective decision making in the private sector such as the giant corporations, trade associations, philanthropic foundations, and coordinating bodies like the National Civic Federation. Many also helped other interventionists to achieve new governmental mechanisms for order, including regulatory agencies, social control devices like prohibition and immigration restriction, and a modern army, navy, and diplomatic service for a more active, interventionist foreign policy.

Others who did not consider themselves progressives also organized and sought to participate in social, economic, political, or cultural relations to improve their position or that of society. Among these were the labor movement, the corporate reorganization movement, and movements for prohibition and immigration restriction.

Recent scholarship on the Progressive Era has to some extent shifted away from a focus on progressivism itself, generally accepting the reform "movement" itself as pluralistic, to the context in which the reformers operated. As the historian Daniel Rodgers aptly concluded in the 1980s, much of the new scholarship

> inquired less about the progressives themselves than about their surroundings; less about the internal coherence of the progressive "movement" than about the structures of politics, power, and ideas within which the era's welter of tongues and efforts and "reforms" took place.

Regarding politics, the new scholarship emphasized a dramatic change: the explosion of aggressive, politically active pressure groups that rushed to influence public policy at a time when old party loyalties were evaporating and the electorate was contracting as voters were excluded or simply stopped voting. Facing this decline and the unsettling emergence of new issue-oriented, extraparty pressure groups, the nineteenth-century system of "distributive governance," in which political parties sought to retain power by distributing favors all around, rapidly eroded. The fragmented, fluid, issue-focused politics that replaced the strong party system enabled some independent politicians to vault into office and permitted both "reform" and "antireform" coalitions to proliferate. In the reduced electorate, voters interested in progressive issues generally felt specific loyalties, even if they were in flux in the varying coalitions that categorized the politics of the era. Most important, historians now recognize that the struggles among the progressives, their enemies, and their allies were played out against a backdrop of much greater structural change: the rise of the weak-party, issue-oriented politics that would last the rest of the century.

Even more substantial change took place in the organization of economic and social power. The local, informal group so characteristic of small-town and agrarian society was superseded as the basic framework of American life by immensely larger, hierarchically structured formal organizations. Most prominent in what some historians called the organizational or bureaucratic revolution were the large corporation and regulatory government. The organizational movement's response to industrialism was fueled in part by an increased emphasis on social efficiency, systematization, and scientifically adjusted harmony. Some historians posited a role for a "new middle class" of educators, engineers, doctors, lawyers, social workers, and others in conveying new bureaucratic values, from reordering their own professions to reorganizing government and social services in a more efficient manner, but the linkage was far from complete, and the professions remained highly entrepreneurial.

Many observers focused on the organizational revolution in big business, for it was in the corporations that the concepts of efficiency, rationality, and predictability were being made an integral part of large-scale organizational operations. Although the fierce competition of market capitalism continued in some industries, in retail goods and services, and in many nonindustrial sectors of the economy such as agriculture, it is clear that at the turn of the century the majority of giant corporations in business and finance shifted from an ideology of unrestrained price competition to one of administered prices and more stable economic relationships. In oligopolistic industries, most of the giant firms were more than willing to cooperate with one another, unless their vital interests were endangered, in pursuit of continued, predictable growth. A spate of mergers at the turn of the century made big business a major public issue. Large corporations had marshaled their considerable resources and sought to rationalize their economic environment in a variety of ways, through efficient internal administration, by coordinating the growth of profits and markets, and by attempting to fend off adverse actions by workers, other firms, government regulators, or public opinion.

Particularly in dealing with government and unions acceptable to them, many big business leaders exchanged the tactics of direct resistance for those of cooptation. No more the blatant "public be damned" attitude, as Cornelius Vanderbilt, the railroad magnate, had openly expressed in the nineteenth century. Instead, in the crisis of legitimacy triggered by public reaction to the mergers of the turn of the century and criticism of trusts by many journalists, academicians, labor leaders, agrarians, and politicians, corporations and their defenders developed a series of measures that, although directed at specific assaults, had the overall effect of diminishing middle-class resentment and at least temporarily reducing labor militancy. What historians such as James Weinstein and Martin Sklar have called "corporate liberalism" involved new schemes of business-government cooperation, agreements to accept acquiescent labor unions, and ideals of larger social harmony. The social schemes involved programs by corporate-financed philanthropic foundations and public policy institutes, among them plans for adapting the educational and public health systems to produce healthier and more vocationally trained citizens who would be better workers and less discontented with the system. Corporate liberalism included a belief that social harmony, as well as business profits, would be enhanced by the development of a consumer society and culture that emphasized the importance of the ongoing acquisition of goods and services promoted as offering both a new frontier of economic expansion and a new mechanism for individual happiness and fulfillment.

As the emergence of a culture of consumption suggests, the Progressive Era witnessed significant changes in social thought. Progressives had an inordinate faith in ideas and in their own ability to preach the truth. Like many others, however, they were also prone to exaggeration and vague, partisan rhetoric to minimize differences and build coalitions behind their goals. Although they used many of the same words — *social justice, democracy, public interest* — progressives differed over the meanings. But they were able to draw on what Daniel Rodgers has identified as three distinct clusters of ideas — three social languages or public rhetoric — to articulate their discontents and their social visions: the idiom of antimonopoly, the rhetoric of social efficiency, and the language of social bonds. This last emphasized a larger responsibility to society (progressives differed over whether such bonds were to the state and the nation or to family, community, and neighborhood) in opposition to irresponsible, antisocial acts. Elements of these clusters of rhetoric and ideas existed earlier, and some would continue long afterward. But, as Rodgers suggests, "what made progressive social thought distinct and volatile . . . was not its intellectual coherence but the presence of all three of these languages at once." This time-bound constellation of concepts offered progressives and others a particular manner of addressing the world in which they lived — the political language of an era.

Despite the breadth of the forces for change, the Progressive Era cannot be understood without progressivism. Although it was neither a unified social movement nor a single coalition of voters, progressivism cannot be dismissed for its diversity. Nor can it be disregarded because of conservative aspects of its nature and legacy. Rather, contemporaries correctly saw it as the dominant motif of the period.

The core of progressivism was the progressive ethos — a combination of moral idealism and pragmatic, piecemeal reform with a sweeping vision of democracy and rejuvenated national community. Evangelistic modernizers, progressives had a sense of morality and mission that led them to try to impose their standards on an increasingly diverse society and, in fact, through cultural imperialism, on the rest of the world as well. The reformer Frederic C. Howe, writing his memoirs in 1925, put it candidly:

> Evangelical religion [and] . . . early assumptions as to virtue and vice, goodness and evil . . . explain the nature of our reforms, the regula-

tory legislation in morals and economics, our belief in men rather than in institutions and our messages to other peoples. Missionaries and battleships, anti-saloon leagues and Ku Klux Klans, Wilson and Santo Domingo are all part of that evangelistic psychology that makes America what she is.

The progressives' spirit and rhetoric, like that of the nation's founders, and later the Jacksonians, and much later, the New Dealers, set the style and much of the substance of the agenda and leadership of their time.

Progressivism also provided a significant number of leaders, both in private and public organizations and in government, who translated that spirit into an ideal and a language that helped to mobilize millions of Americans into myriad campaigns for progress. "It is this union of the idealistic and the efficient," a young intellectual named Randolph Bourne wrote in 1913, "that gives the movement its hold on the disinterested and serious youth of today." A generation earlier, in the spoilsman days of the Gilded Age, young people from elite families had avoided politics as disreputable. But progressives resurrected public service and political leadership as honorable callings. Unselfish service came to be seen as an ideal, partly because resurgent Protestant evangelism coalesced with such secular developments as professionalization and bureaucratization. The altruist, the expert, and the civil servant were seen as people who put the good of society above their own interests. Leaders like Jane Addams, Lillian Wald, Gifford Pinchot, Theodore Roosevelt, and Woodrow Wilson — the latter, the most intellectually distinguished presidents since the framers of the Republic — inspired a generation of young men and women to enter community and public service. They also influenced the course of public debate for several decades.

The rhetoric of reform, the common language that progressivism gave to an era, proved more effective in mobilizing action than in analyzing developments. It masked the differences among people who used the same political phrases. The conflicting aims of many progressives and others were muted by the interventionists' emphasis on process — purposeful, intelligent, collaborative decision making — rather than on specific goals such as reducing prices, providing socially acceptable wages, or limiting the size of corporations. The progressive ideal was to establish a general public interest among different and often competing groups. But defining the specific "public interest" might have destroyed the coalition that made possible much of the interventionist legislation. To the extent that progressives and other interventionists stressed larger abstract goals of a higher morality, a general public interest, and a unique mission for ensuring progress at home and abroad, they served as missionaries of a particularly American form of modernization.

"Modernization" in World Perspective

Because of a different environment, culture, and tradition, the United States placed much less emphasis on governmental intervention and acted much more slowly than the industrializing countries of western Europe in establishing a regulatory welfare state. Beginning in the 1880s, for example, the German government under the chancellorship of Count Otto von Bismarck insured industrial workers for loss of income because of sickness or accident and guaranteed them old-age pensions. The Germans established the principle that such risks should be carried by society and not solely by individuals. Under pressure from rapidly expanding trade and craft unions and from socialist labor parties and middle-class reformers, other western European nations adopted similar programs. Britain added a system of national unemployment insurance and, under the Liberal governments of Henry Campbell-Bannerman and David Lloyd George, sought to increase economic and political democracy by restricting the power of the House of Lords and raising taxes on the wealthy to pay for the emerging welfare state.

The United States experienced industrialization and the drive toward political and social democracy somewhat differently because of its relative abundance, the absence of an entrenched landed aristocracy and a restless proletariat, and its emphasis on individualism, laissez-faire, and a relatively free marketplace. America's social democracy was much less oriented toward labor and socialist ideology than Europe's. The lack of widespread class consciousness among industrial workers and notoriously weak labor unions together with the continued power of business and finance contributed to a reform program that was moderate, pragmatic, and problem-centered. More politically influential than labor were the agrarians of the South and the West, the broad middle class, and big business. Religious and missionary traditions also gave American social democracy a particularly moralistic air and an evangelical tone. Furthermore, there was no counterpart on the European continent to the United States' antimonopoly tradition. European political and legal systems proved much more permissive to allowing independent manufacturers to join together in cartels to avoid destructive price competition at home or abroad. Paradoxically, the American antitrust tradition, which outlawed such cartels, furthered the development of the largest integrated supercorporations in the world.

Structural obstacles and suspicion of strong central government helped to limit the growth of governmental power in the United States. Taxes, for example, took only 3 percent of average income, compared to 9 percent in Britain and 12 percent in France. Traditionalists and many fiscal conservatives in Congress, the judiciary, and the media restricted governmental expansion. In the political system, power was fragmented among various branches of government and in the division of the federal-state system itself. The new supercorporations and other powerful interest groups contested many reforms. Given the proliferation of pressure groups, the polity in the Progressive Era may have been more pluralistic than its predecessors, but pluralism did not mean equality of influence. Financial and informational resources and personal access to the media and to decision makers meant greater influence in the political system. The giant corporations were certainly the richest and most powerful private organizations of the era. Although business was seldom united on specific issues, it generally agreed in opposition to radical proposals seen as a threat to the overall business environment. Furthermore, most of the largest corporations were usually adept at making their influence felt. When they joined together, they were particularly successful in obtaining compromises in legislation or appropriations and in achieving sympathetic treatment from regulatory agencies. Although people at all levels of society sought to influence the forces affecting their lives, particularly in the immediate environment in which they lived, the poor and the unorganized had little or no influence in the national political system. Without the vote, the poorest of the poor were completely excluded from politics. Even the majority of voters, generally unaware of the details of pending legislation or administrative actions unless they involved sensational issues, had little direct influence on the precise nature of particular laws, appropriations measures, and regulatory rulings. Even reformers who kept track of issues and legislation were often divided. Finally, progressives overestimated the length of time that reform activism could be sustained before sufficient opposition gathered to blunt it and stop its momentum.

Cycles of Reform

The life cycle of progressivism as a nationwide political movement illustrates the dynamic quality of the American political system. Dramatic events and shifts in public mood can, under favorable circumstances and effective leadership, reduce somewhat the power of previous constraints, at least temporarily. At such pivotal moments a broad national consensus for collective action can lead to the achievement of significant changes. Such a departure generally requires a special combination of occurrences to unsettle the political situation. During the Progressive Era the interventionist, reformist mood stemmed from the traumatic disruptions of the depression of the 1890s, which helped convince many Americans that industrialization would not automatically cure its own ills and that purposeful action was required. Following the depression, the economic growth in the first decade of the twentieth century encouraged optimism, hope, and a sense of generosity among the middle and upper classes. It also increased the expectations and demands of many agricultural workers, miners, and members of the urban laboring classes for a better life in a dramatically expanding economy. Investigative journalists — the muckrakers — helped to encourage and sustain the reform movement through their exposés of social problems, from corruption in business and politics to adulterated foods, fraudulent patent medicines, and unsafe and exploitative working conditions. Though entrenched interests remained, new political leaders came to power promising significant changes.

Progressivism emerged in the cities in the late 1890s and reached its peak nationally in the decade between 1907 and 1917. Then the movement began to divide as more conservative reformers became convinced that new groups in the reform coalition, particularly labor unions and social justice progressives, were rushing the pace of reform and broadening its scope beyond what the more conservative reformers had envisioned. They joined antiprogressive conservatives and traditionalists in seeking to block additional reforms and diluting the effect of some that had already been adopted. American participation in World War I aroused, divided, and then dissipated the militant optimism of progressivism. "We were not used to smelling blood from vast human slaughterhouses," William Allen White recalled. The strains of the war and the struggles over postwar domestic and foreign policies shattered progressivism as a national movement. The political power of conservative interests, particularly big business and the Republican party, was restored. "We poor panting crusaders for a just and righteous order were left on a deserted battlefield," White mourned, "our drums punctured, our bugles muted, our cause forgotten."

In the 1920s progressivism as a broad, national political force faded from American life. The coalitions that had supported its reforms splintered further over ethnocultural issues — prohibition, compulsory "Americanization," and immigration restriction — raised by intensified pressures for certification of a homogeneous Anglo-Saxon Protestant national culture. Further blows were dealt to the movement by the death of its political leaders, including Roosevelt and Wilson, and the aging of others, such as La Follette. Many wealthy patrons of reform movements died; others turned their attention to the arts, religion, or other concerns. Despite considerable economic discontent and some organized liberal and radical dissent, the national focus for most of the decade was on the growth of business, the flood of new consumer goods, mass entertainment, changing lifestyles and gender relations, and the divisive ethnocultural issues that dominated the decade. Although a number of the reforms and reformers continued, the national mood of the Progressive Era evaporated in the boosterism, consumerism, individual self-concern, and aid to business that characterized the 1920s.

The Legacy of the Progressive Era

Despite the demise of progressivism, the era significantly influenced American society. Interventionists of various political hues began to acclimate Americans to new mechanisms for social change and order in a complex and interrelated urban, industrial society. Most progressive and conservative interventionists sought to provide new means of coordination and direction without creating the kind of powerful state apparatus that emerged in Europe. Although they called for modification of laissez-faire and the marketplace ideal, they wanted new private and governmental mechanisms that would ensure progress while maintaining the nation's basic economic, social, and political structure.

Despite the democratic rhetoric of the time, the politics and institutions developed in the Progressive Era provided an ambiguous legacy. In retrospect, most progressives were rather naive reformers. They proved better at obtaining power than at using it. In ousting incumbents they had few equals, but once in office they could not agree on the specific aims of government. They argued for a general public interest, but they did not define it. Given the conflicting aims of the interventionist groups that helped to create the new mechanisms of management, it was perhaps impossible to define a commonly accepted goal. But without such a definition, or adequate guidelines for the exercise of power, the new institutions could be used by interests with other philosophies when the national mood and political power shifted. The regulatory commissions, for example, often became dominated by many of the powerful interest groups they were designed to control.

The fact that the most liberal progressives later claimed that the institutions had betrayed their original purpose was less a reflection of the actual aims of these bodies than of the ambiguity of the democratic rhetoric of the Progressive Era. That rhetoric often masked not only the conflicting aims of competing groups but wide differences in philosophy as well. It was evoked by those who emphasized rights and those who stressed duties; it was employed both to encourage freedom and to increase repression. In the long run interventionists created mechanisms that could be used for different purposes. In retrospect, the ambiguity had been present from the beginning.

In their search for new people and new systems to direct social change, progressives and other interventionists promoted patterns of rationalization, predictability, and efficiency; most important, they created new organizations. To replace what they regarded as reliance on chance and ad hoc local responses, interventionists turned to the methods of scientific investigation — data gathering, analysis, and prognosis — and to the establishment of permanent associations or agencies. Despite their ambiguity, the organizations of the Progressive Era proved one of the period's most important legacies.

Interventionists gave a major boost to the creation of nationally organized voluntary associations to mediate between increasing social demands and the need for some kind of collective action, on the one hand, and, on the other, older American traditions of individual autonomy, private property, and limited government. Although they recognized the need for some expanded governmental power to balance the growth of private power centers, progressives and most other interventionists did not want to end primary reliance on voluntary action and initiative in the community itself. The corporations demonstrated the effectiveness of organization and intervention in the marketplace. As a result, many workers, professionals, producers, shippers, and others formed associations for self-protection and self-promotion.

The Progressive Era also showed that nationally organized voluntary associations could intervene to improve society. The tuberculosis society, the settlement house association, the National Consumers League, the Sierra Club, and youth organizations such as the Boy Scouts, the Camp Fire Girls, the YMCA, and the YWCA tried to alleviate problems by altering environmental conditions, attitudes, and behavior. So, in fact, did more coercive organizations like the Anti-Saloon League and the Immigration Restriction League. The irony of the Progressive Era included not only the ambiguity of its mechanisms of organization and intervention but also the fact that progressives, while espousing a common public interest, joined in creating interest groups that ultimately changed the way the national government functioned and contributed to the rise of the broker state.

Women and Progressivism

Nowhere were the effective role of private voluntary associations and their ultimate impact on the state more evident than in the role of activist women reformers in developing grassroots organizations and national and international lobbying groups to press for an expansion of women's rights in society, including legal and political rights and maternal and child welfare benefits. Women felt the effects of industrialization in ways often different from men, since they also continued the primary responsibilities for home and child care despite the dislocations of a rapidly changing society. Women and children bore the brunt of poverty. They also faced discrimination in the labor force. The proportion of women holding paying jobs increased from 15 percent of women over 16 years of age in 1900 to 23 percent in 1920, but they were almost always assigned to less prestigious and lower-paying tasks. Yet the turn of the century also saw the emergence of significant numbers of college-educated, self-supporting professional women who became the leaders and supporters of the reform, benevolent, and suffrage organizations that made up the women's movement.

Excluded from or marginal to male-dominated political parties, trade unions, and fraternal organizations, women found other means of influencing public policy and protecting themselves. They formed the Women's Trade Union League to promote the growth of women's trade unionism and the National Consumer's League to prevent the exploitation of working women and children through protective legislation and consumer boycotts. As settlement house workers, public health nurses, and members of a variety of women's benevolent associations, women activists also created support services for needy widows, mothers, and children. They did this first through the women's own voluntary associations and then through state and local governments that acted largely as a result of mobilization and lobbying by the women reformers. With the establishment of the U.S. Children's Bureau in 1912, they also established a base in the federal government. Although Congress made a gesture in the Sheppard-Towner Act of 1921, real federal assistance to needy widows, mothers, and dependent children would not be obtained until the New Deal. Nevertheless, the gradually emerging welfare state would almost certainly have been less responsive to the needs of women and children had it not been for the women activists. It was not coincidental that social welfare programs emerged at the same time as the rise of women's social action movements.

One of the major gains of the Progressive Era was also that women finally won the vote. They did so in part by going beyond the voluntary reform groups women had used for some time as vehicles to participate in public life. In the suffrage movement in the 1910s they engaged for the first time in mass and direct demonstrations, the kind of public rituals of solidarity and power that, as Michael McGerr has noted, had been central to male popular politics in the nineteenth century — open-air meetings, parades, and pageantry, designed not simply to demonstrate the mobilization of large numbers but also to emphasize equality, diversity, and participation. Paradoxically, in the aftermath of the suffrage victory with the final ratification of the Nineteenth Amendment in 1920, women abandoned these techniques and, like the majority of men, acquiesced in the political style of the 1920s in which mainstream politics came to be dominated by educational and advertising styles rather than mass demonstrations. Furthermore, despite the importance of the suffrage victory, the enfranchisement of women did not in itself change their special, and generally inferior, status, since discrimination against women was deeply rooted in the structure of society — in the roles assigned to women and in a sexual division of labor that emphasized that a woman's major roles were as wife and mother, not as an autonomous individual.

The New Politics

For all their talk of restoring government to "the people" and curbing "the interests," the progressives obtained mixed results. Many of the insurgents' innovations were designed primarily to help them to gain office by expanding the power of their particular constituency, mainly the middle class. Thus they circumvented party bosses by emphasizing popular government. They enlarged the nominating process by creating direct primaries in several states, and they achieved direct election of U.S. senators nationally through a constitutional amendment. They developed a new kind of personal and issue-oriented politics that party machines usually found difficult to handle.

In practice, however, much of their emphasis on democracy proved illusory. Measures such as the initiative and referendum have been employed most successfully by the best-financed and best-organized special-interest groups, especially conservative organizations. The recall has rarely been effective in removing public officials. And though progressive reforms helped insurgents to gain power, they also diminished the political involvement of many lower-income people — blacks as well as Asian, Hispanic, and European immigrants — whom progressives deliberately disfranchised. Furthermore, the progressives' emphasis on personalities and issues was no substitute for party loyalty and discipline as a means of mobilizing masses of voters. Voter turnout (as a percentage of eligible voters), which had begun to decline after the election of 1896, shrank rapidly in the Progressive Era, evidence of increasing voter apathy despite extensive political activity.

The experience of Europe, where socialist labor and liberal reform parties emerged in these years, was not matched in the United States, where attempts to create substantial socialist and progressive parties failed. The structure of the two-party system remained basically unaltered. The Progressive party died when Roosevelt deserted it, and the Socialist party was drained by Wilsonian reforms and crippled by repression and internal schism during and immediately after World War I. The dominant Republican party repudiated much of Roosevelt's reform activism and statism, and the Democratic party spent much of the 1920s paralyzed by bitter divisions between its urban and rural wings. It took the Great Depression and Franklin D. Roosevelt to unite those elements, enlist millions of new voters, and forge the Democratic party into the new majority coalition that would dominate national politics for more than two decades.

Progressives did, however, create the modern presidency. Theodore Roosevelt and Woodrow Wilson took advantage of the centralizing forces of the period, the mass media, and the growth of foreign affairs to attract popular loyalty and enlarge the public's expectations of presidential leadership. In departing from the limited view of executive power of the post – Civil War period, Roosevelt and Wilson showed that the modern president could sometimes bridge the separation of powers and overcome other obstacles to strong positive governmental action. Herbert Hoover and Franklin Roosevelt continued the expansion of the presidency in meeting the exigencies of the Great Depression. Thus progressives created an institution that could help the nation to take effective action against national problems but could also become an "imperial presidency" that went beyond both consensus and constitutional limitations on executive power. Like the other progressive mechanisms, the modern presidency could be used for good or ill.

Responding to Big Business

By the end of the Progressive Era, national administrators in both major parties had responded to the problem of industrial concentration. Interventionists evolved four different approaches to managing the organizational revolution and the new economic order. These alternatives came to be lumped under general rubrics: socialism, the New Freedom, the New Individualism, and the New Nationalism. The Progressive Era did not resolve the debate among these alternatives, but it left an institutional legacy based on each of them.

The concept of public ownership, central to socialism, was applied primarily to local utilities. Governmental ownership of natural gas and water facilities, and sometimes of electrical production and transit lines, removed these local utilities as sources of corruption and usually meant lower prices for consumers. Public control of water and power and the principle of conservation contributed to the development in the 1930s of the Tennessee Valley Authority, the largest federal experiment in regional conservation and development through public ownership and planning.

But public ownership was vigorously opposed by conservative interests as too radical for most Americans, who supported more traditional concepts like Wilson's New Freedom idea, which had the government intervene in the economy only to the extent necessary to break up monopolies and help to restore the discipline of the marketplace. Attempts to limit concentration included tariff reduction, regionalization and public supervision of banking through the Federal Reserve System, restrictions on business practices through the Clayton Antitrust Act, and the growing antitrust bureaucracy in the Department of Justice. Although virtually abandoned in World War I and the 1920s, the New Freedom idea was restored temporarily during the New Deal through federal regulation of the stock market, limitation of utilities' holding company empires, and a temporary revival of the investigation and prosecution of concentration in industry.

The new "cooperative individualism," as it was called by some progressives, such as Herbert Hoover, envisioned both government and private institutions playing a more positive and cooperative role to encourage socially beneficial economic growth. In a marketplace in which "destructive" price competition was reduced, social duties and many crucial decisions about public policy would be made not by government but by private, voluntary economic associations. In what would later be called corporatism, functional groups in business, labor, agriculture, and other major sectors of the economy would, with advice and cooperation from government, initiate policies to encourage steady economic growth and social harmony. The National Civic Federation, several corporate leaders, and a number of trade associations favored this politicoeconomic alternative to laissez-faire or a powerful administrative state. In the 1920s, Hoover, first as secretary of commerce and then as president, became the leading booster of this kind of partnership among interdependent economic groups. Although corporatism was adopted in a number of European nations, a formalized structure of cooperating national economic power blocs proved too much of a departure from American tradition to be accepted, in the United States, except temporarily in wartime.

The Progressive Era's most substantial legacy in the area of governmental policy was the New Nationalism of Theodore Roosevelt, with its emphasis on national governmental planning and regulation and its contribution to the origin of the managerial and social service state. In the public interest, federal agencies would supervise activities in the private sector that affected the nation as a whole: the consolidation and trade practices of big business, railroad acquisitions and rate making, the manufacture and sale of drugs, food preparation and meatpacking practices, the development of natural resources, and the currency reserves of the banking system. The size of the federal government, which had grown from 95,000 civilian employees in 1880 to 230,000 in 1900, nearly doubled again by 1917, when the civilian employee total reached 430,000. New or expanded agencies such as the Interstate Commerce Commission, the Federal Trade Commission, the Federal Reserve Board, the Forestry Service, the Bureau of Mines, and the Food and Drug Administration greatly increased the federal government's role in the economy. They also served as models for mobilization agencies in World War I, for new regulatory bodies like the Federal Radio Commission (later the Federal Communications Commission) and the Civil Aeronautics Board in the 1920s, and for a host of New Deal agencies, such as the National Recovery Administration, the Agricultural Adjustment Administration, the Securities and Exchange Commission, and the National Labor Relations Board, in the 1930s.

The independent regulatory commission, the key mechanism of most progressives and many other interventionists for maintaining a public interest in certain sectors of the economy, proved complex and ambiguous. Given the contradictory goals of restricting combination and protecting consumers while promoting economic growth and a healthy industry, progressives were never able adequately to define an enduring public interest. Rather, the regulatory agencies tended to become independent bureaucracies concerned primarily with their own status and well-being. Although their original proponents often claimed — with justification — that the commissions had become too responsive to the industries they were designed to regulate, the charge oversimplified the origins, obstacles, and subsequent development of most regulatory commissions. These agencies responded most directly to changes in the power of various groups caused by fluctuations in political circumstances. Commissioners, often drawn from the industries they were commissioned to regulate, saw themselves as operating within a much narrower range of policy options than most progressives recognized. Even when on occasion they sought to act boldly, commissioners found themselves restricted by the courts, the legislatures, business interests, and changing public opinion. Finally, they were limited by the inherent nature of each industry, which in the long run proved to be the single most important context of governmental regulation.

The early history of the Federal Trade Commission (FTC) illustrates the complexity of the problem. Originally, radical progressives hoped that it would control big business and promote fair competition. But many corporation managers expected it to encourage cooperation between business and government to stimulate further economic growth. During its early years the FTC began some investigations of business practices, but during World War I it turned its attention to encouraging cooperation among businesses in order to expand production of war matériel.

After the end of the war the commission returned briefly to investigating business. But when it recommended radical restructuring of the meatpacking industry, including some public ownership, a conservative Congress called for an investigation of the FTC and transferred jurisdiction over the meatpackers to the more friendly Department of Agriculture. During the Republican administrations of the 1920s a chastised and restaffed FTC supported efforts by competing businesses to cooperate through trade associations and provided governmental advice on business opportunities and economic growth. Not until the New Deal did the FTC, with new powers and personnel, again seek to regulate business practices in the public interest. Like the FTC, other regulatory commissions adjusted their roles repeatedly in response to changing appointments, new circumstances, and different public and governmental attitudes toward business.

Regardless of occasional gestures toward antitrust action and some federal regulation, big business and big finance remained relatively unimpaired. Although a few giants, including Standard Oil and American Tobacco, suffered temporary setbacks due to governmental action, the supercorporations lost little of their power or prerogatives, despite widespread public hostility toward the trusts. The most effective challenge to monopoly came from new competitors as the economy evolved toward oligopoly, the concentration of power in a few giant firms in each major industry. In their relationship with government, corporation managers and financiers were not able to obtain everything they wanted or block everything they opposed, but they wielded substantial influence in shaping legislation and especially in modifying its implementation. Although the power of big business fluctuated—greater in the 1890s and the 1920s than in the Progressive and New Deal eras— it was always able to block the most radical efforts against it.

Many Americans feared the complete breakup of big business would create such chaos that it would jeopardize economic growth. Many rejected governmental ownership because they believed in private property and individual initiative and were skeptical of the efficiency of governmental operation. As a result the governmental response to industrial and financial concentration in the Progressive Era did more to help Americans to adjust to the new liberal corporate economy than it did to curb the new centers of power. Not until the New Deal, with its dramatic expansion of the power of government and of other groups such as organized labor, did big business begin to feel significant public influence and constraints.

Continued Harshness of Industrialism

Although some precedent-setting steps were taken to mitigate the harshness of unregulated industrialism, the Progressive Era saw little real amelioration of the conditions of the poor and oppressed. Many states passed laws that seemed to mandate a basic standard of protection for industrial workers—mine and factory safety, worker's compensation, outlawing of child labor, and minimum wage and maximum hour standards for women workers—and provided pensions for particularly needy mothers and widows, but appropriations for enforcement and its implementation were usually inadequate and often nonexistent. Not until the New Deal did the federal government obtain the power to establish wage and hour standards for male and female workers, outlaw child labor in industry (it continued in agriculture and some other fields), and set up nationwide systems of unemployment insurance, aid to the disabled, the elderly, and needy children, and other social security benefits.

Any real gains that industrial workers made during the period came primarily from direct collective intervention in the marketplace. Though espoused among progressives only by social justice activists, trade unionism and collective bargaining agreements between unions and employers over wages, hours, and working conditions emerged as the predominant mechanisms for protecting and improving labor's position. The greatest number of collective bargaining agreements in the period were negotiated during World War I under wartime federal compulsory labor relations laws. These laws were ended in 1920, and compulsory bargaining with unions was not permanently established until the National Labor Relations Act (the Wagner Act) of 1935. Unlike European unions, with their mass membership and socialist ideology, the American Federation of Labor remained limited primarily to skilled workers, moderate in its goals, and only reluctantly political. The AFL barred blacks from most unions and did not vigorously recruit women or recent immigrants. Its membership increased from about 600,000 in 1900 to 4 million in 1920, although it declined sharply thereafter. It was not until the Great Depression of the 1930s that mass production workers were organized by an offshoot of the AFL, the Congress of Industrial Organizations (CIO), and organized labor, numbering 8 million workers (28 percent of the nonagricultural work force in 1938), became an enduring substantial component of a major political party, the New Deal Democratic coalition.

Dangers posed by urban decay and poverty and deplorable conditions in festering industrial metropolises had been of particular concern to progressives. Interventionists' urban reforms helped to make cities somewhat cleaner and healthier places to live. The reformers supplemented church and ad hoc private charities with new, permanent, professional secular organizations of social workers, youth workers, and public health nurses and physicians. However, these efforts and the laws designed to ensure safe water, milk, and meat as well as the creation of settlement houses, parks, and playgrounds sought also in large measure to make cities safer and more attractive places for the middle and upper classes. The City Beautiful movement, for example, sought to upgrade the physical appearance of towns and cities and resulted in a few spectacular civic centers and many small-scale projects involving outdoor art, historic and scenic preservation, and the regulation of outdoor advertising—not areas of major concern to the poor.

Poverty remained widespread, and there was little public relief. Most western European nations had governmental social insurance programs, especially for the unemployed, disabled, or elderly industrial workers, and paid family allowances designed in part to help the poor. But owing to traditional American attitudes toward hard work and self-reliance as well as continued ethnic and racial prejudice and opposition to increased taxes, the United States had no national welfare program. What little state and local government spending there was on relief and welfare went primarily for institutions such as the nineteenth-century almshouses that grudgingly sheltered "paupers," regarded as improvident people dependent on relief; they lost their eligibility to vote when they accepted such custodial welfare. As late as 1923 some 2,046 almshouses in the United States held 85,899 inmates.

In addition, living as best they could in urban and rural poverty were millions of impoverished Americans, among them the disabled, the chronically ill, the aged, women with dependent children, and the marginally and sporadically employed. Although society generally chose to ignore it, dependency was a major source of destitution. In the South, which continued to have the highest incidence of poverty in the nation, a deeply depressed lower class of sharecroppers and tenant farmers, black and white, lived in rough-hewn cabins and suffered heavily from hookworm, pellagra, and malnutrition. It was not until the Great Depression, with its accompanying massive unemployment among the working and middle classes, demonstrated the inadequacy of local efforts that the federal government established the first comprehensive national programs in the United States providing relief for the unemployed, the aged, and the infirm.

Henry George and other national reformers had long pointed to the growing gap between rich and poor. In one of their most important victories, reformers had obtained a federal income tax as a means of tapping the new sources of wealth in the corporate economy. However, keeping tax rates generally low and applicable mainly to wealthy individuals and to corporations, Congress chose to use it to pay for expanding federal expenditures — driven particularly by war and the military — rather than as a device to redistribute wealth. Comparatively, the gap between affluent and poorer Americans widened during the Progressive Era. Wartime taxes did temporarily reduce somewhat the share of national personal income received by the richest Americans. Between 1917 and 1920 the share of national income of the richest 1 percent of the approximately 100 million Americans dropped from 14 to 12 percent; the richest 5 percent's share slipped from 25 to 22 percent. But this slippage was more than recouped in the 1920s. Despite the income tax, the most affluent 10 percent of the population increased its share of total personal income from 34 to 38 percent between 1910 and 1920, while the poorest 60 percent — approximately 60 million people in 1920 — watched its share drop from 35 to 30 percent of the growing national income in the United States.

Social and Cultural Repression

Some of the most repressive interventionist measures of the Progressive Era came from attempts to coerce particular groups into behavior defined by others as the norm. Some of these efforts were designed to keep minorities in inferior social and economic positions. Others sought to force people with various cultural views to accept a single dominant culture, "Anglo-Saxonism," that reflected primarily white, Anglo-Saxon Protestant attitudes and values. Long interwoven with the ideological and religious aspects of the dominant national identity, Anglo-Saxonism became more overtly ethnic and racial in its focus at the turn of the century in response to waves of immigration and new pseudoscientific racial theories. "Americanization" sought to bring immigrants systematically into conformity with the minimal requirements of Americanism. Pessimistically, the nativistic racism and concepts of "racial self-preservation" epitomized by the writings of Madison Grant contributed both to the subjugation of nonwhites and to the immigration restrictions against those whom Grant called "undesirable races and peoples" from southern and eastern Europe and from Asia. However, the seeds for an interpretation of ethnicity and American identity that came to be known as cultural pluralism were also planted in the Progressive Era.

Intensified racism and officially sanctioned attitudes of white supremacy contributed directly to the further subjugation of nonwhites through social segregation, economic discrimination, and mob violence — and, in the case of Asians, exclusion from the country. American Indians continued to suffer under the coercive assimilation policy that cost them much of their land, debilitated their tribes, brought them to their lowest point, and consequently engendered maximum hostility toward whites and the federal government. For the vast majority of blacks, the Progressive Era meant primarily disfranchisement and the solidification of racial segregation in the South, where 90 percent of African Americans resided, and the expansion of urban black ghettos and de facto segregation in the North. Anti-Asian sentiment reached new heights in the Progressive Era, as Chinese and Japanese in the United States were denounced as biologically unassimilable because they were not white and culturally incompatible because their culture differed substantially from the Anglo-American norm.

Like the Asian minorities, Spanish-speaking Americans continued to be victims of a combination of ethnocultural and racial prejudice. The native-born Mexican-American community was swollen by the immigration of more than 700,000 Mexicans between 1900 and 1930, especially into Texas and California, where this propertyless laboring class formed the bulk of the agricultural labor force. Although Mexicans were specifically excluded from the immigration restriction laws, at the request of employers in the Southwest, government officials were able administratively to adjust the supply of immigrants to domestic economic demand, often routing Mexican laborers from their jobs in favor of non-Hispanic Americans and deporting unemployed aliens back across the border. Like Asians and blacks, brown-skinned Chicanos encountered segregated schools, restrictive covenants on residential property, and separate "white" and "colored" sections in theaters and other facilities.

To deal with what they considered the "problem" of the new

immigrants, primarily Catholics and Jews from southern and eastern Europe, conservative and progressive interventionists used a combination of education and coercion. These ethnic groups in the North, like the blacks in the South and the Hispanics and Asians in the West, did not resign themselves to prejudice and discrimination. When their public protests failed, all of these people fell back on their own institutions — families, churches, schools, and community organizations — for protection.

When voluntary Americanization measures worked too slowly, nativists turned to government to restrict or prevent disapproved behavior through efforts to prohibit the use of alcohol, enforce sabbatarian and antivice laws, and suppress foreign-language newspapers and parochial schools. The Americanization movement gained momentum from the chauvinism of World War I and grew during the ensuing hysteria encouraged by ultranationalists and other conservatives over radicals and foreign influence. Extensive immigration restriction, begun in 1917, was expanded and made permanent in the early 1920s through legislation that directly excluded most southern and eastern Europeans and nearly all Asians and Africans.

The issue of the belief and value system that should prevail in America also continued to divide modernizers and traditionalists as they struggled over the direction of change. For example, prohibition, support for which became widespread during the Progressive Era, grew into a major symbolic issue in the 1920s. Some progressive and conservative interventionists had supported it as a means of improving society. But to many of those who were committed to the traditional culture, affirmation of abstinence as a national ideal became intertwined with the desire to uphold the values of small-town and rural Protestant America as opposed to secular and permissive trends or Catholic culture, which they identified with modern metropolitan America. National prohibition, first adopted as a wartime measure, was seemingly made permanent in 1919 by the passage of the Eighteenth Amendment, one of the most extensive examples of national cultural intervention.

Traditionalists and fundamentalists also struggled against many of the changes being made by modernizers in what was being preached in churches, taught in schools, and shown in movie theaters. Their reaction against modernization and secularization became extreme in legislation like the Tennessee law that prohibited the teaching of the theory of evolution in public schools (and led to the conviction of biology teacher John Scopes in the famous "monkey trial") and in the vigilantism of the revived Ku Klux Klan. Despite such resistance, the complex transformation of moral values, religious beliefs, and social and sexual customs that accelerated during the Progressive Era became even more widespread in the following decades.

The International Legacy

Interventionists of the Progressive Era found a new frontier of activism and economic growth abroad, but they did not achieve agreement among Americans over the nation's proper role in the world. Much of the old isolationism remained, despite the internationalists' efforts not to drift in reaction to events but actively to shape and improve the environment for American interests and ideals abroad. Yet the internationalists created a number of new organizations — ranging from trade groups to the ideological associations that made up the modern peace movement — and devised a variety of mechanisms for implementing their policies. Among these were arbitration and conciliation treaties, a world court, a league of nations, and a modernized and expanded army, navy, foreign service, and presidency. The United States intervened in the Caribbean and the Far East. After obtaining a few formal colonies, it developed a string of protectorate client states in the Caribbean. But it also attempted to go beyond imperialism to a new, Americanized world order created through economic investment and trade, scientific knowledge, and moral commitment. And it used economic policies, nonrecognition, and even military intervention to affect revolution in Mexico and the communist seizure of power in Russia. It was a moderate, liberal, capitalistic international order that Woodrow Wilson envisioned in his Fourteen Points and in the concept he supported for a league of nations.

In the Progressive Era, for the first time in generations, foreign relations became a major continuing concern. Americans debated the effect of the new U.S. interventionism on traditions such as isolationism, neutrality, and the Monroe Doctrine, on institutions and ideals, and on the security and prosperity of the nation. The annual cost of the army and navy, for example, increased from $66 million in 1890 to $191 million in 1900, $343 million in 1915, and an astonishing $6 billion in 1918. The postwar reaction led to major cutbacks in the armed forces, including naval arms limitation treaties, and military expenditures dropped to an average of around $700 million a year during most of the subsequent decade. The military remained the main expense of the federal government.

Activism abroad did benefit a number of sectors of the American economy. Exports of manufactured goods, agricultural commodities, and mineral resources between 1890 and 1920 increased dramatically from $910 million to $8.6 billion a year. In America's favorable balance of trade, the excess of exports over imports rose from $87 million to $2.9 billion in those same years. U.S. investments overseas increased exponentially, skyrocketing from less than half a billion dollars in 1890 to more than $7 billion in 1920, giving American corporations and other investors considerable financial gain as well as powerful influence abroad. Growing sales overseas, especially during World War I, helped to sustain an expanding economy at home. Wartime dislocation of international trade patterns also helped American business to capture Latin American markets from the British and the Germans. In international finance, as a result largely of American war loans to the Allies, the United States emerged from the conflict as the world's creditor nation, replacing Great Britain. All of these trends encouraged the expansion of American corporations as well as numerous other business ventures in the 1920s.

Despite the new interest and involvement in world affairs, large numbers of Americans retained much of their former isolationist attitude. American views on foreign affairs lagged behind the altered international situation. Policy and institutions were transformed more rapidly than attitudes. Most Americans assumed that the country could enter the modern world while maintaining its nineteenth-century traditions of relatively free security and freedom of action. The modernizers—militant expansionists and reform internationalists—influenced many people but failed to convince the majority of Ameri-

Cheering wildly as they arrive in New York Harbor, American "doughboys" return from France in 1919 with hopes for a peaceful world and a better life. (*National Archives*)

cans of the need for sustained drastic change. Even Wilson's combination of evangelistic mission with interventionism could not sustain a continuous commitment to active engagement and responsibility in international affairs. The new outward thrust was counterbalanced by traditional American parochialism.

The Unites States' entry into World War I represented both a logical culmination of growing interventionism and the failure of the progressives' hope that Americans could be active abroad and improve international relations at little cost. The era left a dual legacy. Reaction against the war and the Treaty of Versailles led to a resurgence of political and military isolationism, at least outside the Western Hemisphere, that precluded many formal U.S. commitments and interventions. The Great Depression and the rise of aggressive military regimes in Italy, Japan, and Germany increased American isolationism, which reached its peak in the neutrality legislation of the 1930s. But there was also continued internationalism in the form of economic expansion and diplomatic attempts to build postwar cooperation without military intervention. The fragile structure of international relations crumbled in the 1930s, but as the United States moved toward global commitments in World War II and during the Cold War, active interventionism and the Wilsonian ideal of collective security were resurrected from the Progressive Era.

The Progressive Era and the Nature of Modern America

The divided legacy of progressivism, at home and in international affairs, is both symbolic and painfully real, for the Progressive Era was instrumental in shaping modern America, with its achievements and with its failures. In the first years of the twentieth century, with the economy producing vast wealth in the midst of great poverty, interventionists made the first national effort to curtail some of the harsh and dysfunctional features of unrestricted individualism and an unregulated marketplace. They provided new private and governmental mechanisms for consciously improving the functioning of society, the economy, and the polity, at least as seen by the middle- and upper-class men and women who called themselves progressives and made up the bulk of the moderate reform movements called progressivism. A number of their measures were also severely repressive. Progressives asserted that their means were consistent with America's traditions and ideals, but, as the historian Nell Irvin Painter has aptly put it, the emphasis in practice was often on ideals of hierarchy and order over ideals of democracy and equality.

Progressives were creatures of their own time and also part of larger patterns of American culture and reform. Despite the practical, modern nature of many of their devices, their evangelical exuberance made them more like nineteenth-century moral reformers than like later generations of pragmatic liberal reformers who were chastened by the Great Depression, fascism, Nazism, totalitarianism, and two world wars. The progressives' uncritical faith in expert planners and in the malleability of individuals and of institutions for "social improvement" was especially characteristic of their optimistic era.

The progressives demonstrated both the possibilities and the limitations of moderate reform. Their achievements were limited by their own caution. They were also limited by restraints imposed by vested interests, conservatives, and traditionalists who were aided by the many impediments to radical change inherent in separation of powers in the national government and within the American federal system. Things might have gone differently if, for example, Theodore Roosevelt had been able to conquer the old guard and reshape the Republican party into an instrument responsive to industrial workers and ethnic groups instead of primarily to northern business or if Woodrow Wilson had been able to pursue, without the divisions caused by U.S. entry into the war, the progressive agenda of his 1916 electoral coalition, which added many more northern urban progressive and socialist reformers, trade unionists, and ethnic voters to the Democratic party's traditional electoral base in the agrarian South. Nevertheless, although progressivism had a limited life span, it did help to set a public agenda for much of twentieth-century liberalism. It was also, as historian Arthur Schlesinger, Jr., has shown, part of a cycle of reform and reaction that has occurred repeatedly in American national politics.

In retrospect, progressivism, although it gave its name to much of the era between 1890 and 1920, was only a part of much larger developments in the shaping of modern America in those years. Probably the most dramatic change was the organizational revolution that produced the modern giant corporations. This revolution also included the proliferation of functional organizations, from expanded trade unions to reformed professional associations. Part of the larger structural change was the reorganization of the American polity — a decline in party politics and voter turnout and a profusion of politically active, issue-oriented pressure groups.

As the revisionist social and cultural history written in the 1980s and early 1990s has revealed, American culture and society were also being transformed. Men and women from different classes, regions, races, and ethnic groups used a variety of means to sustain themselves in their rapidly urbanizing, industrializing, and modernizing environment. Immigrant working classes, for example, brought a host of new ideas and institutions to the burgeoning cities of America. The growing urban market in turn contributed to the rise of mass entertainment and popular forms of leisure activity, from vaudeville to the movies, from penny arcades to fantastic new amusement parks. The entrance of increased numbers of women into the paid work force and the emergence for the first time of a sizable group of college-educated professional women helped to undermine Victorian concepts of women's proper sphere. Women became wage workers and also voters; they challenged some of the traditional views about women, the family, sexuality, politics, and international relations.

In these years the United States was evolving into a consumer society. Emerging as the first nation to mass-produce consumer goods, it also developed a modern consumer culture that emphasized immediate gratification and self-fulfillment. The culture of consumption, the image of the "new woman," the movies, and many other aspects of modern American society usually associated with the 1920 actually began in the Progressive Era.

The various changes of the Progressive Era, "modernization" and resistance to it, have traditionally been seen as part of a saga of continued upward progress of American civilization. Change can be for good or ill, and clearly many of the developments at the turn of the century —the dramatically increased segregation and subjugation of non-whites, for example—were deplorable. The consumer culture has proved a mixed blessing. Yet there were major gains, such as women's acquisition of important legal and political rights—especially the vote —and their active participation in the public life of the nation.

One of the most important lessons that recent historical scholarship has drawn from the past is that the great masses of people, those previously neglected in most historical accounts, are not passive observers but active participants, trying to sustain themselves in the swirls of change in which they find themselves. The sum of their participation, no less than that of people in positions of great power, is the history of our country.

At the turn of the century masses of Americans from all levels of society were caught up in a period of rapid and dramatic change. That they sought to direct that change, or in many cases merely to survive in it, revealed their determination and courage. In varying degrees they set the course that the nation would follow for the rest of the twentieth century.

Bibliography

General Works: 1890–1920

Exciting and controversial, the subject of the nature of American society and of the dramatic changes of the Progressive Era continues to generate substantial interest and many fine works of scholarship. (This selected bibliography includes primarily only works published after the first edition of *The Tyranny of Change* in 1980.) The best recent guides to the literature about progressivism and the era are the valuable one-volume reference work to the period by John D. Buenker and Edward R. Kantowicz, eds., *Historical Dictionary of the Progressive Era, 1890–1920* (New York, 1988); and two outstanding interpretive treatments: Daniel T. Rodgers, "In Search of Progressivism," *Reviews in American History* 10 (December, 1982); and Arthur S. Link and Richard L. McCormick, *Progressivism* (Arlington Heights, Ill., 1983). There is also a splendid new group of essays on various aspects of the Progressive Era in John Milton Cooper, Jr., and Charles E. Neu, eds., *The Wilson Era: Essays in Honor of Arthur S. Link* (Arlington Heights, Ill., 1991).

In regard to the nature of progressivism, particularly its relationship to the corporations and the state, Martin J. Sklar, *The Corporate Reconstruction of American Capitalism, 1890–1916: The Market, the Law, and Politics* (New York, 1988), has provided the most provocative reconceptualization since Robert Wiebe, *The Search for Order, 1877–1920* (New York, 1967). An alternative and less satisfying interpretation is put forward in Morton Keller, *Regulating a New Economy: Public Policy and Economic Change in America, 1900–1933* (Cambridge, Mass., 1990). Gabriel Kolko's polemical work *The Triumph of Conservatism: A Reinterpretation of American History, 1900–1916* (New York, 1963), neglected or dismissed evidence contradicting his thesis that big business advocated and obtained regulatory legislation. A more persuasive and thoroughly grounded analysis is presented in Thomas K. McGraw, "Regulation in America: A Review Article," *Business History Review* 49 (Summer 1975). David Thelen, *The New Citizenship: Origins of Progressivism in Wisconsin, 1885–1900* (Columbia, Mo., 1972), offers an insightful analysis of consumer-conscious citizens in Wisconsin. Robert M. Crunden, *Ministers of Reform: Progressives' Achievements in American Civilization, 1889–1920* (New York, 1982), stresses religious motivation and includes other cultural analyses of the progressive reformers. Barry D. Karl, *The Uneasy State: The United States from 1915 to 1945* (Chicago, 1983), shows the importance of continued antistatism in early-twentieth-century America. Conversely, the growth of the state is emphasized in Stephen Skowronek, *Building a New American State: The Expansion of National Administrative Capacities, 1877–1920* (New York, 1982); and by Theda Skocpol, who has begun a major recasting of state-centered theory in *Protecting Soldiers and Mothers* (forthcoming); and Peter B. Evans, Dietrich Rueschemeyer, and Theda Skocpol, eds., *Bringing the State Back In* (New York, 1985). Paul Boyer, *Urban Masses and Moral Order in America, 1820–1920* (Cambridge, Mass., 1978) is a work of monumental importance on the Progressive Era and the nineteenth century.

Cultural History

The reexamination of the social and cultural history of the Progressive Era was one of the most fascinating developments of the 1980s. Within the many aspects of cultural history are Howard M. Feinstein, *Becoming William James* (Ithaca, N.Y., 1984); T. J. Jackson Lears, *No Place of Grace: Antimodernism and the Transformation of American Culture, 1880–1920* (New York, 1981); Richard W. Fox and T. J. Jackson Lears, eds., *The Culture of Consumption: Critical Essays in American History, 1880–1980* (New York, 1983); Donald B. Meyer, *The Positive Thinkers: A Study of the American Quest for Health, Wealth, and Personal Power from Mary Baker Eddy to Norman Vincent Peale* (Garden City, N.Y., 1965); William R. Leach, "Transformations in a Culture of Consumption: Women and Department Stores, 1890–1925," *Journal of American History* 71 (September 1984); Daniel Horowitz, *The Morality of Spending: Attitudes Toward the Consumer Society in America, 1875–1940* (Baltimore, 1985); and Warren I. Susman, *Culture as History: The Transformation of American Society in the Twentieth Century* (New York, 1984). Special topics are dealt with in Cecilia Tichi, *Shifting Gears: Technology, Literature, and Culture in Modernist America* (Chapel Hill, N.C., 1987); Joseph J. Corn, *The Winged Gospel: America's Romance with Aviation, 1900–1950* (New York, 1983); Martin Laforse and James Drake, *Popular Culture and American Life* (Chicago, 1981); Ronald Davies, *A History of Music in American Life, Volume 2: The Gilded Years, 1865–1920* (Huntington, N.Y., 1980); John Di Meglio, *Vaudeville U.S.A.* (Bowling Green, Ohio, 1973); Robert Sklar, *Movie-made America: A Cultural History of American Movies* (New

York, 1975); Lara May, *Screening Out the Past: The Birth of Mass Culture and the Motion Picture Industry* (New York, 1976); and Kevin Brownlow, *Behind the Mask of Innocence: Social Conscience Films of the Silent Era* (New York, 1990). See also the volumes in the series, *History of the American Cinema* (New York, 1991–   ), under the general editorship of Charles Harpole.

On religion, see Edwin Scott Gaustad, *A Religious History of America*, rev. ed. (New York, 1990); Anne T. Fraker, ed., *Religion and American Life* (Urbana, Ill., 1989); and Charles H. Lippy and Peter W. Williams, eds., *Encyclopedia of the American Religious Experience* (New York, 1988); see J. Gordon Melton, *Encyclopedia of American Religions*, 2d ed. (Detroit, 1987), on religious groups. Marty E. Marty, *Modern American Religion, Volume 1: The Irony of It All, 1893–1919* (Chicago, 1986), provides an overview of the period. For specialized treatments, see the appropriate chapters in Mark A. Noll, ed., *Religion and American Politics from the Colonial Period to the 1980s* (New York, 1990). For the struggles within Protestantism in the early twentieth century, see Ferenc M. Szasz, *The Divided Mind of Protestant America, 1880–1920* (University, Ala., 1982); William R. Hutchinson, *The Modernist Impulse in American Protestantism* (Cambridge, Mass., 1976); and George M. Marsden, *Fundamentalism and American Culture: The Shaping of Twentieth-Century Evangelism, 1870–1925* (New York, 1980). Various tensions within Roman Catholicism are treated in Thomas T. McAvoy, *The Americanist Heresy in Roman Catholicism, 1895–1900* (Notre Dame, Ind., 1959); and Jay Dolan, *The American Catholic Experience* (Garden City, N.Y., 1986). Judaism's divisions are examined in Jacob Neusner, ed., *Understanding American Judaism: Toward the Description of a Modern Religion*, 2 vols. (New York, 1975); and Marc Lee Raphael, *Profiles in American Judaism: The Reform, Conservative, Orthodox, and Reconstructionist Traditions in Historical Perspective* (San Francisco, 1984). On the intellectual and theological climate of the debate over "modernity," see Bruce Kuklick, *Churchmen and Philosophers* (New Haven, Conn., 1985); and on the struggle between science and religion, see Ronald L. Numbers, *God and Nature* (Berkeley, 1987).

Intellectual History and the Arts

On the ideas of the Progressive Era, see James T. Kloppenberg, *Uncertain Victory: Social Democracy and Progressivism in European and American Thought, 1870–1920* (New York, 1986), a provocative if ultimately unfulfilling examination of the thought of several philosophers and theorists of social democracy and progressivism on both sides of the Atlantic. More effective is Thomas K. McGraw, *Prophets of*

Regulation: Charles Francis Adams, Louis D. Brandeis, James M. Landis, Alfred E. Kahn (Cambridge, Mass., 1984); David Noble, *The Progressive Mind, 1890–1917*, rev. ed. (Minneapolis, 1981); and John L. Thomas, *Alternative America: Henry George, Edward Bellamy, Henry Demarest Lloyd, and the Adversary Tradition* (Cambridge, Mass., 1983). Lewis Mumford, *The Brown Decades: A Study of the Arts in America, 1865–1895* (New York, 1959, 1971), is still valuable.

Social History

The latest social history includes women's history, the history of immigrants and ethnic and racial minorities, and the history of average people—their lives and attitudes. Recent studies of the social history of the Progressive Era include the following: on social mobility, Hartmut Kaelble, *Social Mobility in the 19th and 20th Centuries: Europe and America in Comparative Perspective* (New York, 1986); on class, culture, and political power, David C. Hammack, *Power and Society: Greater New York at the Turn of the Century* (New York, 1982); and Francis G. Courvares, *The Remaking of Pittsburgh: Class and Culture in an Industrializing City, 1877–1919* (Albany, 1984); on the use of leisure time, John Kasson, *Amusing the Millions: Coney Island at the Turn of the Century* (New York, 1978); Steven A. Riess, *Touching Base: Professional Baseball and American Culture in the Progressive Era* (Westport, Conn., 1980); David I. MacLeod, *Building Character in the American Boy: The Boy Scouts, YMCA, and Their Forerunners, 1870–1920* (Madison, Wis., 1983); Dominick Cavallo, *Muscles and Morals: Organized Playgrounds and Urban Reform, 1880–1920* (Philadelphia, 1981); Roy Rosenzweig, *Eight Hours for What We Will: Workers and Leisure in an Industrial City [Worcester, Massachusetts], 1870–1920* (New York, 1983); Perry R. Duis, *The Saloon: Public Drinking in Chicago and Boston, 1880–1920* (Urbana, Ill., 1983); and Kathy Peiss, *Cheap Amusements: Working Women and Leisure in Turn-of-the-Century New York* (Philadelphia, 1986).

A variety of aspects of social history deals with housing, urbanization, and youth. See George Talbot, *At Home: Domestic Life in the Post-Centennial Era, 1876–1920* (Madison, 1976); David Handlin, *The American Home* (Boston, 1981); Dolores Hayden, *The Grand Domestic Revolution: A History of Feminist Designs for American Homes, Neighborhoods, and Cities* (Cambridge, Mass., 1981); Raymond A. Mohl, *The New City: Urban America in an Industrial Age, 1860–1920* (Arlington Heights, Ill., 1985); Kenneth T. Jackson, *Crabgrass Frontier: The Suburbanization of the United States* (New York, 1985); and Joseph F. Kett, *Rites of Passage: Adolescence in America, 1790 to the Present* (New York, 1977). John R. Gillis, *Youth and History: Tradition and Change in*

European Age Relations, 1770–Present (New York, 1981) contains valuable insights into young people in Western industrializing societies.

Other institutions and professions are described in David B. Tyack, *The One Best System: A History of American Urban Education* (Cambridge, Mass., 1974); Lawrence R. Veysey, *The Emergence of the American University* (Chicago, 1965); Charles Rosenberg, *The Care of Strangers: The Rise of America's Hospital System* (New York, 1987); John S. Haller, *American Medicine in Transition* (Urbana, Ill., 1981); Gerald N. Grob, *Mental Illness and American Society, 1875–1940* (Princeton, 1983); John C. Burnham, *Paths into American Culture: Psychology, Medicine, and Morals* (Philadelphia, 1988); David Musto, *The American Disease: Origins of Narcotics Control* (New York, 1987); David Rosner, *A Once Charitable Enterprise: Hospitals and Health Care in Brooklyn and New York, 1885–1915* (Cambridge, Mass., 1982); Judith Walzer Leavitt, *The Healthiest City: Milwaukee and the Politics of Health Reform* (New Haven, Conn., 1982); Allan Brandt, *No Magic Bullet: A Social History of Venereal Disease in the United States Since 1880* (New York, 1985); Edward H. Beardsley, *A History of Neglect: Health Care for Blacks and Mill Workers in the Twentieth-Century South* (Knoxville, Tenn., 1987); Burton Bledstein, *The Culture of Professionalism* (New York, 1976); Robert W. Gordon, "Legal Thought and Legal Practice in the Age of American Enterprise, 1870–1920," in Gerald L. Geison, ed., *Professions and Professional Ideologies in America* (Chapel Hill, N.C., 1983); and Ellen Ryerson, *The Best-laid Plans: America's Juvenile Court Experiment* (New York, 1978).

Women's History

Extremely useful surveys of women's history are Sara Evans, *Born for Liberty: A History of Women in America* (New York, 1989); Mary Ryan, *Womanhood in America: From Colonial Times to the Present* (New York, 1979); and for the twentieth century, William H. Chafe, *The Paradox of Change: American Women in the 20th Century* (New York, 1991); and Lois W. Banner, *Women in Modern America: A Brief History* (New York, 1974). More specialized works include valuable information on this period: on the image of women in the Victorian era, see Carol Smith-Rosenberg's essay in her *Disorderly Conduct: Visions of Gender in Victorian America* (New York, 1985); Hasia Diner, *Erin's Daughters in America*; Alice Kessler-Harris, *Out to Work: A History of Wage-earning Women in the United States* (New York, 1983); David M. Katzman, *Seven Days a Week: Women and Domestic Service in Industrializing America* (New York, 1978); Nancy Schom Dye, *As Equals and as Sisters: Feminism, the Labor Movement and the Women's Trade Union League of New York* (Columbia, Mo., 1980). On the relationship between culture and politics and the changing roles of women through the vehicle of reform movements, see the conceptual articles by Paula Baker, "The Domestication of Politics: Women and American Political Society, 1780–1920," *American Historical Review* 89 (June 1984); and Suzanne Lebsock, "Across the Great Divide: Women and Politics, 1890–1920," in Louise Tilly and Patricia Gurin, eds., *Women, Politics, and Change in Twentieth-Century America* (New York, 1990); also see Nancy F. Cott, *The Grounding of Modern Feminism* (New Haven, Conn., 1987); William L. O'Neill, *Everyone Was Brave: The Rise and Fall of Feminism in America* (Chicago, 1969); and case studies such as Allen F. Davis, *An American Heroine: Jane Addams* (New York, 1975); Mari Jo Buhle, *Women and American Socialism, 1870–1920* (Urbana, Ill., 1981); and Kathryn Kish Sklar, *Florence Kelly and Women's Political Culture: Doing the Nation's Work, 1820–1940* (New Haven, Conn., 1992).

On women's suffrage, the classic work remains Eleanor Flexnor, *Century of Struggle*, rev. ed. (Cambridge, 1975), but see also more recent works such as Steven Buechler, *The Transformation of the Woman Suffrage Movement: The Case of Illinois, 1850–1920* (New Brunswick, N.J., 1986); and Sherna Gluck, ed., *From the Parlor to the Prison: Five American Suffragists Talk about Their Lives* (New York, 1976). Biographies of leading feminists include Ann Lane, *Charlotte Perkins Gilman* (New York, 1990); Ruth Bordin, *Francis Willard: A Biography* (Chapel Hill, N.C., 1986). On birth control, see David Kennedy, *Birth Control in America: The Career of Margaret Sanger* (New Haven, Conn., 1970); James Reed, *The Birth Control Movement and American Society: From Private Vice to Public Virtue* (Princeton, N.J., 1983); and Linda Gordon, *Woman's Body, Woman's Right: A Social History of Birth Control in America* (Middlesex, England, 1977). Gordon's recent study, *Heroes of Their Own Lives: The Politics and History of Family Violence* (New York, 1988), shows how women used what Elizabeth Janeway calls the "powers of the weak" to protect themselves and their children. Also illuminating is Judith Walzer Leavitt, *Brought to Bed: Child-bearing in America, 1750–1950* (New York, 1986).

Women in the professions are described in Margaret Rossiter, *Women Scientists in America* (Baltimore, 1982); Rosalind Rosenberg, *Beyond Separate Spheres: The Intellectual Roots of Modern Feminism* (New Haven, Conn., 1982); Regina Markell Morantz-Sanchez, *Sympathy and Science: Women Physicians in American Medicine* (New York, 1985); and Susan M. Reverby, *Ordered to Care: The Dilemma of American Nursing, 1850–1945* (Cambridge, Mass., 1987). Carl N. Degler, *At Odds: Women and the Family from the Revolution to the Present* (New York, 1980), is a provocative analysis combining women's history and family history. See also Carol Groneman and Mary Beth Norton, eds.,

To Toil the Livelong Day: America's Women at Work, 1780–1980 (Ithaca, N.Y., 1987); Susan Porter Benson, *Counter-Cultures: Saleswomen, Managers, and Customers in American Department Stores, 1890–1940* (Urbana, Ill., 1986); Margery Davis, *Woman's Place Is at the Typewriter: Office Work and Office Workers, 1870–1930* (Philadelphia, 1982); Glenna Matthes, *"Just a Housewife": The Rise and Fall of Domesticity in America* (New York, 1987); Laura Shapiro, *Perfection Salad: Women and Cooking at the Turn of the Century* (New York, 1986); Sarah Deutsch, *No Separate Refuge: Culture, Class, and Gender on an Anglo-Hispanic Frontier in the American Southwest, 1880–1940* (New York, 1987); Susan Glenn, *Daughter of the Shtetl: Jewish Immigrant Women in the American Garment Industry, 1880–1920* (Ithaca, N.Y., 1990); Joanne Meyerowitz, *Women Adrift: Independent Wage Earners in Chicago, 1880–1930* (Chicago, 1988); Meredith Tax, *The Rising of the Women: Feminist Solidarity and Class Conflict, 1880–1917* (New York, 1980); Estelle Freedman, *Their Sisters' Keepers: Women's Prison Reform in America, 1830–1930* (Ann Arbor, Mich., 1981); Helen L. Horowitz, *Alma Mater: Design and Experience in the Women's Colleges from Their Nineteenth-Century Beginnings to the 1930s* (New York, 1984); Barbara M. Solomon, *In the Company of Educated Women* (New Haven, Conn., 1985); and Jacquelyn Dowd Hall, *Revolt against Chivalry: Jessie Daniel Ames and the Women's Campaign against Lynching* (New York, 1979).

Sexuality, sexual matters, and courtship are dealt with in Ellen K. Rothman, *Hands and Hearts: A History of Courtship in America* (New York, 1984); Pat Caplan, ed., *The Cultural Construction of Sexuality* (New York, 1987); John D'Emilio and Estelle B. Freedman, *Intimate Matters: A History of Sexuality in America* (New York, 1988); Lillian Faderman, *Odd Girls and Twilight Lovers: A History of Lesbian Life in Twentieth-Century America* (New York, 1991); Mark T. Connelly, *The Response to Prostitution in the Progressive Era* (Chapel Hill, N.C., 1980); and Ruth Rosen, *The Lost Sisterhood: Prostitution in America, 1900–1918* (Baltimore, 1982). Also instructive are Peter N. Steans, *Be a Man: Males in Modern Society* (New York, 1979); Peter G. Filene, *Him/Herself: Sex Roles in Modern America*, 2d ed. (Baltimore, 1986); and Mark C. Carnes, *Secret Ritual and Manhood in Victorian America* (New Haven, Conn., 1989); and *Meanings for Manhood: Construction of Masculinity in Victorian America* (Chicago, 1990).

Most of the scholarship on black women is quite recent. See, for example, Jacqueline Jones, *Labor of Love, Labor of Sorrow: Black Women, Work, and the Family from Slavery to the Present* (New York, 1985); Paula Giddings, *When and Where I Enter: The Impact of Black Women on Race and Sex in America* (New York, 1984); Hazel Carby, *Reconstructing Womanhood: The Emergence of the Afro-American Woman Novelist* (New York, 1987); Darline Clark Hine, *Black Women in White: Racial Conflict and Cooperation in the Nursing Profession, 1890–1950* (Bloomington, 1989), and Hine, ed., *Black Women in American History*, 16 vols. (Brooklyn, N.Y., 1990); see also the works listed for racial minorities.

Racial and Ethnic Minorities

The best work currently available on African Americans in the Progressive Era is contained in Mary Frances Barry and John W. Blassingame, *Long Memory: The Black Experience in America* (New York, 1982); Herbert G. Gutman, *The Black Family in Slavery and Freedom, 1750–1925* (New York, 1976); Florette Henri, *Black Migration: The Movement North, 1900–1920* (New York, 1975); Joel William Trotter, Jr., *Black Milwaukee: The Making of an Industrial Proletariat, 1915–1945* (Urbana, Ill., 1985), which traces the rise of a northern ghetto; John Hope Franklin, *From Slavery to Freedom: A History of Negro Americans*, 5th ed. (New York, 1980); Louis R. Harlan, *Booker T. Washington: The Wizard of Tuskegee, 1901–1915* (New York, 1983); David Levering Lewis, *W. E. B. Du Bois*, 2 vols. (New York, 1992); Lawrence W. Levine, *Black Culture and Black Consciousness* (New York, 1977); Robert Farris Thomas, *Flash of the Spirit: African and Afro-American Art and Philosophy* (New York, 1983); Eileen Southern, *The Music of Black Americans: A History*, 2d ed. (New York, 1983); John W. Cell, *The Highest Stage of White Supremacy: The Origins of Segregation in South Africa and the American South* (New York, 1982); George Frederickson, *White Supremacy: A Comparative Study in American and South African History* (New York, 1981); Joseph R. Washington, Jr., *Black Religion: The Negro and Christianity in the United States* (Boston, 1964); Gayraud S. Wilmore, *Black Religion and Black Radicalism: An Interpretation of the Religious History of Afro-American People*, 2d ed. (Maryknoll, N.Y., 1983); and James M. Washington, *Frustrated Fellowship: The Black Baptist Quest for Social Power* (Macon, Ga., 1986); and Willard B. Gatewood, *Aristocrats of Color: The Black Elite, 1880–1920* (Bloomington, Ind., 1990).

Excellent summaries of the latest research on immigrants and their communities in the United States are Virginia Yans-McLaughlin, ed., *Immigration Reconsidered: History, Sociology, and Politics* (New York, 1990), especially the essays by Ewa Morawska and Charles Tilly; John Bodnar, *The Transplanted: A History of Immigrants in Urban America* (Bloomington, Ind., 1987); and Thomas P. Archdeacon, *Becoming American: An Ethnic History* (New York, 1983). See also Stephen Thernstrom et al., eds., *The Harvard Encyclopedia of Ethnic Groups* (Cambridge, Mass., 1980). James S. Olson, *Catholic Immigrants in America* (Chicago, 1987), is a valuable summary. For particular ethnic groups, see Samuel L. Baily, *The Italians in Buenos Aires and New York City, 1875-1925* (Ithaca, N.Y., 1992); Kerby A. Miller, *Emigrants and Exiles: Ireland and the Irish Exodus to North America* (New York, 1985); Timothy J. Meagher, ed., *From Paddy to Studs: Irish American Communities in the Turn of the Century Era, 1880 to 1920* (Westport, Conn., 1986); Robert Bach and Alejandro Portes, *Latin Journey: Cuban and Mexican Immigrants in the United States* (Berkeley, Calif., 1985); and Stanley Lieberson, *A Piece of the Pie: Blacks and White Immigrants Since 1880* (Berkeley, Calif., 1980), which compares the experience of the two groups. Interesting, too, is Theodore Hershberg, ed., *Philadelphia: Work, Space, Family, and Group Experience in the Nineteenth Century* (New York, 1981). Nancy Foner, ed., *New Immigrants in New York* (New York, 1987), explores immigrants black and white, foreign and domestic. See also Thomas Sowell, *Ethnic America: A History* (New York, 1981); Frank Bean and Marta Tienda, *The Hispanic Population of the United States* (New York, 1987); Olivier Zunz, *The Changing Face of Inequality: Urbanization, Industrial Development, and Immigrants in Detroit, 1880-1920* (Chicago, 1982); Lucie Cheng and Edna Bonacich, eds., *Labor Migration under Capitalism: Asian Workers in the United States before World War II* (Berkeley, Calif., 1984); Sucheng Chan, *This Bittersweet Soil: The Chinese in California Agriculture, 1860-1910* (Berkeley, Calif., 1986).

Other studies include Calvin Goldscheider and Alan Zuckerman, *The Transformation of the Jews* (Chicago, 1984); Deborah Moore, *At Home in America: Second-Generation New York Jews* (New York, 1981); Moses Rischin, *The Promised City: New York's Jews, 1870-1914* (Cambridge, Mass., 1962); Irving Howe, *World of Our Fathers* (New York, 1976); Judith Smith, *Family Connections: A History of Italian and Jewish Lives in Providence, Rhode Island, 1900-1940* (Albany, N.Y., 1985); Joel Perlmann, *Ethnic Differences: Schooling and Social Structure among the Irish, Italians, Jews, and Blacks in an American City, 1915-1935* (New York, 1989); Thomas Kessner, *The Golden Door: Italian and Jewish Immigrant Mobility in New York City, 1880-1915* (New York, 1977); David Levering Lewis, "Parallels and Divergences: Assimilationist Strategies of Afro-American and Jewish Elites from 1910 to the Early 1930s," *Journal of American History* 71 (December 1984); Mark Stolarik and Murray Friedman, eds., *Making It in America: The Role of Ethnicity in Education, Business Enterprise and Work Choices* (London, 1986); Ewa Morawska, *For Bread and Butter: Life-Worlds of East Central Europeans in Johnstown, Pennsylvania, 1890-1940* (New York, 1985); Charles C. Moskos, *Greek Americans: Struggle and Success*, new enlarged edition (New Brunswick, N.J., 1989); Sylvia Pedraza-Bailey, *Political and Economic Migrants in America: Cubans and Mexicans* (Austin, Texas, 1985); Harry Kitano, *Japanese Americans* (Englewood Cliffs, N.J., 1976); Won Moo Hurh and Kwang Chung Kim, *Korean Immi-*

grants in America (Rutherford, N.J., 1984); John Bodnar, *Workers' World: Kinship, Community, and Protest in an Industrial Society* (Baltimore, 1982); and Tamara Haraven, *Family Time and Industrial Time* (New York, 1982).

The South

Informative are J. Morgan Kousser, *The Shaping of Southern Politics: Suffrage Restriction and the Establishment of the One-Party South, 1880–1910* (New Haven, Conn., 1974); Charles Reagan Wilson and William Ferris, eds., *Encyclopedia of Southern Culture* (Chapel Hill, N.C., 1989); J. Wayne Flynt, *Dixie's Forgotten People: The South's Poor Whites* (Bloomington, Ind., 1979); Joel Williamson, *The Crucible of Race: Black-White Relations in the American South Since Emancipation* (New York, 1986); Jacquelyn Dowd Hall et al., *Like a Family: The Making of a Southern Cotton Mill World* (Chapel Hill, N.C., 1987); David E. Whisnant, *All That Is Native and Fine: The Politics of Culture in an American Region* (Chapel Hill, N.C., 1983); Henry D. Shapiro, *Appalachia on Our Mind: The Southern Mountains and Mountaineers in the American Consciousness, 1870–1920* (Chapel Hill, N.C., 1978); Dewey W. Grantham, *Southern Progressivism* (Knoxville, Tenn., 1983); and Grantham, *The Life and Death of the Solid South: A Political History* (Lexington, Ky., 1988).

Labor, Business, Finance, and Agriculture

The following works provide comprehensive information: Gerald T. White, *The United States and the Problem of Recovery After 1893* (University, Ala., 1982); Alfred D. Chandler, Jr., *The Visible Hand: The Managerial Revolution in American Business* (Cambridge, Mass., 1977); Naomi R. Lamoureaux, *The Great Merger Movement in American Business, 1895–1904* (Cambridge, Mass., 1985); Herbert Gutman, *Work, Culture, and Society in Industrializing America* (New York, 1977); "A Round Table: Labor, Historical Pessimism, and Hegemony," *Journal of American History* 75 (June, 1988); David Montgomery, *The Fall of the House of Labor: The Workplace, the State, and American Labor Activism, 1865–1925* (New York, 1987); Gwendolyn Mink, *Old Labor and New Immigrants in American Political Development: Union, Party, and State, 1875–1920* (Ithaca, N.Y., 1986); Christopher L. Tomlins, *The State and the Unions: Labor Relations, Law, and the Organized Labor Movement in America, 1880–1960* (New York, 1985); Daniel T. Rodgers, *The Work Ethic in Industrial America, 1850–1920* (Chicago, 1978); James Livingston, "The Social Analysis of Economic History and Theory: Conjectures on Late-19th-Century American Development," *American Historical Review* 92 (February, 1987); and Pete Daniel, *Breaking the Land: The Transformation of Cotton, Tobacco, and Rice Cultures Since 1880* (Urbana, Ill., 1985).

Poverty and the Poor

On poverty, see James T. Patterson, *America's Struggle Against Poverty, 1900–1985* (Cambridge, Mass., 1986). Daniel Levine, *Poverty and Society: The Growth of the American Welfare State in International Comparison* (New Brunswick, N.J., 1988), compares social legislation in the United States and several European nations; likewise Sonya Michel and Seth Koven, eds., *Gender and the Origins of the Welfare States in Western Europe and North America* (forthcoming). Updated cost-of-living figures are available from the Bureau of Labor Statistics, U.S. Department of Labor, Washington, D.C.; see also Daniel Pope, "American Economists and the High Cost of Living: The Progressive Era," *Journal of the History of Behavioral Science* 17 (1981).

Politics in the Progressive Era

Two excellent recent overviews are Richard L. McCormick, *The Party Period and Public Policy: American Politics from the Age of Jackson to the Progressive Era* (New York, 1986); and Lewis L. Gould, *Reform and Regulation: American Politics from Roosevelt to Wilson*, 2d ed. (New York, 1986). The fullest biography of any leading figure of the era is Arthur S. Link, *Woodrow Wilson*, 5 vols. (Princeton, N.J., 1947–1965), which goes to 1917. See also Kendrick A. Clements, *The Presidency of Woodrow Wilson* (Lawrence, Kans., 1992); Edmund Morris, *The Rise of Theodore Roosevelt* (New York, 1979); and John Milton Cooper, *The Warrior and the Priest: Woodrow Wilson and Theodore Roosevelt* (Cambridge, Mass., 1983). Other insightful works are Michael E. McGerr, *The Decline of Popular Politics: The American North, 1865–1928* (New York, 1986); David Sarasohn, *The Party of Reform: The Democrats in the Progressive Era* (Jackson, Miss., 1989); Richard L. McCormick, *From Realignment to Reform: Political Change in New York State, 1893–1910* (Ithaca, N.Y., 1981); K. Austin Kerr, *Organized for Prohibition: A New History of the Anti-Saloon League* (New Haven, Conn., 1985); Jon Teaford, *The Unheralded Triumph: City Government in America, 1870–1900* (Baltimore, 1984); Paul Kleppner, ed., *The Evolution of American Electoral Systems* (Westport, Conn., 1981); Richard Oestreicher, "Urban Working-Class Political Behavior and Theories of American Electoral Politics," *Journal of American History*

74 (March, 1988); and Morton Keller, *Affairs of State: Public Life in Late-Nineteenth-Century America* (New York, 1977). On populism, see Steven Hahn, *The Roots of Southern Populism: Yeomen Farmers and the Transformation of the Georgia Upcountry, 1850–1890* (New York, 1983), for a new interpretation; but see also the passionate defense of the populists' message in Lawrence Goodwyn, *Democratic Promise: The Populist Moment in America* (New York, 1976). For other dissent, see Nick Salvatore, *Eugene V. Debs: Citizen and Socialist* (Champaign, Ill., 1982); and David Thelen, *Paths of Resistance: Tradition and Dignity in Industrializing Missouri* (New York, 1986). Too late for inclusion in the present volume are Alan Dawley, *Struggles for Justice: Social Responsibility and the Liberal State* (Cambridge, Mass., 1991); and August Heckscher, *Woodrow Wilson* (New York, 1991).

Environmental History

Among the most instructive works are Susan R. Schrepfer, *The Fight to Save the Redwoods: A History of Environmental Reform, 1917–1978* (Madison, Wis., 1983); and the appropriate chapters in Samuel P. Hays, *Beauty, Health, and Permanence: Environmental Politics in the United States, 1955–1985* (New York, 1987); and Richard L. White, *Land Use, Environment, and Social Change: The Shaping of Island County, Washington* (Seattle, 1980). See also Samuel P. Hays, *Conservation and the Gospel of Efficiency: The Progressive Conservation Movement, 1890–1920* (New York, 1972).

International Relations

The best overall account is Thomas G. Paterson, J. Garry Clifford, and Kenneth J. Hagan, *American Foreign Policy: A History Since 1900*, 3d ed., rev. (Lexington, Mass., 1991). For more specialized studies, see Emily Rosenberg, *Spreading the American Dream: American Economic and Cultural Expansion, 1890–1945* (New York, 1982); David F. Trask, *The War with Spain in 1898* (New York, 1981); Lloyd C. Gardner, *Safe for Democracy: The Anglo-American Response to Revolution, 1913–1923* (New York, 1984); William H. Becker, *The Dynamics of Business-Government Relations: Industry and Exports, 1893–1921* (New York, 1982); Lester H. Brune, *The Origins of American Security Policy: Sea Power, Air Power, and Foreign Policy, 1900–1941* (Manhattan, Kans., 1981); Richard H. Collin, *Theodore Roosevelt: Culture, Diplomacy, and Expansion* (Baton Rouge, La., 1985); William C. Widenor, *Henry Cabot Lodge and the Search for an American Foreign Policy* (Berkeley, Calif., 1980); Charles De Benedetti, *The Peace Reform in American History* (Bloomington, Ind., 1980); and John W. Chambers II, ed., *The Eagle* and the Dove: The American Peace Movement and U.S. Foreign Policy, 1900–1922, 2d ed. (Syracuse, N.Y., 1991). On U.S. entry into the world war, the biographer of Woodrow Wilson summarizes his latest findings in Arthur S. Link, Woodrow Wilson: Revolution, War, and Peace (Arlington Heights, Ill., 1979). See also Lloyd C. Gardner, A Covenant with Power: America and World Order from Wilson to Reagan (New York, 1985); H. W. Koch, ed., The Origins of the First World War, 2d ed. (New York, 1991); and John A. Thompson, Reformers and War: American Progressive Publicists and the First World War (Cambridge, Mass., 1987).

America in World War I

The most recent overall account is Robert H. Ferrell, Woodrow Wilson and World War I, 1917–1921 (New York, 1985), but see also David M. Kennedy, Over Here: The First World War and American Society (New York, 1980). The best account of the economic mobilization during the war is Robert D. Cuff, The War Industries Board: Business-Government Relations during World War I (Baltimore, 1973); and Cuff's essay, "American Mobilization for War, 1917–1945: Political Culture vs. Bureaucratic Administration," in N. F. Dreisziger, ed., Mobilization for Total War: The Canadian, American, and British Experience, 1914– 1918, 1937–1945 (Waterloo, Ont., 1981). William E. Leuchtenburg, "The New Deal and the Analogue of War," in John Braeman et al., eds., Change and Continuity in Twentieth-Century America (Columbus, Ohio, 1964), suggests that the wartime mobilization inspired many New Deal efforts. A recent evaluation is Arthur S. Link and John W. Chambers II, "Woodrow Wilson as Commander in Chief," in Richard H. Kohn, ed., The United States Military under the Constitution of the United States, 1789–1989 (New York, 1991). The draft and its enemies are examined in John W. Chambers II, To Raise an Army: The Draft Comes to Modern America (New York, 1987). The standard military account of America's role is Edward M. Coffman, The War to End All Wars: The American Military Experience in World War I (Madison, Wis., 1986). Recent studies of mobilization agencies include Valerie Jean Conner, The National War Labor Board (Chapel Hill, N.C., 1983); and Stephen L. Vaughn, Holding Fast the Inner Lines: Democracy, Nationalism, and the Committee on Public Information (Chapel Hill, N.C., 1980). The latest examination of the suppression of civil liberties in the war is Richard Polenberg, Fighting Faiths: The Abrams Case, the Supreme Court, and Free Speech (New York, 1988). On the wartime experience for women, see Maurine Weiner Greenwald, War and Work: The Impact of World War I on Women Workers in the United States (Westport, Conn., 1980); and Barbara Steinson, American

Women's Activism in World War I (New York, 1982). Also interesting is Michael T. Isenberg, *War on Film: The American Cinema and World War I, 1914-1941* (Rutherford, N.J., 1981).

Postwar Era

On Wilson's illness and stroke in 1919, see Arthur S. Link, et al., eds., *The Papers of Woodrow Wilson*, Volume 64 (Princeton, 1991). On foreign policy, see Thomas J. Knock, *To End All Wars: Woodrow Wilson and the Creation of the League of Nations* (New York, 1992); Lloyd E. Ambrosius, *Woodrow Wilson and the American Diplomatic Tradition: The Treaty Fight in Perspective* (Cambridge, Mass., 1987); David S. Foglesong, *America's Secret War against Bolshevism: United States Intervention in the Russian Civil War, 1917-1920* (Chapel Hill, 1992); and Joseph P. O'Grady, ed., *The Immigrants' Influence on Wilson's Peace Policies* (Lexington, Ky., 1967). Domestic issues are surveyed in Burl Noggle, *Into the Twenties: The United States from Armistice to Normalcy* (Urbana, Ill., 1977). More specific aspects are treated in David Brody, *Labor in Crisis: The Steel Strike of 1919* (Philadelphia, 1965); Robert K. Murray, *Red Scare* (New York, 1955); Murray, *The Harding Era* (Minneapolis, 1969); William M. Tuttle, *Race Riot: Chicago in the Red Summer of 1919* (New York, 1970); Norman H. Clark, *Deliver Us from Evil: An Interpretation of American Prohibition* (New York, 1976); Francis Russell, *A City in Terror, 1919: The Boston Police Strike* (New York, 1975); Robert L. Zangrando, *The NAACP Crusade against Lynching, 1909-1950* (Philadelphia, 1980); and Alfred W. Crosby, *America's Forgotten Pandemic: The Influenza of 1918* (New York, 1989). For an overview of the 1920s, see also an excellent companion volume in the St. Martin's Series in 20th-Century U.S. History, Ellis W. Hawley, *The Great War and the Search for a Modern Order: A History of the American People and Their Institutions, 1917-1933*, 2d ed. (New York, 1992).

Primary Source Materials

A quick sense of the public debates of the era can be obtained from reading *The Literary Digest*, a weekly periodical that surveyed and summarized the leading newspapers and newsmagazines throughout the country. One of the most important works of the period in the women's movement, Charlotte Perkins Gilman's *Women and Economics* (1898), was reprinted in 1970 with an introduction by Carl Degler. For accounts by other activist professional women, see the lawyer Crystal Eastman, *Crystal Eastman on Women and Revolution*, ed. Blanche Wiesen Cook (New York, 1971); and Barbara Sicherman's biography of an activist physician, *Alice Hamilton: A Life in Letters* (Cambridge, Mass., 1984). The new social history is derived primarily from the common people. For vivid personal descriptions of life for the poor and middle classes, see David Katzman and William Tuttle, Jr., eds., *Plain Folk: The Life Stories of Undistinguished Americans* (Urbana, Ill., 1982), and the extraordinary work by Theodore Rosengarten, *All God's Dangers: The Life of Nate Shaw* (New York, 1984), a remarkable oral-history autobiography by a black southern sharecropper.

Bibliographical Supplement for the 2000 Edition: New Scholarship on the Progressive Era

In the decade since the second edition of *The Tyranny of Change* first appeared, much new scholarship has been published that offers fresh insights or raises new questions about the history of the United States between 1890 and 1920. This selective bibliography is not a complete listing but seeks, rather, to highlight some of the more dynamic areas of recent scholarship.

Important summaries of historical approaches to the period, which include essays and original documents, may be found in Leon Fink, ed., *Major Problems in the Gilded Age and the Progressive Era* (Boston, 1993) and Elisabeth Israels Perry, ed., "The Progressive Era," special issue of the *Magazine of History* 13 (Spring 1999), published by the Organization of American Historians. Steven Diner's *A Very Different Age: Americans of the Progressive Era* (New York, 1998), offers a broad synthesis of the ways that Americans in all walks of life reacted to the reorganization of the world around them.

Research into politics and reform in the Progressive Era has been especially energized by two scholarly developments: the widely heeded call to "bring the state back in" and the surge of interest in women reformers. An important work at the forefront of both trends is Theda Skocpol, *Protecting Soldiers and Mothers: The Political Origins of Social Policy in the United States* (Cambridge, Mass., 1992), which seeks to explain why a male-dominated social insurance movement failed to gain ground in these years, even as a female-dominated, "maternalist" welfare movement was winning unprecedented policy victories. A special emphasis on the dynamics and development of state structures and their relationship to particular groups can now be found in scholarship on an otherwise diverse array of topics: William E. Forbath, *Law and the Shaping of the American Labor Movement* (Cambridge, Mass., 1991); Victoria C. Hattam, *Labor Visions and State Power: The Origins of Business Unionism in the United States* (Princeton, N.J., 1993); Melvyn Dubofsky, *The State and Labor in Modern America* (Chapel Hill, N.C., 1994); Lucy Salyer, *Laws Harsh as*

Tigers: Chinese Immigrants and the Shaping of Modern Immigration Law (Chapel Hill, N.C., 1995); Eric H. Monkkonen, *The Local State: Public Money and American Cities* (Stanford, Calif., 1995); Robert W. Cherny, *American Politics in the Gilded Age, 1868–1900* (Wheeling, Ill., 1997), which summarizes historical debate about the earlier era; Elizabeth S. Clemens, *The People's Lobby: Organizational Innovation and the Rise of Interest Group Politics in the United States, 1890–1925* (Chicago, 1997); Cindy Hahamovitch, *The Fruits of Their Labor: Atlantic Coast Farmworkers and the Making of Migrant Poverty, 1870–1945* (Chapel Hill, N.C., 1997); Fareed Zakaria, *From Wealth to Power: The Unusual Origins of America's World Role* (Princeton, N.J., 1998); and Elizabeth Sanders, *The Roots of Reform: Farmers, Workers, and the American State, 1877–1917* (Chicago, 1999), which argues that agrarian protest was the driving engine behind state expansion in these years.

Scholarship on women reformers has been particularly rich. In this area, important works include Jacquelyn Dowd Hall, "O. Delight Smith's Progressive Era: Labor, Feminism, and Reform in the Urban South," and William H. Chafe, "Women's History and Political History: Some Thoughts on Progressivism and the New Deal," both in Nancy A. Hewitt and Suzanne Lebsock, eds., *Visible Women: New Essays on American Activism* (Chicago, 1993); Noralee Frankel and Nancy S. Dye, eds., *Gender, Class, Race, and Reform in the Progressive Era* (Lexington, Ky., 1991); Peggy Pascoe, *Relations of Rescue: The Search for Female Moral Authority in the American West, 1874–1939* (New York, 1991); Evelyn Brooks Higginbotham, *Righteous Discontent: The Women's Movement in the Black Baptist Church, 1880–1920* (Cambridge, Mass., 1993); Glenda Elizabeth Gilmore, *Gender and Jim Crow: Women and the Politics of White Supremacy in North Carolina, 1896–1920* (Chapel Hill, N.C., 1996); Elizabeth Hayes Turner, *Women, Culture, and Community: Religion and Reform in Galveston, 1880–1920* (New York, 1997); Deborah Gray White, *Too Heavy a Load: Black Women in Defense of Themselves, 1894–1994* (New York, 1998); and Melanie Gustafson, Kristie Miller, and Elisabeth Israels Perry, eds., *We Have Come to Stay: American Women and Political Parties, 1880–1960* (Albuquerque, N.M., 1999). Among the many recent studies of suffrage, see especially Sara Hunter Graham, *Woman Suffrage and the New Democracy* (New Haven, Conn., 1996); Marjorie Spruill Wheeler, *New Women of the New South: The Leaders of the Women's Suffrage Movement in the Southern States* (New York, 1993); Elna C. Green, *Southern Strategies: Southern Women and the Woman Suffrage Question* (Chapel Hill, N.C., 1997); Ellen Carol DuBois, *Harriet Stanton Blatch and the Winning of Woman Suffrage* (New Haven, Conn., 1997); and Rosalyn Terborg-Penn, *African American Women and the Struggle for the Vote, 1850–1920* (Bloomington, Ind., 1998). The period is also covered expertly in Blanche Wiesen Cook, *Eleanor Roosevelt, Vol. I: 1884–1933* (New York, 1992). On the considerable influence of women activists on early welfare state initiatives, see Robyn Muncy, *Creating a Female Dominion in American Reform, 1890–1935* (New York, 1991); Linda Gordon, *Pitied But Not Entitled: Single Mothers and the History of Welfare* (Cambridge, Mass., 1994); Kathryn Kish Sklar, *Florence Kelley and the Nation's Work: The Rise of Women's Political Culture, 1830–1900* (New Haven, Conn., 1995); an historiographical article by Patrick Wilkinson, "The Selfless and the Helpless: Maternalist Origins of the U.S. Welfare State," *Feminist Studies* 25 (Fall 1999); and most recently Sonya Michel, *Children's Interests/Mother's Rights: The Shaping of America's Child Care Policy* (New Haven, Conn., 1999).

The study of gender has not been limited to the history of women. Rebecca Edwards in *Angels in the Machinery: Gender in American Party Politics from the Civil War to the Progressive Era* (New York, 1997) argues for the centrality of gender issues in the history of party politics. Angel Kwolek-Folland explores the influence of gender in the development of the insurance and banking industries in *Engendering Business: Men and Women in the Corporate Office, 1870–1930* (Baltimore, 1994). For studies of manhood and masculinity, see especially Gail Bederman, *Manliness and Civilization: A Cultural History of Gender and Race in the United States, 1880–1917* (Chicago, 1995); Arnaldo Testi, "The Gender of Reform Politics: Theodore Roosevelt and the Culture of Masculinity," *Journal of American History* 81 (March 1995); and Keven White, *The First Sexual Revolution: The Emergence of Male Heterosexuality in Modern America* (New York, 1993). On sexual subcultures in the cities, see Timothy Gilfoyle, *City of Eros: New York City, Prostitution, and the Commercialization of Sex, 1790–1920* (New York, 1992); Madeline D. Davis, *Boots of Leather, Slippers of Gold: The History of a Lesbian Community* (New York, 1993); and George Chauncey, *Gay New York: Gender, Urban Culture, and the Makings of the Gay Male World, 1890–1940* (New York, 1994).

The historical construction of racial and ethnic identities has been a major concern of scholarship in the 1990s. The salience of such identities for the worlds of politics, culture, and labor is discussed in George J. Sanchez, *Becoming Mexican-American: Ethnicity, Culture, and Identity in Chicano Los Angeles, 1900–1945* (New York, 1993); Camille Guerin-Gonzales, *Mexican Workers and American Dreams: Immigration, Repatriation, and California Farm Labor, 1900–1939* (New Brunswick, N.J., 1994); Neil Foley, *The White Scourge: Mexicans, Blacks, and Poor Whites in Texas Cotton Culture* (Berkeley, 1997); Chris Friday, *Organizing Asian American Labor: The Pacific Coast Canned-Salmon Industry, 1870–1942* (Philadelphia, 1994); Mildred Allen Beik, *The Miners of Windber: The Struggles of New Immigrants for Unionization, 1890s–1930s* (University Park, Penn., 1996); James J. Connolly, *The Triumph of Ethnic Progressivism: Urban Political Culture in Boston, 1900–1925* (Cambridge, Mass., 1998); Daniel Soyer, *Jewish Immigrant Associations and American Iden-*

tity in New York, 1880–1939 (Cambridge, Mass., 1997); Elizabeth Clark-Lewis, *Living In, Living Out: African-American Domestics and the Great Migration* (Washington, D.C., 1994); Tera Hunter, *To 'Joy My Freedom: Southern Black Women's Lives and Labors after the Civil War* (Cambridge, Mass., 1997); and for a sweeping overview, Jacqueline Jones, *American Work: Four Centuries of Black and White Labor* (New York, 1998).

Among the most important work to deal with racial issues in recent years has been the wealth of new scholarship on whiteness and white supremacy. A compelling cultural analysis of white identity is Grace Elizabeth Hale, *Making Whiteness: The Culture of Segregation in the South, 1890–1940* (New York, 1998). For a longer view, see Matthew Fry Jacobson, *Whiteness of a Different Color: European Immigrants and the Alchemy of Race* (Cambridge, Mass., 1998); and on black perspectives, see Mia Bay, *The White Image in the Black Mind: African-American Ideas about White People, 1835–1925* (New York, 1999). On racism and nativism, see Roger Daniels, *Not Like Us: Immigrants and Minorities in America, 1890–1924* (Chicago, 1997); Elizabeth Lasch-Quinn, *Black Neighbors: Race and the Limits of Reform in the American Settlement House Movement, 1890–1945* (Chapel Hill, N.C., 1993); and Gwendolyn Mink, *The Wages of Motherhood: Inequality in the Welfare State, 1917–1942* (Ithaca, N.Y., 1995). The brutal underside of white privilege in the South is uncovered in W. Fitzhugh Brundage, *Lynching in the New South: Georgia and Virginia, 1880–1930* (Urbana, Ill., 1993); David Oshinsky, *"Worse Than Slavery": Parchman Farm and the Ordeal of Jim Crow Justice* (New York, 1996); and Alex Lichtenstein, *Twice the Work of Free Labor: The Political Economy of Convict Labor in the New South* (New York, 1996). For a measured appraisal of a hard-won cross-racial alliance, see Daniel Letwin, *The Challenge of Interracial Unionism: Alabama Coal Miners, 1878–1921* (Chapel Hill, N.C., 1998). A broader synthesis of developments in the South is Edward L. Ayers, *The Promise of the New South: Life after Reconstruction* (New York, 1992) or, in its abridged version, *Southern Crossing: A History of the American South, 1877–1906* (New York, 1995). On white southern Progressives, William Link, *The Paradox of Southern Progressivism, 1880–1930* (Chapel Hill, N.C., 1992) is particularly perceptive.

Many scholars now agree that the turn of the century was also a turning point in the rise of a new consumer culture, but they continue to disagree over the nature and significance of the transition. See William R. Leach, *Land of Desire: Merchants, Power and the Rise of a New American Culture* (New York, 1993); David Nasaw, *Going Out: The Rise and Fall of Public Amusements* (New York, 1993); Dana Frank, *Purchasing Power: Consumer Organizing, Gender, and the Seattle Labor Movement, 1919–1929* (Cambridge, Mass., 1994); James Livingston, *Pragmatism and the Political Economy of Cultural Revolution* (Chapel Hill, N.C., 1994); Jackson Lears, *Fables of Abundance: A Cultural History of Advertising in*

America (New York, 1994); Ellen Gruber Garvey, *The Adman in the Parlor: Magazines and the Gendering of Consumer Culture, 1880s to 1910s* (New York, 1996); Richard Ohmann, *Selling Culture: Magazines, Markets, and Class at the Turn of the Century* (New York, 1996); Lawrence B. Glickman, *A Living Wage: American Workers and the Making of Consumer Society* (Ithaca, N.Y., 1997); Pamela ·Walker Laird, *Advertising Progress: American Business and the Rise of Consumer Marketing* (Baltimore, 1998); Kathy Peiss, *Hope in a Jar: The Making of America's Beauty Culture* (New York, 1999); and Nan Enstad, *Ladies of Labor, Girls of Adventure: Working Women, Popular Culture, and Labor Politics at the Turn of the Twentieth Century* (New York, 1999).

A central feature in the cultural history of this era is the growth of the film industry. In addition to path-breaking studies by Charles Musser, Eileen Browser, and Richard Koszarski in the *History of American Cinema Series* (made available in paperback in the mid-1990s by the University of California Press), several important new works on motion pictures address the issue of audiences and spectatorship; among them are Miriam Hansen, *Babel and Babylon: Spectatorship in American Silent Film* (Cambridge, Mass., 1991); Janet Staiger, *Interpreting Films: Studies in the Historical Reception of American Cinema* (Princeton, N.J., 1992); and Linda Williams, ed., *Viewing Positions: Ways of Seeing Film* (New Brunswick, N.J., 1995). For fan magazines and rural audiences, see Kathryn H. Fuller, *At the Picture Show: Small-town Audiences and the Creation of Movie Fan Culture* (Washington, D.C., 1996). Douglas Gomery, *Shared Pleasures: A History of Movie Presentation in the United States* (Madison, Wis., 1992) and Gregory A. Waller, *Main Street Amusements: Movies and Commercial Entertainment in a Southern City, 1896–1930* (Washington, D.C., 1995) are examples of the innovative study of the early motion picture business at the national and local levels. Daniel Bernardi, ed., *The Birth of Whiteness: Race and the Emergence of U.S. Cinema* (New Brunswick, N.J., 1996) deals with the filmic representation of white supremacy and the resistance of minority filmmakers and actors to racial stereotypes. Film images of World War I are examined in Leslie Midkiff DeBauche, *Reel Patriotism: The Movies and World War I* (Madison, Wis., 1997); and from a transnational perspective in John Whiteclay Chambers II, *Visualizing Death: "All Quiet on the Western Front," the 1930 Movie, and the Image of World War I* (forthcoming 2001).

On the corporate consolidation that intertwined so closely with the growth of mass markets and mass culture, see Glenn Porter, *The Rise of Big Business, 1860–1920*, 2d ed. (Wheeling, Ill., 1992); Martin J. Sklar, *The United States as a Developing Country: Studies in U.S. History in the Progressive Era and the 1920s* (New York, 1992); Philip Scranton, *Endless Novelty: Specialty Production and American Industrialization, 1865–1925* (Princeton, N.J., 1997); and William G. Roy, *Socializing Capital: The Rise of the Large Industrial Corporation in America* (Princeton, N.J., 1997).

For stirring biographies of the "barons" behind the economic transformation, see especially Ron Chernow, *Titan: The Life of John D. Rockefeller, Sr.* (New York, 1998) and Jean Strouse, *Morgan: American Financier* (New York, 1999). Hal S. Barron, *Mixed Harvest: The Second Great Transformation in the Rural North, 1870–1930* (Chapel Hill, N.C., 1997) asks how the era's economic and cultural changes played out in rural areas.

The past decade has seen the publication of superb biographies on two of the towering intellects of the age: David Levering Lewis, *W.E.B. Du Bois: Biography of a Race, 1868–1919* (New York, 1993) and Robert Westbrook, *John Dewey and American Democracy* (Ithaca, N.Y., 1991). An important work on the emergence of the social sciences is Dorothy Ross, *The Origins of American Social Science* (Cambridge, Mass., 1991); see also Helene Silverberg, ed., *Gender and American Social Science: The Formative Years* (Princeton, N.J., 1998) and David Moss, *Socializing Security: Progressive-Era Economists and the Origins of American Social Policy* (Cambridge, Mass., 1996). For a provocative analysis of the discipline of psychiatry, see Elizabeth Lunbeck, *The Psychiatric Persuasion: Knowledge, Gender, and Power in Modern America* (New York, 1994). On intellectuals' efforts to engage "the public," see Leon Fink, *Progressive Intellectuals and the Dilemmas of Democratic Commitment* (Cambridge, Mass., 1997).

The emergence of the United States as a dominant world power is forcefully interpreted in Walter LaFeber, *The American Search for Opportunity, 1865–1913* (Cambridge, 1995). Institutional and cultural aspects behind the industrial nation's embrace of expanded military power are treated in G. Kurt Piehler, *Remembering War the American Way* (Washington, D.C., 1995); Paul A. C. Koistinen, *Mobilizing for Modern War: The Political Economy of American Warfare, 1865–1919* (Lawrence, Kans., 1997); Kristin L. Hoganson, *Fighting for American Manhood: How Gender Politics Produced the Spanish-American and Philippine-American Wars* (New Haven, Conn., 1998); Manfred F. Boemeke, et al., eds., *Anticipating Total War: The German and American Experience, 1871–1914* (New York, 1999); and John Whiteclay Chambers II, ed., *The Oxford Companion to American Military History* (New York, 1999). On specific wars, see John L. Offner, *An Unwanted War: The Diplomacy of the United States and Spain over Cuba, 1895–1898* (Chapel Hill, N.C., 1992); Louis A. Pérez, Jr., *The War of 1898: The United States and Cuba in History and Historiography* (Chapel Hill, N.C., 1998), a rich analysis both of the war itself and of its subsequent treatment by historians; John S. D. Eisenhower, *Intervention! The United States and the Mexican Revolution, 1913–1917* (New York, 1995); Anne Cipriano Venzon, ed., *The United States in the First World War: An Encyclopedia* (New York, 1995); David F. Trask, *The AEF and Coalition Warmaking, 1917–18* (Lawrence, Kans., 1993) for a highly critical view; and David S. Foglesong, *America's Secret*

War against Bolshevism: U.S. Intervention in the Russian Civil War, 1917–1920 (Chapel Hill, N.C., 1995). Diverse popular and cultural influences on foreign policy are discussed in Elizabeth McKillen, *Chicago Labor and the Quest for a Democratic Diplomacy, 1914–1924* (Ithaca, N.Y., 1995); Elliott P. Skinner, *African-Americans and U.S. Foreign Policy toward Africa, 1850–1924* (Washington, D.C., 1992); and Hazel M. McFerson, *The Racial Dimensions of American Foreign Policy: A History* (Westport, Conn., 1997). Aspects of American peace movements are explored in Charles Chatfield, *The American Peace Movement: Ideals and Activism* (New York, 1992); Harriet Hyman Alonso, *Peace as a Women's Issue: A History of the U.S. Movement for World Peace and Women's Rights* (Syracuse, N.Y., 1993); and Frances H. Early, *A World Without War: How U.S. Feminists and Pacifists Resisted World War I* (Syracuse, N.Y., 1997).

Lastly, among the most promising developments in Progressive Era scholarship is a growing awareness that many subjects, traditionally studied within a strictly national context, may in fact be better understood as transnational or global phenomena. Here, Daniel T. Rodgers's study of progressive reformers, *Atlantic Crossings: Social Politics in a Progressive Age* (Cambridge, Mass., 1998), makes a seminal contribution by tracing the lines of influence that link progressive reforms in the United States to movements that first gathered steam in Europe. Other studies of the transnational dimensions of reform movements are Ian Tyrrell, *Woman's World/Woman's Empire: The Women's Christian Temperance Union in International Perspective, 1880–1930* (Chapel Hill, N.C., 1991); Seth Koven and Sonya Michel, eds., *Mothers of a New World: Maternalist Politics and the Origins of Welfare States* (New York, 1993); Paul T. Phillips, *A Kingdom on Earth: Anglo-American Social Christianity, 1880–1940* (University Park, Penn., 1996); Leila J. Rupp, *Worlds of Women: The Making of an International Women's Movement* (Princeton, N.J., 1997); and J. Lawrence Broz, *The International Origins of the Federal Reserve System* (Ithaca, N.Y., 1997). William G. Robbins, *Colony and Empire: The Capitalist Transformation of the American West* (Lawrence, Kans., 1994) explores a "West" that stretches from Mexico to Canada and relates the dynamics of its transformation to the rhythms of world capitalism. Walter Nugent's important synthesis, *Crossings: The Great Transatlantic Migrations, 1870–1914* (Bloomington, Ind., 1992), resituates immigration to the United States within "the demographic mosaic of the transatlantic region"; in this regard, see also the innovative study by Mark Wyman, *Round-Trip to America: The Immigrants Return Home, 1880–1930* (Ithaca, N.Y., 1993). Moreover, as is made clear in several new studies, even when migrants had planted new roots in local American communities, they remained intricately involved in transnational communities as well; see especially Winston James, *Holding Aloft the Banner of Ethiopia: Caribbean Radicalism in Early Twentieth Century America* (New York, 1998); Douglas Monroy, *Rebirth: Mexican Los Angeles from the Great*

Migration to the Great Depression (Los Angeles, 1999); and Nancy Hewitt's study of the many fractured dimensions of women's activism in the polyglot city of Tampa in *Forging Activist Identities: Latin, African American and Anglo Women in Tampa, Florida, 1870s–1920s* (Urbana, Ill., 2000).

(Bibliographical supplement compiled by Patrick Wilkinson.)

Index

About the Author

John Whiteclay Chambers II is professor of history and former chair of the history department at Rutgers University, New Brunswick, New Jersey, where he has taught since 1983. He received his Ph.D. in history from Columbia University (1973). Chambers has written *To Raise an Army: The Draft Comes to Modern America* (1987) and *Visualizing Death: "All Quiet on the Western Front," the 1930 Movie, and the Image of World War I* (forthcoming 2001). He is editor or co-editor of *American History* (1983), *The Eagle and the Dove* (2d ed., 1991), *The New Conscientious Objection* (1993), *World War II, Film, and History* (1996), and *The Oxford Companion to American Military History* (2000). His articles have been published in *American Heritage, Historical Journal of Film, Radio, and Television, Labor History,* and *Political Science Quarterly*. Recipient of Rockefeller and Fulbright Fellowships, major grants from the Ford Foundation and the National Endowment for the Humanities, as well as an Outstanding Teacher Award, Chambers has also taught at Columbia University and has lectured at universities and conferences around the world.